British Identities, Heroic Nationalisms, and the Gothic
Novel, 1764–1824

British Identities, Heroic Nationalisms, and the Gothic Novel, 1764–1824

Toni Wein

First published 2002 by
PALGRAVE MACMILLAN
Houndmills, Basingstoke, Hampshire RG21 6XS and
175 Fifth Avenue, New York, N.Y. 10010
Companies and representatives throughout the world.

PALGRAVE MACMILLAN is the global academic imprint of the Palgrave Macmillan division of St Martin's Press, LLC and of Palgrave Macmillan Ltd. Macmillan® is a registered trademark in the United States, United Kingdom and other countries. Palgrave is a registered trademark in the European Union and other countries.

ISBN 0–333–97171–X

This book is printed on paper suitable for recycling and made from fully managed and sustained forest sources.

A catalogue record for this book is available from the British Library.

Library of Congress Cataloging-in-Publication Data

Wein, Toni, 1952–
    British identities, heroic nationalisms, and the gothic novel, 1764–1824 / Toni Wein.
        p. cm.
Includes bibliographical references and index.
ISBN 0-333-97171-X
    1. English fiction – 18th century – History and criticism. 2. Horror tales, English–History and criticism. 3. English fiction–19th century–History and criticism. 4. Gothic revival (Literature) – Great Britain. 5. Nationalism and literature–Great Britain. 6. Literature and society – Great Britain. 7. Identity (Psychology) in literature. 8. Group identity in literature. 9. Courage in literature. 10. Heroes in literature. I. Title.

PR858.T3 W45 2002
823'.0872909'09033–dc21

2001056136

10   9   8   7   6   5   4   3   2   1
11 10 09 08 07 06 05 04 03 02

Printed and bound in Great Britain by
Antony Rowe Ltd, Chippenham and Eastbourne

For Helen, always and forever

Contents

Part III   Tailgating on the Gothic Myth

List of Illustrations

Acknowledgments

Books spring from community. Professionally, the Andrew Mellon Foundation and the Provost's Office of Gettysburg College made available time and money (necessary luxuries) to pursue my research and writing. The librarians of the Sadleir-Black Collection of the University of Virginia, the New York Public Library Rare Books Division, and the British Library gave me vital assistance in locating rare works.

My deepest gratitude goes out to those individuals who nurtured this work through their support, encouragement, and, most salutarily, naked criticism. Steven Knapp and Ernest Machen fought to exorcise my writing and exercise my mind. Catherine Gallagher, Carol Clover, Morton Paley, and Frederick Crews helped refine my focus. Thane Pittman, Leila May, and Don Palmer heroically urged me to express my ideas clearly and succinctly. Members of the Gettysburg College English Department – Temma Berg, Beth Lambert, Mary Margaret Stewart, and especially Leonard Goldberg – nursed the book's growing pains. Ellen Geist and Flossie Lewis shared the invaluable perspective of non-specialist readers. Eleanor Birne, my editor at Palgrave, and her assistant Rebecca Mashayekh responded with grace and insight; my (anonymous) readers at Palgrave generously guided me. My niece, Zoe Wein Shiovitz, inspired the beginning of this book; my niece, Brynn Wein Shiovitz, adapted an eighteenth-century drawing and my description of the book into the perfect cover illustration. No list of acknowledgments would be complete without the mention of my immediate family, whose love enabled me to see the importance of generational continuity and whose family ghost stories elucidated the elastic meaning of nation.

Introduction: Punctuating Disequilibrium

> I want a hero: an uncommon want,
> When every year and month sends forth a new one,
> Till, after cloying the gazettes with cant,
> The age discovers he is not the true one:
> Of such as these I should not care to vaunt,
> I'll take therefore our ancient friend Don Juan –
>
> (Byron, *Don Juan*, Canto I)

'Tell it again!' To those who fancy themselves storytellers, no words from the lips of an auditor deliver as much pleasure. Accompanied by their silent cousins, eyes and mouth cavernous in wondering amaze, those words signal the heartfelt approval of teller *and* tale, the successful summoning of chills, dread, sorrow, joy, despair – the gamut of emotions conjurable in an audience. Most of the time, such a reaction confines itself to young audiences, children beguiled at bedtime. Yet such responses, and such a call for repetition, accompanied the Gothic.

The attraction exerted by the Gothic on readers, authors, publishers, and booksellers bound them in a 'cultural intimacy' that lasted for 60 years.[1] But the spell was slow to weave. Despite the popularity of Horace Walpole's *The Castle of Otranto* (1764), a fact indicated by the rapid progress of editions, 14 years elapsed before another Gothic novel appeared. That novel was Clara Reeve's *The Champion of Virtue*, first published in 1778 but reissued a year later with a different title, the now more familiar *The Old English Baron*. Again, Reeve's novel initially produced an enthusiastic reception, followed by a curious lull. Not until 1789 did the genre take hold, with Ann Radcliffe's *The Castles of Athlin and Dunbayne* followed in quick succession by her 1790 *A Sicilian Romance*, 1791's *The*

Romance of the Forest, and 1794's *The Mysteries of Udolpho*. At that point, a host of imitators swarmed into the marketplace, most notable among them Matthew Lewis's *The Monk* (1796). From then on, 'about a third of all fiction published in volume form between 1796 and 1806 was frankly "Gothic" in character' (Mayo, 1962, 349). This surprisingly retarded development contravenes all theories of originality, production, marketing, and consumption.[2] Therefore, in order to understand the nature of the Gothic's ultimate attraction and the intimacy it constructed, we have to know why climatic conditions delayed its maturity.

1764, 1778, 1789 – beyond literary history, these dates commemorate tidal shifts in the nature, composition, and prospects of Great Britain. After the Seven Years' War, the strains of absorbing the returning military population, over 200 000 in number, were overmatched by the tensions produced by military success (Colley, 1992, 101). Because they had conquered peoples foreign in race and religion (vast territories of Asia; 70 000 French Catholics in Quebec alone), and because the geographical sweep of the victories mandated new administrative machinery to manage those subject peoples, the victories of the war challenged dearly-held myths about the nature of the British people as Protestant, commercial, and liberty-loving. Furthermore, since the war had proved the loyalties of those earlier suspected of Toryism and Jacobitism, increasing pressure came to open up circles of power to those formerly marginalized, whether on the edges of Great Britain or the frontiers of empire: 'At home, John Wilkes and his supporters launched a turbulent campaign for old English liberties and new English rights, while English patriots more generally felt themselves under threat from Scottish ambition and Scottish constructions of Great Britain' (Colley, 1992, 105). In the same year that Wilkes and his supporters began their agitation, Horace Walpole began his Gothic novel.

Like a Gothic villain, the British people and government quickly adjusted to their new power. The embarrassment expressed over the victories of the Seven Years' War lasted a bare two decades. Then, the loss of the American colonies produced a fever for empire, and the government responded in paroxysms of Acts designed to assert authority. A concurrent movement to solidify control at home accompanied these foreign edicts. But, at home, authority wore a gentler face, administering its doses through 'a far more consciously and officially constructed patriotism which stressed attachment to the monarchy, the importance of empire, the value of military and naval achievement, and the desirability of strong, stable government by a virtuous, able and authentically British elite' (Colley, 1992, 145). The pages that follow represent my attempt to coax that gentler face of patriotic indoctrination out from one of its lurking places, the Gothic novel. Both the correspondence of dates, the 'punctuated equilibrium' of Gothic production, and the nationwide response testify to the Gothic's successful imagining of a nationalist community.[3]

Invoking the concept of nationalism obliges me to discriminate between the nation and the state. I take it as axiomatic that the nation codifies itself into the state only when institutional and bureaucratic apparatuses are in place. In the pre-dawn of the state, the social and the political have not yet separated, a symbiosis delineated by thinkers as diverse as Gramsci and Habermas. Yet I would wish to distance myself from Gramsci's vision of nationalism as driven from the top down.[4] Instead, the Gothic nationalism of eighteenth-century fiction corresponds to the process described by an anthropologist like Michael Herzfeld (1997), where it forms part of the 'cultural poetics' of existence, encompassing both critique and celebration in an ambivalence that Herzfeld characterizes as 'disemia.' Thus, in articulating the role played by the Gothic in the invention of a British nation, I shall necessarily be tracing the intersections between nationalist discourse in the spheres of life that Habermas has characterized respectively as public authority, synonymous with 'state-related' jurisdictions and 'endowed with a monopoly over the legitimate use of coercion' (1992, 19); the public sphere, self-nominated with the task of engaging in critical public debate over the protection of a commercial economy and the regulation of civil society at large (1992, 52); and the truly private, because uneconomic, domestic realm. Our access to these bygone realms and the roads linking them will lead through parliamentary debates, political pamphleteering, periodical literature and non-fiction essays, architecture, visual art, and, above all, the novel, with a vital foray into private readers' comments, all screened against a panoply of events, domestic and foreign (wars, economic growth and mercantilist ideals, social and political legislation), stretching out over the period in question. Our quest will require as adjunct that we take the measure of late eighteenth-century aesthetics and its role in social formation along the way, a topic most explicitly addressed in Chapters 1 and 7.[5] For even those theorists of nationalism most enamored of a top-down bias admit the crucial role played by the print medium both in disseminating cohesive identities and, more importantly, in retrospectively attributing a mythical coherence and eternity to those identities.[6]

In consequence, analyzing nationalism demands not only an explanation of the *what* and *why* of its existence but even more so the *how* of its discourse. I call the Gothic novel nationalist discourse because it so aptly fits the description offered by Deniz Kandiyoti: it 'presents itself as both a modern project that melts and transforms traditional attachments in favor of new identities and as a reaffirmation of authentic cultural values culled from the depths of a presumed communal past' (1994, 378).[7] This restructuring of personal and public history takes place on two planes, formal and substantive.

Formally, the Gothic novel is a harmonizing fiction: from its inception, it announced as its project a hybridization of romance and novel. According to Walpole in the Preface to the second edition of *The Castle of Otranto*, modern romance failed because the 'strict adherence to common life' constrained the imagination. Yet the license of ancient romance meant that the 'actions, sentiments, conversations, of the heroes and heroines of ancient days were as unnatural as the machines employed to put them in motion' (1963, 9). To the reconciliation of apparently incompatible ideals, boundless invention (ancient romance) and the rules of probability (the modern novel), Horace Walpole gave the name 'Gothic story' (10). This famous announcement of his bricolage encapsulates an aestheticized version of nationalist discourse's paradox.

Substantively, whether responding to fears of a lost British identity as the outline of the nation changed, or embracing the extended reach of British imperialism, Gothic novels reaffirm 'authentic cultural values culled from the depths of a presumed communal past.' They do this first by copying the ways of the past, rather than breaking sharply with it. Further, Gothic novels do more than rehearse the past; they figure that past as a lost Golden Age that can be recovered.

The yearning expressed in that backward glance helps us distinguish the Gothic novel from the historical novel with which it has frequently been compared, and with which it shares an episodic, retrogressive structure. Leland's *Longsword* is commonly credited as the first historical novel: advertising its source in 'the antient English historians,' it imagines the lived reality behind those circumstantial accounts. Set in the reign of Henry III, the action features the exploits of an actual figure of the late twelfth and early thirteenth century, William de Longespée, or Longsword, third Earl of Salisbury and, according to legend, the natural son of Henry II. However, the fictionality of *Longsword* is foregrounded in several ways. Most immediately, Leland's Preface announces that he has taken liberties by enlarging and altering the accounts. Such an admission would never have been made by the Gothic novelists, who are diligent to preserve the illusion of authenticity. Leland's alteration would have been apparent to anyone familiar with the historical records, for he interposes to revise the hero's almost senselessly tragic demise by making his novel end happily for all the 'good' characters. Despite Leland's scrounging in the bin of history to furnish his tale, he evinces little preference for ancient ways. In Book V, a transparent reference to the present tense of the book's composition occurs in a fantasia, where George III is eulogized as a 'glorious Monarch' (117–18).[8] Since this paean to an unspecified Solomon must be couched as an inspiriting vision in order to maintain narrative continuity, it depends upon a notion of the past as debased in comparison with the glorious future that awaits. And this attitude towards the past is made explicit in the lines immediately preceding the vision:

> Good heaven ... When shall our distracted country feel the blessings of a wise and virtuous rule? Shall faction and tumult for ever disturb the land, and sordid avarice and slavish adulation for ever surround the throne? Is the insolence of ill-gotten power to know no controul [*sic*]?
>
> (117)

Longsword is a chauvinistic tribute to the homeland, but only to the homeland of Leland's immediate present. In contrast, the Gothic recapitulation of the past reinvents that past to be adaptable to the present at the same time that it glorifies it.[9]

Moreover, the Gothic reinvents the present to make it adaptable to a glorified past. Specifically, the Gothic transfiguration took advantage of the very conditions of modernity in print and visual culture that threatened the past. Mechanical techniques of reproduction spurred desire for original genius; the demand for originality pressured the very definition of authenticity. As Benjamin averred, '[T]he presence of the original is the prerequisite to the concept of authenticity... The whole sphere of authenticity is outside technical – and, of course, not only technical – reproducibility' (1968, 222). The cultural construction of Gothic authenticity did not depend on the 'protocol of displacement' common or endemic to novels' relationships to other novels, whereupon they insisted on their originality and freedom from indebtedness.[10] If anything, Gothic novels flagged their dependence through repetition and allusiveness. More than a 'proper' legitimating function, Gothic allusiveness is narcissistically self-referential and self-reflexive. To the extent that Gothic reflexivity confines itself to the act of reading qua reading, in staged scenes of instruction and entertainment, whether complimentary or critical, it resembles other fictional forms of the period. To the extent that Gothic reflexivity explicitly mediates the place and function of literature in society, it betrays the authors' concern not only with the public sphere but also with their place within that sphere, as I will demonstrate more fully in Chapter 7.[11]

While Michael McKeon's magisterial work on the origins of the novel deflates anxiety about authenticity after the Richardson–Fielding debates of the 1740s, a developing novelist like Frances Burney still cannot draw an easy breath on the subject in 1778:

> In all the Arts, the value of copies can only be proportioned to the scarceness of originals: among sculptors and painters, a fine statue, or a beautiful picture, of some great master, may deservedly employ the imitative talents of younger and inferior artists, that their appropriation to one spot, may not wholly prevent the more general expansion of their excellence; but, among authors, the reverse is the case, since the noblest productions of literature, are almost equally attainable with the meanest. In books, therefore, imitation cannot be shunned too sedulously; for the very perfection of a model which is frequently seen, serves but more forcibly to mark the inferiority of a copy.
>
> (Preface to *Evelina*, 8)

Burney's comments coincide with the passage in England of new copyright legislation, a topic still reverberating in the pages of pamphlets, periodicals, and newspapers. In those years the discourses on originality and proprietorship converged.[12] Both the origins of the Gothic novel and the imitations that sedulously followed bespeak a similar anxiety about originality, property, and authenticity, at the same time that they instance a very different novelistic solution.

Implicitly, Gothic novels insist that authenticity is reproducible in several ways. First, the initial works, like those of Walpole, Reeve, and early Radcliffe, draw on the romance convention of the discovered manuscript, thereby presenting their works as transparent transmissions or translations of an authentic, original text. Despite our modern awareness of the complexity of translating, traces of which are retained etymologically, eighteenth-century audiences were less suspicious. Walpole may have been playing with the doubled meanings of translation, as I will argue in Chapter 2, but those who employed the convention after him did so with far straighter faces, and even his early readers took the production to be genuine. What we might consider gullibility on the part of readers resulted from a curious redoubling of efforts at authenticity: conscious that their novels were stamped by mechanical techniques of reproduction as they spewed from the presses, Reeve and Radcliffe went to some lengths to reproduce the authentic material conditions of discovered manuscripts, giving them a spurious patina of age by adverting to the damaged leaves and by omitting portions, as though eradicated by time, a hoax impervious to detection for those lacking the carbon-dating sophistication of post-structuralist theory. Once the hallmark conventions of the Gothic – the embodiment of situations, settings, character types; the iconology of type, illustrations, and title words – had been firmly established, their very familiarity lent them a specious authenticity.

Whereas only the nobility could inhabit the physical remains of the past, the technical reproduction of that past in book form turned it into a consumer item, available to all. Since the seventeenth century, it had been a rhetorical commonplace to endow a book with the properties of an architectural space.[13] Fielding recapitulates the idea when he metaphorizes the narrator of *Tom Jones* as a host of a 'public Ordinary' (31). But because Fielding's metaphor emphasizes the public entertainment aspect of his novel, temporality is involved only insofar as it is a durational requirement of the entertainment. In the Gothic novels that rely on the presentation of their contents as authentic manuscripts, the reader is invited into a space that is simultaneously the distant past and the immediate present. Within its often claustrophobic confines, the notion of book-as-building meets the idea of building-as-book, one which encodes the territorial struggle for power and encrypts a warning to its innocent inhabitants. Narrative detail becomes the ordering of space, a grammar of shape, texture, and light embodying idealized versions of the past and wishful thinking about the future.

The fictionalized versions of authentic British documents made that history available to social groups whose financial means prevented them from acquiring such artifacts. But as Homi Bhabha reminds us, '[S]uch a bringing to light is a question of the provision of visibility as a capacity, a strategy, an agency' (1995, 110). By using their novels to rehearse the past and thereby reformulate the present, Gothic novels prepared the conditions of growth for nationalism. As Ernest Gellner has argued, nationalism requires a shift in the role of culture; no longer the guardian at the gate, maintaining the hierarchical distinctions in the old agrarian form of society, it must move to become the means whereby cultural and hierarchical differences are to be homogenized (1983, 64). It is not necessary for a work of art to advocate homogenization explicitly. Instead, it can be more subtly promoted through heightened literacy and distribution of the materials of culture. Gothic's widespread dissemination as a cultural ideal, in literature, art, architecture, and politics, made it a perfect vehicle for nationalist sentiment.

For that reason, the Gothic novel corresponds somewhat to Debord's definition of the spectacle; as he argues, the 'spectacle is not a collection of images but a social relation among people mediated by images' (1970, aphorism 4). However, unlike Debord's spectacle, in resurrecting an artifically rosy past and presenting that past as a solution to present ills the Gothic novel sutures over the experience of alienation. As we will see, because it does not emanate as the product of a separate sector, the Gothic spectacle made the spectator feel more at home, rather than less. In its simulation of the past, the Gothic novel made the past visible in the present, providing, as Baudrillard describes, 'a visible continuum, a visible myth of origin to reassure us as to our ends' (1993, 19). Still, we must not conflate the Gothic spectacle or the Gothic simulation with poststructuralist notions of these phantasmatic operations.[14] Baudrillard's notion of simulation starts from the '*radical negation of the sign as value*, from the sign as the reversion and death sentence of every reference,' contrasting representation, 'truly' or 'falsely' mimetic, with simulation, which swallows the entire edifice of representation as 'itself a simulacrum' (1993, 11). Instead, the Gothic moment stands as an outpost on the way to such a self-consuming end, pointing still behind at the possibility of recovery and restitution.[15]

And both those hopes concentrate in the person of the hero.[16] Most of the best new work on nationalist discourse has focused on national cohesion as a reaction to confrontations with an Other. Applied to literary studies, it has led to stimulating work on the monstrous, the villainous, and the demonized. Conversely, in postcolonial theory, interest has sided more with the monstrous, the villainous, and the demonized as producers of a conflictual or hybrid identity. But if, as Homi Bhabha pleads, we need to understand 'processes of subjectification,' to see that the discourse for the dominated subject also contains within it the strategic placing of the dominant (1995, 67, 72), then we need also to scrutinize portraits of 'simple' goodness. Goodness may be unfashionable; still, it is the necessary obverse pole around which a national identity can be constructed.

In what follows, I will argue that the Gothic novel figures a nationalist community through its imagining of a hero.[17] Byron's comments in *Don Juan*, which furnish the epigraph, may mock the national obsession with heroes, but at the same time he enters into the discussion.[18]

Crafting a new hero for the post-Waterloo world, more follower than leader, a piece of flotsam on the tide of history, Byron will redefine the Gothic hero in as radical a manner as had his reworking of the Gothic villain into anti-hero through his Eastern tales, *The Giaour, Lara, The Siege of Corinth*.

Models of manners and integrity, Gothic heroes bear many conventional attributes of the romance hero: they are honest, courageous, disinterestedly interested (another version of impartiality), chivalrous to women, humble, and handsome. They are also willing to fight for their principles, their rights, or their ladies. Above all, these are men in tights. That costume is significant, because it reminds us that the bulk of Gothic novels are set in the distant past, and sometimes also in distant lands. Yet their very reliance on the past and on romance conventions enables Gothic novels to furnish heroes in tempo with contemporary concerns.[19] Combativeness in defense of rights is carefully modulated to distinguish it from the French Revolution's rallying cry of Natural Rights. The heroes have been robbed of their birthrights, so they must go to war, but the kind of battle they conduct can be distanced and idealized by its remote setting. Public violence is refined; private violence is increasingly anathematized as the resort of inexperience or of villainy. By draining the blood, smoke, and lead from fictionalized accounts, these airbrushed portraits of war respond to a growing preference in the literature of the period for bloodlessness rather than bloodletting.

In place of brute force, these heroes substitute empirical logic. In actuality considered as indispensable to a commercial career, empiricism's alliance with industry and scientific investigation did not preclude its desirability and utility from crossing social boundaries in the later eighteenth century, as elegance strove to replace virtuosity with connoisseurship.[20] The gift of nature, improved by hard work rather than the effortless gift of birth, empirical logic as a desideratum for heroes represents the symbolic extension of talents to all. Empiricism is romanticized as thoroughly as is noble blood.

These new/old heroes must be carefully discriminated from the Gothic villains, with whom they are all too often conflated.[21] To read the Gothic as always or only concerned with its villains does the novels and their audiences a disservice. It ignores what those readers and critics said about the novels they experienced firsthand.[22] For instance, in 1785 Hannah More praised Walpole's *Otranto*, along with 'the courtly ease of the style of Addison, the sinewy force and clear precision of Swift,' for its 'elegant vigour ...

untainted with this spreading corruption,' the Frenchification of the English language. All three authors 'exhibit models of taste in their several species of composition' (Lewis, 1973, 31:224). As More's grouping illustrates, literary products and producers are valued for diffusing an elegance characterized as simultaneously masculine, hygienic, and British.[23] That masculinity, hygiene, and citizenship also inhered in aristocrats means that the Gothic novel stands in direct contrast to the sentimental novel's representation of effete aristocratic libertines. Moreover, the characters of the Gothic novel become the carriers of these values. When Mrs Fenn, an author of children's works published anonymously under the pseudonym Mrs Teachwell or Mrs Lovechild, praised *Otranto* as a moral story in her *The Female Guardian. Designed to Correct Some of the Foibles Incident to Girls, and Supply Them with Innocent Amusement for Their Hours of Leisure*, she did so by excerpting 'beauties,' a practice promoted by the literary journals; but instead of the graceful prose, graceful characters were exhibited as worthy of emulation.

But as much as we need to discriminate the Gothic hero from the Gothic villain, so much also must we recognize the new openness with which masculinity is defined.[24] No 'simple, single, coherent concept linked to a single locality,' manliness was 'a portmanteau term which embraced a variety of overlapping ideologies regionally interpreted, which changed over time and which, at specific moments, appear to be discrete, even conflicting, in emphasis' (Mangan and Walvin, 1987, 3). The delicacy of sentiment Gothic heroes exhibit is almost feminine. Instead of the delicacy of sentiment we find delineated in the periodicals and in earlier didactic literature, where it arises from aristocratic taste and education, Gothic sentiment appears in the heroes' and heroines' responses to nature, even or especially when looking out at that nature from between the bars of a prison. Nature and scenes of domestic affection frequently make them swoon. Heroes, as much as heroines, are also prone to swoon when confronted with tyranny or supposedly supernatural visitations. More important, women share empirical ability. Both heroes and heroines employ empirical observation to aid them in their escapes from imprisonment, and to detect imposture and social injustice. In fact, Walpole's Isabella makes possible the escape of Theodore from his underground prison by finding the ring to the trap door. By distributing these heroic traits across gender lines, Gothic novelists make them seem generally available. At the same time, because the characters who exhibit these traits are so attractive, they become desirable models for attainment.

This new technology of masculinity contrasts with the picture developed in critical accounts of the novel's evolution. When they address the nature of the hero, current critics rehearse the debates of two centuries ago: hero as secularized bourgeois or as feminized anti-bourgeois.[25] The Gothic complicates this simple binarism: the 'feminized' hero maintains an agency that theorists of the feminized hero deny. The cross-gender attributes of heroes and heroines militate against recent interpretations of the Gothic and romance as bifurcating into male and female forms.[26] One central tenet of my work is that the Gothic hero and heroine share attributes, without necessarily being feminized or masculinized.

If the heroines' and heroes' qualities migrate across conventional barriers of gender behavior, so their attributes cross class lines. Predominantly noble heroes are imbued with middle-class virtues. If we return again to Walpole's Preface, quoted above, with the question of ideological investment in mind, the language he employs ostensibly in the sole service of formal matters suggests a further purpose: what constrains in modern romance is adherence to *common* life; in ancient romance, too much *license* turns heroes into machine-like cogs acting automatically and hence unnaturally. By implication, Walpole wants heroes who will share the nobility exclusive to romance heroes, but because he wants worthy, 'natural' models for human behavior, he sees a certain amount of restriction necessary in their action. And this same tempering of heroism with prudence will be true, to varying degrees, in all the heroes who fill the pages of Gothic novels. Unlike Jacobin, sentimental, or domestic novels, servants are given a voice and an opportunity to become heroes in their own right. When they speak, we see them learning empirical observation and logical inferences from their masters. Novelistic elements of 'realism' enabled Gothic novelists to naturalize and domesticate members of the aristocracy by subjecting them to the same problems and granting them the same virtues as the middle class; the romance topos of disguised noble origins that Walpole imported into the Gothic novel heightened the illusion of access to the aristocracy, since readers could internalize that romantic view of themselves as inherently noble.[27]

Because the hero forms but one part of a social whole, his relations with that whole, his manifestations of civic virtue, must also be considered. If the amount of violence permissible in those dealings with others becomes a recurring theme, discussed in Chapters 2, 3, and 4, so also will the hero's institutional relations, as exemplified by the law, come under scrutiny in Chapters 3, 4, 5, and 7. In order to regain and exercise his proper role, the hero must circulate among members of his community. Therefore, circulation becomes a theme of these texts, as the texts' forms of reproduction and distribution themselves trope the act.[28]

This imaginary community reinflects current discussions about identity politics. Occulted identities initially strangle the loyalties of heroes and heroines to self and to society. That such paralysis occurs in plots which suggest archetypal fears has led to the predominance of archetypalist or psychological criticism on the Gothic to date.[29] Yet, if we ignore the spooky atmospherics, we realize that Gothic plots tremble over the potential loss of their protagonist's integrity, an integrity imaged as bundling together the political and social with the private and sexual.[30] Their corporate identity corresponds to that 'fictitious identity' of the 'bourgeois public sphere,' described by Habermas as composed of two roles: 'the role of property owners and the role of human beings pure and simple' (1992, 56). As I hope to make clear, the Gothic novel argues time and again that identity inheres in the performance of one's role, not in isolated action.[31] And as the following chapters will show in greater detail, critics, professional and amateur, prized the Gothic novel for its vision of an organic society, and for its analysis of human nature.

If Gothic novels instance processes of identification in transit, both locally for readers and more globally for citizens of the nation, they do so in good company. That the need for an organic vision was felt by British society at the time, and that the hopes for satisfying such a need centered on a new definition of heroism, speaks through the periodical literature running concurrent with the production of Gothic novels. Periodical journalists echo Byron with a straight face; the national litany, 'I want a hero,' finds its call and response there.

Periodical literature shows us how frequently the image of the hero arose in mundane arenas. For instance, writing for the Anglican *British Critic*, the author of a piece on Matthias's *The Pursuits of Literature* commends Matthias as the 'patriotic champion of morality, religion, and sound principles, literary and political' (1797, 303), a characterization that places Matthias on a Gothic charger. Usually, the desire for heroes sounds even more loudly in prospectuses and editorials than it does in literary reviews, where it takes comparatively muted form. But the search for heroes is limited neither to one department or branch of letters, nor to one political faction. All periodicals, whatever their party stripe, join an avowedly conservative organ like the *Anti-Jacobin, or Weekly Examiner*, in calling upon us to 'Reverence LAW, USAGE, PRESCRIPTION' (Prospectus, 20 November 1790). Competing suggestions swirl over the correct means to obtain those goals. Martial discipline combats senti-mental tenderness, with common sense adjudicating the fight.

Sometimes these contradictions show up within the pages of the same journal. In its Prospectus, the *Anti-Jacobin* trumpets the accom-plishments of military heroes. The editors proclaim themselves 'Admirers of military heroism, and dazzled by military success in common with other men,' as long as these other men are British, and frequently invoke the names of Howe, Jervis, and Duncan.[32] Nevertheless, in the same issue's extended paeans to British life, they blazon a type of hero whose plastic spirit makes him seem more senti-mentally fluid than the rigid disciplinarian we might expect in heroes martially derived.[33] A fictitious letter to the editor opens the first volume by rejoicing over the vast improvements in daily conditions. The post, newspapers, conveyances, cooking, food supplies, and prosti-tutes, plus the latter's treatment by 'Watchmen of the Night': such cat-egories indiscriminately mingle food for British thought and British bodies, all testifying to progress. Despite the letter writer's attempt to pin down the sources of this renovation, he can only offer a series of abstract qualities as having produced this revolution in concrete details. Taking these in turn, he offers a salute

> To the prevailing spirit of CANDOUR, which dictates a gentleness of construction upon all actions, of whatever nature or tendency, that entirely takes away all harshness and invidiousness of distinction and discrimination; to that LIBERALITY which disdains to bind the conduct of any one individual to the rigid maxims that are arbitrarily drawn up for all, without reference to the difference of temper, feeling, or taste, which must in polished society mark the characters of differ-ent minds; to that exquisite DELICACY OF SENTIMENT, which throbs in the heart and swells at the eye; – which soars above the pedantry of rules, and feels its energies called forth sometimes on one side the question, sometimes on the other; and which a man of true feeling would always wish to see err, because it is so beautiful, so lovely in repentance – finally, Sir, to that system of general TOLERATION, IMPARTIALITY, INDULGENCE, FORGIVENESS, CONCESSION, & ACCOMMODATION, which can alone render the OPERATION OF MORALITY certain, because it alone makes the practice of it easy.

Institutions can reform because they have been renovated by their members. At the same time, the author blurs the boundaries between institutions and persons; the individual qualities of a hero are pro-jected onto a social body writ as large as the ghost of Alfonso the Good

in *The Castle of Otranto.* Yet, while his catalogue literally and figuratively incorporates British civic heroism, the competing attributes
threaten to shiver this harmony to pieces. Already we can see some of
the different emphases that will divide the Gothic from the Romantic
ideal of heroism. The *Anti-Jacobin* writer wants tradition maintained, at
the same time that he prizes individualism – a shift notable in the
characterizations of both liberality and delicacy of sentiment as superseding rules and as enabling individual decision. Moreover, it is
unclear who must practice candor in order to benefit society: the one
who discriminates or the one who is being discriminated against.
Toleration, concession, indulgence, and forgiveness clasp hands with
delicacy of sentiment in promoting the welfare of prostitutes, but
guardians of morality may view this embrace with skepticism. Of greatest significance for the argument that follows, the gendered outlines of
this heroic body lack firm detail. Liberality and forgiveness, tradition-
ally identified with a chivalrous gallantry the preserve of males, are
eroticized through the throbbing eyes and hearts 'so lovely in repentance' and feminized through 'CONCESSION' and 'ACCOMMODA-
TION,' so that the image of 'energies called forth sometimes on one
side the question, sometimes on the other' becomes an apt symbol of
the fluidity of gender identification, a fluidity that will have important
consequences for readers' responses to the Gothic novel.

The passage above indicates the lack of stability shoring up notions
of a national hero. It is far easier to enumerate the social conditions
desired than to imagine how to arrive at them. Perhaps the *Anti-Jacobin*
is less forthcoming on this subject because, despite its overt allegiance
to individualism, as evidenced by the first passage quoted above, so
many of the improvements depend upon a centralized state power.
Hence, in the issue of 7 May, which again airs self-congratulations, the
letter from 'Muceus' calls our attention to the decrease in duelling and
gambling and the increase in education for female children, the
'improved situation of women in society,' and the 'decency and morality' of modern dramas, as compared with those penned by Congreve
and Centlivre (1791, 203), without citing any specific reasons for the
change. But the very conjunction of technological advances in communication, enhanced access to material goods, enforceability of the
law, and dissemination of education with dramatic and literary amend-
ment, especially when accompanied by an outline of social temperament resembling a sentimental (or a Gothic) hero, shows the habit of
linking the political and the literary even in British minds given to
conservative leanings. Whether we examine the periodical reviews

such as *The Monthly* and *The Critical*, run by Dissenters and supporting reform, the ostensibly neutral *Gentleman's Magazine*, or the avowedly conservative *Anti-Jacobin*,[34] we repeatedly discover delighted pronouncements that literature and politics cavort in the same bed, an obsession that predates our modern fascination with the alliance.[35] Time and again, literary reviews second this opinion. This belief in the didactic/prophylactic nature of literature has important consequences for the way Gothic novels will be reviewed, as I discuss at greater length in Chapter 1. It also testifies to a climate of opinion pervading readers as they encountered the new genre.

Belief in, or desire for, heroes also affects the reviews' self-representations, lending weight to my contention that the written word, and its producers, operated in a theater of war for the affections of the British public. Thus, when we come to consider the reviews of Gothic novels in Chapter 1, we must first bring their pronouncements down from the Olympian heights reviewers ventriloquized, remembering that the reviewers both participate in debates over heroic nationalism and attempt to construct themselves as the arbiters of that debate. So promiscuously did these couplings of literature and politics take place during the heady days of Revolution that the *Critical Review* attempted to legitimize the union.[36] An Advertisement in the first volume dated under the new style, 1791, announced that the *Review* had changed its format accordingly. A new Appendix would now review numerous political and literary works. 'A review of this kind, without the violence, the illiberality of party, neither dictated by a bigotted attachment to old forms nor an impetuous fondness for every innovation, cannot fail to be agreeable to the dispassionate reader, and will serve to connect, what the practice of mankind has already united, the political and literary department.' This advertisement serves my turn in several ways. First, it offers testimony, unmediated by critical interpretation or deflected through hearsay, that eighteenth-century men (and women) thought of literature and politics as inextricably tied. Second, it unconsciously demonstrates the influence of one on the other. For the *Review*'s self-representation tallies well with portraits of disinterested heroism circulating within its own pages and among its competitors. Neither menacing a shotgun wedding, disinheriting the offenders, nor constructing an imaginative Plato's Retreat for the wanton, the *Review* depicts itself as a commonsensical, tolerant parent, acceding to changes and trying to make the best of them.

In deciding the shape of its publication, the editors adopt characteristics of leadership they had earlier located in the political realm.

Inspecting Burke's *Speech on the Debate on the Army Estimates,* the reviewer says:

> Nothing can in our opinion be so different, so opposite in *appearance,* tendency and effects as the revolutions of 1688 and 1789: the one was conducted by a set of wise, enlightened politicians, the other by the eager violent phrenzy of *innovation*: the one was marked by beneficial *alterations*; the other by furious destruction: the one ended in increased energy and respectability; the other is apparently proceeding to national debility and bankruptcy.'
>
> (1790, 475; emphasis added)

Great leaders must distinguish alteration from destruction. Both involve change, but the leaders of the English Revolution had the good sense to impose change incrementally and with respect for tradition. While revolutions are here personified as leaders, they share with literary periodicals character traits whose oppositions we see again (and again) in novels: the hero is wise, cautious, a deliberate politician, with no pejorative meaning attached; the villain is rash hasty, imprudent, a gambler.

Despite the wide solidity of opinion concerning the union of the literary and the political, less agreement attended the requisite qualities for political or literary leadership than the *Critical's* assured moderation or Byron's modulated outrages would lead us to suspect. While the Gothic novel ultimately downplays the role of individualism, it furnishes heroes who amalgamate all the disparate characteristics desired by the *Anti-Jacobin.* By comparing the values urged by the periodicals with those incorporated by the Gothic novels under survey, we see most clearly how the Gothic participates in the construction of a British national identity through its imagining of a hero, entering into rather than acquiescing in a conversation.

Thrumming through that conversation is the question of access or barriers to membership in that national identity. The iconographic status of heroes and heroism becomes even more prominent when we look beyond the luxury editions, printed in three volumes and accompanied by stiff prices, that found their way into the hands of many both through booksellers and the circulating libraries. Such editions form the 'canonical' works of study today, insofar as Gothic, once considered a marginal branch of popular culture, can be said to have attained the status of canonical. But while the multiple printings and multiple title lists indicate a high level of activity, they alone did not suffice to quell the public appetite. The Gothic trod the stage in dramatic form; equally popular and prolific were the chapbook versions and redactions, whether by translation or abridgment, of published novels. The very existence, let alone significance, of these Gothic replications has gone unmentioned if not unrecognized.[37] That the Gothic spoke to its times in ways we have perhaps not yet discerned resounds in this sheer output and variety of forms. Accordingly, I read the luxury editions against these more plebeian forms. Through their techniques of production and distribution, these 'low-brow,' popular versions extend the invitation to participate in the Gothic nation, at the same time that they herd members of the nation into traditional enclosures, segregating the aristocratic heroes from servants and women.

The question of membership preoccupies those who chose to write the Gothic because it is the genre of choice for members of groups who were marginalized either because they occupied the liminal affective ground of female gender or 'deviant' sexual orientation, or because they inhabited the contested geographical ground of Ireland or Scotland.[38] Inevitably, the substantive and formal imbrication of the Gothic with matters economic, political, and social means that we cannot automatically brand the intention or the fruit of these authors' imaginings as conservative or subversive. Or, perhaps, better put it that we cannot necessarily decide issues of political affinity on the grounds of plot alone. Because women novelists depicted fictional heroines as incarcerated does not necessarily mean that they viewed all women as slaves to marriage, even though this was a trope available to them. Nor do the happy marriages that succeed their liberation from such prisons tip the scale in the opposite direction. Complaint is not the only mechanism of subversion, nor must the complacent celebration of conjugal happiness necessarily entail only conservatism. Just as we can condition women to seek more by harping on their injustices, so we can also inspire them to search by painting pictures of the better life attainable. As long as that better life rests on a meeting of equal individuals, then marriage will not have to deform into the 'slavery' decried by Wollstonecraft and Macauley. By attributing to their heroes qualities conventionally linked to the feminine, women authors promoted such equality.[39]

For their characters, women authors' subversiveness lay not merely in an anti-marriage, quasi-libertine liberationism. For themselves, they could be equally subversive by laying claim to the kind of authority previously the preserve of male authors. That authority takes two forms. On the one hand, it is professional. The women who wrote

Gothic novels thought of themselves foremost as participants in a literary tradition and expected (or hoped) that their works would assume a place in the general society. Even when their aims were overtly feminist, as I will argue was true for Clara Reeve, they expected male readers to be among their audience and knew that their works must appeal to readers of both sexes in order to receive the financial rewards they desired as much as fame.[40] On the other hand, or at the same time, it is political: the authority to speak of political affairs and the social, broadly defined. Such a reach was both necessitated and empowered by their turn to the Gothic.

The positions of Gothic novelists at the borders of the dominant social order invite us to recognize the extent to which these authors invest in nationalist imagining. And if the novelists give us heroes and heroines whose attributes make them worthy leaders of the nation, they construct *themselves* as heroes at the same time. Their self-reflexive eruptions into what would otherwise be seamless romance linearity foreground questions of production and reproduction. By insisting on the authenticity of their works, they concurrently assert authority for their productions. The relevance of these techniques to the nationalist vision of the Gothic novel becomes the subject of Chapter 7.

By reuniting these (fictional and fiction-writing) heroes and heroines with the (fictional and non-fictional) social milieus in which they move, we clarify the differences between the nationalist imaginings of the Gothic and those of the Romantic, whose formulations either confound the Nation and the cult of the individual, or suffuse the Nation with a transcendental philosophy in which only the authentic, subjective self has value.[41] By implying that private experience matters only insofar as it affects the public domain, Gothic novels enlarged readers' horizons beyond the domestic sphere emphasized by the novel proper: they substituted the good of the nation-state for identification along class lines.[42] And if that same nationalistic fervor sought to instill itself by 'reading nationalisms *genealogically* – as the expression of an historical tradition of serial continuity' (Anderson, 1991, 195), we should look to the concerns about genealogical transmission that govern the plots of Gothic novels as reflective of that nascent fervor.

If I offer an oblique angle to the work on the Gothic novel that has preceded me, I do so with the dual aim of intervening in our notions of how people read.[43] The feminine qualities attributed to the hero help us moderate Laura Mulvey's 1988 palinodic assertion of an 'immasculation' of the viewer/reader, and support a view of identification as complex, an 'extremely fluid and shifting process'

(Horrocks, 1995, 44). As Horrocks notes, men in film and sports have been spectacularized in much the same manner as have women. The same holds true for the Gothic hero, who not only draws our attention in the narrative but also constitutes one half of our visual pleasure in the illustrations accompanying the works.[44] Gothic novels call our attention to a technology of masculinity by spectacularizing the male. At the same time, because these heroes have character traits that cross gender barriers, they open up a cross-gender identification and suggest that masculinity is as much a subject position to be occupied for men as femininity is for women. Theorists of film have increasingly chipped away at the concept of visual representation as demonically unidirectional.[45] I would apply their insights to the narrative and visual features of the Gothic novel as well. Because readers left marginalia and commentaries, both on the 'high-culture' products of Gothic and on their 'popular' cousins, the chapbooks, we can gain insight into the way the Gothic helped form interpretive *and emulative* communities. Such a historical reception study can help us cure what Catherine Gallagher has called the naive tendency to take the text as a constant, 'the very instability of which is stable across time' (1989, 44).

Thus, studying Gothic novels and chapbooks from the perspective of nationalist discourse sharpens our ears to the desire for heroes constant over the period (if not indeed over time), at the same time that we can detect this refrain accommodating new strains. Estranged from earlier cultural and social ideals, Gothic novelists and eighteenth-century periodical writers present their solutions 'as acts of repair or adaptation,' preluding the same motif struck with obsessive frequency by those mid-Victorian connoisseurs of the heroic, Carlyle and Thackeray: that heroism must be made over to their own needs and that it requires a new footing in 'enlightened good sense' (Ousby, 1981, 152–3). However, unlike their Victorian successors, Gothic technicians of the heroic aim not to shrink heroism to fit 'the restricted scope that modern life affords' but to expand modern life to fill the contours of an earlier enlarged age. Their championing of heroes and heroism is mimetic 'not by virtue of imitating the externals of some historical situation but by imitating a *moral attitude* which, however moribund at present, may be brought to life in any age of human history' (Dowling, 1981, 114). As Dowling goes on to claim, such mimesis aimed to help 'men or entire societies' create, or recreate, themselves in this image. In succeeding chapters, we will examine how Gothic mimesis merged with contemporary ideas about heroism to shape novels and their reception.

An effort must be made to reclaim *all* the hidden layers of the palimpsest that is Gothic. Joel Porte says that 'the critic searching for something like a unified field theory of Gothic fiction will certainly be tempted to throw down his pen in despair' (1974, 42). For me, the diversity represented by the entire field of Gothic, whether literary or extra-literary, is matter for celebration. I would like to replace Porte's idea of a unified field theory with a quantum approach, in which minute discriminations are drawn, each of which may temporarily destabilize our sense of secure knowledge. Ultimately, a survey of the discrete particulars making up the universe of Gothic may lead us to a better understanding of the cultural work performed in the buried life of the Gothic novel.

Part I:
Tailoring the Gothic Myth

1
Bearing Repetition

> Times are bad. Children no longer obey their parents, and
> everyone is writing a book.
>
> (Marcus Tullius Cicero)

In 1793, a group of Americans toured the estate of the quondam
Englishman and financier of the American Revolution, Robert Morris.
This group was a family, the Constables. What brought them there,
who they were, what their connections, national affiliations, or means
of acquaintance with so prominent a member of society: on all these
topics, history has little to say. Nor do we know the purpose of their
visit with any certainty, or the conversation that passed among them
as they promenaded the grounds. We can, however, imagine their surroundings. Cookham forms the northwest parish of Windsor; the
Castle is but one of many historical structures decorating the landscape, and the topography itself undulates with numerous other graces:
chalk hills ring the town, while the Thames cuts through the valley,
watering heath, parklands, and Windsor Forest, with Eton visible
across the river. Perhaps memory can serve if imagination fails: Austen
gives us Elizabeth perambulating Pembroke with Darcy, or Catherine
Morland being shepherded around Northanger by Henry; Pope epically
bodies forth the landscape's lushness, its productive nurture of
England's greatness, furnishing both human leaders and creature comforts. And perhaps both of these aims lent motive to the Constables'
visit beyond the usual curiosity of tourists, just as the Bennetts and the
Morlands, less consciously, designed. For the Constables had a daughter, and that daughter seems to have made an impression upon the
mind, if not the heart, of Morris's son, at least insofar as one of Ann
Radcliffe's novels can testify. On the end-leaf of volume I of her *The*

Romance of the Forest, second edition (1792), we find the moment etched for posterity: 'Given to Anne Marie Constable by Robert Morris son of our great financier Robert Morris[1] – while on a visit at his country residence at Cookham England with her parents in 1793 –.' While history also fails to record the subsequent fate of these young people, the fact of the book as a medium of exchange is suggestive. It hints at a Gothic novel's propriety, its status as a proper instrument to forge relationships between people.

Nor are these two young readers of Radcliffe anomalous. Equally tantalizing evidence exists, suggesting that audiences for the various types of Gothic production I outlined in the introduction – the 'high-quality' novels and their 'low-brow' imitations, the redactions, the chapbooks – remained neither rigidly stratified nor exclusive.[2] Despite many recent critical assertions denominating the Gothic the province of women or of the lower classes, men and women of means or position seem to have been equally eager consumers of Gothic, as witnessed by the flyleaf inscriptions or bookplates of owners' names still affixed to the early editions housed in the magnificent Sadleir-Black Collection at the University of Virginia, a collection which forms a representative cross-section of the genre. For instance, the flyleaf of the 1797 Dublin edition of Ann Radcliffe's *The Italian* bears the inscription 'Sir John C. Carden, Bart, Templemore, October 12, 1797'; this edition also carries a price of £8. 8s. The 1795 American edition of *The Mysteries of Udolpho* records two owners, William Oliver, 1799, and Elizabeth Dorr, 1853. The fourth London edition (1799) of the same novel attests to its transmission through several hands: the name 'E. L. Haven, Calcutta, 1849' is followed by a Boston Library sticker, then the notice that the book was given to the Roxbury Athenaeum 11 October 1886. The fifth London edition announces Lady Le Fleming, Rydal Hall, as its owner. And the first edition owned by the University of Virginia carries the suggestive name Eliza Shelley, the two dots after the 'a' implying that the name is an abbreviation for Elizabeth and that the owner thus is Percy's sister. The first edition of Matthew Lewis's *The Monk* is graced by the armorial bookplate of W. Richard Whatham of Liverpool. A Bennett Wood Green, MD, of Warwick City, Virginia, owned the second edition. Two copies of the 1818 edition exist at Virginia. The first contains the armorial bookplates of Herbert Wilson Greene and of Hugh Walpole, and the bookplate of W. C. Brackenburn. The second copy wears the bookplate of Sir Benjamin Morris. While the chapbook versions undoubtedly were purchased by people of lesser means and standing, they were also collected by children of sufficient means to amass a substantial collection and to have those individual works bound, in leather, into private volumes to which they then attached titles like *The Entertainer* or *Tales and Romances*.[3] For instance, in volume I of *Tales and Romances*, we find 17 chapbooks bound together. These chapbooks were originally issued by a variety of publishing houses. None of the title pages of these individual works carries a publishing date, but the date at which they were purchased is inscribed. It ranges from 1810 to 1818, the year in which binding took place. Perhaps part of this cost was defrayed by the children's generosity: the individual works were passed from brother to brother to sister, each of whom would inscribe his or her name and the date at which he or she finally obtained the longed-for possession. This evidence about readership not only demonstrates cross-class and cross-gender interest in the Gothic novel, but also portrays the Gothic novel as forming around it a society of its own, a portrait tacitly confirmed, if overtly ridiculed, by Austen herself in *Northanger Abbey*.

To those familiar with the history of animus against the novel, the idea that any type of novel could be a means of communication or of formation for a society must seem perverse. Yet that very idea threads through contemporary reviews of Gothic novels. Rather than siding with Wordsworth's theory that the taste for Gothic novels evinced a pervasive mental aberration, a population suddenly obsessed with sanguinary dreams, contemporary critics, professional and amateur, found in the Gothic novel their own dreams of a nation, past, present, and future. Reviewers of Gothic novels not only ignore the 'supernatural horrors' so fascinating to modern readers but they also tacitly acknowledge the sociality of the Gothic novel by praising its evocation of 'sympathetic emotions, whether of pity or terror' (*Monthly Review*, 15 (1794): 279).

Because these critics viewed the Gothic novel as underscoring the link between individual humans and their society, their example should help us distinguish the Gothic from the novel of manners. It might seem as though a close connection subsists between the two. Both were produced at the same moment, that era of rapid social change, both record changing social standards and values, and both were widely read. Yet we should not be led astray by such similarities as to impute more fundamental sympathies.[4] I would maintain that a signal difference between them lies in the features to be emulated. For the Gothic, it is the notion of the heroic national character, as set over against the subjective or individual. When Gothic novels fail to provide such a socialized self, they draw invective. For instance, the review of *Adeline de Courcy* praised the character Zodisky for his 'honour, generosity, and disinterested love' as not only 'pleasing to the reader's imagination,' but also as having 'a good effect on his heart.' However, the fact that Zodisky takes it upon himself to punish the villainous Marquis de Rozancourt produces unease: 'however defective our laws may be in avenging crimes ... the most destructive to the peace and happiness of society, danger may arise from every man's assuming a right to redress himself, when injured; and the practice of duelling should never meet with countenance and encouragement from those who are capable of reflecting on the evils which attend it' (*Monthly Review*, 26 (1798): 107).[5] The interest in a technology of the 'self' does overlap with the thematic and ideological desires of the Gothic novel; nevertheless, we read anachronistically when we recognize that 'self' as a hauntingly familiar modern bourgeois or hear these texts interpellating a 'self' that has not yet been constructed. As the evidence I adduced above about the cross-class and cross-gender interest in the Gothic novel suggests, we cannot confine our interest in the audience of Gothic to any one group. I believe that, in order to understand these desires and their technological transmission properly, we must consider how the Gothic was perceived by those who read, and wrote, it first.

For example, the *Monthly Review* and the *British Critic*, diametrically opposed politically, united in praise of the heroes of Ann Radcliffe's *The Italian*.[6] The latter found her hero and heroine to have merit, not the least of which was that they were 'occasionally, disguised into characters which afford a commentary upon the customs of the country' (1791, 266). The former found '[T]he impetuous Marchesa, the stern, intriguing, terrific Schedoni, and the amiable, pensive Olivia' become doubly interesting 'by their connection with Vivaldi and Ellena' (283). Although these records may not celebrate Gothic heroes as openly as did Fenn, More, and Barbauld in my introduction, they do praise the moral tendency of the works. And, as we will see, morality equals social utility equals heroic character.[7]

Morality and social utility become increasingly important categories in the reviews. Commenting on Clara Reeve's *The Champion of Virtue*, the writer opines that 'the story being well contrived, agreeably told, and not very long, may be ranked among those which afford a tolerable degree of amusement, *without any dangerous tendency* (*Critical Review* (1777): 154, emphasis mine). To the *Critical Review*, Reeve's story has a negative virtue; it amuses without danger because it does not too long distract from more serious work. The reviewer of *The Abbey of Saint*

Asaph complained of the author's 'compliance with the present rage for the terrible' by his inclusion of a 'horrid cavern,' a 'fiery spectre,' and a 'moving and shrieking skeleton'; nevertheless the reviewer held the novel a 'pleasing performance' with 'good moral reflections ... interspersed' (*Monthly Review*, 15 (1795): 229).

Charges of subversion in the Gothic novel appear only with regard to the literary decorum of diction. For instance, George Moore's *Grasville Abbey* earned this terse dismissal: 'A dismal story, related (if we may use a familiar phrase) in a stile *dismally bad*' (*British Critic* (1798): 305). Joseph Fox drew fire for his *Santa-Maria; or, The Mysterious Pregnancy*, because the subject matter and the style equally offended the reviewer (*British Critic* (1798): 183–4). But critics undermine their own linkage of probable plot with truthful characterization when they separate the two.[8] Ministers of the King betrayed no anxiety about the subversive tendencies of *The Mysteries of Udolpho*, unlike the attitude they took to Godwin's *Caleb Williams*, published the same year. Writing about Godwin's novel, the *British Critic* said:

> This piece is a striking example of the evil use which may be made of considerable talents, connected with such a degree of intrepidity as can inspire the author with resolution to attack religion, virtue, government, laws, and above all, the desire (hitherto accounted laudable) of leaving a good name to posterity.
>
> In this extraordinary performance, every gentleman is a hard-hearted assassin, or a prejudiced tyrant; every Judge is unfit, every Justice corrupt and blind. Sentiments of respect to Christianity are given only to the vilest wretch in the book; while the most respectable person in the drama abhors the idea of 'shackling his expiring friend with the fetters of superstition.'
>
> In order to render the laws of his country odious, the author places an innocent prisoner, whose story he (avowedly) takes from the Newgate Calendar of the first George's reign, in a dungeon; the wretched state of which he steals (as avowedly) from one of the benevolent Howard's painful descriptions of a worse gaol than common...
>
> When a work is so directly pointed at every band which connects society, and at every principle which renders it amiable, its very merits become noxious as they tend to cause its being known in a wider circle.
>
> (1794, 70–1)

Whereas the *British Critic* censured Godwin in the strongest language, compare the same journal's estimation of the merits of *The Mysteries of Udolpho*:

> We so very seldom find, in a work of imagination, those qualities combined, which are necessary to its successful accomplishment, that when the event does happen, we distinguish it as a place of repose from our severer labours, and are happy to beguile the hours of weariness and chagrin beneath the shade which fancy spreads around. A tale, regularly told, neither offending probability by its extravagance, nor fatiguing by its want of vivacity or incident, has ever been esteemed among those labours of the mind which the critic cannot disdain to commend, ... and when it is further embellished by the charms of good writing, is the vehicle of ingenuous sentiments, and inculcates the purest morality, it eminently takes the lead in that class of writings, which is professedly designed for entertainment.
>
> (1794, 110)

The improbabilities of romance cannot damage readers so much as a willful attack upon society and its heroes. Two decades later, John Dunlop enters the same opinion about the 'virtuous' effects of Gothic romances (1814, 587).[9]

Even Flammenberg's *The Necromancer* betrays a social function:

> Exclusive of the entertainment arising from this narrative, it has in view an additional purpose, of greater importance to the public. It exposes the arts which have been practised in a particular part of Germany, for carrying on a series of nocturnal depredations in the neighborhood, and infusing into the credulous multitude a firm belief in the existence of sorcery.
>
> (*Critical Review* (July 1794): 469)

The supernatural no longer forms merely a supplementary value to entertainment. By the time of the French Revolution, the supernatural announces a critique of the mummeries by which the populace can be manipulated.

When we realize that the respectable periodical press interpreted Gothic novels as pointing to contemporary political events, Joanna Southcott's 'divine analysis' of Ann Radcliffe's *The Romance of the Forest* appears less eccentric. Although Southcott's millenarian views may strike us as extreme (or eerily familiar) today, she had literally thousands of followers. Southcott reads Radcliffe's novel on two levels: the first agitates over the day of judgment; the second, more mundane level, burns a path to France. As Eugene P. Wright, whose researches uncovered the unpublished manuscript, reports: 'The evil Marquis is a symbol of the French people, who had murdered their King and replaced him with Napoleon, one infinitely more evil. Adeline is identified as a symbol of England, for just as the evil Phillipe de Montalt pursued the virtuous Adeline, so was the corrupt France then intending to destroy England' (1970, 385).

As the French Revolution caused people to alter their ideas of the supernatural and of villainy, so it produced a need for a new hero. Hester Thrale Piozzi exemplifies this uneasy blending of real and fictional tastes, worn so lightly by those living through it. Piozzi repeatedly praises Burke. According to her editors, political stability in England was more important to her than class identity (1989, 16). In her outrage at French actions, she approved Pitt and George III's suspension of Habeas Corpus in 1794 and accepted the Treasonable Practices and Seditious Meetings Acts (17). Piozzi dismissed the idea that mutineers were justified in their objections to wretched conditions on board; she wanted mutinies to be ruthlessly suppressed and their leaders executed, because she feared that mutinies would lead to mob rule and the anarchy of France (18). She seeks the same sort of exemplary 'leadership' in her fictional heroes. The Gothic novel stood to the ready with its apposite alternative. Writing to her daughter on 25 October 1796 about Matthew Lewis's work, she acknowledges his resonance with public taste, a taste she herself ratifies:

> The taste in this City is altered since she [Frances Burney] last wrote – People are tired of figures in just proportions, – some going to Court, some crying Fish, moving across a Camera Obscura in St. James Street; They want Gyants again and Dragons, and with Respect for the German Valour, there is stolen in a revived liking for Runic and Scaldic Imagery, – from the same Country.
>
> (391)

She goes on to recommend that her daughter read Lewis's verse ballad, 'Alonzo the Brave and Fair Imogine,' which had been reprinted from his novel in *Gentleman's Magazine* (66, 1796), and had also appeared in the *Morning Chronicle* for 27 July.

Nathan Drake perceived the supernatural elements of the Gothic novel as 'calculated to soothe and support the mind' (1800, 62–3).

While Drake prizes these elements as awakening our feelings to heavenly inspiration, a more concrete interpretation of such 'awakening' existed in the rhetoric of the new European nationalisms, which characterized themselves as 'awakening from sleep' (B. Anderson, 1991, 195).[10] Since the hero awakened to the evils contaminating his realm through the agency of dreams and supernatural visitations, this political metaphor may be seen to underlie the imagery of dreams and the subconscious figured in the Gothic novel.

The Gothic novel was uniquely positioned to capitalize on the grudging acceptance gradually granted the fact of the novel's preeminence as a genre. The Gothic novel's special status arose from the history of Gothic as an ideological force in nationalistic discourse, from the romance revival which celebrated medieval culture and literature as elevating the British nation above all others, and from the immediate social conditions surrounding the emergence of the subgenre, which melded those historical precedents to fit the keenly felt need for heroes I've outlined in the introduction. This chapter will rehearse that history, beginning with the distaste articulated by cultural guardians, and continuing with the subtle inducements to acquire a taste for the novel urged by its defenders.[11] From there, I will retrace the history of Gothic as a political and aesthetic category, before showing how that history was seized upon by the romance revivalists of the mid-eighteenth century.

Invading forces

Optimism about the novel as a means of communication had not always prevailed. Shaftesbury had early posited an analogy between the aesthetic and the moral. But as the century's debates over leadership and the public sphere evolved into a competition between 'a conception of property which stresses possession and civic virtue with one which stresses exchange and the civilization of the passions' (Pocock, 1985, 115), possession of moral taste and the modes of acquiring it came under increasing pressure. Fiction especially exacerbated that tension.[12] Later critics, corroded by anxiety that fiction's moral status impinged on the social to the extent that it amounted to the quasi-political, would more eagerly sever the two. Indeed, the mid-eighteenth century saw numerous treatises deriding fiction and novel-reading as isolating. In analyzing the rise of 'aesthetics' as a socio-politically mediated intellectual field, historians and sociologists usually concentrate on Hume, Kant, Schiller, or Rousseau. But Kames and Monboddo serve us better here for two reasons.[13] First the temporal proximity of their work makes their ideas more germane to the genesis of the Gothic novel. Their works represent the fracture point in notions of culture's role. Second, the theories they create to solder over that fracture anticipate and prepare the way for solutions employed by the Gothic novel.

A career of successive editions and responses, pro and con, to *Elements of Criticism* (1762) by Henry Home, newly created Lord Kames, speaks to its influence.[14] Even though Kames refrains from directly attacking the novel, as later writers will do, he omits it from the categories of fine arts that he establishes. This omission speaks volumes about his fears. When he does occasionally discuss literary works qua solitary reading exercises, he confines his few examples to poetry, history, and rhetoric. Holding a Longinian theory of the type of reader response produced by good literature, he deems it of little consequence whether the kind of literature read be fable or 'true history,' and admits that fable is often more effective in raising an emotional response (1830, 50–1). Still, since fable 'operates on our passions … by deluding us into a conviction of reality' (394), Kames urges that fablers borrow from history to foster the delusion. As though he were writing a prescription for a Gothic novel, he cautions that 'the subject chosen must be distant in time, or at least in place' (ibid.).

Kames addresses the question of a common human nature, a communion that might be presumed by the notion of taste. Artistic adherence to commonality promotes accomplishment in the arts and underwrites their expense. For Kames, as for Shaftesbury, common standards only exist with respect to morals and fine arts. Furthermore, the 'common sense' of taste is restricted to a narrow compass. Laborers are 'totally void of taste'; the wealthy consult only their vanity and desire to overawe (444–5). This is fortunate, because it permits men to hold different stations in life without experiencing discontent: 'a taste too refined would obstruct that plan; for it would crowd some employments, leaving others, no less useful, totally neglected' (440). Accordingly, Kames limits his definition of the fine arts to those which preserve uniformity of taste. The social benefits of the fine arts emerge from their ability to knit men of different classes together:

> The separation of men into different classes, by birth, office, or occupation, however necessary, tends to relax the connection that ought to be among members of the same state; which bad effect is

in some measure prevented by the access all ranks of people have to public spectacles, and to amusements that are best enjoyed in company. Such meetings, where every one partakes of the same pleasures in common, are no slight support to the social affections.

(443)

The crucial element in this passage is his reference to public spectacles, to art that can be enjoyed as a communal event. It follows naturally that his examples derive from perceptible objects like painting, nature, gardening, and architecture; that when he discusses literary works, he relies heavily on cases drawn from the drama.

Kames's emphasis upon public spectacle announces an underlying fear about social disaffection, a fear that will reach a crescendo in the latter half of the century. Kames's solution is to ignore or downplay the very genre producing those fears. Unlike Kames, James Monboddo, in his 1773 *Of the Origin and Progress of Language,* adverts to the eminence of the new novelistic genre when he cites Fielding's and Swift's perfections (1786, 195–6, 296–7). Yet this praise for the novel cannot stand unqualified: he calls Fielding one of the 'greatest *poetical* geniuses of his age' (298, emphasis added). Monboddo's conversion of Fielding into an epic poet is consistent with his privileging of Greek literature as the exemplary model. Behind the comment, though, we can also locate a wishful transportation of novel-reading's insularity to the public arena of an epic poem.

The class-inflected fears articulated by Kames and Monboddo resemble Wordsworth's strictures against 'frantic novels,' although Wordsworth fulminates in a different register (Preface to *Lyrical Ballads,* 1802, 145). Wordsworth heard the taste for 'German horrifications' as speaking to a need for stimulation, produced by the deadening labor of industrialization and the pressure of crowded cities. While his characterization of the Industrial Revolution may have accurately represented the condition of the masses, his strictures against novels presume or portray a readership not fairly reflective of actuality. Instead, we can see through the screen of his remarks his apprehension that poetry no longer holds the preeminent position in letters, and his reinvention of a common human nature as requiring the intervention of a bardic calling.[15]

If, as for Daniel Cottom, the 'taste' of Kames and Monboddo represents not only 'the aspiration to attain the status or recognition of the aristocracy but also the aspiration of the aristocracy to fulfill the idea of itself' (7), Wordsworth's comments announce the attempt of the literati to fulfill their idea of themselves as aristocratic. Critics whose fears about the novel struck another vein seem to have been inspired by a similar sense of guardianship. Within the same period that Kames, Monboddo, and Wordsworth were denouncing the novel for locking readers into isolation, critics began warning about contamination through imaginative conjunction. The *Critical Review*'s 1778 review of *Evelina* can stand in for a host of similar comments in this vein. While the writer admires Burney's work, he bemoans the practice of depicting noble characters:

> We could wish her husband had not been a lord, and that her father had been less rich... The purchasers of novels, the subscribers to circulating libraries, are seldom in more elevated situations than the middle ranks of life – The subjects of novels are, with a dangerous uniformity, almost always taken from superior life. – The satirists complain with justice of the want of virtue in our modern nobility; when the hero and heroine of every novel hardly ever fail, sooner or later, to turn out a lady or a lord. What effect has this upon the readers? They are convinced that happiness is not to be found in the chilling climate of low life, nor even, where one of our poets so truly fixed it, in the temperate zone of middle life. – Rank alone contains this unknown good, wealth alone can bestow this coveted joy.... What is the consequence? Their fates have perhaps destined them to be a petty attorney or a silver smith's daughter, a grocer's son or a clergyman's heiress; fortune *positively* refuses to realize any of their romantic dreams; and a quarter of an hour's perusal of an unnatural novel has embittered all their lives.
>
> (203–4)

How fortunate for Burney that the reviewer *liked* her novel! Nevertheless, the reviewer worries that readers will internalize such idealized representations of the aristocracy. Detached from anchoring personal attributes, nobility floats as a free signifier of wealth, falsely equated with happiness. Novels become unnatural because they inspire a desire for consumption beyond the means of the reader and for an imagined identity similarly detached from any traditional demarcations of belonging.

   While no agreement about the reason for fear emerges, we can witness through these juxtaposed comments a progress of social unease. Kames and Monboddo envision fiction-reading as a solitary endeavor that damages sociality, because its reinforcement of social stratifications makes those divisions visible and hence targets for demolition. With Wordsworth, the demotic art of fiction becomes demonic, an arm of the factory that mass-produces men and machines. The *Critical Review*'s writer acknowledges that fiction has become a social event; even though the individual act may be performed in isolation, knowledge about the content of that act, if not the actual experience, helped bridge the divide. But this bridging is no longer viewed as desirable, as it had been for Kames and Monboddo. Instead, art as communion gets translated into art as consumption, eating away at rather than reinforcing or smoothing over traditional barriers.

As E. J. Clery has argued, and as the *Critical Review* passage illustrates, the 'attack on novels and novel-reading in this period was part of the wider opposition to consumerism' (1995, 7). In the *Critical Review*, we see a stepped-down version of convention: no longer even securely middle class, novel readers purchase aristocratic dreams. But the fantasy purveyed is not alone that of noble birth; to be valuable, rank must be accompanied by wealth. Those who wished to defend the novel against such detraction used the same logic, while purifying away any material consequences of consumption.

For instance, Hugh Murray, in his 1805 defense *Morality of Fiction*, begins by assuming that the universal taste for fiction validates its morality *and* utility. These twin qualities arise from fiction's ability to 'exhibit examples of conduct, superior to those which are to be met with in ordinary life' (3). Murray is everywhere concerned to prove the *practical* effect of reading (9). Examples of human life and manners can protect a person from committing errors upon entering life that might cripple fortune and happiness, a conjunction analogous to that of utility and morality. Enough examples will furnish forth a 'science of domestic life' (4), two more terms that invoke the sanction of enlightenment philosophy and morality, and thereby temper the equation of fortune with happiness. However, founding philosophical ideas upon any other basis than an empirical one endangers reason and logic (10–13). Murray saves reading from such threats by making imaginative identification a kind of empirical lesson. His fears about undermining empirical habits of thought and action seem to have been anticipated by the Gothic novelists, who repeatedly emphasize the empirical qualities of their heroes and heroines.

Murray, too, values the exhortation of superior examples; these best harness man's innate propensity to imitation (18). As if in confirmation of his own theory, Murray calls to his aid the writings of Kames, Johnson, and Blair, thus giving his ideas a pedigree and history and making them a species of the very imitation he advocates. Like Kames, Murray urges that we select the grounds of our imitation very carefully, rejecting cold perfection for warm courage and active virtue. In other words, we want a hero. Answering minutely quibbles about the novel, Murray asserts that reading about or contemplating heroes will form an 'habitual disposition to act conformably... and be ready to manifest itself at the first favourable opportunity' (27). Moral fiction will create the equivalent of a standing army without the attendant dangers of well-armed men. In the next section, we see why a novel denominated 'Gothic' could furnish such an army of readers.

Out of the Gothic past

As an ideological construct, 'Gothic' had long been poised to fill a powerful role. Etymological history at first obscures this potential potency, since 'Gothic' initially takes divergent paths. One path gives access to seventeenth- and eighteenth-century politics; the other leads us to aesthetic concerns about literature, art, and architecture during the same period. Critics of many schools and disciplines have treated these two branches as distant relatives, deriving merely from a common root, especially because the former usually carries a positive while the latter carries a negative charge. Despite the apparent divide, the two branches are near kin. Common elements either in the rhetoric employed or in the impulses driving the debates link them. These impulses include the desire to retroactively construct a national genealogy, to found the genealogy on heroic ancestors, and to use that heroic ancestry both as a panacea for social divisiveness and as a prophylactic against competition from other European nations.

Politically, the Gothic story had a long and independent chapter. Early Gothic theorists subdivided as Continental or English; but, in either case, their creation of the term 'Gothic' as a general, broadly based category of peoples was in each originary moment an act accessory to the foundation of a nationalist myth.[16] Both versions of the Gothic myth connected the Goths with the Germanic tribes: on the Continent (with the obvious exception of Germany), the heritage was seen as an oppressive burden to be overthrown; in England, Germanic traditions were felt to have bequeathed an inherent love for liberty that would color debates over the division of power in England and, subsequently, Great Britain.[17]

Early in seventeenth-century England, the budding myth of Gothic origins shows promise of the political fruit that myth could bear. In

England, the term 'Gothic tradition' had two, principally democratic, meanings: the Saxon custom of *witenagemot* and the Kentish institution of *gavelkynde*. *Witenagemot* meant free tribal assemblies, which invested power in elected chiefs; the chiefs deliberated over minor matters, while the whole tribe voiced its opinion on larger questions such as the proclamation of war.[18] *Gavelkynde* equalized heritable property distribution. The first Society of Antiquaries zealously promoted the notion that ancient political liberties furnished a legacy for the present. The story they disseminated, that these political liberties included an elective parliamentary assembly whose members then chose one of themselves as a provisional king, proved the democratic character of those liberties and formed perhaps the Society's most seditious idea.[19]

Whereas James I could suppress the first Society of Antiquaries by abolishing it in 1604, on allegations that this Society was political in nature and that its members were hostile to the King, he could neither silence their rhetoric nor stamp out the politicization of history. The subsequent debates over Gothic origins show the two egalitarian prongs of *witenagemot* and *gavelkynde* converging, as adversaries attempt to decide whether the monarchy is a 'free gift' or an 'inheritance.' The controversy eddies around specific genealogical questions: how old is the Constitution? how much power should be delegated to Parliament? is that power a free gift of the monarch and consequently revocable, or is it part of the Saxon inheritance? if an inheritance, was the entailment curtailed by the Norman conquest? and indeed, did a conquest per se ever occur, or was William invited into the kingdom with the proviso that he honor the Saxon custom of *witenagemot*? Charles's opponents claimed to fan the ardor for Gothic nationalism because they prized such a pyramidal structure as *witenagemot* as the seed of English parliaments. Whether their love was born of experience or of expediency, Parliamentary leaders seized the epithet 'Gothic' to defend their rights against Charles I's encroaching claims of royal absolutism. The year 1688 marked the juncture of 'modern' politics and the 'Gothic' myth. The contractual agreements reached in the Glorious Revolution permitted Englishmen to rewrite history with a second 'Norman invasion' over which they exercised full control. Englishmen reasserted their right to hold a king to Constitutional prescriptions at the same time that they justified the apparent breach of power by reference to the unbroken continuity of Parliament.

While current historians debate whether 'Gothic liberty' more properly belongs to Whig or Tory camps, the identification of the trope as congruent with either party is irrelevant to my purposes.[20] Indeed, Bolingbroke's application of the convention in the *Craftsman*, a use not considered by the historians, would make such a unilateral assignment problematic. I am concerned, however, to demonstrate that the idea of Gothic as the locus of traditional British liberty is pervasive in England from the mid-seventeenth century forward; and, for that reason, the decision to use the very epithet to characterize one's work cannot be utterly divorced from the political associations which the term had carried up to the time when it is employed by Walpole et al.

If the identification of Gothic as a nationalist political formation had obtained a secure footing by the Glorious Revolution, its footing as an aesthetic category was far more shaky. We can see this dual valuation clearly in William Temple's 1690 series of essays, *Miscellania*, Parts I and II. Temple's work demonstrates the nascent concatenation of politics and aesthetics, a union that will be celebrated by eighteenth-century theorists of romance and ratified by periodical writers at the end of the century, as I have already argued in my introduction. However, Temple's attitude towards 'Gothic' wears a Janus-face: 'Gothic' politics have positive value; 'Gothic' aesthetics represent a debasement of Roman language and poetry into Romance languages and tales respectively.[21] Temple's allegiance to classicism in literary matters is well known, and accounts for his dyslogistic allusion to romance. Nevertheless, present in these two essays are a constellation of associations that will be repeated in the Gothic novel: the fight against barbarism, the hero as leader of a new civilization, chivalry, and the supernatural. This constellation foreshadows the merger of substantive and stylistic elements in subsequent discussion of Gothic.[22] Once eighteenth-century aestheticians have reevaluated romance, providing it with a legitimate genealogy, the cluster of ideas will furnish the means whereby the next wave of 'Gothic' assimilation can occur.

The curve of history

Given the history of Gothic as a political construct, it perhaps comes as little surprise that the springboard upon which Gothic aesthetics leapt to prominence was nationalistic identification, although this fact has been neglected in recent critical discussion. As early as 1689, John Shurley proclaimed the reading of romance valuable because it could inspire readers to emulate its heroes and thus 'to raise the very name of the British empire, as formerly it was, to be the Terror of the World.'[23] It was no accident, however, that Shurley was a publisher/bookseller, and that his proclamation of benefits appeared in abridged and revised versions of traditional romances that he peddled to the lower classes. In consequence of his professional interest, Shurley advocated romance as a highway along which peasants and artisans could traverse the limitations of their class. His romances would provide mental exercise for 'Country-Swains,' teaching them to discover in their rural pursuits opportunities for 'Martial Atchievements,' so that theirs might imaginatively be transformed into 'Princely' minds. Of his edition of *The Seven Champions of Christendom*, Shurley held it equally suited to the 'meanest Capacity' and to the learned. In keeping with this goal, 'the writers of the prefaces still clung to the courtly quality of the works.'[24]

The eighteenth-century revival of interest in romance proceeded from the same transposition of class identification, motivated by similar professional interests, and covered up by the same appeal to a nationalistic impulse. Spearheaded by the antiquarian movement, scholars at mid-century reacted against the Greek and Roman models exalted by the neoclassical Augustans. Ironically, the same allegiance to order, discipline, and reason that gave rise to neoclassical literature also resulted in numerous treatises that sought to classify and trace the origins of literary kinds. This process of classification was accompanied by theories of the origins of romance. The great antiquarian disseminators of romance theory and practice – the Wartons, Percy, and Hurd – were all members of institutions fighting for a larger and more influential role in society: Percy and Hurd were bishops; Thomas Warton was Professor of Poetry and later of History at Oxford, and was ultimately rewarded with the Poet Laureateship.[25] Whether their strategy was consciously designed or not, its success before the explosion of Gothic fiction may be measured by George II's granting of a royal charter to the Society of Antiquaries in 1751. That antiquarian interest in Gothicism, political and aesthetic, was now perceived as conducive to national glory may have resulted, in part, from the long-standing association of Gothic with things Germanic: at this juncture, a house of German kings occupied the throne of Britain.

Like Paul-Henri Mallet, who advocated the study of Northern religions because they shed light on the customs and attitudes of modern Europe, English antiquarians urged the study of romance because it would shed light on the sources of British literary greatness.[26] In making this claim, scholars exceeded the more modest aims of tracking possible analogues of and influences on the work of Spenser, Shakespeare, and Milton. They intended nothing less than the laying title to the originals, by proving that romance originated in the Anglo imagination.[27]

Through MSS collections available at the newly formed British Museum and in private collections housed at Oxford, Cambridge, and in the archives of the Society of Antiquaries, evidence accumulated that romances had remained popular throughout the sixteenth and seventeenth centuries. Antiquarians trumpeted this information as justification for their own interests. Romance, it was claimed, could do more than inform scholars about the origins and development of English literature, although this alone was a worthy recompense for scholarly labors. Because romances were considered the characteristic product of the Middle Ages, the study of romance could furnish rewards for historians seeking knowledge of medieval history and geography. Romances were culled for their abundant details of chivalric feasts, costumes, architecture, jewelry, armor, and hunting since, even if idealized, these details represented the range of the conceivable (Johnston, 1964, 13). Exceeding the provision of education about the past, the study of romance could lead to a wholly new mode of aesthetic appreciation. When information about medieval life was welded to the knowledge of medieval literature, as exemplified by Chaucer, Spenser, Shakespeare, and Milton, the medieval world's superiority to the classical world would shine forth. And the specifically English nature of that superiority would inspire nationalistic pride.

The need for such a fiction originally had been spurred by the very bloodless revolution fought on 'Gothic' ground. One hundred years later, relative political stability was producing economic growth; but economic growth was rocking social stability. As the balance of economic power shifted in the newly formed Great Britain, the pre-1688 debate renewed itself and gathered impetus as the number and social status of people agitating for access to political power broadened. The rhetoric of 'free gift' versus 'inheritance' in the Gothic debate over the nature of government began to dovetail with the Gothic notion of *gavelkynde*, when invoked by the propertyless classes seeking to assert their rights to the political power ensured by Gothic traditions. The question, or problem, of access would be answered by the extension of Gothic politics through Gothic aesthetics.[28] Binding together the disparate phenomena of medieval art or the fragmented clusters of the eighteenth-century population, 'Gothic' romance would give evidence of an organic nationalist culture.

The aesthetic conflicts provoked by the romance revivalists speak to a growing awareness of literature's fitness for ideological service. Their arguments on its behalf testify to the increasing importance of reading as a mode of entertainment. Like their opponents, the revivalists saw the solitary nature of reading as posing a threat to social cohesion, a threat that could be overcome only if literature fostered the illusion of commonality by providing a myth of noble origins that would apply to members of all classes.[29] That myth lay ready to hand in the romance topos of discovered origins. By linking romance to a feudal order of life, they saw the fictions resulting as simultaneously uniting readers and reinstilling the desire for social hierarchy. As we shall see, Bishop Richard Hurd's 1762 arguments for the unity of Gothic design depend on his unifying the multiple actions of romance by their purported relationship to a transcendent common purpose. By 1778, the unity of Gothic aesthetics, as revelatory of a social order, will become a commonplace.[30]

Hurd's work demonstrates the general trends I have sketched above and represents the dovetailing of historical, political, and literary interests. The first of the new breed of scholars in England to distinguish between 'classical' and 'romantic,' Hurd's use of Gothic is the second citation recorded by the *OED*, after Shaftesbury. Furthermore, Hurd's very specific advocacy of romance stands in opposition to competing aesthetic guides written by members of the aristocracy like Kames and Monboddo,[31] who preserve the neoclassical preference for Greek and Roman models. Hence, by comparing his position to those of Kames and Monboddo, we can sift the social agendas underlying each branch of aesthetic theory. Judged by the popularity of the Gothic novel, the competition of tastes is won by partisans like Hurd who base their appeal on a seemingly more inclusive notion of common human nature that paradoxically reinforces aristocratic temperament. Kames and Monboddo restrict this aristocratic temperament to those who do not perform bodily labor; romance would make the myth of noble origins available to all.[32]

Hurd's principal work is exactly contemporaneous with Kames's; both *Letters on Chivalry and Romance* and *Elements of Criticism* appeared in 1762. Both men rely on the notion of a common human nature for their arguments. Despite this insistence on commonality, both betray their fears that social realities create a polarization that can only be patched over by works of art. Hurd differs from Kames in this by attributing adhesive properties to the Gothic.

At first, this Gothic is imaged solely as a social institution. He opens this subject in 1759's *Moral and Political Dialogues*. Dialogue III is titled 'On the Golden Age of Queen Elizabeth, Between the Honorable Robert Digby, Dr. Arbuthnot, and Mr. Addison. Occasioned by a View of Kenilworth Castle, in the Year 1716.' Arbuthnot is Hurd's mouthpiece. The initial premise of the dialogue centers on the value of Gothic . Arbuthnot urges that we prize Gothic chivalry for three things: its hospitality, which prevented individualistic luxurious pursuits and made amends for the disparity of wealth and social position (1911, 49); its promotion of civility and gallantry through tournaments (52–3); and its promotion of the arts (64–73). Addison, speaking for the ignorant vulgarity of the parvenu, argues that the system merely supported the 'pride and insolence of the old nobility' and led to the enslavement of the people (50). Arbuthnot counters that the Crown's attempt to disenfranchise the nobility sunk the authority of the Crown with it and resulted in the debasement of people's liberty. 'It was thus discovered, but a little of the latest, that public freedom throve best, when it wound itself about the stock of the ancient nobility' (51), an argument that will be repeated almost verbatim by Burke in his *Reflections*. Hurd's metaphor evokes both the caduceus and grotesque ornamentation, apt precursors for the salubrious effect shortly to be claimed for the Gothic romance (and symbols that will recur in the illustrations to Gothic novels and bluebooks). Three years later, with his *Letters*, romance enters the lists as the substitute champion of values that can no longer be met with in real life.

Hurd compares Homer to medieval romance, and declares the corpus of Shakespeare, Spenser, and Milton more formidable.[33] He awards the palm to romance over epic in general because of 'the improved gallantry of the feudal times; and the superior solemnity of their superstitions' (1963, 108). In this, he follows Temple, who found the origin of romance in the 'adventures and successes of the first Christian, pretended heroes and their combats with Pagans and Saxons,' as instanced by the Arthurian cycles.[34] Romance may contain superstitious improbabilities, but the improbabilities are less so than pagan ones. Moreover, elves and fairies are more charming than pagan gods; while 'for the more solemn fancies of witchcraft and incantation, the horrors of the Gothic were above measure striking and terrible. The mummeries of the pagan priests were childish, but the Gothic enchanters shook and alarmed all nature' (110). At this juncture, horror and terror are almost conflated and both are equally prized as being Christian.[35]

His appeal to the fundamental truths of Christianity, which underlie the marvelous of romance, lends credence to the historicity he claims for romance in general. Romance manners are neither artificial nor monstrous, but a factual representation of the behavior of people in the Middle Ages. One instance of the reasonableness of romance/chivalric conventions appears when the source of gallantry towards women is rightly understood to partake of pecuniary interest. In feudal times, women could succeed to estates; knights were gallant partially because they were vying for the affections of a potentially rich heiress (104–5). Chivalry's other characteristics (prowess, generosity, and religion), along with a gallantry now deprived of potential reward, are to be prized and preserved in the modern era. With this admonition, Hurd voices a subtle critique of the current age. His strategy of using Gothic institutions and romance to launch this critique is fundamental to the Gothic novel, as I will argue in my next chapter.

While Gothic has been viewed prejudicially by contemporary critics of architecture,[36] Hurd states that it is vital to understand the aesthetic canons of Gothic historically. The unity of Gothic design lies in the respect which a number of related actions have to a common purpose, a goal he opposes to classical models which insist upon a unity of action.[37] He continues the argument put forward by the conservative branch of the seventeenth-century pamphleteers that chivalric institutions derived from the 'Feudal Constitution.' Hence, romance was born of chivalry and the feudal organization of society. Yet the codes of honor and of behavior are remarkably consistent between Homeric times and those of modern knight-errantry, because a similarity in composition exists between feudal Europe and the political state of Greece, likewise compounded of an infinite number of petty governments.

So far, Hurd's analogies have bridged the ancient and the feudal worlds. But a third axis extends the analogy into his own moment. The necessary reliance upon 'petty governments,' the rotating cast of small powers entering and exiting the orbit of the various alliances, were recent topics of concern in the wars of the eighteenth century. Hurd writes as the Seven Years' War winds to a close. Moreover, Hurd's insight into the affinities between political institutions widely separated in time leads him to interpret both the themes and the supernatural machinery of 'barbaric' romances and epic poetry as metaphors for political insurrection. Homer's two epics sequentially expose the social cost of independence, which produces a private dissension and public insolence that can only be restrained by a wise leader (43).[38] Romance giants encode oppressive feudal lords; 'savages' resolve into dependants of the lower orders, who lack a castle but are equipped with 'lurking places.' Balancing between attacks on the aristocracy and on the mob, conjured up in the ripe image of 'lurking places,' the political takes on social relevance. As will be true in the Gothic novels that follow, Hurd's version of romance sees overreaching aristocrats and rebellious servants as equally destructive of the social order.

Hurd's *Letters* rustle with nostalgic sympathy for ancient honor against the prevailing climate of rational skepticism.[39] His aesthetic resurrection of Gothic prefigures the way Gothic novels will record and reconcile two contemporary, contradictory causes of the aristocracy's precarious position: the perception that their imputed immorality was to blame for society's ills; and the actual extinction of old peerages occurring on a fairly regular basis during the period between 1714 and 1782 (Keir, 1966, 327). His politicized reading of the castle opens the significance of setting to a new light. Gothic novels excavate the castle and find the decay pervading the contemporary social scene.[40] In keeping with my interpretation, Hurd and the Gothic novelists who follow him seem to argue that the castle *should* represent the order of the aristocracy, but it is always an order that has decayed because its principle function, as well as its principals, has been overthrown.

These ancient castles also enclose secret chambers, rest atop dungeons or are riddled beneath by dank caverns. Thrust into these inaccessible and remote places, Gothic protagonists stumble upon the signs of familial disorder: putrefying corpses, disintegrating skeletons, immured prisoners long rumored to be dead or whose existence has been concealed. The rotting carcases or skeletons which are discovered in the subterranean passages of these castles not only symbolize the disruption of the status quo, they are often the literal remainders of the *status quo ante*. And the work of the plot is to both uncover that corruption and to cure it with the healing rod of justice.

Hurd's introduction of the term 'Gothic' into his defense of romance does more than bring earlier political and historical debates into a central position in aesthetic theory; it crystallizes the cultural code ready to be written into the Gothic novel. The close temporal connection between Hurd's work and the inauguration of the Gothic novel implicates the adjective chosen by Walpole and his successors to describe their literary project.[41] The aesthetic realm can now seem to take over the democratic function of Gothic liberty. By so doing, it can alleviate fears about the social ramifications of reading. No longer must novels be idealized as free-verse epic poems, as Monboddo had done,

or swept utterly out of sight, as by Kames, in favor of painting, picturesque sightseeing, architecture, or drama. Gothic structures could be
used to counter the aestheticians' fears that the 'appetite' for novel-
reading, destructive of the social good because of its private activity,
could, in fact, represent a very social 'taste.'

Clara Reeve predicates her defense of romance on just such a claim
for enhanced sociality. In *The Progress of Romance* (1785), she compares
romance to the woman behind the throne, at the same time that she
celebrates authors as the 'good citizens' of 'the Republic of letters'
(II.98), a metaphor that reveals the way the infrastructure of publishing
and bookselling condenses tensions experienced by individuals of the
period between self and state.[42] Formally, romance is aristocratic by
virtue of its lineage, which Reeve traces back to ancient Greece and
Rome.[43] Substantively, the morals and manners disseminated by
romance are those of a chivalrous nobility (*Progress*, I: 7, 67–8), best
suited to promote the 'health and prosperity of a state' (I: 25).
Romance literature may be aristocratic, but in order to fulfill its potential for social utility, romance must circulate freely in the marketplace.[44] The even-handed attention given to each of these two facets of
romance demonstrates their equal importance. Of 259 pages in the two
volumes of *The Progress of Romance*, 71 pages are devoted to romance's
lineage and 73 to the possible social and material benefits which
mandate that romance be sold and read. Thus the history of romance's
status also pleads for a reconsideration of romance's stature in contemporary letters, one that would be rewarded pecuniarily. Ultimately, *The
Progress of Romance* disguises the desire for the kind of economic mobility conventionally associated with middle-class aspirations as a more
broadly based than usual effect of kinship relations, applied to create a
new social order.

Back to the future

Even those critics like Kames and Monboddo who anathematized the
novel believed immersion in the fine arts to be a necessary concomitant of leadership. Their confused accounts of the value of taste
testifies to a 'growing moral imperative' during the period, 'an insistence that human virtue can be measured only by its immediate social
value' (Plumb, 1973, 84). As John Brewer characterizes the period, the
changed emphasis:

> ... helped perpetuate a distinction between those who worked for
> the public good or as public servants and those who worked for

private gain or profit. The obligation to fulfill public duties was viewed as an essential component of gentility ... Office-holding was therefore compatible with the gentlemanly ideal in a way that trade, business, and finance were not.

(1988, 206)

Unfortunately for the aristocracy, a decreasing number of venues were available to them to fulfill that newly manifest destiny. The twin mechanizations of industrial revolution and the bureaucratization of government jarred the status quo and forced a redistribution of class dominance. In tandem with this redistribution came a shift in career aspiration for the younger sons of the gentry. Unlike the seventeenth century, second sons were no longer being apprenticed to trade in the city; the preferred careers were now the army, the navy, or government. Superseded by their younger siblings, as well as by the middle class and City interests, the eldest sons of the aristocracy had, perhaps, only their taste to recommend them.

With the coming of the Peninsular War and the growth of Britain as an economic force, authors faced a new quandary: creating a hero who could inspire without depressing, who could become all things to all people. As Hugh Murray described this new needed image: ' his merit ought to be as much as possible intrinsic, and independent of outward circumstances. At the same time, to make him strikingly deficient in qualifications which command so much of the admiration of mankind, would lower his character in the eyes of most readers, and would tend to throw contempt on those moral qualities, which are held forth as objects of imitation' (1805, 32). Merit and birth must unite. Money creates a larger problem. The hero's dignity and happiness must be independent of cash; he should exhibit 'respectability and usefulness' in a 'moderate and humble sphere,' yet demonstrate his qualifications to discharge duties 'of the highest and most important situations.' Recognizing the glaring fictionality of such opposed traits, Murray recommends that the hero 'experience various vicissitudes of fortune' in order adequately to test all his talents (35–6). Hugh Murray's ideal hero reflects the changed tempo of British life. Liberated comparatively from constraints of rank or wealth, ceaseless activity forms the predominant burden on him.

Although he does not say so here, the perfect formula for such a cross-class hero had been developed with the earliest romances.[45] Their topos of disguised birth enabled heroes to move between the borderlands of rank, just as their callings as knights of chivalry later enabled them to traverse domestic and martial virtue, as we will see with Clara

Reeve's work. While Gothic plots feature heroes whose births have been disguised, as is common to Greek romance, these disguises are not initially willed but have been imposed, often without the knowledge or consent of the protagonist.[46]

The disguised births of Gothic heroes (and later, in the fictions of Ann Radcliffe, of Gothic heroines) mean that the protagonists have been bereft of their social birthrights, whether these birthrights entail access to political dominion or genealogical legitimacy. This occluded identity enabled authors to combine in their Gothic heroes the intrinsic merit and the noble status Murray found so desirable. The characters' recovery of their displaced origins has a dual function. Just as in the traditional romance formula, the discovery of one's identity permits marital union with the loved one. Furthermore, that discovery purges the polity of evil. By that means, Gothic novels both advocate domestic tranquillity and sanction such tranquillity as nationally valuable.

Coleridge lacked sympathy with the Gothic project. Seeing it as provoking only curiosity, he drew aesthetic and professional distinctions: 'The love of poetry is a taste; curiosity is a kind of appetite, and hurries headlong on, impatient for its complete gratification' (*Critical Review* (1794): 369). Coleridge's attitude may have resulted from his recognition that such novels posed serious competition to his own work, as Wordsworth's complaints in the Preface to the *Lyrical Ballads* more whiningly confess.[47] Like an addict attempting to abjure his habit, Coleridge ends by declaring that '[T]hese novels will not bear repetition.'

Coleridge knew he lied. In one sense, Coleridge's remark functions as an in-joke: the novels will not bear repetition in the sense of rereading, since they bear repetition in the form of recurrent motifs, settings, characters, and situations. On a more serious level, the novels' frame tales, recounting the discovery of an original, factual manuscript which the 'editor' now transmits to posterity, use repetition to assert authenticity and authority, an attainment Coleridge's statement denies. The Gothic myth, as retailed in novels and poems, had borne repetition in the very multiplication of heroes competing on the stage by the time Byron came to write *Don Juan*, and in the appetite pervasive among the public for such heroes. But the Gothic myth had long been bearing repetition. In the next chapter, following the myth forward to the moment of its fictional incarnation, we will survey its specifically political relevance, the agency, or loss thereof, envisioned in the fecund image of 'bearing.'

Part II
Retailing the Gothic Myth

2
When Everything New is Old Again: Horace Walpole's Heroic Bequests

> L'Histoire n'est fondée que sur le témoignage des Auteurs qui nous l'ont transmise. Il importe donc extrêmement, pour la sçavois, de bien connoitre quels étoient ces Auteurs. Rien n'est à negliger en ce point; le temps où ils ont vecû, leur naissance, leur patrie, la part qu'ils ont eue aux affaires, les moyens pour lesquels ils ont été instruits, et l'intérêt qu'ils y pouvoient prendre, sont des circonstances essentielles qu'il n'est pas permis d'ignorer: delà dépend le plus ou le moins d'autorité qu'ils doivent avoir: et sans cette conoissance, on courra risque très souvent de prendre pour guide un Historien de mauvaise foi, ou du moins, mal informé.
>
> (Horace Walpole, epigraph to *Historic Doubts on the Reign of Richard III*, 1987).[1]

Christmas 1764 witnessed the birth of a new cultural hero. Theodore, the first 'Gothic' hero, was the product of as unlikely a couple as that Galilean family. The family resemblances go beyond the 'miraculous birth' myth attending both creations. War and taxation set the stage for the story in both cases. And like that earlier foundational birth, the new hero arises at a moment of 'tyrannical oppression.' Yet the class targets of that oppression have been reversed. The prosecution of the Seven Years' War paradoxically damaged aristocratic autonomy. Because the war left most European nations in debt, governments were forced to streamline the efficiency of their taxation and to impose taxes on the rich. The English aristocracy countered by charging royal tyranny and the abrogation of ancient liberties (Butler, 1982, 14).

Taxation was not the only reason that the aristocracy was feeling its privilege slip away. The Seven Years' War also marked the erosion of the Whig aristocracy's power, based on its commercial interest in the monopolistic trading companies. Tipping the scales, the independent City merchants were gaining power (Spector, 1966, 84). Furthermore, industrial specialization brought with it a concurrent development of administrative specialization in the departments of government (Brewer, 1988, 84). The professionalization or bureaucraticization of government led to advocacy from within for reform, since an increase in work could no longer be delegated to underlings working for lower wages; that fact, and the inability of professional administrators to cash in on the traditional financial perquisites of office, tendered as bribes by Whig power brokers, decreased the political influence held by aristocratic Whig ministries since Sir Robert Walpole's tenure.

 With the trial of John Wilkes on charges of treason and seditious libel for his role in *The North Briton*, no. 45, the perception spread among members of the aristocracy that personal animus and social tyranny converged. Wilkes had been apprehended but discharged from custody by the Court of Common Pleas on the grounds that his position as a member of Parliament protected him. When Wilkes was tried by his peers in the House of Commons, King George and his ministers moved Parliament to consider their contention that the 'privilege of Parliament does not extend to the case of writing and publishing seditious libels.'[2] Horace Walpole found himself doubly threatened by the ministerial position, as a member of Parliament and an author/publisher. Accordingly, Walpole allied himself with the Opposition for the first time. The King's forces prevailed and Wilkes was expelled. In the wake of Wilkes's defeat emerged *The Castle of Otranto*'s chivalrous knight.[3]

 Detecting a cause-and-effect relationship between the chronological events outlined above, as I have, and thereby taking Walpole's endeavor seriously poses several dangers, primarily because Walpole is such a devious man, who so often betrays those who place confidence in him. One example of his deviousness can be seen in the way he used his friends and correspondents to craft a carefully controlled posthumous reputation. Men of parts and letters who thought that their correspondence was solicited out of an impersonal interest quickly learned that Walpole employed them as sounding boards, especially when he requested they preserve and return his letters to them for inclusion in his published works. Other correspondents may have died before they had a chance to learn that they were being instrumentalized; we can read backwards into their fate when we see Walpole replacing their loss with another conversant in the same category of thought.

Perhaps the most famous examples of Walpole's deviousness cluster around the very novel I wish to discuss, and these multiple hoaxes have bedeviled friends and critics from 1765 right up until the present moment. The first hoax concerns his authorship. His masquerade as 'William Marshall' deflected attention and averted possible criticism; his presentation of the fable as an ancient manuscript, written sometime between the launching of the First Crusade and the blossoming of the Italian Renaissance, fooled even supposedly discriminating members of the public such as the schoolboys at Cambridge led by Thomas Gray and his antiquarian friend, the Reverend William Mason. Yet he ultimately acknowledged his authorship, only to insert two more disclaimers: the claim to diffidence as the motive for the hoax, and the explanation that the story had originated in a dream of a giant hand on the staircase of Strawberry Hill.

Two consequences have rippled from his posturing. First, proclaiming the work a dream has led some contemporary critics to dismiss any notion that significance attaches to the work. Instead, Walpole's fascination with the past remains an example of his delight in flaunting convention, a tendency critics alternately celebrate or deplore. *Otranto* reduces to an anomaly in the history of the Gothic, whether for its fairy-tale quality 'even when it strives for the horrific' (Punter, 1980, 49), or as a 'jeu d'esprit, magnifying comically' some of Walpole's own narcissistically beloved eccentricities and signifying his 'intentional and privileged shuffling off of responsibilities of all kinds' (Napier, 1987, 74–5). At least an earlier generation of Gothic critics offered a more romantic, if no more dignified, interpretation. Both Montague Summers and Oswald Doughty imagined Walpole as an evanescent figure gradually retreating into his imaginary construct of a medieval world, where he lives only in dreams (Summers, 1938, 179, 181, 410; Doughty, 1929, xxvii, xxxii, xxxiv).

Yet despite Walpole's efforts to cover his traces, including his giving the manuscript out to William Bathoe and Thomas Lownds to publish rather than printing it at his own Strawberry Press, the record of his activities during the writing of *The Castle of Otranto* shows a far more active intelligence and engagement at work.[4] And some critics have acknowledged this, and have begun to counter the derogation he has suffered by finding confirmation of their own critical theories in the work. Walpole's hoaxing produces a different consequence here. The sheer variety of interpretations that compete today for attention suggest that Walpole's gamesmanship has confused the scent. The little worry that has gone into the choices he made respecting the title of the work betray the backward nature of the glances critics have cast at the meaning of Gothic as a literary construct, since they retrospectively attribute meanings to the phenomena that derive from more current concerns. If Walpole's interest lay mainly with the villain, as has so much of the criticism, why not call the novel *Manfred*?[5] If his emphasis truly lay in creating a fantastic structure through the use of the supernatural, why not *St Nicholas* as the title? Or *Alfonso the Good*? Or perhaps, most fitting of all, an American tabloid-type parody title: *Ghost-Buster*? Moreover, while the legend that Walpole built his castle in a dream before committing it to paper has been exploded, we still don't savor the phrase 'A Gothic Story' enough. Why Gothic? If he meant no more than an architectural reference, a sly allusion to the space he bequeathed us at Strawberry Hill, then the subtitle functions as an in joke, whereby Walpole calls his own novel an ersatz tale. If, as some have argued, the word Gothic bespeaks the hybrid style of the novel, then the subtitle functions as proleptic marker of his intention to publish the second Preface before he'd written the first. So what was he thinking of?

As the epigraph to this chapter indicates, the question is more than an idle one. Even the inclusion of St Nicholas as the patron saint, a detail against which Thomas Gray fought, is more than coincidence. Beyond its historical accuracy, the use of Nicholas points as much to the evolution of myth, to the mythologizing habit of mind, as it does to Christmas (Walpole's publication date), since Nicholas was patron saint of thieves and pawnbrokers before he patronized elves.[6] Occupying a highly ambiguous position, St Nicholas perfectly signifies the eighteenth-century tradition of infusing political allegory into their fables.[7] By reading *The Castle of Otranto* as a jeu or by seeing Walpole as a daydreamer, critics have failed to see the deadly earnest with which Walpole pursued his game. At stake, in his mind, were the unique rights of the minor aristocracy and gentry.[8]

To consider Walpole as a 'Gothic' historian, then, we will begin by considering the qualities he lists in the epigraph as contributing to a historian's bias: his birth, education, country, and interest, comprising both the affinities he felt as a result of those early affiliations and the power he was able to exercise in assuming his part. From there, we will go forth to consider the specifically British elements of his story, before turning to the British heroes he constructed out of these materials.

Family lessons

Reduced to skeletal form, *The Castle of Otranto* details the ill effects upon an imaginary Italian kingdom of a usurpation of power by an imposter, and the restoration of that kingdom to its rightful heir. As an antiquarian collector, Horace Walpole would have been all too aware that the epithet 'Gothic' had very little to do with Italy. While the extent of his familiarity with the diverse theories of Gothic ancestry traced out in the previous chapter cannot be specified with certainty, he had a unique slant on the way Gothic could be used to political advantage. The epithet 'gothic' had been employed in his own time and against his own father, by the so-called Country Party of Bolingbroke and Oxford. In his *Craftsman* papers, Bolingbroke championed Gothic liberty as the antidote to what he portrayed as the executive branch's meddling in Parliament, all in a ploy to break Sir Robert's power. The first *Craftsman*, issued 5 December 1726, established the credentials of its 'editor,' one 'Caleb D'Anvers, the second son of an ancient Northern family, born 1660.' Walpole's use of a fictional 'editor,' William Marshall, mirrors Bolingbroke's not only in tactic but also in the Northern address. This is not the only similarity: *Craftsman* 16 features a 'Gothick' dream called the 'Vision of Cameleck.' Set in medieval times, it purports to be a vision about the Magna Carta recorded in a Persian manuscript brought to England by Spaniards and translated at D'Anvers request. The Wilkes affair might have sparked memories of Bolingbroke's 'Gothic' antics. According to J. H. Plumb, Walpole resented Bute's part more than George III's, largely because Bute 'preach[ed] the doctrines of Bolingbroke and goad[ed] the King to action which was unconstitutional by convention, if not by law' (1973, 116).

This series of associations would have been underlined by the schooling Horace had received from his father to view the press as an adjunct of politics.[9] He himself had deftly applied these lessons during the 1740s and 1750s in an effort to improve his own political and financial position.[10] Walpole's thoroughly politicized upbringing militates against the notion that he viewed literature as an idealized aesthetic pursuit divorced from more materialistic ambitions, as is urged by those who see *Otranto* as a retreat from politics.[11] And the individual lessons he received from his father and his father's enemies regarding literature as a species of political agitation conform to attitudes dominating the customary approach of essay-journals and magazines in the 1750s and 1760s, as well (Spector, 1966, 14). In a letter to Horace Mann (31 July 1762), Walpole insists that all party writings in the current papers operate by parallels to historical figures.[12]

Walpole's interest in politics, antiquarian history, and literature lent him a natural means of drawing parallels when his own interest was threatened. At the same time that the characterization of the novel as 'Gothic' points to the story's relevance for contemporary political events in England, the foundations discernible beneath the tale apply equally well to English history.[13] And these resonances are no accident. The villain Manfred's actions can easily be read in counterpoint to those of Henry VIII.[14] Like Henry, Manfred desires to divorce his wife in order to produce a *male* heir. His allegation that their marriage was illegal, despite the dispensation granted, because they were related within the forbidden degrees of affinity (1963, 51) exactly mirrors the assertions of Henry VIII in his attempt to dispose of Catherine of Aragon. Henry, too, had obtained a papal decree permitting his marriage to his deceased brother's widow; like Hippolyta, Catherine's other children had all died, leaving only Mary to inherit a throne pressed by foreign enemies; and like her, Catherine was then past the age of childbearing. Perhaps most interestingly, Henry cited a biblical curse as responsible for the downfall of his dynasty.[15] Henry also sought a second papal ruling to annul the effects of the first dispensation, as does Manfred (51–2). These eerie 'Italian' echoes of familiar English history might have encouraged readers to take up the 'editor's' call for a hermeneutic reading, an incitement for which they were prepared by their exposure to the heroic romances and *romans à clef* that had so scandalized and delighted English audiences earlier in the century, and by contemporary justifications being offered for the rediscovered value of romance.

This parallel between Manfred and Henry VIII with respect to their attitudes towards the Church and towards their wives appears on the surface of the tale. As a well-known facet of English history, they might have encouraged readers to translate the Italian setting to one closer to home. To the sensitive reader, a second, more oblique angle could then be detected, one in which the situation with George III is reflected. Here, the date assigned to the printing of the 'recovered manuscript,' 1529, takes on new significance. In that year, Wolsey's power over Henry VIII finally reached an end. Wolsey's reign was marked by his domination over all facets of administration and judiciary. Conciliar machinery (via the Star Chamber) began to replace the courts of common law, exceeding nominal jurisdiction in deciding cases of titles to property. Wolsey's control over local authorities and his use of special commissions undermined local institutions. Parliament met only once in 14 years. So in addition to the linkages between Manfred/Henry VIII/George III, we can map Wolsey with Bute.

Certain of Manfred's actions can be construed as relevant to my contention that Manfred represents, if not the person then the actions of, George III. Manfred's exercise of artful policy to deceive his subjects (1963, 19–20) could refer back to the King's deceptive description of the recently concluded treaty as an economic victory for England (in a speech written by Bute). Manfred's irrational attack on Theodore, culminating in the hero's imprisonment for making empirical observations (18–19), could be likened to George III's willful ignoring of common law in his use of general warrants, ultimately deemed an illegal violation of individual liberty.[16] So, too, could Manfred's conflation of libel with breach of the peace echo George's reaction to attacks against the King's ministers.

But we should not hear in these reverberations of English history an outright attack on the King. Despite Walpole's occasional dissension from the policies of the king, he is always deferential in the language he uses to refer to George III and in the concern he expresses for His Majesty's well-being. While the King's illnesses receive frequent mention in Horace's letters to Englishmen residing abroad, he never voices any concern about the protracted regency that would be forced upon the nation in case of the King's insanity or demise until 26 March 1765, in a letter to Horace Mann. Far from regarding the Hanovers as usurpers, he extended his view of their legitimacy to include the King's mother. Siding for the only time with the detested Bute, Horace urged that the Princess Dowager be included among those named in the May 1765 Regency Act, since she was the direct lineal descendant of George II.[17]

Nor is there any evidence that Walpole would subscribe to a sentimentalized, nostalgic yearning for restoration of the 'true' Stuart line. His infrequent mentions of the Stuarts are far from complimentary. Rome is a 'Catholic dunghill,' where the Stuart 'phantoms' are 'nosed' (Lewis, 1973, 22: 237, 253–4).[18] This Hamlet-like aside serves more as an intimation that Walpole wanted to write an anti-Jacobite warning, if we bear in mind the first Preface's animadversions upon Roman Catholic political agitation disguised as theology.[19] The 'central issue' of the novel may well be 'legitimacy,' as it defines both the right to rule and the reproduction of that royal lineage; however, Walpole seems to argue not so much that George III's power is illegitimately derived as that his manipulation of that power in the case of Wilkes, and by inference his attitude towards members of Parliament, is illicit.[20] Justice consists in a restoration of the rights of the true nobility. The doubled directions of ancient Italy and England cancel one another out, so that the marker of Otranto in the title becomes less important, in the final analysis, than does the emphasis upon the Castle, the ancestral home, the locus of lineage and power.

These twin foci recur in the plot of Theodore's disguised birth, in the Biblical curse that simultaneously sings the praise of blood. The notion of blood as a river that connects and nourishes a people runs through the discourse of nationalism. In the particularist forms of nationalism or kinship theory espoused by Muslim and Jewish cultures, the fervor for nationalism still allows those outside the kinship pod to exist and have civil liberties. In Roman and later Christian hands, the fervor becomes a fever. Marc Shell (1993) describes the universalist theory of kinship developed by those cultures as the doctrine 'all men are my brothers,' meaning that, if you are not my brother, i.e. don't share my values and opinions, then you aren't human. Manfred's treatment of Isabella, his willingness to jettison Hippolyta and to pander Mathilda to Frederick, seem to instance a Christian notion of kinship if seen as critically by Walpole as by Marc Shell. When Walpole speaks through his mouth-piece, William Marshall, and claims that the manuscript is the work of a Roman Catholic priest attempting to enslave the population, he seems to take such a critical stance toward Catholic doctrine. However, the novel's insistence on blood lineage rejects the universalist embrace of brotherhood as equality. If this double-speak weren't complicated enough, Walpole has more twists lurking in the names he chose for his royal families. The deceased cynosure of kingship, Alfonso, echoes an eleventh-century Christian monarch Alfonso VI (sometimes called 'El Bravo'), who offered limited protection to Muslim subjects in Léon and Castile.[21] Alfonso designated as his heir a son by Zaida, daughter of the Muslim king of Seville. The Muslim-Christian king Frederick II of Sicily is another exemplar of tolerance towards Muslims and Jews (Shell, 1993, 212, n. 6). Recognizing this hidden agenda helps us make sense of the multiple dates Walpole gives for the 'provenance' of his text. Combined with Walpole's overdetermined satirizing of Christian theology (the 'sins of the fathers') and Providence (the theatricalized deflation through romance 'coincidence'), his rulers' names instance Walpole's interest in a particularist nationalist ideology in contrast to the universalist inter-pretation urged by Elizabeth I as she sought to consolidate her throne.

Yet neither of the two fictional monarchs in the story qualifies as the heir of Otranto. Even if Alfonso's death hadn't disqualified him, his tol-erance seems to have led to his usurpation; and Frederick's lust for Mathilda, which overcomes his scruples, unfits him for the job even if another, more immediately direct descendant weren't available. While a particularist ideology seems to govern the transmission of power, the joke remains that everyone *does* seem to be coincidentally related to everyone else of stature in this world. In this regard, Otranto resembles Spain, which mandated the purity of bloodlines, despite the fact that universalist kinship should transcend consanguineous (Shell, 1993, 27). However, whereas members of the Spanish gentry excluded from this blood purity fought against such exclusion by rhetorically basing nobility on deeds rather than on blood (Shell, 1993, 29), Walpole creates Theodore, a sign that unifies those opposing values.

Family values

That the Wilkes's contretemps inspired Walpole to ponder heroic qualities appears in remarks Walpole makes about the nature of the man he had just championed in the Parliamentary debates. He describes Wilkes as 'as bad a fellow as ever hero was, abominable in private life, dull in Parliament, but, they say, very entertaining in a room, and certainly no bad writer, besides having had the honour of contributing a great deal to Lord Bute's fall' (Lewis, 1973, 22: 136–7). Wilkes may fail to exhibit the requisite politesse; Walpole cures this modern-day failing by constructing a hero who is a model of integrity *and* manners in *The Castle of Otranto*.

He is also a hero modeled on Horace's cousin, Henry Seymour Conway.[22] That Walpole idealized Conway can be seen from the mythic proportions with which he invested Conway's actual military exploits. Writing to Horace Mann of Conway's siege of the castle of Waldeck, Walpole reports: ' ... it was impregnable without cannon; he had none and his powder was spent. He made them believe he was preparing to storm it, and they instantly surrendered' (22: 55–6). This letter is dated 31 July 1762, and its account is completely contradicted by the newspaper version published in the *London Chronicle* for 27–29 July (xii), where the surrender is said to follow upon a brisk bombardment by seven cannon and nine mortars and howitzers for two days, a fact that Walpole nowhere acknowledges. By draining the blood, smoke, and lead from his fictionalized account, Walpole makes Conway's achievement analogous to that of Shakespeare's Henry V at Harfleur (Act III, scene 3).

How much the danger posed by the recension of Parliamentary privilege weighed in Walpole's thinking is difficult to ascertain with certainty.[23] But Conway lost his post in the King's Bedchamber and his regiment as a direct consequence of Walpole's advice with respect to the Wilkes contretemps.[24] In the paper war that Walpole mustered to recover Conway's position, one, moreover, which overlaps in time with the composition of *The Castle of Otranto*, we can discern a clear analogy between Walpole's public and private representations of Conway, and the character and deeds of the novel's hero, Theodore.

Like the novel, Walpole's first defense of Conway appears pseudonymously. Perhaps of greater significance, it, too, features what I call an act of ventriloquism, a species of the double-voicedness that is a hallmark of Walpole's version of Gothic. This first act of ventriloquism appeared in the same *London Chronicle* that had carried news of Conway's victory two years earlier. On 3–5 May 1764, the paper ran an 'Address From the Corporation of Thetford' to Conway. Drafted by Walpole and circulated surreptitiously to the press, the 'Address' articulated the following message:

> We the Mayor, Aldermen, and Corporation of Thetford, desire to return to you our most unfeigned and grateful thanks for your late spirited, conscientious and unbiased conduct in Parliament, particularly on that most important question to the liberties of us all, the seizure of private papers by the warrant of a secretary of state; a question, which remaining undecided, must make every Englishman tremble, and which till declared to be illegal, leaves the Glorious Revolution imperfect.
>
> Your behaviour, Sir, on that occasion, was worthy the unblemished integrity which you have always manifested. Superior to bribes or menaces, you have demonstrated your civil courage to be equal to your military. You have fought the battles of your country against *domestic* and foreign enemies; we know your services; and we have heard that they were particularly recommended to favour by that great judge of martial merit, Prince Ferdinand.
>
> *These honours*, Sir, cannot be taken from you. Some sort of rewards may be envied you by selfish and designing ministers, who may know that you scorn to support unconstitutional measures; but your country (and may it continue this free country) in whose cause you have fought from the noblest and most disinterested motives, will join in conferring the best of rewards – *its applause*. There are seasons when it would be a disgrace not to be disgraced. Continue to act as you have done, and may every borough in the kingdom be as worthily represented as the Corporation of Thetford.
>
> Dated at our Guildhall, the 28th of April, 1764.[25]

Walpole's chivalrous defense of his cousin did not end with his pseudo-nymous venture. According to his *Short Notes*, he began an answer to a pamphlet against Conway on 29 May. This rejoinder was completed 12 June, but not published until 2 August. The same source records that Walpole began *Otranto* in June and finished it 6 August, so that Conway's affairs were very much in Horace's mind while he was writing.

If Conway in the *Address* becomes a type of all that should govern England, that type of leader reappears in the character and deeds of Theodore. Walpole makes his hero, Theodore, return from overseas to save Otranto. John Stevenson reads this as a return from exile, a fact which he sees as substantiating Theodore's resemblance to the Stuarts. But Theodore's recital of his history reveals that he and his mother had been kidnapped by corsairs from the coast of Sicily, their home. When his mother dies a year later, Theodore is pressed into service with the corsairs, whom he serves for the next 14 years. The corsairs are eventually captured by a Christian vessel, whose captain frees Theodore and returns him to Sicily.[26] Learning that his father had abandoned his devastated castle and 'retired into religion in the kingdom of Naples,' Theodore sets off on a quest to recover his remaining parent. This quest, occupying the past two years, has culminated in his accidental arrival in Otranto (1963, 84–5). Thus, Theodore has no prior physical connection to the country that is lineally his; the acclamation of the people to his accession, following the 'divine Will' that manifests his selection through the shade of Alfonso (113), makes him a national hero and ruler in the tradition of William of Orange. Finally, this allusion ties Walpole's fictive hero together with the reference to Conway's heroism in defense of the rights won by the Glorious Revolution.

While less pacific than the airbrushed portrait of Conway in battle, Theodore's martial actions still register a growing preference for blood-lessness over bloodletting. Politics, morals, and aesthetics combined to produce a 'major cultural shift away from Homeric and towards more pacific ideals,' a shift attributed to the century's martial ravages which 'nonetheless required anti-war psychology – of war to end war, or war only to repel a terrible enemy, or war to protect God's people' (Weinbrot, 1993, 146). Walpole's novel further suppresses the identification of martial conduct with noble value. Theodore's one act of violence, his hand-to-hand combat with Frederic, occurs as a result of mistaken identities. Each man suspects the other of aiming to injure Isabella. Frederic compounds his malefactions in Theodore's eyes by his haughtiness and his easily inflamed resentment, qualities the narrator underscores as if to guide our sympathies. But the deck is not stacked completely in Theodore's favor, unlike Walpole's treatment of Conway. While Frederic first lashes out at the youth, Theodore is no saint; he returns the blows, roused as much by Frederic's 'pride and wrath' as he is by his own long-'smothered' valor. The rush to hardy deeds appears equally valorous and impetuous (77). As another way of tempering such questionable haste, Theodore's impetuous kindness acts as a counterweight to his martial impetuosity. No sooner does he wound Frederic than he sheds tears of 'pity and generosity' and works as hard to save Frederic's life as he had to take it (77–9). Theodore's Gothic heroism bathes him simultaneously in the martial prowess of the chivalric knight and the tears of the eighteenth-century sentimental hero.

But whereas eighteenth-century audiences might have expected prowess military and amatory from their heroes, the class or status of those heroes had been under siege for some time. Theodore is also *genuinely* noble, despite his apparent peasant origins. *The Castle of Otranto* thus reads as a parodic mirror version of Pamela's romance. The 'one great *Proof*' derived by contemporaries from Pamela's history was 'that Advantages from *Birth*, and the Distinction of *Fortune*, have no Power at all, when consider'd against those from *Behaviour*, and Temper of *Mind.*'[27] Walpole takes the conventional novelistic representations of 'a degenerate aristocracy, with its traditional license, and the middle classes ... with their new wealth, their social consciousness, and their sober Puritan morality' (Beasley, 1982, 19), and deliberately inverts the schema.[28] Yet, in so doing, he does not vilify the middle classes; his villain, Manfred, is below that, having risen from the status of personal servant. Instead, Walpole suggests that the middle-class virtues depicted in precursor fiction inhere in noble status.

Both Conway and Theodore bear many conventional attributes of the romance hero: they are honest, courageous, disinterestedly interested, chivalrous to women, humble, and handsome. Like Conway as imaged in the letter from the Corporation of Thetford, Theodore proves himself 'superior to bribes or menaces.' The villain Manfred's fulminations when he discovers the young peasant freed from his confinement under the steel helmet in the courtyard fail to rattle Theodore. He denies Manfred's accusations that he is a traitor. His equanimity is matched only by his integrity. 'My veracity is dearer to me than my life ... nor would I purchase the one by forfeiting the other... Ask me what I can answer ... and put me to death instantly, if I tell you a lie,' he offers, almost provokingly, in assertion of his innocence (30).

Yet, despite his ill-treatment at Manfred's hands, when servants interrupt his interrogation to report their sighting of a ghost, Theodore volunteers his services in Manfred's behalf (34). His disinterested willingness to concern himself in the distresses of others is not actuated by a desire to improve his condition. When Matilda, Manfred's daughter, offers to reward his assistance of her, Theodore refuses any compensation, even though her offer does not constitute a bribe: 'I know not what wealth is: But I do not complain of the lot which heaven has cast for me: I am young and healthy, and am not ashamed of owing my support to myself – yet think me not proud, or that I disdain your generous offers' (42). This selflessness in service of citizen and country stands in sharp contrast to the self-interestedness which actuates Manfred.

The 'noble and disinterested motives' attributed to Conway are encoded in Theodore's character as a combination of chivalric manners and the topos of the Christian hero. But, like Conway in the *Address*, Theodore's chivalric manners appear as much civil as they do military courage, because he is beset by domestic enemies. He repeatedly signifies his willingness to lose his life, which he little values, to combat 'tyranny' (1963, 28, 54, 58, 72). His faith as a Christian knight is attested to by his renunciation of sanctuary. 'No, Princess, sanctuaries are for helpless damsels, or for criminals. Theodore's soul is free from guilt, nor will wear the appearance of it. Give me a sword, Lady, and thy father shall learn that Theodore scorns an ignominious flight' (73). At the same time, his faith makes him profess humility as a knight: 'If heaven has selected me for thy deliverer, it will accomplish its work, and strengthen my arm in thy cause – ...' (76). Hauled into the courtyard for beheading, he receives his sentence with calm resignation. 'The only boon he deigned to ask, was, that he might be permitted to have a confessor, and make his peace with heaven' (55). Granted this request, he is unfazed by Manfred's warnings to be brief. 'My sins, thank heaven! have not been numerous; nor exceed what might have been expected at my years ... This is a bad world; nor have I cause to leave it with regret' (56). When he freely pardons Manfred, the priest sorrowfully predicts that neither Manfred nor himself can 'hope to go, where this blessed youth is going!' (ibid.).

Physically, as well, Theodore repeats the handsome face and figure given to Conway by Walpole.[29] Early correspondence between Walpole and Conway reveals Walpole's estimation of Conway as a romance hero. Writing after the battle of Fontenoy, in May 1745, in which Conway first seriously distinguished himself, Walpole chides him for lacking the 'charming violences' necessary to the 'perfect hero':

Can your friends flatter themselves with seeing you one day or other be the death of thousands, when you wish for peace after your first engagement, and laugh at the ambition of those men who have given you this opportunity of distinguishing yourself? With the person of an Orondates, and the courage, you have all the compassion, the reason, and the reflection, of one that never read a romance. Can one ever hope you will make a figure when you only fight because it was right you should, and not because you hated the French, or loved destroying mankind? This is so un-English, or so unheroic, that I despair of you! (Lewis 1973, 37: 195)[30]

As Walpole's jesting comments indicate here, Conway's 'defects' arise from his humane rationality. Conway's fictional stand-in, Theodore, preserves this unique blend of romance chivalry and rational judiciousness.

Walpole emphasizes Theodore's reason as a means to create a modern romance that would combine the probability of the novel with the heroic adventure of the ancient romance. The 'novelistic' strains in Theodore's personality, the characteristics that ally him with other eighteenth- and nineteenth-century fictional heroes, include his equanimity, his innocence, and, above all, his integrity, both in the sense of virtue and of a harmonious wholeness of parts, physical and moral. But what lifts Walpole's contribution beyond all these is his insistence on Theodore's intelligence, specifically Theodore's talent for empirical observation.[31]

This talent forms one way that Walpole melds the middle class with the noble. In fact, Theodore no sooner appears in the novel than he demonstrates this habit of mind, making the connection between the monstrous helmet that has just crushed Manfred's heir and the helmet capping the statue of Alfonso the Good in the church of St Nicholas (18–19). Walpole underscores the importance of his perspicacity by contrasting it to the chaotic mentality of the mob. When peasants who have forayed to the church return to report the statue's helmet missing, the mob mistakes the missing ornament for the casque in the courtyard and joyfully accedes to Manfred's declaration that Theodore is a sorcerer. Walpole's scorn insists on the faulty reasoning of the mob:

The mob, who wanted some object within the scope of their capacities, on whom they might discharge their bewildered reasonings, caught the words from the mouth of their Lord, and reechoed [them] ... never reflecting how enormous the disproportion was between the *marble* helmet that had been in the church, and that of

steel before their eyes; nor how impossible it was for a youth, seemingly not twenty, to wield a piece of armour of so prodigious a
weight ... The generality were charmed with their Lord's decision,
which, to their apprehensions, carried *great appearance* of justice, as
the Magician was to be punished by the very instrument with which
he had offended: Nor were they struck with the least compunction
at the probability of the youth being starved, for they firmly
believed, that, by his diabolic skill, he could easily supply himself
with nutriment.

(19–20, emphasis added)

If the mob's inability to reason leads to their consequent manipulabil-
ity, making them hollow guns that can only repeat at another's commands, Walpole also lets us see why Manfred in every case must resist
empirical reasoning and treat Theodore's observations as treasonous:
empiricism poses a threat to Manfred's control over his people.

The conflation of nobility with empiricism goes beyond the depiction of the mob as incapable of such factual discrimination mentioned
above. Theodore's actions consistently demonstrate the soundness of
his observations. When Manfred deduces that Theodore has bribed the
guards and threatens to make them pay for their disloyalty with their
lives, Theo calmly responds, 'My poverty ... will disculpate them: ...'
(29). Manfred proposes to torture the youth to learn who has helped
him escape; Theodore smiles and cheerfully indicates the crack in the
pavement which had permitted him to reach the dungeons below.
Such observations enable Theodore to deflect Manfred's threats gently
and to shelter others from his wrath, thus permitting a chivalric
pacifism.

To underscore his point, Walpole provides more than one character
whose talent for empirical observation contributes to a heroic nature.
Theodore's gifts are matched by those of Isabella. She demonstrates the
sharpest eye and the most acumen at reading human nature, making her
'victory' at the end and her eventual alliance with Theodore seem
natural. We see these qualities in her from the first, since her role as
potential victim brings them to the fore. Seeking to escape from
Manfred's incestuous attentions, she runs mentally through her options:

There she stopped, not knowing whither to direct her steps, nor
how to escape from the impetuosity of the Prince. The gates of the
castle she knew were locked, and guards placed in the court. Should
she, as her heart prompted her, go and prepare Hippolita for the
cruel destiny that awaited her; she did not doubt but Manfred

would seek her there, and that his violence would incite him to double the injury he meditated, without leaving room for them to avoid the impetuosity of his passions. *Delay might give him time to reflect on the horrid measures he had conceived*, or produce some circumstance in her favour, if she could for that night at least avoid his odious purpose. – *Yet where conceal herself! How avoid the pursuit he would infallibly make throughout the castle!* As these thoughts passed rapidly through her mind, she recollected a subterraneous passage which led from the vaults of the castle to the church of St. Nicholas.

(25, emphasis added)

Isabella brings observation, analysis, foresight, and memory all to bear in her behalf. Lest we miss the significance of her mental gymnastics, the narrative verges within her mind. Throughout, the narrator speaks in consonant psycho-narration with his heroine, as witnessed by the exclamation points and the urgent dashes of the second italicized example.[32] The collapsing of perspectives encourages us to assent to the soundness of her mental proceedings.

Even when at her most terrified, Isabella's habits of thought can restore a modicum of equanimity.

Every suggestion that horror could inspire rushed into her mind. She condemned her rash flight, which had thus exposed her to his rage in a place where her cries were not likely to draw any body to her assistance. – Yet the sound seemed not to come from behind, – if Manfred knew where she was, he must have followed her: She was still in one of the cloysters, and the steps she had heard were too distinct to proceed from the way she had come.

(26)

Only when her sense perceptions are incapacitated does she panic and resort to prayer (27). Moreover, she never gives up the attempt to help herself through empirical observation for long. When Theodore accosts her and offers his aid in chivalric clichés, she cuts him off mid-flourish and demands the only assistance worthy of the name, help in locating the trap door that she presumes will be located nearby (28).

By distributing these heroic traits across gender lines, Walpole makes them seem generally available. At the same time, because the characters who exhibit these traits are so attractive, they become desirable models for attainment. Empiricism is romanticized as thoroughly as is noble blood. Even though the plot depicts the suitability of a marriage partner as determined by external obstacles, in time-honored romance fashion, rather than by a novelistic emphasis on subjective judgment, the 'basic mode' of the story is empirical. While Walpole would have disagreed with Locke's assertions about natural rights, he appears to concur with the primacy accorded by Locke to physical sensation as the road to knowledge. In the characters' encounters with the supernatural, and in their flight from pursuit by living humans, the verbs betray the distinction accorded to the five senses. Sight allows Jerome to recognize his long-lost son (56), Isabella to realize Theodore's love for Matilda (89), and the inhabitants of Otranto to claim their rightful ruler (115). Indeed, in this last instance, Manfred waives any documentation of Theodore's claim because the vision of St Nicholas 'corroborate[s] thy evidence beyond a thousand parchments.' The sound of Theodore's voice and the 'tone' of his words attest to his gentlemanly nature long before his birth is revealed (45). These sensations teach the characters how rightly to value what is good.

That lesson can only obtain when sensation applies itself to the discovery of genuine knowledge. The individual's experience must accrue from his senses of '*the world outside himself*' (Greene, 1970, 100); a reliance on empirical data disputes human reason's ability 'to attain knowledge through its own *isolated* activity' (Greene, 101, 1970 emphasis added). Otherwise, the stress on sensation might promote individualism at the expense of social harmony.

This second stage in Walpole's redefinition of heroism, the firm binding of personal heroism to the public good, had already appeared in the redefinition of valor. Even though *Longsword* bemoans the hardships war imposes upon the populace, its English heroes uphold individual rights; they articulate the belief that chivalry or friendship transcends national boundaries (1957, 27–31, 39–40, 44).[33] Walpole's insistence on public good at the expense of private happiness repeats in the internal battles his characters wage. All of these characters, so praised by contemporary reviewers for their fidelity to truth, wrestle the demons of allegiance. As individuals, they are awash with desire for personal autonomy; as members of a larger whole, they flounder in their attempts to reconcile that autonomy with the needs of others.

And just as sensation, rightly used, can provide a tow rope out of the morass, so sensation wrongly used can further those who seek to hitch others to their star. Manfred demonstrates this potential flip-side of empirical argument, its alliance with self-seeking, when he boasts to Isabella that union with him will ensure her a husband who knows how to rightly value her beauties, as indications of her ripeness to produce offspring (23). I want to turn now to examine this dark reverse of glamorized empiricism because it has been misread by critics as indicating Walpole's preference for a purely narcissistic life of the heart.

To counter this tendency, Walpole repeatedly stresses the dangerous link between passion and reason. Frederic's desire to wed Matilda partakes of both. Although Frederic realizes 'that heaven declared itself against Manfred' and that union with Matilda would involve him in the curse on Manfred's family, his 'increase of passion' (106) weakens his scruples. Moral 'scruples' quickly modulate into mercenary considerations about the effects of such a marriage upon his independent claim to the kingdom: 'the principality of Otranto was a stronger temptation, than the contingent reversion of it with Matilda' (105).

Walpole's critique reveals that excessive passion or excessive rationality lead to the identical social outcome. In both cases, integrity, in the sense of a wholeness that includes the social community as well as individual consistency, is compromised. Because both excessive passion and excessive reason foster individualism, they facilitate the breakdown of social bonds. Thus both destroy private and public happiness. Walpole's polemic buttresses his political agenda: were either empiricism or rationalism seen as an uncomplicated good, middle-class readers might assume they could navigate for themselves.

The need for guidance appears in two cases affecting the hero and heroine of the tale. On the surface, these two dilemmas seem disparate. Isabella confronts parental authority, wondering whether her father can 'enjoin a cursed act' (91) in ordering her to marry Manfred, and, if so, whether she is duty-bound to obey it. Theodore confronts parental authority when he is told to relinquish his love for Matilda. The selfishness of his preference is emphasized when we are told that he spends the night pleasing himself 'with visions of love' (94). When Jerome objects to the union, Theodore has 'little curiosity to learn the Friar's reasons, and less disposition to obey them' (ibid.). His misguided solipsism is blamed on his early separation from parental authority, with which he is only now being reacquainted. Theodore learns to adjust his desires to parental dictates. Isabella learns that she must invoke divine and human laws, as administered by the community, to guard her against her father.

Yet the apparent contradictions dissolve when we examine the underlying logic. Each case tests the good of the nation-state. When fathers thwart that good, they must be rejected. When they serve that good, they must be obeyed. A ruler like the 'good Alfonso,' the '*father* of his people' and 'the delight of mankind' (95, emphasis added), had once provided such a cynosure. Virtuous discretion, which Theodore and Isabella will learn, results only from conformity to the public good. Failure to conform is made to seem so outlandish that audience sympathy is enlisted on the side of the conventional. In this respect, the manners of the novel reflect in miniature the ideology of policy that governs the analysis of Manfred, since, like an ill-timed or illegitimate pregnancy, the ghost's display of its inflated injuries prevents the further concealment of Manfred's familial breaches.

Theodore's selfish indulgence in affective anticipation of the delights of physical sensation may be his only fault; just the same, it is not lightly dismissed. Raptures over Matilda produce a 'pleasing melancholy' that usurps control of his mind (74). This pleasing melancholy resembles the exhortations to retirement and solitude voiced by so many poems on melancholy written from the late 1740s on.[34] These homages to 'withdrawal into country seclusion from the distractions and corruptions of the city and the court' envisage an 'aristocratic and sophisticated sort of retirement' (Sickels, 1932, 17). In spite of his aristocratic bias, Walpole does not condone selfish seclusion. Instead, at the end of the novel he has Theodore return to a very differently imagined state of melancholy, one in which social bonds and social utility can be maintained.

This sharing of sorrow and responsibility is the highest good to which the individual can attain, in Walpole's fictive universe. Although the evil empire of Manfred has ended, and the rightful ruler is restored to the throne, the world does not seem a better and brighter place. The castle may self-destruct, but a new hierarchy and a new castle will simply replace the old. No brave new world of egalitarian interchange is envisioned. A conservative return to true nobility entails merely the assurance that one will have empathic company with whom to share nostalgic reminiscences.

Family legacy

I have been arguing that Walpole's novel inaugurated a new species of Gothic discourse, whereby a dream of extensive community could fasten its hopes to a heroic figure representing attributes of middle class and aristocracy alike. The response of Walpole's contemporary readers, like the response of his first critics, make Walpole's work seem congruent with the purpose of other eighteenth-century novelists, as estimated by John Preston: 'to project as one of the resources of their fiction an appropriate role for the reader. At their best they will be assisting the reader to be at his best; they will in effect be creating the pattern of an ideal assumption of the role' (1970, 210). By 1784, *The Castle of Otranto* was figured prominently in the work of Mrs Fenn, an author of children's works published anonymously under the pseudonym Mrs Teachwell or Mrs Lovechild, as I mentioned in the introduction. In *The Female Guardian,* two essays, 'Refined Morality' and 'Heroic Sentiments,' praise *Otranto* as a moral story. Her edifying commentary observes, 'The whole work is replete with refined morality ... A mother would surely be glad to select for her daughter such sentiments as may be met with in the mouths of that constellation of exalted characters, *Theodore, Hippolita, Matilda,* and *Jerome.* It is impossible to resist the inclination I feel to introduce my young readers to a slight degree of acquaintance with these respectable persons' (Fenn, 1784, 90). Hannah More's approbation, already cited, is significant not only for its association of the novel with a hygienic British masculinity, but also because of her endeavors to bring such 'refinement' to the lower classes. And Elizabeth Hamilton's 1806 comments reflect on the sturdy worth of the novel in general, at the same time that they reveal the epistemological lessons lying beneath the glittery or gloomy surfaces: it matters not 'when or where they lived, or indeed whether they lived at all. The sole question to be asked is, whether such and such dispositions and opinions would naturally and inevitably lead to such and such conclusions' (212).

Hamilton's rational analysis of behavioral propensities validates one of Walpole's goals. According to Walpole, 'personages under the dispensation of miracles and witnesses to the most stupendous phenomena, never lose sight of their human character: whereas in the products of romantic story, an improbable event never fails to be attended by an absurd dialogue' (Preface to the Second Edition, 10). However, his proclaimed fidelity to 'natural' speech carries an inherent class bias: heroes, heroines, villains, and monks preserve the elevated diction of the aristocracy. To vary the otherwise uniform refinement of language, Walpole introduces servants who maintain 'suitably' low diction and consequently provide comic relief, a device he claims to have learned from Shakespeare (11). This taxonomic assignment of linguistic style controverts Bakhtin's notion of heteroglossia as fundamentally dialogic (1981). Instead, Gothic heteroglossia confirms Franco Moretti's analysis that heteroglossia 'embodies a principle *hostile* to dialogue':

Its most typical habitat is, symptomatically, traditional societies, 'status' societies – those rigidly classified worlds that generate all sorts of local and professional jargons, of almost sumptuary distinctions and nuances ... Heteroglossia here flourishes because such worlds do not tolerate dialogue, which by nature is *anti*classificatory, as it implies equality, spiritual mobility, interchangeability of positions.

(1987, 194–5)

Given the appearance of *The Castle of Otranto* in just such a 'status' society, it should come as no surprise that Walpole's taxonomically assigned elevated diction seemed 'natural' to the reviewers, who praised characters they considered well-drawn and probable, despite the improbability of events.[35]

The romance trade-mark of heightened diction, and the question of who has the right to speak it, will provide a convenient measure of shifts born of social contingency as we move into a next phase of Gothic development. Clara Reeve's *Champion of Virtue* instances the 'proliferation of myths of origin and signs of reality; of second-hand truth, objectivity and authenticity' (Baudrillard, 1993, 12). With the loss of the American colonies, the time ripens for nostalgia to assume a new meaning, one where the 'resurrection of the figurative' replenishes the nation.

3
The Prince in the Pauper: Clara Reeve and *The Old English Baron*

> It may indeed be possible for us ... to exaggerate the impor-
> tance of law; we may say ... that it is only the skeleton of the
> body politic; but students of the body natural cannot afford to
> be scornful of bones, not even of dry bones; they must know
> their anatomy.

(Maitland, Collected Papers, II: 3)

In *The Castle of Otranto*, the mechanism of restoration and transmission occurs at an inflated distance. The kingdom comes to Theodore as
the result of prophecy fulfilled: 'that the Castle and Lordship of
Otranto should pass from the present family, whenever the real owner
should be grown too large to inhabit it' (1963, 15). Although the narrator tells us that the prophecy makes little sense, it establishes an
inverse relationship. The ghost of Alonso seemingly keeps pace with
the maturation of Theodore. The ghost becomes 'too big' to inhabit
the castle because its rightful owner is now big enough to replace it. In
The Old English Baron, past and present collaborate. Set a trial by ordeal
to clear his honor, that of having to spend three nights in the abandoned wing of the castle to ascertain whether it be haunted, Edmund
is rewarded for his courage not by the representatives of the present
order but by the ghostly law of the past:

> He thought ... there entered a warrior, leading a lady by the hand,
> who was young and beautiful, but pale and wan: the man was
> dressed in complete armour and his helmet down. They approached
> the bed; they undrew the curtains. He thought the man said, 'Is this
> our child?' The woman replied, 'It is; and the hour approaches that
> he shall be known for such.' They then separated, and one stood on

each side of the bed; their hands met over his head, and they gave him a solemn benediction. He strove to rise and pay them his respects, but they forbade him; and the lady said, 'Sleep in peace, oh, my Edmund! For those who are the true possessors of this apartment are employed in thy preservation: sleep on, sweet hope of a house that is thought past hope!'

(Reeve, 1883, 66–7)

This dream sequence enacts nationalism's rehousing of the dead in this world. As Tom Nairn says, the agency of nationalism memorializes the past into time present and thus bequeaths it a future (1997, 4). While nothing can reclothe these dry bones with flesh and blood, the body politic can be rejuvenated by Edmund's efforts, just as his fictional 'body natural' reanimates his biological line.[1]

Nevertheless, the nature of the aristocracy and social order in Reeve's version represents changes from that of Walpole's. Reeve annexes a vigilantly ethical foundation – her constant championship of merit, across class lines – to an utterly unsentimental story of the mechanisms by which financial status and advancement usually proceed. In this regard, her diagnosis and prescriptions resemble those of Edmund Burke. In his 'Speech on Economical Reform' (1780), Burke was to urge that reform of the royal household could only proceed when men were salaried for their services. Self-sacrificing virtues, which Burke calls 'rare and heroic,' may be a disguise for ambition that will overthrow modesty when its aims are achieved. To ignore such subconscious motivation is particularly dangerous: '[F]or as wealth is power, so all power will infallibly draw wealth to itself by some means or other' (258). Like Burke, Reeve repeatedly demystifies human relationships by emphasizing the extent to which lucre provides motivation, whether consciously or not.

Her belief in the need for concrete stimuli accounts for the dense materiality of both her nature and her supernature. The ghostly parental figures who appear to Edmund in a dream do not maintain the dignified, mysterious silence of Walpole's spectres; they are prosy and prolix (1883, 44–5). Neither does she skirt graphic description of the desecrations of vice. The villain confesses that his hired assassins had returned to him for orders after murdering Edmund's father: 'I sent them back to fetch the dead body, which they brought privately into the castle: They tied it neck and heels, and put it into a trunk' (105). When commissioners are sent with Edmund to investigate the crime, they discover a breastplate of armor stained with blood and the trunk, whose cords have rotted to dust, containing the skeletal remains of the torqued body (131).

Yet, at the same time, she remystifies the relationship between humans and abstractions by correlating wealth and merit, rank and talent. In the process, *The Old English Baron* imagines a communal splendor only temporarily (in the long view of history) misplaced. As such, Reeve's novel fulfills wishes we find articulated in other venues, like 1781's 'The Ancient Briton.' An imaginary dialogue between a coin representing Briton and a human discoverer of the coin, the poem praises the fact of the king having been 'Briton born' and describes his empire as extending 'As far as ocean rolls his foaming tides'(*Critical Review*, 1781, 72). Each member of Reeve's fictional community, no matter to which economic group he or she belongs, resembles that coin: communal splendor affords security and happiness to all. If Walpole hints that the resumption of aristocratic privilege and place cannot cure a world riven by melancholic division, Reeve's fictional resolution dissolves the potential for dissension, whether caused by the pull between a status and a class orientation, between the competing needs of the individual and the needs of the state, or between the kind of circulation representative of mercantilist capitalism and a land-based stability. This remystification takes concrete shape when habitual benevolence finds immediate recompense. Moreover, the resurrection of the polity occurs because all members work in harmony, unlike the divisions existing between masters and servants in *Otranto*. Reeve's message in *The Old English Baron* thus encompasses a broader spectrum of society than had Walpole's. This broad reach extends to the borders of the kingdom as well. Whereas Otranto solidifies once more into an autonomous kingdom governed by its rightful heirs, the marriages at the end of *The Old English Baron* help compose an isolated region of England into a federation incorporating essential elements of what would become Great Britain.

Colonial betrayal gothicized

More concretely than any other Gothic novelist, Clara Reeve's literary practice licenses us to see the nationalist ideal beneath the Gothic fiction. She first forayed into literary publication with a translation of Barclay's *Argenis*, which her publisher forced her to title *The Phoenix* (1772). Reeve's selection of Barclay's work as the vehicle through which she could pursue her theoretical goals was consistent with the original's tenor. Romance and politics dovetail in *Argenis*, a confluence Reeve acknowledges in her Preface. She calls Barclay's tale 'a romance, an allegory, and a system of politics. In it the various forms of government are investigated, the causes of faction detected, and the remedies pointed out for most of the evils that can arise in a state' (A3).[2] Like its original author and subsequent editors, Reeve furnishes a key to identify the historical personages intended, thereby signaling the work's kinship to other seventeenth- and eighteenth-century *romans-à-clef*. Sicily represents France, from the civil wars under Henry III to the crowning of Henry IV. Competing with Sicily is England, headed by Hyanisbé, stand-in for Elizabeth I. Lycogenes and his friends are the Lorraine party, headed by the Duke of Guise; Radirobanes, Phillip II of Spain. Each additional character is further identified as some historical player in the fight over French succession at that time (A6).

Despite the bravado of her prefatory prediction, the public did not love *The Phoenix*. Still, it remains a valuable document, if only because it demonstrates Reeve's active interest in political issues.[3] The romance touches on a great number of diverse topics: the correct manner by which kings should choose their ministers and remain independent and separate from parties and factions (I.1: 6); the prudence of securing ministerial talent by financial reward (I.1: 10); the nature of the best form of government: republic, oligarchy, hereditary or elective monarchy (I.1: 18–19); the desirability of maintaining hierarchical class discriminations; the social consequences of welfare and the proliferating legalistic mentality, both of which are lamented (III.3: 22); the proper (privatized) mode of tax collection and the protection due citizens against arbitrary taxation to finance war (rights advocated by the queen, Hyanisbé (IV.4: 18).

While we have already seen these issues as troubling Reeve's contemporaries, a crucial 'Gothic' aspect is missing from *The Phoenix*: public events are not dissected in the light of their consequences for private experience. The problems consuming the heroes and heroine of *The Phoenix* remain strictly aristocratic. More critics (and readers) than Walpole found *The Phoenix* to be a still birth, in the sense that no identification with the characters was possible. Unlike *The Phoenix*, where political morals appear as undigested set-pieces, *The Old English Baron* embeds its political morals in the narrative form. Private events are constructed in such a way that they necessarily impinge on the public realm. This melding of public and private enabled Reeve to cure the lack of interest readers found in *The Phoenix* by providing characters and situations with which readers could identify.

Reeve's narrative revisions respond as much to market realities as they do to alterations in political and social reality. Between 1772 and 1778, the need for a 'stately fable' resolving political unrest had intensified. Even though the sources of social unease recorded fictionally in *The Phoenix* glance at external realities, their sheer number and the episodic manner of their presentation indicate a more diffuse sense of menace. The colonists' revolt, in full swing by the writing of *Baron*, threatened the political stability of the nation and touched off anxieties about external and internal relations.

Domestically, the rebellion especially stirred up doubts about the general nature of kinship relations among members of the polity. The longstanding, commonplace comparison of the kingdom to a great family made these questions cut both in the direction of one's loyalty to the King and government, and to one's immediate kin. As ties loosened, the proliferating legalistic bent Reeve had discerned and bemoaned in *The Phoenix* began more frequently to leverage individual rights. While the analogy between the family and the state reaches back to the writings of Filmer, Reeve's application of that analogy suggests her support of Sir William Temple's view that such a political organization was Gothic in origin. Moreover, Reeve's fictional embodiment of the analogy in romance form seems implicitly to chastise Temple's splitting of Gothicism into two faces, political and literary, as I discussed in Chapter 1. Further, Reeve's fusion of these two sides into a single aspect supports my contention that, by 1778, Gothic novelists saw a generic function as interwoven with certain generic features. If *The Phoenix* reverberates distantly with the growing clamor in England over the colonies' bid for independence, in that some of the topics enumerated echo Burke's speeches and the colonists' position during the period, *The Old English Baron* thematizes the American Revolution and its aftermath, first by telling multilayered stories of betrayal, and then by accommodating individual and social rights.

Since *The Old English Baron* is the least well-known of the full-length Gothic novels I will discuss, a brief précis of the plot will familiarize us with the surface emphasis on the private realm. Upon his return from the Crusades, Sir Philip Harclay journeys from the north to the west of England in search of his bosom friend, Sir Arthur Lovel. At Lovel Castle, he discovers the recent purchaser, Baron Fitz-Owen, installed with the extended Fitz-Owen family; he learns that Lord and Lady Lovel are deceased, as is the infant she was carrying. Among the Baron's family is an impecunious youth, Edmund Twyford, who has been adopted as an upper servant and companion to the Baron's boys.

Harclay takes an instantaneous liking to Edmund, and entreats the Baron for him. The Baron leaves the decision to Edmund, who prefers to remain with the Fitz-Owens. Harclay leaves, promising the lad his assistance should he ever require it. Edmund accepts that offer when the hostility of the Baron's eldest son and his two nephews drives him from the house. He tells Harclay of the supernatural events that have revealed to him his true paternity as the son of Lord Lovel, information subsequently corroborated by his foster mother. The hearsay testimony of the Lovels' elderly servant, Joseph, suffices Harclay to charge the 'trecherye and crueltie' of the Lovel's 'nearest kinnesmanne,' Sir Walter Lovel, with the murder of Lord and Lady Lovel. Harclay champions the boy by challenging Sir Walter to a duel, to be adjudicated by northern and Scottish lords in the marches. The villain is defeated and confesses his crime; the tale ends with Edmund's restitution as the heir to Lovel Castle and his marriage to Fitz-Owen's daughter.

The historical setting Reeve chooses for her Gothic novel contains special relevance for the immediate circumstances in which it is produced. Like England in the actual day of writing, the England of Reeve's novel is a place where colonial betrayals necessitate battles to recover territory. While the main action takes place in the minority of Henry VI,[4] the events conjured up reach back to the turn of the fifteenth century. The 'true' old, in the sense of former, English Baron had participated in Henry V's battles to put down the Welsh rebels. The story transpires against a backdrop in which England engages in the attempt to recover French possessions revolting to the Dauphin. These French territories had been ceded to Henry V through the combined effects of conquest and alliance. As Hal's son, Henry VI is the rightful ruler of France. In a manner reminiscent of the tactic used by Walpole, the oblique allusion to the situation vis-à-vis America has duplicate value. Not only are the colonies in revolt in 1777, but France has joined the war on their side.

But Reeve does not seize the occasion to launch a direct critique of the French,[5] as had Leland, or of the colonists. Precisely because the past is viewed as positive, we know that, in this Gothic novel, it is being invoked to conjure up a vision of the national purpose that has been lost. This nationalism is not directed against external enemies, but against internal foes who have alienated the values endemic to England, which are shown as having constituted her greatness. Consequently, Reeve uses the theme of betrayal to draw a double-edged analogy. Kinsmen of the Baron Fitz-Owen disseminate a seemingly paranoid discourse about the intentions of Edmund to destabilize the harmony of the extended family into which he has been adopted. The kinsmen imply that Edmund is like the proverbial cuckoo in the nest, suggesting to the Baron that his disappearance is only apparent and covers his concealment within the familial structure until the time is ripe for him to 'rush out in the night, and either rob or murder us, or, at least, alarm and terrify the family' (73). The policy the kinsmen impute to Edmund aligns him with the colonists, in that Americans were portrayed as children revolting against their parent.[6] When the Baron questions why Edmund should shut himself up to be starved, the disaffected kin reply in language that gestures towards the relationship between the colonists and France. Edmund, they say, has friends in the house 'who will not suffer him to want any thing: Those ... will lend a hand to help him in time of need; and perhaps, ... assist his ingenious contrivances' (73–4).

Reeve exonerates Edmund and turns the accusation back upon his accusers. That they are the source from which the evil emanates is hinted by the narrator's repeated use of the word 'cabal' to describe them (26, 28). Admittedly anachronistic, given that Reeve presents the story as a translated manuscript dating from the fifteenth century, the word yet resonates with more than the hollow thud of a false note, since the word was employed both by regicides and cavaliers to characterize their opponents' activity and ultimately came to be associated with misguided alliances with France.[7] The revelation that envious kinsmen could be capable of such intrafamilial malice only heightens the sense of betrayal. Thus, while the setting immerses us in the domestic affairs of a household, not in the political realm of a principality as Walpole's novel had placed us, that household becomes a microcosm of events in the immediate state of Reeve's writing and the site from which Reeve, as a member of the Habermasian public sphere, will launch her critique.[8]

Edmund's restoration as the rightful heir results in the polity being purged of disaffected members. While Edmund may not directly serve as the agent of this change, he does serve as its pretext, thereby contradicting Bakhtin's characterization of the Gothic as a novel of ordeal in which 'the hero does not affect the world, he does not change its appearance; ... [he] does not alter the social face of the world, nor does he restructure it' (1986, 16). Bakhtin claims that there 'is no place for generations in ... the novel of ordeal' because generations 'introduce the contiguity of lives taking place at various times' which 'provides an entry into historical duration' and hence encapsulates a notion of historical time (18). Just such a notion of historical time appears in the summary genealogy which concludes the tale, which delays and extends the closure it nonetheless ultimately provides. More significantly, the generational aspect of the battles for sway between Fitz-Owen, his sons, and his kinsmen conveys a sense of historical time, as does Edmund's championship by three figures of an older generation, Oswald, Harclay, and the elderly servant, Joseph.

And this dispersal over time, this broadcast interrogation of affiliation and degree, necessitates a slight adjustment in my procedure. While Edmund once again displays all the trade-mark characteristics of a romance Gothic hero that I enumerated in Chapter 1 (he, too, is honest, handsome, courageous, disinterestedly interested, chivalrous to women, and humble almost to a fault, nearly losing his beloved because he so exasperates her with his humility), Reeve's novel locates heroism more in social interchange than in individual action. Accordingly, I want to focus on the models that her heroes provide for aristocratic governance and duties.

Bringing the colony home

Such new aristocratic duty scruples neither to weigh proprieties of time and place nor to solicit the spiritual, as well as the physical, well-being of its object, even when the two are no longer necessarily intertwined. We witness this extension of the concept of duty first in the actions of the characters. Harclay undertakes his journey accompanied only by an elderly servant, who dies on the morning of the journey's third day. His loss occasions great concern to the Knight; he orders a funeral, attends it himself, and sheds a 'tear of humanity over his grave' (8). The redefinition also appears by analogy: when a peasant fears that he is 'unable and unworthy' to entertain Harclay, the Knight expresses his allegiance to the tenets of Christ, who 'accepted the invitations of the poor, and washed the feet of his disciples' (13).

When her virtuous characters turn their attention to physical needs, the charity they practice combines older notions of noblesse oblige with more modern instances of bureaucratized charity, in that randomness has been replaced by methodicalness and solitary acts by collective dispensation. Sir Philip maintains 'twelve old soldiers who had been maimed and disabled in the wars, and had no provision made for them; also six old officers who had been unfortunate and were grown grey without preferment' (83), in addition to Zadisky, the servant he has won in the wars and converted to Christianity. Besides these, we are told 'there are many others who eat of [his] bread and drink of his cup ...; his ears are ever open to distress, his hand to relieve it, and he shares in every good man's joys and blessings' (84). When he offers his estate to the Baron Fitz-Owen at the end of the novel, so that Fitz-Owen can vacate Edmund's estate, Harclay assures the Baron that another house exists on his lands that has been shut up for years: 'I will have it repaired and furnished properly for the reception of my old men: I will endow it with a certain sum to be paid annually, and will appoint a steward to manage their revenue' (147). All these provisions will be assured for the life of the first inhabitants; and it is suggested that the institution will be continued for later generations through the auspices of his adopted son, for which purpose Harclay will endow him. Through the portrait of Harclay, we can glimpse the era's new emphasis on public service to which I adverted in Chapter 1. With his heightened attention to circumstantial detail, Harclay sounds very like a one-man welfare state.[9]

Edmund not only regains his inheritance through Harclay, but through Harclay he also refines his notions of aristocratic virtue to purify them of vainglory. Prior to his accession, Edmund suffers 'flames of ambition' kindled by internal and external acknowledgments of his superior qualities (25). These flames must be stifled because his 'low birth and dependant station' offer no outlet for his merit. War cures that lack of opportunity: his worth can be tested and made serviceable when he is permitted to accompany his noble friends to the battlefield of France (26). Still, individual merit cannot fight in its own behalf, unsupported by authority. When Edmund later objects that the responsibility to fight in defense of his rights rests with him, Harclay rejoins: 'And do you think he [Walter Lovel] will answer the challenge of an unknown youth, with nothing but his pretensions to his name and title? Certainly not' (90). If this passage makes apparent an inequity of the laws, that access to justice depends upon circumstances of place and birth, Reeve's revival of feudal kinship relations makes such patronage seem the solution. Aristocratic action on behalf of those proscribed can circumvent contingencies and safeguard the status of all.

Edmund applies those lessons when he must judge his foster father. His foster father is guilty of crimes past and present: he had obscured the evidence of Edmund's birth and buried the discovered corpse of Edmund's mother secretly; responsible consequently for the growing Edmund, Twyford had first beaten and then driven him from home. Edmund's kind treatment of Twyford not only exceeds the generosity of

Walpole's hero but also demonstrates Reeve's variant conception of the nature of aristocratic virtue. Proclaiming his forgiveness, Edmund vows:

> I shared your poverty, and you will share my riches; I will give you the cottage where you dwell, and the ground about it; I will also pay you the annual sum of ten pounds for the lives of you both; I will put out your children to manual trades, and assist you to provide for them in their own station; and you are to look upon this as paying a debt, and not bestowing a gift: I owe you more than I can ever pay.
>
> (149)

He has incurred this debt because Twyford saved his infant life, fed and clothed him. While the objects of compassion in the sentimental novel may be drawn from a wider panoply of humankind than those in *The Old English Baron*, the compensation given them for their distresses is also more superficial.[10] In Reeve's fictional universe, the aristocracy earn their reputations as virtuous because charity is conceived and carried out as a duty, not just as an optional, spontaneous benevolent action to be undertaken solely to bolster one's self-esteem.[11]

Edmund's incorporation of charitable precepts combines the active and literary qualities of Harclay's two acts. He gives his story a spiritual and literary cast by making his own life into an individual instance of *felix culpa*. Since Twyford's cruelty had brought Edmund to the notice of the Fitz-Owens, 'parental' abuse had only been part of the divine plan to effect Edmund's restoration. This heroic Christian humility and involvement with spiritual needs divorced from physical needs is unique to Reeve. Edmund supplies his foster father with more than the means for future physical comfort; he eases his shame and guilt by 'reading' Twyford's behavior and furnishing psychological justification for Twyford's ill treatment of him (149).

Reeve's extension of innate nobility to characters across the ranks makes hers the most democratic of the Gothic novels. Nevertheless, like that of all early Gothic novels, Reeve's plot hinges on status inconsistency. McKeon's argument that attention to status had been superseded by a class orientation by 1778 (1987, 419) might make such a plot choice seem out of step. In McKeon's view, the period of the Civil War strengthened notions of absolute ownership and the heritability of private property at the same time that it weakened belief in the inheritance of nobility. The fundamental relation of lineage, political right, and temporal power became increasingly viewed as tenuous.

Regicide, and the settlement of succession in William III, made the fiction of inherited authority expendable. In such a climate, indifference to genealogical inheritance as an explicit article of the theory of English kingship became obligatory. The divine workings of providence were substituted for the divine right of kings. In secular terms, personal merit replaced hereditary right (McKeon, 1987, 180–1). While Reeve holds tenaciously to respect for merit, as I will show in greater detail below, she nevertheless also adheres to the idea of lineage, whether of manuscripts or of 'orphans.' Her conflicting values testify elegiacally to her sense that a world in which virtue and truth could be known by knowing one's parentage was vanishing.

Lineage may no longer signify character; but character can signify nobility, despite one's de facto origins. In keeping with the empiricist bent of Walpole's novel, Theodore *knows* his heritage, because his mother had bound 'a writing around my arm under my garments, which told me I was the son of the Count Falconara' (1963, 84). Clara Reeve's hero, Edmund, also bears the characters of his birth, but they are not bound around his arm.[12] Instead, these graphic indices shine through in moral, behavioral, and physiological traces of inheritance, transparent to all who behold him but opaque to Edmund himself. Thus, rather than claiming his patrimony as Theodore does, his patrimony claims him. In so doing, Edmund's accession melds two types: the 'gentleman' as 'aristocrat of character' and 'aristocrat by birth.'

By making her middle- and lower-class characters emulate the values and manners of the aristocracy, she projects the intangible accoutrements of status onto members of a group increasingly encouraged to view themselves as a class. The virtuous aristocrats, represented by Baron Fitz-Owen and Sir Philip Harclay, champion a meritocracy; the virtues of the 'peasantry' are contrasted favorably with the criminal, or merely ill-mannered, tendencies of the false 'nobility.' Servants are uniformly industrious, virtuous, and well-versed in sentimental attitudes (1883, 25, 44, 64–5). This projection of quality onto people never before considered 'the quality' distinguishes Reeve's beliefs from those of Walpole, and suggests one source of his animus towards her novel. Walpole's novel depicts middle-class virtues as inhering in the nobility, at the same time that empirical evidence, said by McKeon to be prized among those elements of society most captivated by a materialistic outlook, underwrites traditional institutions. Reeve makes the confluence run in both directions: the aristocracy participate in middle-class virtues, while the middle and lower classes have internalized noble manners. Reeve's idealization of the servant class stands in marked distinction not only to Walpole's portrayal of servants but also to that of Radcliffe and Lewis. Radcliffe's servants may be industrious and ultimately virtuous, but their indiscriminate garrulousness betrays their social inferiority. Lewis's lower classes maintain the same distinction as Radcliffe's between virtuous action and speech; he ironizes their utterances of sentimental platitudes as indications of their vanity, an affective as well as linguistic overstepping of boundaries. In Reeve, linguistic boundaries function like geographic and social borders; they dissolve, to be crisscrossed as magical thresholds over which people pass to new stages.

As a result of their moral and linguistic resemblance, a new web of relations can be woven between the classes. If Edmund is the warp, then the new kinship lines which attach themselves to him as his enfeoffment takes shape are the weft of this tapestry. And like a medieval tapestry, the shifting planes of the picture allegorize more than one meaning: if, on the one hand, the story stands as a synecdoche for transcontinental traitors, it also metonymically represents domestic relations along a horizontal axis on the other. Eighteenth-century inhabitants of England felt the palpable reconfiguration of kinship systems. Stripped of political, economic, educational, and organizational functions, they were reduced to markers governing the construction of sex and gender.[13] Reeve reverses this historical process, eradicating kinship systems' influence over sex and gender but preserving their palliative effect in political, juridical, and economic spheres.[14] She replaces the nuclearization of the family with a colonialist thrust that incorporates through marriage geographically, politically, and socially discrete groups. The family engorges on the cumulative portions that accrue from these alliances, among which are the 'accumulated wealth and the maintenance of differential access to political and economic resources; ... [and] the consolidation of high-ranking persons into a single closed strata of endogamous kin' (Rubin, 1975, 209).

If the shift from affiliation through hereditary ties to identification along class lines caused social rifts, the new kinship relations woven by Reeve's plot provide emotional upholstery for those rents. Edmund's history also signifies a fictional resolution to the competition between capitalist individualism and progressivism and adherence to more stable forms of society because his growth as an individual smooths out at the same time that it reflects the historical trajectory. As such, the Gothic novel becomes a *Bildungsroman* in which both self and society are fashioned. When Edmund's martial prowess is brought to the attention of Richard Plantagenet, the Regent proposes to confer a knighthood upon him. This gesture of honor is thwarted. Edmund's enemies protest that his status prevents it. The Duke of York agrees. Reeve implicitly criticizes the hierarchical prejudice by showing the Regent as motivated by his own pride of birth (30). Discovering an honorable substitution, the Regent makes amends: 'Though I cannot reward you as I intended, I will take care that you shall have a large share in the spoils of this night; and, I declare publickly, that you stand first in the list of gallant men in this engagement' (ibid.). The episode illustrates that gentility does not inhere merely in birth, and it foreshadows the way pecuniary remuneration and verbal tribute will become satisfactory compensations when the meritorious, unlike Edmund, are discovered merely to resemble, rather than to be, the noble.

Circulation at home and abroad

In the novel, Reeve expands the feudal ritual of gift exchange to accord more closely with nascent capitalist enterprise. Fitz-Owen and Harclay barter over competing claims: the castle and its property become the appropriate mediums of exchange to compensate Fitz-Owen for his expense in raising Edmund and housing him as weighted against the service received by the Baron while the hero has acted as his page. Middle-class concerns appear most clearly in the homely details of egg-and-bacon breakfasts, and in the descriptions of private quarters for the boys – an architectural innovation characteristic of middle-class housing but alien to Gothic castles.[15] More than charming eighteenth-century errata, like the anachronistic spectacle of aristocratic heroes suffering toothaches (Tompkins, 1932, 229–30), the pervasive, incessant images of exchange, and the widespread applicability of such images, leave ineffaceble traces of ideological debate. Just as her portrait of social relations negotiates differences (between a status and a class orientation, between the individual and the state), so her economic relations expunge the sense of alienation usually charged to capitalist enterprise.[16]

Both material goods and human beings become exchangeable and interchangeable; each can equally be the object of circulation. That human beings must percolate through society is thematized from the first page of the novel in the history of Zadisky, a soldier of Greek extraction brought up by a Saracen officer, captured by an Englishman in the service of the Greek Emperor (Harclay), converted to Christianity, and translated to England with his captor, who has become his benefactor and friend (7). Both Zadisky and his master illustrate the way duty demands our willingness to circulate, for the good of self as well as of others. And that duty applies alike to noble and commoner. Despite the presence of this wartime comrade, Harclay feels profoundly alienated upon his return. Essentially reduced to the condition of a stranger in his homeland, Harclay combats the melancholic longing to seclude himself which results. Like Walpole's Theodore, Harclay 'could be contented to give up the world, and retire to a religious house.' But his realization that others depend on him stays his inclination, and he finds a further rationale in the thought that 'he might be of service' to those as yet unknown (17).

Harclay's sense of duty counterpoints the poetic version of melancholy, sung in the latter half of the eighteenth century as an aristocratic paean to rusticated isolation (Sickels, 1932, 144). And even the novel's inhabitant of rustic isolation, Fitz-Owen, agrees with Harclay that active participation is of greater service than retirement. Although he may not circulate personally, he opens his home as a way station. Hence, he receives his two nephews and their companions, and adopts the unwanted Edmund. This latter kind of charity seems to Fitz-Owen more effective than mere alms or passive donation to the Church, since ecclesiastical 'servants did not always make the best use' of one's fortune (17). Expense of spirit must be accompanied by an expense of pocket whose outlays are carefully shepherded by the individual.

This notion of circulation as a desirable end also governs purely affective economy. Harclay vows to be thankful for the blessings spared to him, and promises to 'endeavour to replace those I have lost' (9). Human relationships are envisaged as interchangeable because they facilitate vicarious experience. The young servant, John Wyatt, is exhorted to transfer his allegiance from Harclay to Edmund. In thus transposing his feelings he will demonstrate his attachment to Harclay: 'in serving my friend, you will serve me' (87).

Servants are not the only people to serve as counters of emotion. From the very beginning, Edmund's propulsion along the trajectory that will culminate in his restitution depends on his transudation through familial economies. Beloved by all the villagers except his putative father, he takes up errand-running for the Fitz-Owens and is incorporated into their family as reward, initially with the intent of placing him in service. The intensified contact that ensues teaches the Baron to value Edmund more highly, with the result that he educates him as the companion of his children; before the plot gives Edmund's destiny a different spin, he has come to be regarded as 'a faithful servant of the upper kind, and an useful friend to my family' (18). At first sight of Edmund, Harclay desires to own the boy (18–19).

Like Emma, then, whose role as a heroine is muted comparatively to Isabella in *Otranto*, Edmund serves as a cipher onto whom desire can be projected by others. The resemblance between them crystallizes in their only pre-nuptial courtship scene, where both young people delicately minuet around their feelings, displacing onto the 'friends' they invent their occulted desire for one another (1883, 98–9). Although Emma answers her father's query if she will marry Edmund by acknowledging her affection, she modestly qualifies the expression of her own longing:

> My lord and father's goodness has always prevented my wishes; I am the happiest of all children, in being able to obey his commands, without offering violence to my own inclinations. As I am called upon in this public manner, it is but justice to this gentleman's merit to declare that, were I at liberty to choose a husband from all the world, he only should be my choice, who, I can say with joy, is my father's also.
>
> (1883, 202).

Even though Fitz-Owen has indeed granted Emma the 'liberty to choose her husband from all the world,' the economy, affective, political, social, or financial, requires that she restrict her compass. But the strong arm of necessity bows like a gracious yielding to coincidence. This is Sedgwick's homosociality run in all possible configurations of gender.[17] And such a fiction of a fortuitously closed circulation of desire reappears when Harclay must console himself for his inability to 'possess' Edmund (or any man) in the manner he had envisioned: instead, Harclay learns to cherish Edmund as a remnant of his friendship with Edmund's father (89), and Zadisky suggests that Edmund will supply Zadisky's absence as well (137). Ultimately, Harclay becomes Edmund's father, not only by adoption (88, 94), but by literally treading in the footsteps of Arthur Lovel when he comes to reside with Edmund.

Even the villain must be kept in circulation, albeit at a distance.[18] Walter Lovel, who has engineered the murder of his kinsman in order to usurp his title and estate, and in the hopes of gaining his wife, is given the opportunity of making financial and spiritual restitution. If he willingly surrenders the title and estate to the rightful heir, and disposes of his own proper fortune to his relatives, he can choose between retirement to a religious establishment or voluntary exile. In either case, he will be allotted 'a decent annuity, that he may not want the comforts of life. By the last I disable him from the means of doing further mischief, and enable him to devote the remainder of his days to penitence' (122). Public vengeance is renounced in favor of a private code of justice that is depicted as more in accord with Heavenly dispensations than the law of the land: 'If Heaven gives him time for repentance, man should not deny it' (ibid.).

Reeve's treatment of the supernatural also tropes circulation. Immaterial events in the story take on flesh, and recapitulate the osmotic nature of relationships as a whole. Dreams infiltrate the membrane between the conscious and the unconscious, between illusion and reality, and between human minds. Early in the novel, Harclay dreams that he follows Arthur Lovel into a 'dark and frightful cave, where he disappeared, and in his stead he beheld a complete suit of armour stained with blood, which belonged to his friend, and he thought he heard dismal groans beneath' (14). Edmund later has that very experience (53–4). Harclay realizes other points of his own dream (13, 98), just as aspects of Edmund's come true (43–4, 145). But Lady Lovel's vision and legacy offer perhaps the clearest instance.

Although Lady Lovel is already dead when the novel begins, her presence is more than spectral; she sets the pattern for the translation of Christian passivity (domestic virtue) into secular activity. Like a true sentimental heroine, she faints away upon learning of her husband's death. She revives, at first resigned to her widowed state and committed to the welfare of the child she is carrying who will represent the continuity of her race. This patient renunciation for the benefit of the future is abruptly abjured. Claiming that she has been visited by the ghost of her husband, who has communicated his murder, she calls simultaneously upon God and King to revenge his death and give her justice. Her powers of speech frustrate the villain's attempt to invalidate her accusations by declaring her mad, just as her refusal to be imprisoned in the iconic female body of the aristocracy permits her to elude the villain's efforts to incorporate her through marriage (51). His misreading of her apparent compliance opens the space for her escape at night into the common fields where she delivers her child alone before she dies. Although her aristocratic body is stripped by the peasants who find it (60), this dismantling does not dissolve the hierarchical world order but merely transmits that identity from one generation and one gender to the next. Since she had swaddled her infant in her cloak, wrapped up with the signets of his house, her abandoned identity can be reinstated later when he is recognized as the heir.

Likewise, in the figure of Zadisky the disparate realms of material and immaterial are compressed or collapsed; and the inclusive significance of his successive translations is symbolized structurally by the fact that his peregrinations form a parenthesis to the tale proper, since at the end he returns to the Holy Land as chaperone to the expelled villain. Years after his return, he finally gives Harclay his reasons for desiring to leave: the discovery of a son, presumably unknown to him, living in Palestine. Zadisky had been so thoroughly acculturated that he had declared all countries alike to a wise man (136). As proof of this philosophy, he pursues the same system with his son. Upon discovering him, father converts son to Christianity, then persuades the new convert to retire with his father to a monastery, in retreat from the downfall of his newly readopted empire (152–3). It is appropriate that the novel should proleptically signal its end with this retirement, for elsewhere retirement from the world is equated with silence (9). The formula silence:speech::passivity:action is demonstrated by Edmund's view of words as his inheritance, before the revelation of his identity permits him to give more concrete proof of his benevolence (25), and by Lord Clifford's intercession with Lord Fitz-Owen, whom he begs to judge of the surprising revelations with 'that justice and honour that speaks your character' (109).

Language thus becomes another medium for diffusion, especially because proper names take on predicative capacity.[19] A proliferation of names accompanies Edmund's transversal of status boundaries. While his claim is being prosecuted, Harclay convinces him to drop the patronymic of his foster father (Twyford) and to replace it with the name Seagrave, which Harclay dredges up from his own mother's family (88). When, before the single combat that will decide the issue of Edmund's claim, Harclay makes a will, he appoints Edmund his heir 'by the name of Lovel, alias, Seagrave, alias Twyford' (94). The muniment of nominative transmission to the second and third generations carries both legal and emblematic function. In Reeve's eyes, predication may be superior even to sexuality: the adoption of some of Edmund and Emma's children by William and Harclay circumvents the negotiation of power through heterosexual union. These adoptions are symbolized, in William's case, through the imposition of a name – a marking *of* character by the inscription of characterological significance: William bequeaths to the boy both his estate and his predilection for the single life (152).

The evidence adduced thus far concerns mainly social and economic factors of circulation as types of mobility. One of the best examples in

the novel of such mobility is the fact that the Fitz-Owens have purchased their estate. Although no aspersions fall on the antiquity of
their name as a result, Harclay does express surprise that Sir Walter
Lovel should have left 'the seat of his ancestors' (10). The servant who
provides Harclay the information explains that Sir Walter had married
his sister to Fitz-Owen and had retired, after the sale, to build a new
estate in the north. It remains unexplained why Fitz-Owen should
have needed to acquire paternal lands on the open market. Before
meeting the Fitz-Owens, Harclay dreams that he receives a message
from his deceased friend, who tells him that he still commands the
domains from beyond the grave: 'none can enter these gates without
my permission' (13); and he calls upon Harclay to preserve the hopes
of his house. As we have already seen, that preservation requires that
the lands be restored to Edmund; but, once again, the restoration
occurs through a legally enacted transmission accompanied by the
exchange of monies.

Restricting the arm of the law

Their ability to effect this exchange among themselves, without the
need for recourse to some legal institution, is one instance of the
romanticization of legal jurisdiction. Nor is this the only example of the
individual's capacity to prosecute the law in his own behalf, as I will
argue below. By restoring the juridical domain to the individual, the
novel seems directly to counter legal tendencies in the world of fact.

The complaints Reeve had voiced in *The Phoenix* about litigiousness in
the population increasingly find echoes in journalistic outcries against
proliferating laws. For instance, the reviewer of *The Laws Respecting
Women, as they regard their Natural Rights, or their Connections and
Conduct* (*Critical Review*, 1778) seizes the occasion to enter his own plea:

> That the great bulk of the body of the laws of this country is a
> public grievance, few, who are in the least acquainted with the laws
> under which they live, will deny. It is a melancholy truth, that,
> during the present reign, of only sixteen sessions of Parliament, our
> statute law has swolen [sic] to a size equal to all the statutes from
> Magna Charta down to the death of Queen Anne – a period of five
> centuries... Notwithstanding these are days of patriotism, more
> hands are employed, we fear, to break the laws, than to mend, or to
> explain them ...

(44)

In his 'Letter to the Sheriffs of Bristol' (1777), Burke mourns that 'our subjects diminish as our laws increase' (1960, 177). As Burke says, the war has been conducted not only by virtue of martial arms but also by the hostility of the laws (188). The animus displayed towards the colonists has perverted natural and national sympathy; the antidote is 'to revive the old partiality to the English name' (193). By this, he means allegiance to the type of 'Gothic liberties' that opponents of the colonists have abrogated.

Reeve's fictional antidote preserves the myth of Gothic liberty discussed in Chapter 1 by returning the law to the jurisdiction of individuals. Here we see that Reeve is not so much defending earlier values under attack as trying to justify new values by recourse to older models, to show them not as a break from tradition but as part of a natural social and historical continuum. Beyond the familiarization of the strange, through the literal domestication of capitalist ideology, *The Old English Baron* conversely makes strange the increasingly familiar bureaucratization of the state, by privatizing justice and welfare in a resurrection of the seigneurial.

The first such privatization, and domestication, of justice occurs at the home of Fitz-Owen. The two principal agitators against Edmund, Fitz-Owen's nephews Markham and Wenlock, are divided against one another by Father Oswald, who then persuades Markham to bear witness against his kin. The Baron conducts a private trial, and privately condemns the boys to banishment (95–7), although once again the offenders are kept in purgatorial reserve for circulation within the family economy. Markham's punishment especially resembles reward for his testimony, since his banishment consists in his being sent abroad on business for the Baron: 'that shall put you in a way to do credit to yourself, and service to me' (97).

Credit accrues from individual action, as long as this action serves the self in a tangential by-product of serving the greater good. In that case, no competition between the two poles of demand is envisioned, and Heaven itself is judged to advocate human self-reliance. Virtue and merit, repeatedly stressed, often take this form of self-sufficiency. When Harclay learns of Walter Lovel's perfidy, he ponders the best means to bring him to justice: 'Shall I go to court, and demand justice of the King? or shall I accuse him of the murder, and make him stand a publick trial?' (90). Lovel's falsely gained nobility poses a legal conundrum. If he is treated as a Baron of the realm, the title by which he is known, he is entitled to a trial by his peers. But the peerage may be less than honestly sympathetic to the claims of a peasant lad, whose only evidence is the supernatural testimony of his dead parents, and the confirmation of an elderly servant to his family. If Lovel is stripped of his title, he will be tried at a county assize, where the chances of justice are greater, but reason must be given why he should be deprived of that title. Edmund points out a further complication. Since Lovel's sister had married the Baron Fitz-Owen, any degradation of Lovel's title will shed disgrace on Fitz-Owen. This conundrum suggests the private cost of public justice. Harclay insists that Edmund's first duty is to the memory of his injured parents. Yet he proposes a solution that will elude both the legal and the emotional problem: 'I will challenge the traitor to meet me in the field; and, if he has spirit enough to answer my call, I will there bring him to justice' (90).[20]

This privatization of justice accords with the attitude towards dueling expressed by the aristocracy throughout the eighteenth century. Dueling devolved from the ancient trial by battle, a system of legal adjudication first introduced by the Gothic tribes (Rush, 1964, 1), and became an accepted part of the theory of divine and human justice as early as the sixth century (Baldick, 1965, 12–13). Accuser and accused were supposed to fight each other in person, but women, invalids, men over sixty, and eventually priests were exempted. In consequence, both abroad and in England, the Crown took to using 'approvers' or inform-ers to fight on the Crown's behalf. Gradually, a class of proxy fighters came into existence, known as 'champions.' These proxies were merce-nary, willing to fight on either side for hire. Their materialistic disregard of true equity makes of Reeve's original title, *The Champion of Virtue*, an oxymoron.[21] From the trial by battle came the duels of chivalry, used to settle scores of law, possession, or honor (Baldick, 1965, 22). In keeping with the aristocratic code of chivalry, participation in such duels was more tightly restricted than the judicial duels had been. Lists of persons not qualified to take part included 'whosoever doth not live suitably upon his lawful rents and income, but debaseth his dignity by buying and selling' (24). Such miscreants were to be beaten instead.

The modern duel as we know it today from novels and the pictorial arts thrust itself onto the English stage much later than it did on the Continent. Up until the late sixteenth century, private quarrels in England were settled by means of 'killing affrays' or attacks by hired gangs of assassins. V. G. Kiernan correlates the appearance of codified rules for violence with periods of class upheaval:

By the ritual of the duel, private resentments were lifted above the merely personal level of revenge; the combatant's honour merged into that of the class to which both he and his antagonist were making obeisance. It was this corporate honour that all its members were bound to uphold ... acceptance of the standards of conduct epitomized in the code of honour could help to incorporate middle-class candidates, native or immigrant, in an old aristocracy, or in later times to promote a partnership. It could form one part of what has been called the 'invention of tradition,' the adjustments by which ... the newcomer to 'good society' is induced to identify himself with its ways of thinking and behaving.

(1988, 15–16)

Kiernan calls the practice of dueling an 'assertion of superior right, a claim to immunity from the law such as a ruling class is always likely to seek' (53). Just as the ideological codes of knight-errantry had provided a buffer that screened the real jockeying for honors among the nobility as feudal allegiances withered, in the sense of emoluments from the monarch, so private dueling set a stamp of uniqueness to the aristocracy threatened with submergence in the eighteenth century.

The battle between Harclay and Walter Lovel partakes of all three types of dueling enumerated above. As in the judicial duel, the vanquished Lovel is considered a prisoner, to be detained for further punishment (102). The fight itself is attended with all the pomp of a chivalric duel. It is overseen by Lord Graham, who is accompanied by 'twelve followers gentlemen, and twelve servants' (98). Harclay's retinue includes an esquire, a page, two servants in livery, Edmund and his servant, and Zadisky with his. Lord Clifford, the judge of the field, brings one esquire, two pages, two livery servants, his eldest son, a nephew and that nephew's gentleman friend, as well as a 'surgeon of note' to attend the wounded, a distinctly eighteenth-century touch. The rest of the ceremony preceding the actual combat conforms to feudal details; nevertheless, we can discern more modern customs in the fact that the fight takes place in an open field. Even more notable is the location of that field, in the Scottish marches, and the time of the fight, dawn. Such secrecy was a constant of contemporary duels, since royal and religious disapproval meant that combatants, as well as their seconds, were subject to prosecution for participation, even if the duel only went so far as the issuing of challenges. Despite its ostensible setting in the late Middle Ages, the participants in this fictional duel register appropriate eighteenth-century anxiety over their criminal liability: when Lovel is wounded, Lords Clifford and Graham, the judges of the field, advise Harclay to have his prisoner conveyed to Graham's house 'on this side of the borders till they saw what turn his health would take' (102).[22]

Retrieving the character of the nation

Just as the marches of Scotland offer a border where public and private needs can be mediated, so her Gothic form mediates the ongoing separation of literature from history, by implying historicity through the romance topos of the discovered manuscript. Likewise, her plot calibrates the disjunction of self from society. As Bourdieu has argued, social powers occupy social space, taking up symbolic volume measured by the amount and type of 'capital', economic and cultural, they possess (1990, 128). Bourdieu's theory finds retrospective confirmation in the seventeenth-century architectural theory of 'convenience,' advocated by exemplars like Christopher Wren. 'Convenience' denoted the complementarity of form with function, the harmony of external and internal, to signify the agreement between the appearance of the building and the moral quality of its owner.[23] Reeve recognizes the wishfulness of this correlation. Lord Fitz-Owen professes to have been hoodwinked by Markham and Wenlock, and declares that 'It is no wonder that princes should be so frequently deceived, when I, a private man, could be so much imposed upon within the circle of my own family' (96). Yet Reeve elides the issue by refusing to give physical descriptions of those co-conspirators. Instead, each mention of them is interjacent to sibilants: they are the 'sisters sons,' who 'secretly' envy Edmund and 'strive' to undermine him by their 'malicious insinuations' (23). The evocation of serpent-like treachery is completed when Wenlock is sent into exile (96–7); the Edenic conditions of Castle Lovel thus become ripe for restoration. In a further effacement of the problematical nature of the fit between exterior and interior, characters' emotions, even those of the villains, are continually described as legible,[24] with tears serving as the watermarks to seal the features' involuntary confessions.

In fact, the notion of 'character' itself fragments into three component meanings; each type of 'character' is depicted as increasingly durable. The first import of 'character,' already touched on, resides in the sense of reputation, which coexists with or influences status or position. While this type of 'character' derives from fundamentals of action and personality, it is also vulnerable, that is, because it circulates in the world, it is subject to augmentation or attrition. Edmund articulates the real threat his enemies pose to him: ' if ... I should be put out of the house with disgrace, what will become of me? I have nothing but my character to depend on; if I lose that, I lose everything; ... ' (35). Yet that same circulation of reputation, if broad or long-lived enough, can overcome merely local detractors because one's 'good name' acquires additional patina as it travels either in time or space (67). Edmund attempts to forestall the criticisms of the envious kinsmen by putting both time and space between himself and his accusers when he flees the castle and seeks sanctuary with Sir Philip. He is successful: Harclay welcomes him openly because he has 'heard a great character' of Edmund from those acquainted with him in France (85).

That this 'good name' or 'good word' has economic value is suggested by the actions of the villain, Walter Lovel. In the novel, Walter forfeits his reputation, not because he has caused the murder of his cousin, but because he attempts to escape after having given his captors his word that he will comply with their demands. They refuse to rely further on his word, or to place 'faith in your fulfilling the conditions of our agreement.' Their disappointment in his behavior indicates the way a verbal assurance takes on, or is held to take, the overtones of a contractual arrangement. Harclay echoes this economic valuation when he insists to the villain that the new arrangements they propose will leave him 'indebted' to their clemency (135).

Character is also equated with identity. This second significance is essentialist and personal; like character in the sense of reputation, it is empirically observable. When young John Wyatt urges himself as a replacement for Harclay's deceased servant, his 'earnest looks' and impatient blush speak as loudly in his favor as his proud enumeration of an 'honest heart,' 'willing mind,' and 'light pair of heels' (21–2). Harclay responds that he has observed the boy's 'qualifications,' much as he had earlier been impressed with Edmund's merit on the basis of his appearance.

Reeve's advocacy of belief in the connaturality of moral and physical identity is a compensatory fiction. It allays the fear generated by dependence upon intangible qualities like virtue and truth, as these impinge on the moral and physical realms. The old servant, Joseph, recognizes Edmund's true worth because he so resembles the late Lord Lovel. Furthermore, Edmund's 'gentle manners, his generous heart, his noble qualities so uncommon in those of his birth and breeding, the sound of his voice' (52), all signify the internalization of patrician qualities in a pre-Lamarkian scheme of behavioral genetics.

While fears that the moral and the physical might divaricate had a venerable genealogy, contemporary economic realities would have caused anxiety about identity to escalate. The growth of credit and trade, and the widespread dissemination of such investment techniques throughout all classes of eighteenth-century England, created new common bonds as one's economic well-being became inextricably involved with the prosperity of one's debtors and creditors (Brewer, 1988, 186–8). We can see the intervolution of the fictional and the real at the outset of the story. Upon returning to England, Harclay discovers that his estates have been sequestered in the control of commissioners under the assumption that he has died, leaving no heirs. 'He was obliged to prove the reality of his claim, and the identity of his person' (8).[25] This is easily accomplished because of generational continuity: old servants of his family recognize the younger man they had known beneath the ravages of time, and their testimony ensures that his possessions are restored.

In its third sense, 'character' refers to writing, both as penmanship and as the impress of literature. In both cases, this form of character can be either invisible or legible. As applied to her heroines, this shape of character takes on a proto-feminist cast. Lady Lovel and Emma demonstrate a readerly ability beyond the same talents of the men, because they can read the motives and behaviors of others while disguising their own interiority from the intrusive gaze of outsiders. Just as the architectural space of the castle permitted the incorporation of the private into the domain of the public while protecting its autonomy, so graphical manifestations can be used as public markers or as private disguises to facilitate anonymity.[26] To forward their design, Father Oswald and Edmund conspire to leave unsigned letters, delivered mysteriously. These letters serve a dual purpose: Baron Fitz-Owen is contacted so that his clan will be frightened away from the haunted apartment; William receives a letter to relieve his apprehensions at Edmund's disappearance (64). Oswald writes and delivers these letters; strangely enough, no one with whom he lives in the household recognizes his 'character,' though as the resident priest, he may be assumed to have been fulfilling clerkly duties.[27]

Edmund's history collapses or compounds the definitions of characters as identity and literature. His foster mother explains that, from childhood, he was 'sickly and tender, and could not bear hard labour.' An old pilgrim, who single-handedly comprises the professions of scholar, soldier, and religious, providentially wanders into the district and teaches Edmund to read. He tells the boy histories of 'wars, and Knights, and Lords, and great men; and Edmund took such delight in hearing him, that he would not take to anything else' (61). The implication of this episode is that Edmund had already engraven on him the predilection for narrative, as though it waited, unseen, to be fleshed out by the encounter with the storyteller who is so closely related in avocation, and whose emotional and intellectual proximity is signaled by the similarity of his name, Edwin. Fulfilling both his destiny and his education, Edmund neglects the work assigned to him as part of the Twyford family responsibilities to read and do errands for the neighbors. A vessel for the preservation and dissemination of literary values, Edmund is readied for translation to his paternity, where he will also propagate material culture and cultivate social relations.

Still, as the novel repeatedly thematizes, he cannot nor should he suffice alone. Thus, Reeve provides copious marital alliances. The marriages contracted at the end draw together families from the marches of Scotland with inhabitants of Yorkshire, Cumberland, the west of England, and Wales. Edmund stands at the center of this circle, since his adoption by Harclay makes him a son of Yorkshire, at the same time that his accession to the title of Lovel unites Yorkshire and the west of England. When he marries Fitz-Owen's daughter, Edmund 'ingrafts' onto the Fitz-Owen family his newly earned names, titles, and estates (125); the birth of their third son brings the Fitz-Owen family property in Wales into the Lovel fold. Fitz-Owen's eldest son, Robert, espouses the eldest daughter of Lord Clifford of Cumberland, and they repair to Sir Walter's estate in Yorkshire; Lord Graham of Scotland marries his eldest nephew and heir to Clifford's second daughter. As the narrator says: 'The company separated with regret, and with many promises of friendship on all sides; and the Gentlemen of the North were to cultivate the good neighborhood on both sides of the borders' (140). These newly allied groups compose a federation, which replaces the lost affiliations to kinsmen expelled from the family circle for irreconcilable goals and desires.

The ending of the novel not only provides closure, but it also brings us full circle to where I began. The colonists' revolt, in full swing by the writing of *Baron*, threatened both the political and the economic stability of the nation. Merely replacing the lost home markets with other, unaffiliated clients would not restore that stability. As John Brewer notes: 'Great states required both the economic wherewithal and the organizational means to deploy resources in the cause of national aggrandizement' (1988, xv). Trading partners, unconnected by any more profound ties, could not be relied upon to furnish those organizational means. The history of Holland, a country simultaneously weak and prosperous, had already furnished a lesson that technological change and commercial expansion alone could not suffice to make a nation a world power. The characters' marriages discover that interests cross local borders, at the same time that they testify to the forging of an identity that is specifically British. In her hands, the Gothic quest for traditions that will promote social welfare seeks not only religious icons but also the Holy Grail of wealth and power.

4
Radcliffe, Revolution, and the Romance of Heroism, 1789–94

> The age of chivalry is gone. – That of sophisters, œconomists, and calculators, has succeeded; and the glory of Europe is extinguished forever.
>
> (Burke, 1989, 89)

A chasm, almost as vast as those fissuring Ann Radcliffe's fictional terrains, opens between her heroic characters and those of Clara Reeve. These differences will help us see how accusations that Radcliffe painted black-and-white portraits of good and evil overstate the case. Admittedly, her settings frequently give good reason for such an accusation, especially when the scene starkly ('cruelly' as Radcliffe would have it) contrasts with the feelings of the characters. Then we find the 'chequer-work of human life.'[1] Yet Radcliffe's character studies, particularly as character traits bear on definitions of heroism, display far more chiaroscuro than they do high relief. In all his trials, Edmund remains a paragon. Long before they are tried, Radcliffe's heroes seem fallible, if chivalric.

Their frailties encompass contemporary debates about the desirable attributes of masculinity. These contested traits include the proper degree of devotion to ideals of politeness and sentimentality; the permissible degree and type of violence and/or aggression employed in the maintenance of honor; the recourse to forms of civility, such as legal settlements or verbal disputation, to counter the tendency to excessive violence; and the relative merits of active as opposed to passive virtue, a heading under which these subgroups of gentlemanly behavior coalesce.[2]

The composition of their private characters also responds to charges leveled at public, aristocratic leadership. No longer confined to the radical political press, as they had been during the decades preceding the 1780s, such complaints about patrician authority and leadership had begun to shrill in the mainstream venues. The aristocracy was charged with interfering in the electoral process, with graft, with the prosecuting of expensive and protracted wars to enrich themselves, and with thereby inflating taxes. According to Linda Colley, '[S]uch analyses were damaging not because they were correct in detail (they were not), but because they treated the landed interest as a separate class parasitic on the nation, rather than as part of the nation and as its natural leaders' (1992, 153). Indeed, Burke's rhetoric in the epigraph, ostensibly the opening shot in the battle the French Revolution provoked between those attempting to conserve an older vision of English society and the English *philosophes*, actually reflects most of these more longstanding social and political issues.[3]

On the defensive, the English aristocracy countered by making themselves British citizens. Through land purchase and marriage, they increasingly acquired estates that gave them footings in England, Scotland, and Wales. Eschewing continental affiliations, they bought British art and traveled to remote internal destinations, lending an exotic interest hitherto reserved for foreign spots to the British Isles. To appear more public-spirited, they opened their private art collections for viewing and founded galleries in London for commercial visitors (thus putting a benevolent patina on private gain); they also sent their sons in large numbers to public university, reversing a centuries-long trend of private education at home. Finally, they elevated a small quota of landless men of talent to their ranks and accommodated commercial and industrial interests.[4]

These gestures involved concrete acts. But perhaps the most successful salvage job was also the most superficial. Employing window-dressing, the aristocracy costumed itself as military heroes. This new fashion departed from the 'great masculine renunciation' and consequent 'inconspicuous consumption' David Kuchta (1996) has traced to the revolution of 1688, whereby aristocratic leadership dressed its claims to virtue in a 'manly' simplicity of sober cloth and color. As Kuchta relates, the late eighteenth century saw this virtuous dress appropriated by the middle classes in their bid for leadership. The newly fashionable cult of heroism thus became a doubly valuable public relations ploy, because it allowed the aristocracy a new way to distinguish itself from the middle classes and because that distinction cast an aura of diligence and self-sacrificing devotion over the aristocracy.

With the outbreak of war, pressure on the notion of the heroic leader surged from within and without, a cliché harnessed by newspaper commentators of the day to address domestic and foreign policy. Bombarding an already fraught social climate, the first shock wave of news from France deepened suspicion as to the 'naturalness' of leadership. As alarm about violent reaction grew, so, too, did the need to reshape social vision and redefine heroism.

Accordingly, one task in this chapter will be to document Radcliffe's attitude to that revolution. I concentrate on her first four novels, penned between 1789 and 1794, before the Terror ratcheted the stakes and before Radcliffe had a chance to travel in Europe and see the human ravages for herself. Radcliffe's first novels speak directly to domestic discomforts; by portraying her heroes as imperfect, they accommodate changing estimates about the nature of British leaders. Her optimism about the ease whereby social relations could be transformed appears in her cross-dressing her chivalric knights as 'œconomists and calculators.' This optimism arose from her early faith in what would become the single most overriding strain on public opinion, the French Revolution. Establishing her initial reaction as corresponding with the rhetoric of the day will also enable us to chart her changing response, as evinced in her novelistic representations.

The Revolution in the press

Radcliffe's position with respect to the Revolution has caused almost as deep a division in her critics as it did among those experiencing it first-hand. One camp argues for her conservatism, while others equally forcefully contend that her longings inclined her to radical subversion. Neither group has examined the record left by her husband in his capacity as editor of *The English Chronicle*, a tri-weekly newspaper. Yet her prefatory remarks to her 1795 *Journey through Holland and the Western Frontiers of Germany* encourage us to view William Radcliffe as his wife's tutor in matters political:

> The Author begs leave to observe, ... that, her journey having been performed in the company of her nearest relative and friend, the account of it has been written so much from their mutual observation, ... where the oeconomical and political conditions of countries are touched upon in the following work, the remarks are less her own than elsewhere.

When we examine his writings for the period of her first two novels, 1789–90, we find an attitude wavering between support and skepticism.[5] But whatever the attitude articulated, William's comments, whether made *in propria persona* or permitted to appear by editorial fiat, establish the relevance of revolutionary rhetoric to plot and character choices made by his wife.

The initial volley, appearing prophetically on 13 July 1789, establishes a pattern that will be repeated in succeeding issues. First, the Revolution is seen as justified, particularly by aristocratic abuses. More important, conditions in France are constantly compared with those in England, whose constitution and judicial constraints have always formed the centerpieces of English nationalistic self-congratulation. But the *Chronicle* writers seldom find comparisons that work to England's benefit. Holding that the National Assembly should tether their abstract leanings to concrete necessities, the *Chronicle* praises the Assembly when it resolves to create equitable political representation in November. Their actions make the rotten boroughs of the English constitution fester more noticeably in the public's eyes (28 November – 1 December 1789). William's editorial of 4–6 March 1790 joins these two themes: 'the French are employed in revising, renovating, and improving a constitution long since ruined; we are suffering ours quietly to go to decay.' French equality even extends to religious persuasion: 'The French have given unlimited toleration, and an universal partition of privileges even to the Jews; our Parliament denies the same even to Protestant Dissenters. In the various questions that come before the Legislature, we find interest substituted for principle, and that possession is law.'[6]

Criticism levels not only at English institutions, but also at English leaders. On 14 July, the correspondent from Paris castigates Pitt's withholding of food supplies from the French, exonerating at the same time 'even the prejudiced populace' from such 'indifference and inhumanity'(3). Pitt's parsimony has broken the bonds of affection that subsisted between the French and the English. By characterizing those bonds as fraternal, the correspondent invokes the rhetoric of the Revolutionary leaders, at the same time that he casts Pitt into the role of the elder brother, inheritor through primogeniture of benefits that should be shared with his neighbors/siblings. Not even the uneducated English population can be guilty of such a breach of fraternal affection.

Pitt's taxation policies feed additional resentment. In the issue of 22–24 October 1789, two specific complaints reveal the nexus of foreign affairs, aristocratic self-representations, domestic policy, and commercial interests. First, Pitt levies taxes only against the middle class, because he thereby gains the concurrence of both Parliamentary houses. Second, he debases aristocracy by selling titles to the highest bidder. 'What will the Historian, in treating of these times say, of Mr. PITT's promotions? What title can he select that was conferred on real merit and positive service? Such dishonourable honours may gratify the tools on whom they are bestowed; but posterity, as well as the present time, will consider them only as brands of disgrace.' Although the article does not elaborate the connection, we can see how taxation and titles might fit together in the editor's eyes. Taxing the middle class exclusively makes them fully responsible for England's welfare, a responsibility that receives no credit, since to be accredited, it is still necessary to purchase a bogus title.[7] Conversely, purchasing titles offers a way out of the tax burden, an escape which portrays the middle class as eager to escape their responsibilities. Both aristocrats and the middle class are tarred by the practice.

Ann's attitudes may deviate somewhat from her husband's opinions, especially from his class fears, but they show an equal aptitude for nuanced socio-political reasoning. Over the span of her first four novels, several paradoxes arise. Ann's initial support of the Revolution leads her at first to portray her heroes as drawn primarily from the nobility. They reflect revolutionary ideals insofar as they are young aristocrats. As foreign and domestic events nudge her sympathies, so, too, do her class loyalties shift. She distributes heroic characteristics across the class spectrum far more even-handedly, thereby extending the romance of heroism. To some extent, Radcliffe's heroes repeat the conventional attributes: they possess manly grace, accomplished minds, elegant manners, and a countenance expressive of 'a happy union of spirit, dignity, and benevolence' (*Sicilian Romance*, 1993, 11). At the same time, Radcliffe pays increasing attention to the role and plight of women, portraying them less as victims than as equally vulnerable heroes in their own right.[8]

Conversely, virtues and qualities normally prized as heroic – such as passion, prudence, forthrightness, silence, pride, independence – reveal their contrary face. Because they participate in the identical failings and exhibit an identically imperfect grasp of the same talents as her heroes, Radcliffe's heroines show her struggling to redefine not only notions of masculinity but also cross-gendered ideas of heroism *in toto*. To take the temperature of Radcliffe's response to domestic and foreign conflict, I will concentrate less on the conventional positive face of her heroes' virtues than on that mirror image. Ultimately, heroism fissures: individual heroes furnish only moral guidance; political and social justice becomes the province of institutional forces whose very invisibility and mystery makes them analogous to the supernatural beings her novels are said to explain.

Undivided loyalties: the brotherly nation of *Athlin and Dunbayne*

Ann Radcliffe's first novel, *The Castles of Athlin and Dunbayne,* repeats the strategies employed by aristocrats under attack, as outlined above. Unlike any of Radcliffe's other novels published during her lifetime, its exotic locale is twelfth-century Scotland. Further, this is a martial society. The novel opens with a history of clan wars, before depositing us at a yearly festival held at Athlin which all attend dressed in arms, a custom commemorating a surprise attack by a hostile clan during one of the annual celebrations of this festival (1995, 9). Entwining aristocrats, martial prowess, and ancient Britons, *The Castles of Athlin and Dunbayne* fashions things British as objects of aesthetic value.[9]

At the same time, aesthetic value has political relevance. While her Scotland maintains its clan structure, the plot pits the deleterious aspects of clan organization, personified in the villain, the Baron Malcolm of Dunbayne, against a benevolent feudal paternalism as represented by the hero, Osbert, young Earl of Athlin.[10] Good and evil take a palpable shape, tied to the land. Evil resides in Dunbayne and its master because he represents the failed policies of feudal tenure; Malcolm's greed makes tillage of the land unprofitable for his tenants, and consequently much land that could otherwise be productive lies fallow. In the struggle between Malcolm and Osbert, we witness the distinction being drawn between aristocratic heroes who are 'parasitic on the nation' versus those who are 'a part of the nation, and its natural leaders.'

A gentle harping on fraternity plays throughout the *Castles*. Unlike the two earlier precursors to her novel, Radcliffe's first work underscores the importance of sibling relations. Osbert is a gentle and generous brother, who refuses to play the role of patriarchal authority when it comes to his sister's love, at least when it is the Count de Santmorin who sues for her hand (1995, 82).[11] Fraternal relations aid in the idealization of a paternalistic feudalism. Discontented soldiers of Malcolm's clan decamp and join with the forces seeking to free the Earl. The deserters report that the Baron's people, which designation must signify his serfs as well as his soldiers, chafe under his tyranny and await an opportunity to 'resume the rights of nature' (56), Rousseauian language enlisted more on the side of enlightened feudalism than pure republicanism. When the Baron finally launches a surprise attack on Athlin and is repulsed, his people desert in droves (86). Here we see one version of the possible 'fatal consequences' warned about in William's editorials that can ensue when brotherly or neighborly obligations are neglected.

We see Osbert's qualities of leadership being construed as natural from the very first pages, the product equally of nature and nurture (4), which meet in his military prowess: 'He excelled in all the various accomplishments of his rank, but chiefly in the martial exercises, for they were congenial to the nobility of his soul' (5). Congenial as those talents may seem to him, the movement from 'martial exercises' undertaken in dilettante fascination to a soldier's campaign conducted against a real enemy meets with resistance, chiefly from his mother. The clan of the late Lord had adored him and desired vengeance for his murder, but had been 'oppressed by the generous compassion of the Countess' (5), so that they gradually stifled their murmurings but not their desire for revenge. Matilda likewise forbids her son to lead the cause for armed justice; he, too, submits in silence and attempts to stifle his emotions (5). Ultimately, though, to assume his 'natural' leadership, Osbert must conduct military forays.[12]

From a military standpoint, Osbert's defense of his castle against Malcolm's surprise attack seems masterfully planned. We are as much surprised by his preparedness as is Malcolm, for we have only been told that he fears Malcolm has killed his messenger, not that Osbert has set his clan in an elaborate counter-trap. When Malcolm's party sweeps down the hills and think they have gained Athlin in complete slumber, they find archers and men raining down weapons of defense from the battlements. Osbert himself has donned armor, along with the Count; soldiers throng the courtyards and vestibules of the castle; and the clan lurks in the surrounding countryside to swoop around the attackers and enclose them in a perfect net of men. But because this is a feudal society, no cost to the public ensues. Because this is an idealized representation of a feudal society, not even human lives pay the price for prosecuting war.

Still, victory does not come easily. If Osbert initially fails in his attempts to avenge the wrongs done his family, the novel does not function so much as a war manual as it does a conduct book outlining the psychological toll exacted both by social inequities and by the decision to cure those inequities through war. The longstanding hostilities, the old Earl's murder, the present conflicts of the novel's setting: all produce internal dissension (35). Very few of the characters remain free from such a battle within. In some cases, the struggle strains the bond between past and present; for others, the tension pressures relations between genders or generations.

For instance, Osbert's mother, Matilda, suffers contending emotions that paralyze her upon hearing that the Baron wants her daughter in marriage as the condition for her son's release (43). The Baron's demand divides Matilda's loyalties between two men, her husband and her son, thus between two generations. Not even her earlier reckoning that Osbert's enterprise affords honor to her husband's memory and brings retribution upon the head of his murderer can serve to ease Matilda here (12). Malcolm's demand also divides her gender loyalties, since she knows that marriage to the Baron condemns Mary to a life of torment. The conflict maddens her to frenzy.

Mary experiences similar imaginative and affective terror. In the description of the disseveration she feels, we can see that the point of such plot devices is to conjure up a notion of the past impinging upon the present and future. Since Malcolm is her father's murderer, she has a history of hatred towards him, and can envision a future of misery. Yet, at the same time, the past memories of her brother and the kinship bonds she shares with him prohibit making him the sacrifice to her virtue (44–5).

We might think that only women can be put in this untenable position, since the conflict centers around marriage. Almost all Radcliffe's heroines find themselves straddling such a dilemma: Julia in *A Sicilian Romance*, Emily in *The Mysteries of Udolpho*, Ellena in *The Italian* all arrive at crises of decision that pit their virtue and affective loyalties against the lives or welfare of others. But the hero of *Castles* finds himself likewise challenged. The opposition to war of his mother tears Osbert into two (11). He has so internalized his mother's ideas and values that, when he contemplates vengeance, she appears to him as a weeping image (7). Silent and languid in their grief, the beseeching postures of his mother and sister almost break Osbert's resolve, except that 'the figure of his dying father arose to his imagination, and stamped his purpose irrevocably' (11).[13] Moderating a too hasty engagement with violence on the part of its heroes, the novel grudgingly portrays the need for martial prowess.

Having placed her heroines and hero in such a difficult dilemma, we must surmise that the novel will work to imagine a society in which the claims of potentially opposed groups, cleft by gender, age, or status differences, will be able to live in harmony. Tracing the causes of such torn loyalties, the novel also draws a picture of the way to heal such breaches. And it suggests that only a people unified within themselves can present a sufficiently united front to prevail.

While the novel speaks to the social tensions between groups in England, the year of its composition, 1789, furnished an emergent need for such a fiction. Inhabitants of Britain in that year were also experiencing divided loyalties produced by the French Revolution. The novel reflects this political crisis by creating two heroes, one the young earl of Athlin and the other a loyal 'peasant,' bound to the Earl's clan by ideals.[14] Like *The Old English Baron*'s Edmund, Alleyn will also discover in the course of events his noble paternity. Before that discovery, Alleyn's love for Osbert's sister, Mary, places Osbert in a predicament. Seeming both 'worthy' and 'unworthy' at the same time, the character of Alleyn dramatizes the contest between belief in a meritocracy and belief in the inherent nobility of character bestowed by birth.

Since he functions as brother-in-arms to Osbert long before he seeks to become a brother-in-law, Alleyn should garner an equal consideration. Certainly, his personal qualifications establish his rights. Like Osbert, Alleyn exhibits an 'air of benevolence' at first sight. Throughout the novel, we witness him saving the lost or distressed.

In some regards, Alleyn even exceeds Osbert. Like the other Gothic heroes we have met, Osbert is capable of empirical observation. But impatience and the resort to brute force disable him from productively employing his observations (51). Alleyn seems to have a superior grasp of empirical details of the landscape (6), although this may only be an illusion produced by the fact that he is on home territory at this point. But even if the heroes' abilities are evenly matched, Alleyn manages to marry empirical observation to rational calculation about the significance of those observations. He sees and hears his guard striking the pavement with his staff each time he's about to leave the cell; Alleyn deduces that some escape route must lie underneath (21). Thus, unlike Osbert, Alleyn effects an escape.

Alleyn succeeds because he weds intellectual strength to physical endurance. Discovered in his attempt, he wrests the sword from the guard and threatens him, but grants him his life and follows him back to the cell. He acquiesces this way partly because he is too virtuous to take the life of another man, and partly because he pragmatically knows that if the guard is missing, his companions will search him out and Alleyn will be in greater difficulty, numerically (24).

Alleyn's thought processes do not merely revolve around his own physical safety. He is a thinker about political and social justice; he knows agricultural economy (the observations about the Baron's misguided agricultural policies, mentioned above, come from him).Yet he maintains all the sensitivity and ardor of the sentimental hero, feelings loosed especially in demonstrations of fealty to the family of Athlin. Combining a sound heart with a sound head, the character of Alleyn fictively represents a world where the superintendence of facts and of virtue has not yet separated.[15] Peasant, benefactor, social analyst, warrior: in Alleyn's character, the myth of social mobility coalesces, since a number of the novel's characters join the narrator in insisting on Alleyn's fitness to wed a noble bride, long before his noble antecedents are revealed in the penultimate pages.

Because his adventures occur within a martial society, they resemble the conditions of men in England's army at the time. I began this chapter with the attempt of England's aristocracy to portray themselves as military leaders. This guise had two advantages: not only did they seem disinterestedly devoted to their country, but they also portrayed themselves as participating in a meritocracy. The contrast between this myth and the actuality is recorded by Colley, who cites the high percentages of men from old landed families holding parliamentary, military, or naval leadership roles (1992, 191). Osbert's ambivalence about Alleyn makes him seem similarly manipulative of social reality. He simultaneously encourages and blocks true mobility. Of all Osbert's weaknesses as a leader, weaknesses that events will teach him to rectify, his greatest failing is his inability to measure worth by any other yardstick than that of birth.

Learning of Alleyn's love for his sister, after all Alleyn's benefits to him, Osbert reacts 'with a mixture of concern and pity; but hereditary pride chilled the warm feelings of friendship and of gratitude, and extinguished the faint spark of hope which the discovery had kindled in the bosom of Alleyn' (80). The more Alleyn proves his worth, the greater become Osbert's struggles with 'hereditary pride.' This is the language of cliché, but the convention has gained political momentum from its contemporary application to Pitt's behavior vis-à-vis the French. When Mary refuses the Count's offer, explaining that her heart belongs to Alleyn but that he shall never know it, Osbert congratulates her on remembering the respect due her rank and position. Sympathetically, he bemoans that 'worth like Alleyn's is not impowered by fortune to take its standard with nobility' (84). Osbert's doublespeak instances Herzfeld's disemia. On the one hand, Osbert utters a meritocratic wish. On the other hand, he blames the impossibility of such a wish on 'fortune,' a medieval attitude in keeping with his acquiescence in a fixed system and belying a social fatalism at odds with the

liberal spirit of the meritocratic wish. Osbert's entrapment in competing systems of belief leads to his emotional paralysis and suffering from
this refusal of closer affiliation; his victimization, even if self-inflicted,
shields him from too strong a readerly distaste and enables readerly
sympathy. But each time the conflict between merit and birth arises,
the narrator condemns Osbert's reaction in ever stronger and more
explicit language.

Osbert's innate sense of fairness battles a 'pride of birth' instilled in
him by 'the authority of early prejudice' (88, 108–9). 'Early prejudice'
speaks in a public voice; the 'characters of truth' are graven on his
heart at birth, but the silent monitor cannot make itself heard in the
competition. To a large extent, the public voice overwhelms Osbert's
instinct because it emanates from his mother: '[T]he proud nobility of
her soul repelled with quick vivacity every idea of union with a youth
of such ignoble birth' (38). Deluding herself both as to the right course
of action and the grounds justifying such a course, Matilda rationalizes
her behavior in language drawn from the social debates of the period:
'she regarded the present attachment as the passing impression of
youthful fancy, and believed that gentle reasoning, aided by time and
endeavour, would conquer the enthusiasm of love' (ibid.). Reason
opposes an enthusiasm pejoratively identified. Matilda's assignment of
value reflects linguistic history, at the same time that Radcliffe's use of
the term 'enthusiasm' – e.g. the polemical coloring of Alleyn's 'noble
and disinterested' conduct as 'enthusiasm in the cause of justice' –
reverses those values. Toleration and civil incorporation, like that
advocated for Dissenters and granted by the French, should be
extended to Alleyn.

'Interest' refers to a personal ambition privileged over the national
good.[16] This misdirected focus motivates Osbert and Matilda's injustices. To drive home this point, the narrative gives us opposed pairs
whose behavior contrasts selfishness with selflessness. One such is a
pair of brothers, soldiers belonging to Malcolm. We know we should
attend to them because, unlike most of the plebeian participants in the
novel, they are given names.[17] James, the brave and 'noble' half, freely
casts his lot with Alleyn after Alleyn has escaped and while he meditates how to free Osbert. James informs Alleyn that his brother,
Edmund, guards Osbert, and can instruct them (56). Edmund is less
admirable than James; he fears aiding in the escape until he is tempted
with a reward; then, self-interest overcomes his scruples (57).[18] In this
example, self-interest serves as a lever to pry loose virtuous action.
More frequently, it forms a temptation to divert virtue. Servants of the

family act as individualistic social climbers by accepting a bribe from Mary's abductors to resign her into their clutches easily (102–3). However, their innate sensitivity to injustice and cruelty overwhelms their initial greed: when the ruffians threaten to gag Mary, the servants fight for her. As the narrator explains, these servants 'were not yet so entirely lost to the feelings of humanity' (103).

Radcliffe's sanguine faith in the inherent morality of the serving classes stands in sharp relief against her husband's more typical fears. Interestingly, the only time a group of peasants in the novel conduct themselves as a mob is when they desert Malcolm's ranks, which action is applauded. Ann's fiction transcends her husband's (and the populace's longstanding) fears. By so doing, she gains not only the smooth course of chivalric romance, but also imaginatively overleaps obstacles to a national community. Poverty or inferior status alone will not make men abjure virtue completely.

Nor can noble birth necessarily inoculate the upper classes against selfishness. At least one of Radcliffe's aristocrats, the Count de Santmorin, acts mercenarily. Rescued by Osbert as a stranger from a storm-beset ship, the Count has a 'dignified aspect and manners' that indicate him to be a man of rank (76). As they become better acquainted with him through conversation, Osbert's family find their initial bias rewarded. He displays in his conversation a 'manly and vigorous mind, acquainted with the sciences, and with life; and the cast of his observations seemed to characterize the benevolence of his heart' (77). However, Radcliffe here plays off a conventional truism to undermine it. Revealing the Count de Santmorin as less than honorable frustrates a naive reliance upon appearance; it gives a salutary shake to the full faith that nobility marks its bearer such that no scrutiny of actions is necessary.[19]

The Count fails in two domains. The first concerns the proper attitude towards kinship as evidenced through inheritance. The Count relates that he has come to Scotland 'upon a report of a death of some relations, at whose demise considerable estates in Switzerland became his inheritance. That the income of these estates had been hitherto received upon the authority of powers, which, if the report was true, were become invalid' (81). At first glance, the Count's actions could be interpreted as fidelity to family, as the correct desire to maintain paternal estates intact. But the Count violates that implicit trust when he demonstrates that monetary concerns, via inheritance, take precedence over kinship relations. Having been reunited with the Baroness and Laura, he abandons them and the Mary he supposedly loves so much to go off with the aim of recovering yet another bequeathed estate (100).

This last inheritance is spurious, an excuse trumped up by the Count to absent himself so that he can abduct Mary. If his second, and far more calculated, delinquency results from unrestrained passion, it nevertheless connects to his behavior around money. Both actions indicate a headstrong individualism. The very fact that the Count urges greed as an acceptable excuse shows that he fails to understand his loyalties properly. Finally, he suborns the loyalty of the Earl's servants to effect Mary's undoing.

The Count's actions differ little from those of Malcolm. Both treat women as objects of desire and pawns. Both abuse their trust as heads of families and as masters of men. Neither cares for territorial aggrandizement unless it enriches him personally. Yet, while Osbert fights for political and territorial regeneration, he is swept into the orbit of these two men by his blindness about rank. His most generous act highlights his selfishness in that regard: Osbert forgives the Count when he learns of the plot the Count has set on foot (106). In Osbert's scheme of justice, crimes of passion committed by one of your own kind are excusable; omissions of birth are not.

Unlike the Count, the character of Alleyn conflates merit *and* birth. His aims represent the perfect, if delicate, balance: national ambition appears in his desire to avenge the Earl's death and Osbert's imprisonment, to right injustices; his personal ambition centers on the desire to perform deeds worthy of Mary's love, to remove the insult to her of her attempted abduction (32). Unlike Osbert, these two goals cause him no psychic pain. Instead of being divided, Alleyn manages dual loyalties. When his birth has finally been discovered and he is called by his birth name, Philip Malcolm, the narrator tells us he was 'yet Alleyn in everything but in name' (112). The narratorial distinction between conduct or character and identity, the attribute of birth and lineage, forms one key means by which Radcliffe advocates a meritocracy.

The merging of class characteristics runs in both directions. It can be discerned in the description of Louisa's father, who is a Marquis from Switzerland, a place associated in the public mind of the time with republicanism and Rousseauism (60). At the other end, Alleyn's 'father,' the peasant who has raised him, exhibits a moral nobility. Offered a lot of land by Osbert as a reward for Alleyn's services, Old Alleyn declines the gift. He declares that his needs have been sufficiently met and that he feels attached to his old cottage (75). Old Alleyn thus exhibits a loyalty to place similar to that of Louisa's father, who is noble.[20]

In designing such a reward, whether accepted or not, Osbert acknowledges his feudal responsibilities. His offer of land hints at a future ability to support a limited mobility. However, the romance convention of discovered birth at the end mutes this message. It substitutes the fantasy that each of us, given a noble character, might discover we have an identity to match. Mobility must be obtained through deflection. Summing up Alleyn's actions, Osbert opines that 'those virtues which stimulated him to prosecute for another the cause of justice mysteriously urged him to the recovery of his rights' (113). Reward must come obliquely, lest the aristocracy become commercialized.

The benevolent and progressive feudalism of *Athlin and Dunbayne* refines away any tawdry financial considerations and replaces them with an idealized portrait of a free and open exchange. Restored to his home, Osbert's people clamor to see him. He descends into the hall, where the people have gathered. 'An universal shout of joy resounded through the walls on his appearance. A noble pleasure glowed on the countenance of the Earl at sight of his faithful people; and in the delight of that moment his heart bore testimony to the superior advantages of an equitable government' (75). The pleasure runs two ways: it gratifies the people to behold their leader, and he gains an access of feeling from their gratification. Like the public relations men of the King and of the aristocracy, Radcliffe builds a case for the reciprocal delights to be gained from idealized leadership.

Civil war civilized: inheriting the nation in *The Sicilian*

The heroic culture of Athlin and Dunbayne is no country for old men. As we have seen, the Count de Santmorin forms the only potential role model among the over-twenty set, and he is more vulnerable than they to the ravages of passion. We see no evidence that he can surmount his individual weaknesses to lead a people. Instead his affective individualism is mirrored by his economic individualism. Time and again, we see him acting as a parvenu, crisscrossing the country in search of inheritances that must have fallen to him through the failure of his relatives to produce offspring, and thus to promote their lineages, and his own failure to choose an appropriate love interest means that his estates will likewise devolve out of his family.

This bias in favor of youth most likely resulted from the ideology of the French Revolution, with its emphasis on a world reborn.[21] While the terrain in Radcliffe's next novel, 1790's *The Sicilian*, shifts to southern latitudes, the warmth there, too, emanates predominately from the young. The novel places such a premium upon the desires and rights of youth as compared with the desires and demands of parentalism that the tensions of a generational war vibrate across the pages. The unselfish generosity of the younger men vividly contrasts with the self-interested actions of the older generation, as either domestic or institutional father-figures (1993, 48, 121, 127).

However, the novel finally reveals a belief in too easy progress as one of the false idols which we must renounce:

> The rude manners, the boisterous passions, the daring ambition, and the gross indulgences which formerly characterized the priest, the nobleman, and the sovereign, had now begun to yield to learning – the charms of refined conversation – *political intrigue and private artifices*. Thus do the scenes of life vary with the predominant passions of mankind, and with the progress of civilization.
>
> (116, emphasis added)

Where we expect a Whig version of history, we encounter a far more tough and skeptical view. True progress will come not from specious accomplishment but from good solid work. As much as this novel celebrates 'individual virtue based on social affections,' that emphasis does not necessarily *substitute* 'a bourgeois ethic ... for the aristocratic code of honour,' as Alison Milbank claims for it (1993, xxv). Radcliffe melds bourgeois qualities with the perquisite noble blood to guarantee virtue, social affections, and hard work alike. Ferdinand must disown his father's inheritance symbolically. He does so by abandoning the castle of Mazzini. At the same time, something must be saved from the past. Ferdinand takes up the mantle of his position as leader, inherited from his father, by relocating to Naples and accepting a command in the Neapolitan army. '[A]midst the many heroes of that warlike and turbulent age, [he] distinguished himself for his valour and ability. The occupations of war engaged his mind, while his heart was solicitous in promoting the happiness of his family' (199). No longer, as in his father's day, are these two demands at war with one another. Instead, their status has become virtually metonymic.[22]

Incorporating the father in *The Romance of the Forest*

Restoration in the world of Radcliffe's second novel shrinks to a Habermasian realm, in which private individuals occupying essentially private spaces discourse on and represent a public reality. In her third novel, 1791's *Romance of the Forest*, potential models of heroism come to us from every age group, social and professional class. Members of the military, the clergy, and private life, whether gentleman or servant, each take the stage, shining with virtues peculiar to their station. No matter which qualities the hero possesses – fire, sweetness, dignity, modesty, or compassion – these attributes compete without detracting from the main qualification of manliness. As a result, each nascent hero draws our attention as much as he vies for Adeline's. For example, Theodore's gallantry reasserts his masculinity. Although that masculinity arises in response to the social and economic demands of patriarchy,[23] strength of thought meets a strength of arms that shelters rather than threatens. At the same time, Theodore's feminine qualities enhance his complementarity (1986, 95). Theodore's delicacy permits Adeline to unfold the nobility of her mind, allowing each to perceive their resemblance in taste and temperament. This scene rewrites Foucault's definition of sexuality as 'an especially dense transfer point for relations of power' (1990, 103); instead of producing suspicion or inequality, the transfer allows for equality. Likewise, education is said to have heightened their natural endowments of taste and genius, rather than creating divisions. As a result, literature furnishes common matter and cements their mutual regard (190). Here, we see the benefits of a cross-gendered heroism.[24]

Moreover, each station seems to allow for a meritocracy. No apparent class bias prevents servants from participating in nobility of action, either.[25] In their sympathetic regard and active benevolence, these heroes gain a quasi-nobility. They take up the duties formerly belonging to the aristocracy. These portraits of heroism distribute nobility across class and gender lines.

Plethoric plenitude redounds, though, when we realize how anemic these heroes and heroines are, their shortcomings amounting to a lack of compact wholeness.[26] Even before we learn of specific failings and fail to discover a singular heroic savior, the narrative management of the story foreshadows the problematic. For instance, Theodore disappears from the narrative for the bulk of its length; he appears as a memory recurring to Adeline as she travels through Switzerland, Italy, and France, but we do not learn his fate until page 304. Paragons being dead, their excellences have been divided up and dispersed among the population.[27] The very amplitude of heroes suggests that no *one* will suffice. Their contributions must be pooled in order to sustain the woes that confront them. The free and open exchange envisioned in *The*

Castles of Athlin and Dunbayne merges with the aristocratic leadership offered in *A Sicilian Romance* to produce a society in which confederation becomes the key. This fictive union mirrors the felt need among Englishmen for the greater security of a British nation.

The novel's vision of an alliance of heroes extends kinship beyond the limits of blood.[28] Because those heroes emerge from all walks of life, the novel holds out the hope that each member of society can contribute heroically. At the same time, it argues that such incorporation demands the leadership of an authoritative figure. And that stewardship must come from the reassertion of institutional authority. In the novel, the law rises majestic once again; the parliamentary and royal courts dominate the story's close.[29]

This melding of individual action with institutional guarantees reflects the reality of changing circumstances in England at that moment, as Terry Pickett describes. Prior to the French Revolution, sentimental individualism had held sway: 'The dead mechanisms of ancient rule were to be swept away in a new order of individual freedom and self-expression.' The concrete logical extension of this philosophy in France drove such dreams back into the shadows: 'within a generation, the advocates of the new anthropology were turning to the mediative force of the state ... They hoped only for a few modifications and changes in government's organization ... The despised instrument of princely oppression became the cherished source of freedom and self-expression, and all people required was a new story that justified it' (1996, 1). *The Romance of the Forest* forms one such story. Despite the pastoral implications of its title, England's emblematic association with the oak, its characterization as 'this green and pleasant land,' makes it shelter a national signification.

Radcliffe's humanizing of institutional authority restores the world to the justice lost with Henry's death. It also marks a shift in Radcliffe's attitude to the French Revolution, as descried through the two earlier novels. Harbingers of this reversal have appeared from the start of the tale with Radcliffe's representation of the villain. She consistently identifies Montalt with things Roman, now pejoratively viewed.

As Simon Schama notes, the 'French Revolution was obsessed with the model of the Roman Republic' (1989, 169). Revolutionaries prized the Republic for its fusion of 'private morals and public virtues' (170), as well as for its rhetoric. Unlike many of her contemporaries, Radcliffe had previously shared their enthusiasm.[30] In *A Sicilian Romance*, Roman virtue stands as a model for the highest values attainable, comprised in the actions of Cornelia's father, who 'united in an eminent degree the mild virtues of social life, with the firm unbending qualities of the noble romans, his ancestors, from whom he was proud to trace his descent' (1993, 119). One year later, in *The Romance of the Forest*, Roman virtues have deteriorated into vices, their decorum become decor.

Adeline encounters these debased traces of former glory upon her forced entrance to Montalt's chateau:

> They came to another door; it opened and disclosed a magnificent saloon, splendidly illuminated, and fitted up in the most airy and elegant taste. The walls were painted in fresco, representing scenes from Ovid, and hung above with silk drawn up in festoons and richly fringed ... From the center of the ceiling, which exhibited a scene from the Armida of Tasso, descended a silver lamp of Etruscan form: it diffused a blaze of light, that, reflected from large pier glasses, completely illuminated the saloon. Busts of Horace, Ovid, Anacreon, Tibullus, and Petronius Arbiter, adorned the recesses, and stands of flowers, placed in Etruscan vases, breathed the most delicious perfumes.
>
> (1986, 156–7)

In this palace of pleasure, Adeline hears a distant song, whose words advocate a *carpe diem* insouciance. Upon his entrance, Montalt attempts to use rhetoric to seduce; his perversion of morality the narrator deems 'sophistry' (160). Unsuccessful in his pursuit, Montalt permits Adeline to retire, perhaps hoping that the lavishness of her bedroom will win over her reluctance. Again the room reeks of voluptuous appeals to the senses, anchored by classical scenes (164).[31]

Montalt wields a linguistic palette with similar style. Whereas La Motte had resorted to swindling gamblers at play, Montalt attempts to swindle La Motte's very soul, by hiring him to kill Adeline (222–3). Montalt here invokes a Rousseauian primitivism, which he then applies in the service of a natural rights philosophy divorced from any consideration of natural law, a technique of which the French revolutionaries were also accused. The warning to attend carefully to his words and their perversion of moral theory knells in Radcliffe's description of his voice as 'slow and solemn,' an observation about intonation that the narrator almost never makes for her other characters, and one which mimics at the same time that it underscores Montalt's trickery of rhetorical declamation.[32] His entire speech, running to two pages, distorts French revolutionary rhetoric and depicts it as working only in the interests of individualistic self-aggrandizement.

The general thrust of the novel cleaves Rousseau in half: the political thinker of *The Social Contract*, whose ideas were believed to have been appropriated to revolutionary ends, splits off into the villainous Marquis; the apostle of sensibility remains embedded in La Luc, whose history and natural religion philosophy mimics the Vicaire Savoyard of *Emile* (245).[33] Montalt urges, 'It is the first proof of a superior mind to liberate itself from prejudices of country, or of education' (222). La Luc is 'partial to the English; he admired their character, and the constitution of their laws, and his library contained a collection of their best authors, particularly of their philosophers and poets' (261). In fact, so interested is La Luc in the value to be gained from national affiliation that he engages Verneuil in debates about the merit of national temperament. Granting the English wisdom in their 'laws, writings, and conversation,' Verneuil faults their inability to be happy, citing especially 'the frequency of suicide among them.' Conversely, he deems the French the embodied union of happiness and folly (268–9). La Luc agrees that, since the happiness of the French results more from 'constitution' than from thought, 'it deserves not the honours of wisdom' (269).

'Constitution' carries a double charge in the context of contemporary events. In his admiration for England, La Luc redirects our attention away from seventeenth-century France and back to late eighteenth-century England. Radcliffe footnotes this part of the conversation on Verneuil's side with a reminder how to properly understand it: 'It must be remembered that this was said in the seventeenth century' (269). Nevertheless, her husband's newspaper of a year before had carried editorials lamenting the high suicide rate, along with increased notices of suicides in the Bills of Mortality. The fictional conversation sets the body of law and the bodies of legal subjects on a collision course. English laws lend a constitution external to its subjects, one that can lead them to wisdom but cannot elevate their spirits. The French have a physical propensity for happiness, but no written constitution to codify and regulate it. Neither nation takes precedence; each needs revision. While individual heroes can bond together in a compact of virtuous action, they need the strong arm of the law to defend that compact and a wise leader to oversee all. Failing that, all citizens are, like Adeline, quasi-orphans.

As always, Radcliffe's dream of a national family depends upon a fiction of innate nobility. Adeline meditates upon precisely that theme. Musing on the gap between 'her own condition and that of other persons, educated as she had been,' Adeline consoles herself with the belief that 'surely I am not born to be for ever wretched' (242). The plot confirms her optimism: she moves from the wretched hovel of Peter's sister to the opulent comfort of La Luc's chateau (243). But the wealth of surroundings alone reveals another, more covert aspect of the novel's dream. Money and merit will equally provide the means of transportation.[34]

Adeline's translation in material circumstances requires her undergoing a period of literal unconsciousness (244). But literal unconsciousness connects with the work of the imagination, as evinced first in the 'Song of a Spirit' played by the Marquis to 'withdraw [Adeline's] mind from the present scene, and enchant it in sweet delirium' (161). There, the 'spirit' circulates with ease and rapidity from the celestial to the cavernous, from the picturesque to the sublime:

> In the sightless air I dwell,
> On the sloping sun-beams play;
> Delve the cavern's inmost cell,
> Where never yet did day-light stray:
>
> Dive beneath the green sea waves,
> And gambol in briny deeps;
> Skim ev'ry shore that Neptune laves,
> From Lapland's plains to India's steeps.
>
> (ll. 1–8)

Though these airy gambols beckon us to innocent pleasures, our reading must resist that temptation. These aesthetic perambulations draw a zone among the world's markets, as well. Further, with articles lamenting the loss of ships of the line, bewailing the disadvantaged position of the British as compared with the French and Spanish navies, and urging Britain's 'natural' naval advantages running through the periodical press of the time, the spirit's 'natural' ability takes on a new coloring.[35] At the same time, her sojourn in 'the cavern's inmost cell' aestheticizes the work of British and Indian miners who, like her, 'delve.'

Adeline does not merely consume poetry; she also creates it. Like the poem above, the 'comfort and delight' she imagines in her poetry as she struggles against her 'grief and despair' (244) reveal the novel's 'political unconscious.'[36] Wrapped in her sorrows, Adeline pens a poem, 'Titania to her Love.' She longs for escape to 'isles that gem the western deep' (l. 2). These imaginary isles soon take on a concrete presence and relevance:

Swift hie we to that splendid clime,
Where gay Jamaica spreads her scene,
Lifts the blue mountain – wild – sublime!
And smooths her vales of vivid green.

Where throned high, in pomp of shade,
The *Power of Vegetation* reigns,
Expanding wide, o'er hill and glade,
Shrubs of all growth – fruit of all stains:

She steals the sun-beams' fervid glow
To paint her flow'rs of mingling hue;
And o'er the grape the purple throw,
Breaking from verdant leaves to view.

There, myrtle bow'rs, and citron grove,
O'ercanopy our airy dance;
And there the sea-breeze loves to rove
When trembles Day's departing glance.

And when the false moon steals away,
Or e'er the chacing morn doth rise.
Oft, fearless, we our gambols play
By the fire-worm's radiant eyes.

And suck the honey'd reeds that swell
In tufted plumes of silver white;
Or pierce the cocoa's milky cell,
To sip the nectar of delight.

(ll. 17–40)

Sugar (the 'honey'd reeds'), cocoa, and citrus, the fruits of Jamaica's land (and the labors of her slave population), nurture this visionary land of milk and honey. Slavery cannot mar this bounty; instead, Nature's 'stains' imprint on the landscape a naturalized reciprocity (ll. 21–4).[37]

Adeline's poetic efforts have a noble genealogy, inspired as they are by 'having read that rich effusion of Shakespeare's genius, "A Midsummer Night's Dream"' (284). Radcliffe here demonstrates what I have argued in Chapter 1: the revival of interest in romance, the attendant elevation of Shakespeare as representing a lost British glory, the accompanying identification of Britain as Gothic space, all converge with national aspirations. Now, a revivified nationalism extends its sway as colonialism: Jamaica becomes variously a land to be presented as a gift to a lover, a possession securely British, both figuratively as Shakespeare's country of the mind and literally as a God-given paradise of fruits and commodities for British tastes (284–5).

A second effusion tumbles out upon the first. Four pages later another poem, entitled 'Morning, on the Sea Shore,' reprises Titania and the evocation of British colonial might. So powerful are these images that they get singled out for praise: in the *Monthly Review*, the critic excerpts the 'Song of a Spirit', and notes that '[S]everal other poetic pieces, of at least equal merit, are introduced during the course of the romance, particularly, Titania to her Love, – and Morning on the Sea-shore' (1792, 85). In the latter poem, Titania resides in 'India's spicy groves' (l. 14), visiting the 'honey'd buds' of Jamaica as vacation like an eighteenth-century visitor to Club Med (l. 47). India complements Jamaica's riches with her stores of pearl and 'gold from India's deepest caverns brought' (ll. 59–61). Just as particularities of culture, nationality, religion, and geography lose their outlines in the poems, mingling to become a single Indies as source for British markets (288–90),[38] so *The Romance of the Forest* cobbles together seventeenth- and eighteenth-century history, France, and Switzerland, to produce a foretaste of the British future.

Trading places: the mystery of *Udolpho*

Anticipated with relish, that future contained not only the sweets of empire but also a newly leavened society, as represented in the social themes we have encountered thus far. These include a need for a free and open exchange of people and goods, with a concomitant desire that the aristocracy not become commercialized (*Castles*); the desirability of practicing a wise passivity (*Sicilian*), coupled with an active benevolence (*Romance*); and a growing emphasis upon a confederation staffed by meritocratic reward and spearheaded by institutions (*Romance*). Because trade requires open borders, confederation embraces even countries normally perceived as enemy threats, so that, at the onset of the French Revolution, anti-Gallic sentiments are chastised (*English Chronicle*).

New roadblocks appeared in the way to the British future's fruition when France extended revolutionary ideals and war beyond its borders. Nevertheless, Ann Radcliffe's next novel, 1794's *The Mysteries of Udolpho*, is less militant about foreign relations than it is about these internal social themes. Despite being published after England's entry into war with France, the novel is set in France and represents those countrymen relatively even-handedly, in contrast to the Italians. Moreover, symbols of the very valorous traits propagandized for militant English nationalism transplant themselves onto French soil: in search of shelter from a storm, the Count de Villefort stumbles with his party onto an ancient fortress 'built of grey stone, in the heavy Saxon-gothic style... ;[I]n this court of entrance stood the gigantic remains of an oak, that seemed to have flourished and decayed with the building, which it still appeared frowningly to protect by the few remaining branches, leafless and moss-grown, that crowned its trunk, and whose wide extent told how enormous the tree had been in a former age' (1970, 606). Nor do her heroes or heroines celebrate military engagement. Valancourt seeks advancement in the military, and Emily admires the Italian soldiery for the brilliance of their 'high martial air, mingled with the haughtiness of the noblesse of those days,' and the 'gallantry' of their dress (173). But the novel also condemns *some* militarism as indistinguishable from thievery: Valancourt's initiation into vice and Paris occurs under the auspices of his military career and brethren; Montoni couches his depredations against the purses of traveling victims under the banner of the civil wars percolating throughout Radcliffe's fictional Italy. Anguishing over the wedding of war and finance, the novel divorces them by muting political concerns (the immediate engagement in war against France) and trumpeting the social (economic and ethical progress).[39]

Contradictory attitudes compete throughout *The Mysteries of Udolpho*. On the one hand, the novel seems critical of war, in that the gaudy mercenaries who swell Montoni's ranks can be said to resemble the English volunteer militias raised by the gentry, many of the men in both cases raised from tradesmen or from the laboring classes, and both decked out in a hyperbolic aristocratic notion of military splendor, crowned by varying lengths of avian vanity to signify rank. On the other hand, the novel rumbles over threats to trade, a fear also motivating the raising of private defenses. Radcliffe's placing of the private armies under the control of those dedicated to commandeering the profits of honest traders seems to underline the point with all the more force. Yet, if she identifies the government's early reliance for defense on volunteerism with an abdication of responsibility, she also cures that omission fictively by making the government step in to restore Emily's lands.[40] In sum, government or institutional forces become heroes in this novel by virtue of their increasing invisibility and invulnerability to error. At the same time, the novel offers a new British hero in its portrait of Ludovico, the servant who voluntarily rises from the ranks to protect, if not British trade, then the rights of the British gentry.[41]

These contradictory strands, and their resolution in the figure of Ludovico, can shed light on public attitudes contested by historians of nationalism. Gerald Newman sees the voluntary associations as chiefly spawned by and among the middle classes, and interprets their actions as aggressive: the 'scaffolding of middle-class ambition,' whereby the middle classes seized the reins of public spiritedness that the state and the patrician classes had dropped (1997, 63–122) in a bid for control. In contrast, Colley argues that the activity of the middle class in forming voluntary societies demonstrates the close links between the trading community and their superiors (1992, 92). One reason for such links was the need for protection – for trading ships, for orders to manufacturers during wartime. The evidence in *Udolpho* suggests an additional interpretation. Whether the result of a felt national imperative or the consequence of a bid for national dominance, the societies operated by the very type of social emulation fostered and encouraged by the Gothic novel.

More veiled than the waxen monition Emily uncovers at Udolpho, a pointed anxiety about the danger posed to trade by war beats beneath the surface of the novel in the numerous fantasies about shipwrecks strewn through the interpolated poems, supposedly penned by the young heroes and heroines. The importance of the sea to commercial enterprise is attested to by Hobsbawm, who cites the prohibitive costs and delays of transporting goods across land as compared with the relative ease and cheapness of water transport (1996, 9). Naval power was equally crucial to England's security as a nation, and the sea would furnish the first great testing-ground against Napoleon. So the poems' refusal to name the impetus for their imaginary journeys points in both directions at once.[42] In Emily's 'Storied Sonnet,' the 'traveler' catapults from an Alpine bridge to the churning waters below. Here, we seem clearly in the social realm, as we do in other poems about pilgrimage and in Valancourt's 'Shipwreck,' as he fancifully casts his fears that he has lost Emily (558–9). But as these nervous strains climax in two poems towards the close of the novel, the possibility of entwined motive appears. The first is called 'The Mariner.' Emily pens this poem while she awaits embarkation at Leghorn, having just escaped from Udolpho, circumstances that might actuate an interest in sea travel. Equally plausible, military concerns arise as Emily's companion there, Du Pont, learns of his regiment's embarkation for France (462). While we do not know why the poetic mariner journeys, unlike Emily, he and his crew sail into wintry seas; their danger is foreshadowed from the first lines of the poem, where their casting off is called 'the last dread moment' (463). And in 'To the Winds,' an Emily restored to France, friends, and finances (though not yet to Valancourt) makes evident what had before been only implied (641).

Fear of death at sea colors even the landscape, so that clouds become 'billowy surges' or seas of vapor, condensing a torrential 'world of chaos' (165).[43] Poems that appear innocuous daydreaming merely embroider these playful visions above a stormy center: in 'The Sea-Nymph,' the speaker prides herself on her ability to charm mariners with her song and to intervene in their doom. To thwart her beneficence, she tells us, Neptune binds her to the rocks so that the 'drowning seamen cry in vain' (181). Fiction or poetry can only stave off for a bubble of time the 'elemental war' that lurks behind every appearance of calm. Radcliffe's attributing of a pervasive generality to the conflict detoxifies the virulent anti-Gallicism of England's war machinery.

The alarums of war quickly give way to alarums of peace, as recounted in Count de Villefort's history of the Pyrenean fortress chateaux (604–5). Like a traveler in one of her own landscapes, Radcliffe has her eye trained on the long view. In that view, mutual duties to uphold virtue bind merchant and government. Hence, whether prompted by 'timidity' or greed, the 'commercial senate' of Venice must cease conniving at Montoni's scavenging, suppress his power, and correct his 'outrages' (521). Even though her novel celebrates commercial liberty and circulation, as I will demonstrate more fully below, Radcliffe opposes the dominant attitude taken by her English government towards such economic activity. As characterized by Eric Hobsbawm, the government dictum propounded the idea that 'the maximization of private profit was the foundation of government policy' (1992, 2). Instead, like other Gothic novels, Radcliffe argues that private profit, pursued solely for its own ends, can be destructive of the public good. Once obligations are satisfied, reciprocity can come into play. Virtuous commercial enterprise deserves military protection (44). Governments charged with protecting the travel and trade of inhabitants must let neither timidity nor greed prevent them from executing impartial justice, especially because, in seeking to privatize justice, the outlaws undermine the very concept of impartiality (404).

Montoni's actions, and those of the other smugglers and pirates who picturesquely decorate the book's landscape, pose a threat because their operations so closely resemble those of the governments they defraud. Like a government waging war, they take prisoners whom they hold for ransom; to conduct their operations, they hold councils of parley to strategize their attacks; they also act as mercenary soldiers for the highest bidders. Worse yet, when Montoni cannot directly destroy an enemy, he resorts to the government to do the job for him. Dropping a hint into the 'Denunzie secrete, or lion's mouths, which are fixed in a gallery of the Doge's palace, as receptacles for anonymous information, concerning persons, who may be disaffected towards the state' (423), Montoni secures his revenge. While the Venetian prison resembles its fallen twin, the Bastille, so each is associated with Britain through the emblem of the oak, the emphatic fear of naval disaster, and pleas to protect trade. Just so, the network of spies available both to observe and report on men's activities, real or imagined, like the person Montoni employs to drop the accusation, disseminates Italian rumors that carry the whisper of a French accent and the choked glottals of British lips.[44]

If circularity ensnares, circulation saves. But this time, instead of the unseen circulation of wealth being the crucial factor (as in *The Romance of the Forest*), the unseen circulation of men provides the fiction of salvation. Once again, the poetry repeats this theme in a more mercantilist register. In a poem modestly entitled only 'Stanzas,' Emily reanimates the unseen landscape and the fallen heroes of Troy with a 'little story' (206). Initially ruminating on Greece and feeling that 'pensive luxury' produced by 'viewing the scenes of ancient story, and … comparing their present state of silence and solitude with that of their former grandeur and animation'(206), Emily elides Greece with Troy. This displacement makes keen the poem's relevance for British society and trade, since Troy had long been mythologized as the hive of the British nation. A weary merchant drives his camels across the deserted plains and ruined fragments of glory. There, instead of the princes of song, the 'proud columns of deserted Troy' now shelter shepherds and traders such as himself:

From distant lands with merchandise he came,
His all of wealth his patient servants [the camels] bore;
Oft deep-drawn sighs his anxious wish proclaim
To reach, again, his happy cottage door;

...

The robber Tartar on his slumber stole,
For o'er the waste, at eve, he watch'd his train;
Ah! who his thirst of plunder shall control?
Who calls on him for mercy – calls in vain!

(207)

Hamet is saved by two 'servants': first, a camel startles and awakes him in time to avoid the death-thrust of the robber; second, an 'unknown hand,' revealed as belonging to a hiding shepherd, launches a volley of arrows that kills the Turk. The sense of mutual rights and duties causes this shepherd to assume heroic proportions: 'He fear'd his own, and sav'd a stranger's life!' In reward, Hamet removes the shepherd to the safety and domestic bliss of his own home.

Ludovico's history translates the poem into a novel middle-class fantasy. Introduced to us by Annette's description in volume two, Ludovico, the self-made man and only true hero of *Udolpho*, seems an unpromising candidate, serving, as he does, the Signor Cavigni. Annette prizes him for all the wrong reasons: she sees only a young man who is tall, handsome, dresses with panache, rows a gondola, and sings sweetly (246–7). Moreover, Ludovico's disappearance from the story for the next two hundred pages encourages us to dismiss him. But from then on, his repeated appearances and disappearances teach us to read these more as thematizing a circulation of heroism where it would be most invisible to the conventional eye. Prudent, discreet, able to plan an escape and effect it, Ludovico demonstrates that he can think on his feet and seize 'circumstances,' a word that first appears in conjunction with Ludovico and which echoes throughout the remainder of the novel.[45] Through deception, he wins not only escape but also a weapon of defense from one of the castle's guards, jokingly referring to himself as a hero at the very moment that he fulfills that prophecy (451). His only shortcoming is complacency; once safely beyond Udolpho, he 'congratulated himself ... not a little on the address, with which he had deceived the sentinel, and conducted the whole of this affair' (453). Still, pride in one's own accomplishments or self-esteem differs from a peacock vanity or from the kind of class arrogance that makes Du Pont determined to accompany Emily back to France, even though he should rejoin his regiment, because he cannot bear to let Ludovico be the hero alone (455).

Again, as compared with Du Pont, Ludovico surpasses his social better in empirical ability. Though both are Frenchmen, Ludovico has conned the geography and topography of the land through which his movements have been restricted, compared with Du Pont's explorations there while with his regiment, so that only Ludovico can lead them to safety (455). Despite his centrality to the expedition, Ludovico neither assumes superiority nor forgets his feudal obligations. Du Pont offers to stand guard while the escapees sleep, but Ludovico desires to 'spare him this trouble'(457) and so takes up the servant's post.

Ludovico's actions help us see Radcliffe discriminating between two definitions of nationalism, as described by Ernest Gellner. In the first type, the cultural, meaning systems of ideas, signs, associations, and ways of behaving and communicating, determines national affiliation. In the second type, affiliation becomes 'voluntaristic': 'A mere category of persons (say, occupants of a given territory, or speakers of a given language, for example) becomes a nation if and when the members of the category firmly recognize certain mutual rights and duties to each other in virtue of their shared membership of it' (1983, 7). Ludovico's sense of feudal obligation to the man he adopts as his master furnishes him the opportunity to exhibit his greatest heroism. In gratitude for the 'kindness he had received from the Count,' Ludovico offers to watch in Chateau-le-Blanc's 'haunted' chamber (1970, 543–4). While Ludovico disclaims any desire for pecuniary reward, the fact that the Count offers it shows his acknowledgment of their 'mutual rights and duties,' expressed as part of the growing cash nexus. This episode repeats that in *The Old English Baron*, where Edmund serves in a similar capacity. Like that novel, also, the old wing of the chateau is closed off and separated from the more modern additions (479–80). But unlike Fitz-Owen in Reeve's novel, the Count desires not to incorporate the older wings but to keep his servants from deserting in their fear. Thus, both in its architectural lineaments and in its characterological differences (Ludovico does not discover his noble antecedents, as does Edmund in that setting), *The Mysteries of Udolpho* substitutes the idea that the past and the present can be amalgamated for a more progressive and materialist message.

Once in the 'haunted' chamber, the description of the respective leaders encapsulates the role reversal characteristic of *Udolpho* (546). Within this tableau we can see a metonymic analogue with the

Revolution: the Count represents the enlightenment *philosophes*, Henri the middle-class provisioners of revolution, and Ludovico the brave men ready to cast their lives on the altar of ideals. The necessity for such brave men to save the country reappears when the Count and his family are captured by the banditti who plot to murder them (612–13). Ludovico arises from their ranks, having been taken by the banditti from the 'haunted' chamber (in fact, they are the ghosts that persecute the peace of the chateau), and orchestrates once more their release. Having now been longer schooled in adversity, Ludovico has added new talents to his former ones; he can not only save them and provide for their escape but can also minister physic to their wounds (616–17).

But, after all, the novel fantasizes as much about the return of peace as it does about the new hero who will inhabit that age. As St Aubert says, 'happiness arises in a state of peace, not of tumult. It is of a temperate and uniform nature, and can no more exist in a heart, that is continually alive to minute circumstances, than in one that is dead to feeling' (80). Peace comes when the government restores Emily's lands, when the financial collapses that initially impelled her into the arms of careless guardians have been equally mysteriously retrieved, and when Emily learns to remove her family holdings from the 'Gothic realm of non-economic superstition' and to open the land to 'the market and rational exploitation' (Hobsbawm, 1996, 152).[46] Wisely, she makes Ludovico the steward of her father's family estate. Knowing that the future has been connected to the past and is in capable hands, she and Valancourt can retire to the sentimental benevolence of the aristocracy, while the real work of building the nation goes on in the name of their kin, just beyond their ken.

Part III
Tailgating on the Gothic Myth

5
Speaking Shadows

> Am I obliged to prove juridically all the Virtues of all those I
> shall see suffering every kind of wrong, and contumely, and
> risk of Life, ... before I endeavour to excite an horrour against
> midnight assassins at back stairs, and their more wicked abet-
> tors in Pulpits? What, are not high Rank, great Splendour of
> descent, great personal elegance and outward accomplish-
> ments ingredients of moment in forming the interest we take
> in the Misfortunes of Men?
>
> (Edmund Burke to Philip Francis, 20 February 1790,
> quoted in Zerilli, 1992, 47)

Mobilized manpower and mobile credit, that two-fisted engine of war,
stirred up demands for proof of virtue after 1794. The aristocracy's par-
adigmatic responsibilities, the people's rights under government, the
'heroic' locus of allegiance: each came under scrutiny, accompanied by
calls for reform. Although these summons to adjudication appeared in
separate venues and as distinct debates, a questioning of the relationship between social duty and private desire unifies them.[1]

The aristocracy was doubly beset. Pressured to reform their manner and
morals in order to influence the poor,[2] their secure footing in 'honor' and
'virtue' also slipped away as economic realities shifted. Ultimately, the
conflict would pit real against mobile property.[3] Domesticated by the
'culture of civility,' honor migrates into an interiorized evaluation of reputation; 'virtue' gets entangled with economic reality.[4] And a new reciprocity between the categories heroism, virtue, and economics emerges.

But as much as the aristocracy was the cynosure or the cinder of
the public's eye, so also was the state of the nation or the rights of

the people as a collective whole of concern. Spokesmen for the people responded with their own sense of demotic *oblige*. In 1795, a newly published pamphlet entitled *A Remonstrance in Favour of British Liberty, addressed to the Right Hon. W. Pitt, First Lord of the Treasury, &c. By a Country Gentleman* demonstrates Habermas's hypothesized public sphere rising to defend its prerogatives. Once again, Pitt's actions exemplify the threat, this time to 'the people's right of *petitioning* government for the redress of grievances, and of *assembling* for that purpose' (*Monthly Review* (1795): 452). This 'shackling of British liberty,' the writer fears, will soon cost the further rights of trial by jury and freedom of parliamentary debate. Employing slavery rhetoric throughout, the reviewer slyly buttresses the anonymous writer's points. The reviewer ends with the only direct quotation from the pamphlet, an exhortation '*to the people*' to preserve the 'inestimable jewel they inherit from the *virtue* and *heroism* of their ancestors' (453, emphasis mine). The very next article echoes this position. The anonymous author of *A Letter to the High Sheriff of the County of Lincoln* expresses an alarm about the sanctity and security of the Constitution shared by 'at least one half of the nation.' His support for individual action as a safeguard receives sanction from the *Monthly Review*, which deems the author a well-known and 'worthy watchman of the state' and applauds his language for being as 'noble and nervous' as is consistent with decent usage (453). The *Monthly Review's* epithet for the writer restores to the individual the role assigned to the 'night-watchman state' by Gramsci, where it 'operates as a repressive apparatus which comes into play whenever its borders or regulations are directly challenged' (1971, 21),[5] hinting that, in the period concerning us, at least, border crossings occurred in both directions.

Both letters capture a paradox of political rhetoric: while critical of institutional abuses of power, the writers nevertheless express faith in British traditions to protect the liberties of the individual. Their dissent from current procedures can wear the face of patriotic nationalism, because older British traditions muster against British leaders.[6] This uneasy plenitude indicates all the more thoroughly that ideas of nationhood and of heroes, heroism, and the heroic within that nation participate in an agonizingly slow evolution, provoked by debate and controversy.

Doubly reactive, to literary and social events, three works in particular cry out for attention in this chapter: Matthew Lewis's *The Monk* (1796), inspired by *The Mysteries of Udolpho*; Ann Radcliffe's 'rebuttal,'

1797's *The Italian*; and the 1802 anonymous redaction of *The Italian, The Midnight Assassin: or, Confession of the Monk Rinaldi*.[7] This interchange between the 'authentic' and the 'ephemeral,' the elite and the common, simultaneously comments on the competition between privatization and mediation, between honor and virtue. Here, border crossings create surprising affinities. In Radcliffe and Lewis, the bald emphasis upon commerce and circulation that we found in *The Romance of the Forest* and *The Mysteries of Udolpho* reappears in more idealized form. This idealized form returns us to the Habermasian public sphere, always already an outgrowth of commercial interests, and plunges us into discussions of virtue as opposed to honor. However, despite historical evidence that the terms 'honor' and 'virtue' lose their sharp, distinguishing edges, Radcliffe's and Lewis's novels reinscribe the distinction. Whereas honor and virtue equally drove the representations of Walpole's Theodore and Reeve's Edmund, Radcliffe emphasizes virtue, while Lewis awards the palm to honor.

Lewis's honorable and Radcliffe's virtuous hero may share the 'neo-Harringtonian devotion to the public good and his engagement in relations of equality'(Pocock, 1985, 48); nevertheless, that devotion and those relations are no longer unproblematic. Instead, a pull between the desires of self and the needs of society afflicts all the characters. In *The Monk*, Raymond and Lorenzo escape this pull only when they associate as an oligarchic brigade. Mirroring antique notions of honor derived from a 'farmer-warrior world of ancient citizenship or Gothic *libertas*' (Pocock, 1985, 48), the oligarchy's honor consists in the rights and responsibilities of the citizen to keep and bear arms while disassociating civil defense from any institutionalized authority.[8] In *The Italian*, Radcliffe makes conflicting duties to self and society the central dilemma facing her hero and heroine. Using the term 'virtue' repeatedly, meaning thereby an internalized ethos of civility, Radcliffe's model heroes come from all ranks, a tendency normally associated with republicanism. But her sympathy with monarchy and with institutions, evident in the denouement to *The Romance of the Forest*, takes even more pronounced form in *The Italian*, where institutions of authority take center stage as heroes above and beyond her individual actors. Clinging clumsily to dual allegiances, monarchical *and* republican, Radcliffe's work illustrates Herzfeld's contention about the existence of social poetics in nationalist discourse. Thus, Montesquieu's 1748 dictum that 'honor is the principle of a monarchy, the principle of a republic is virtue' cannot help us correlate a Gothic preference for virtue over honor to political faction.[9]

The redaction, belonging to 'low-brow,' popular culture, should conform to the emergence of a radical underworld of literature posited by liberal pluralists.[10] Instead, the redaction's elimination of tension between social and individual desires discovers its individualistic stance, like that of the chapbooks in general, to be a deliberate reaction to Radcliffe's institutionalized fealty. Like Lewis's novel, the redaction privatizes authority and objectifies the female. Nevertheless, like Radcliffe's novel, the redaction promotes the myth of voluntary association. Class mobility simultaneously expands and contracts.[11] On the one hand, servants play an increasingly larger role. On the other hand, servants reject full autonomy as a reward for those roles, preferring to remain economically and socially subordinate. This myth of voluntary association counters the revolutionary charges against 'mastering' men.

Peeling away the comforting certainty of political labels such as conservative or radical, these works also transcend the limiting literary categories into which they have recently been placed. Lewis's work has been said by critics to inaugurate the 'Male Gothic'; Radcliffe's work has been held variously to represent 'Female,' subversive Gothic or a deeply conservative strain. Instead, these works contravene assumptions about gender and class characteristics of Gothic novels. In the 'underworld' literature of the redaction, the absence of narratorial mediation paradoxically facilitates a greater fiction of equality between readers and noble heroes.[12] Moving us closer into a world of individuals and isolation, *The Midnight Assassin* thus shows in embryo what will happen in the self-enclosed universe of the chapbooks, obsessed with modes of production and dissemination, and with readers, as discussed in the next chapter.

Through this obsession we can spy one difference between the Gothic in its various formats and verse romances such as those written by Wordsworth and Scott: whereas the Gothics metaphorize the state as chivalric knights and thematize the need for a 'concentrically ordered web of kinship,' they also reveal the 'machinery of modern nationalism, the fact that it functions like a series of interlocking cogs, fueled by coal and capital' as much as by a feudal or patriarchal loyalty (Ross, 1991, 58). Charting new territory for the domain of the nation as well as the novel, we see that the cultural work performed by authors of the Gothic makes them founders of discursivity as well, creating 'a possibility for something other than their discourse, yet something belonging to what they founded' (Foucault, 1994, 350).

Spectacular honor in *The Monk*

Far from dividing the attention, as reviewers claimed, Lewis's doubled plot offers us a diptych, two sides of the same coin: family loyalty and responsibility versus family alienation and anomie; social power corrupted and social power flowing through its proper channels to its proper ends.[13] Joining Satan in observing that people are virtuous 'from vanity, not principle,' in *The Monk* Lewis privileges honor and shows virtue as a sham (1952, 418). Sheltered by corrupt institutions, virtue's counterfeits appear in four principal arenas: education, sexuality, parenting, and religion. Dematerialized simulacra, these refinements of virtue have withered human relations. Lewis reanimates the social realm with spectacle, reactivating power through an enforced regard for aristocratic honor.[14]

Religion, education, and false virtue

Religious education is spuriously virtuous. When monks instruct Ambrosio, they repress 'grandeur and disinterestedness' as 'ill suited to the cloister':

> Instead of universal benevolence, he adopted a selfish partiality for his own particular establishment: he was taught to consider compassion for the errors of others as a crime of the blackest dye: the noble frankness of his temper was exchanged for servile humility;... He was suffered to be proud, vain, ambitious, and disdainful: he was jealous of his equals, and despised all merit but his own: he was implacable when offended, and cruel in his revenge.
>
> (1952, 238–9)

Like Ambrosio, Antonia's education comes early at the hands of those unfit, in this case her nurse, who loads her with superstitious beliefs that not even Elvira's later lessons can eradicate (309). But Elvira's editorializing undermines her efforts. She permits Antonia to read the Bible for education, but bowdlerizes it to restrict the extent of her knowledge:

> That prudent mother... was convinced that, unrestricted, no reading more improper could be permitted a young woman. Many of the narratives can only tend to excite ideas the worst calculated for a female breast: every thing is called plainly and roundly by its name;

and the annals of a brothel would scarcely furnish a greater choice of indecent expressions.

(258)

While the passage continues to connect Biblical education with an introduction to morality, Elvira's complaint about explicit naming and linguistic impropriety shows how false education and religion can overlap. Later we will see that Lewis's preference for graphic detail lines up with his interest in honor preserved through the strong arm of vengeance. The narrator's facetious insistence that Elvira would have preferred romances such as the *Amadis de Gaul, The Valiant Champion, Tirante the White, Don Galaor,* and the *Damsel Plazer di mi vida* to the Bible connects the works as fictions, and speciously authorizes Elvira's making a fiction of a fiction, for a delusory education.

While the ridicule of monastic life and of pious education might persuade us that religious skepticism confines itself to Catholicism (313), the critical outrage unleashed by the novel shows that its contemporaries read the message as applying to Protestantism as well. For instance, the *British Critic* gave as a 'canon of criticism' which it deemed 'irrefragable': 'That, in speaking of a sacred book, no person who has a spark of religion, or regard for it, will, or can, use such expressions as evidently tend to depreciate it, in any respect, below the most trivial and contemptible works' (1798, 319).[15] For Lewis, Pharisees come in all denominations.[16]

Religious education perverts a healthy sexuality as well, producing instead sexual hypocrisy. As the narrator admonishes, 'vice is ever most dangerous when lurking behind the mask of virtue' (103). Even when the 'mask of virtue' forms a comedic interlude, as with Leonella, revulsion results:

> She affected the airs of a love-sick virgin, and carried them all to the most ridiculous excess. She heaved lamentable sighs, walked with her arms folded, uttered long soliloquies, and her discourse generally turned upon some forsaken maid, who expired of a broken heart! Her fiery locks were always ornamented with a garland of willow. Every evening she was seen straying upon the banks of a rivulet by moonlight; and she declared herself a violent admirer of murmuring streams and nightingales.

(246)

Staging sexual virtue, Lewis parodies the delicate and pure sensibilities of Radcliffe's heroines.

Honorable, as opposed to 'virtuous,' education has an honorable purpose and honored representatives such as the duke of Villa Hermosa, a nobleman venerated by Raymond for his 'abilities and knowledge of the world' (113). The duke urges Raymond to mingle with the lower classes to derive the maximum benefit for his future role as leader:

> Do not confine yourself to the illustrious of those countries through which you pass. Examine the manners and customs of the multitude: enter into the cottages; and, by observing how the vassals of foreigners are treated, learn to diminish the burthens, and augment the comforts, of your own. According to my ideas of those advantages which a youth destined to the possession of power and wealth may reap from travel, he should not consider as the least essential, the opportunity of mixing with the classes below him, and becoming an eyewitness of the sufferings of the people.
>
> (114)

Such education prepares young leaders to become good fathers of their nation, honoring the demands placed upon them by their responsibilities. In order to acquire a universalist perspective, Raymond must eschew the partiality shown to rank by traveling incognito. Unlike Ambrosio, whose 'long absence from the great world, and total unacquaintance with the common dangers of life, made him form of them an idea far more dismal than the reality,' Lorenzo's and Raymond's immersion in university studies must be rounded out by the Grand Tour, by participating in the splendors and dangers of the great world.[17] Because Raymond can move about in the world, while Ambrosio (his half-nephew) is immured in the convent, Raymond can freely gather participants for the new society that will be formed by the end of the novel.

Gendered honor

Ambrosio's education destroys his leadership qualities and his manhood:

> Had his youth been passed in the world, he would have shown himself possessed of many brilliant and manly qualities. He was naturally enterprizing, firm, and fearless: he had a warrior's heart, and might have shown with splendour at the head of an army. There was no want of generosity in his nature: the wretched never failed to find in him a compassionate auditor: his abilities were quick and

shining, and his judgment vast, solid, and decisive. With such
qualifications he would have been an ornament to his country.

(237–8)

Bereft of this native 'manliness', the 'virtues' inculcated into Ambrosio
mark him out as feminized.[18] His 'selfish partiality for his own particular establishment' mirrors Dame Jacintha's fears for hers; his lack of
compassion repeats the Prioress's rigid sternness, as does his implaca-
bility when offended and his cruelty in revenge; his 'servile humility'
resembles that of Antonia (whose humility is at least genuine) and
Leonella (whose is not); his superstition finds a chord in almost all the
nuns and in Cunegonde;[19] and his pride, vanity, ambition, and
disdain, his jealousy of equals and scorn for all merit but his own
resounds in the portrait of the Baroness Lindenburg, with a minor echo
occurring in Leonella. Similarities between Ambrosio's and Antonia's
experiences underscore the monk's feminization. As father confessor to
his flock, and superior of the abbey, then, Ambrosio cannot but fail in
his duties.

Lewis's leveling of gender in Antonia's and Ambrosio's education
does not serve an egalitarian message, as it does for Radcliffe. Instead,
it forms part of the misogyny of his text.[20] Gender equality shimmers
when Matilda implores Ambrosio to be merely her friend (85, 108). But
to win that boon, Matilda must dematerialize her self as a female presence (102); moreover, the vision quickly resolves into a mirage.
Matilda's 'education' shows what becomes of the dream for a female
Bildungsroman. Raised by an uncle of 'solid judgment and extensive
erudition' (82), she gains access to knowledge not only forbidden other
females but hid from view at large. These researches into natural philosophy, geology, botany, and astronomy devolve into the sorcerer's
arts. Worse yet, they turn the soft Matilda into a commanding masculine female (233); the 'delicious languor' in which she clothes herself
to intoxicate Ambrosio evaporates after the heat of passion, and she
barks orders at the monk who, having realized his 'manhood,' has
become unmanned (230–6).

Lewis replenishes the sense of loss caused by the absence of virtue
with a restored emphasis upon honor. Here, the 'Inscription in an
Hermitage' furnishes an apt motto:

> I saw mankind with vice incrusted;
> I saw that Honour's sword was rusted;
> That few for aught but folly lusted;

> That he was still deceiv'd, who trusted
> In love or friend

(75)

Rather than retreat into seclusion, Lewis tries to burnish off that rust. But his reforging of honor downplays traditional elements such as martial ability and chivalric relations to women, insofar as chivalry acknowledged female power. Instead, the metaphor of 'Honour's sword' aptly telegraphs Lewis's gendering of honor as a homosocial bond. Women's sense of honor derives as much from self-interestedness as it does from noble disinterestedness, as we see when Agnes and Elvira demand a sexualized respect from Raymond and Lorenzo, respectively (160, 221), and when the Prioress anguishes over the reputation of her 'house' (72). Men's honor rises above petty considerations, in keeping with the 1764 definition of honor given by Lord Lyttelton as 'something distinct from mere probity, and which supposes in gentlemen a stronger abhorrence of perfidy, falsehood, or cowardice, and a more elevated and delicate sense of the dignity of virtue, than are usually found in vulgar minds,' where honor subsumes virtue.[21] Although he fails to protect Agnes's honor by preserving her virginity, Raymond always plans to restore her honor to wholeness by marriage (161, 194, 197), a feat he holds on through almost mortal illness to achieve. Knowing that refusing Rodolpha's attentions endangers his relationship with Agnes, Raymond nevertheless insists that 'Honour obliges me to inform you, that you have mistaken for the solicitude of love what was only the attention of friendship.' He exhorts her to 'Recollect yourself, noble lady! recollect what is owed by you to honour, by me to the baron' and he refuses to violate the 'laws of hospitality' (149). Raymond's distinction between a woman's wider public obligations and a man's more narrowly defined debts to other men reiterate Lyttelton's annexing of honor to a patriarchal, aristocratic code and self-image: honor belongs to 'gentlemen' with an '*elevated* sense.' The 'gallantry' of Raymond's 'nation' (120) fuses with the gentleman's code of honor, revered by male aristocrats, enabling his 'nation' to transcend the borders of Spain.

Parental honor

If Ambrosio's flaws prevent him from being a good father to his flock, so parental relationships in the novel reveal the specious nature of parental virtue. In fact, parents, whether construed as individuals or as institutions, come in for the largest share of the blame in the novel. Individually, only moments of good parenting break through in the novel to form counter-examples. Marguerite's father welcomes back his prodigal daughter. Agnes feels such a protective love for her child while yet unborn that she forgives Raymond in order to secure her child's happiness and safety (195). She constantly begs for mercy from her captors on the grounds of that child's innocence, in a reversal of Walpole's exordium on the sins of the father. Her maternal loyalty, even to the child's corrupted corpse, may seem excessive and grotesque, but a world of fierce disloyalty could produce its extreme opposite. More typical examples instance parental selfishness, cruelty, and irresponsibility. Marguerite's husband takes to crime after squandering his patrimony and being disowned by his family; he joins a troop 'chiefly composed of young men of family in the same predicament with himself' (137). Seeking to escape the wrath of his father at his marriage to Elvira, Gonzalvo and his new wife abandon their two-year-old son, Ambrosio. Incensed at his defeat, the old Marquis de las Cisternas throws Elvira's father into prison and seizes the boy, whom he, too, abandons, this time anonymously to an abbey (40). Agnes's parents doom her to the convent out of superstition: they promise to bestow their first-born child as a reward for Donna Inesilla's recovery from illness (144). Realizing the selfishness of their intent, especially as the growing Agnes expresses her reluctance, they sequester her from the rest of the family and hide their purpose from them.[22] Beatrice, too, had been forced into the convent by her parents (182).

Beatrice, Ambrosio, and Agnes thus are all oblates: children donated to religious institutions, in which case allegiance towards the adoptive institution was supposed to take precedence over familial connections. The tradition of oblation extends back into Biblical time: we find mention of the practice in Hannah's promising Samuel to the priests at Shiloh. But the donation of their children in this novel does not result from any piety or virtue; instead, the motives driving these various parents derive from a sacrificing of ultimate good to present comfort, analogous to Ambrosio's moral barterings.

Lewis wrests family ties from biological and geographical constraints. A deeply felt sense of place can tether individuals in an imaginary kinship; place can form the backbone or central spoke of a radiating affinity. This elongation of family corresponds to nationalist rhetoric, in that countrymen first identify themselves as 'sons' of a particular land and only later as members of a specific nation. At the same time, affinity can cathect individuals not only to a new family but also to a new locale, a permutation perhaps influenced by the age's enthusiastic adoption of the concept of 'spreading circles of affection.'[23]

However, the proper road to a (male) universalism cannot be found in colonialism, which provides the satisfactions neither of emotional nor of geographical bonds. Despite the fact that colonial adventure in *The Monk* proceeds from a justified self-preservation, it breaks loyalty to kin and country. Thus colonialism appears as a misguided expansionism that quickly collapses into exile, an identification we can see in Gonzalvo's plangent exercise, 'The Exile,' one of the two most popular inset poems in the novel:[24]

> No more my arms a parent's fond embraces,
> No more my heart domestic calm must know;
> Far from these joys, with sighs which memory traces,
> To sultry skies and distant climes I go.
>
> Where Indian suns engender new diseases,
> Where snakes and tigers breed, I bend my way
> To brave the feverish thirst no art appeases,
> The yellow plague, and madding blaze of day.
>
>   (219)

The longing for homeland produces a fever worse than the boiling blood and delirious brain caused by Indian climes. Mental and emotional incapacitation makes it impossible to reap the profit from colonial exploits that Lorenzo vainly imagines of his estates in Hispaniola (112, 217), as Gonzalvo's family finds (41). Instead, colonial possessions confer death either by attacking invisibly, as in the contagion of slow, tropical fever, or visibly, by animals whose poison leaks from their native islands, once contacted by Europeans.[25] Even when exile has occurred voluntarily, as is the case with Elvira's servant, Flora, it must be reversed for ultimate well-being (399).

Lewis's animadversions on exile and colonialism may be the self-dramatizing utterances of a young boy, situated at The Hague during the outbreak of war as apprenticeship for the kind of political position held by his father and the reluctant heir to slave plantations in Jamaica.[26] Nevertheless, they connect with the novel's thematization of alternate forms of parenting, in its portraits of orphans, adoption, adrogation, and oblation, to suggest the nationalist implications of kinship and parenting. Three oblates in the novel could be mere coincidence or plot necessity. But the tandem presence of an equal number of orphans underscores the significance of family. Lorenzo's father having died, he has been raised by his uncle; Matilda tells us that she, too, had an uncle to thank for her upbringing, her father being dead; Raymond's father dies in the course of the narrative, as does Antonia's remaining parent, her mother. (Interestingly, this is the only mother to appear; none of the other 'orphans' mention theirs.) With the exception of Antonia, each finds an acceptable substitute from within the family to restore the place of guardian or guide, even though technically Lorenzo and Raymond are of sufficient age to be on their own.[27] In these sketches of families failed and newfangled, we find the greatest resonance with French Revolutionary rhetoric and practice, and with fears and hopes for the British nation.[28]

To build the new family, Lewis pierces the 'honorable' myth that class lines be maintained intact. Each of the heroes and heroines who falls passionately in love with someone beneath him or her – Gonzalvo, Lorenzo, Marguerite – and marries out of her or his rank betrays the code of honor supposed to protect the family name (50).[29] Don Christoval becomes the mouthpiece for the traditional sentiments of family 'honor' and patriarchy against which Lorenzo's heroic benevolence can sound all the more loudly. Hearing that Agnes has taken the veil, which Lorenzo construes as the loss of a sister, Christoval exclaims at the gain to Lorenzo's pocket (51). Christoval uncovers the material profit underlying family 'honor.' Neither egalitarian nor meritocratic, the novel is 'liberal' in that wealth can equalize disparities of birth, provided that the family 'thinks liberally upon the subject.' As little as Lorenzo would profit from his sister's fortune, even less would he profit his own sense of honor at the expense of her happiness. Enraged with Raymond at first for impregnating Agnes (110–11), he draws a distinction between selfish and selfless notions of honor (198). Taking Lewis's designation of Lorenzo as 'our hero' at face value (54, 55), in him we see the code of family honor stretching to a pliancy more responsive to the exigencies of the times.

If Lorenzo's heroism consists in his consideration of an equal, how much more heroic and honorable appears Raymond's consideration for those beneath him. Raymond's voluntary relationship to Theodore combines autonomy and affinity in a newer version of the family.[30] Assailed by Theodore to be taken into Raymond's 'service,' Raymond views the prospect with distaste (142). At first chivalrously dubbing Theodore his page, Theodore's 'qualities' soon cause Raymond to treat him 'rather as an adopted child than a domestic' (179).[31] Raymond's emotional paternity exceeds the kind of paternalism voiced by Percy in *Castle Spectre* (1992, 160). While Lewis is less 'radical' in *The Monk* insofar as the lack of noble birth must find wealth as a compensating factor, he is more 'radical' insofar as the bonds between members of disparate ranks can grow so strong as to constitute a permanent union of equals.

Minority honor

Raymond's new 'family' is a nation open to all talents; unlike Radcliffe's, though, it is not meritocratic insofar as loyalty alone can win a place.[32] Theodore impresses Raymond by his acuity, which he puts to strategic use:

> He observed in silence what was going on, nor strove to make himself an agent in the business till my interests required his interference. I equally admired his judgment, his penetration, his address, and his fidelity. This was not the first occasion in which I had found him of infinite use, and I was every day more convinced of his quickness and capacity.
>
> (158)

The 'judgment' and 'penetration' he exhibits prepare him to be more than pander or valet. He adds to his 'address' the ability to speak several languages, so that he could equally become a servant of the state (158). Coupled with his theatrical talents for disguise, Theodore can move easily among all levels of society. In Theodore's ambition, we discover remnants of a Renaissance heroic ideal, theoretically lasting only to the middle of the seventeenth century, according to Ariès, but still present in the Gothic novel (1962, 386–8). It appears there not as a marker of historical accuracy but as reflecting a drive for social mobility.

Theodore's qualities leave little room for discrimination between him and the other heroes in the novel, Raymond and Lorenzo. This relative equality stands in sharp contrast to contemporary social attitudes not only to those of the lower classes, but especially towards foundling children. Since the last Jacobite revolt, fears of a French invasion and recognition of France's superior numbers had spurred support for indigent children, seemingly benevolent but in reality motivated by the desire, should the need arise, for cannon fodder.[33] By the time of *The Monk*, children were viewed as targets for patriotic indoctrination and as counters in that wider process (Colley, 1992,

226–7). While Lewis's use of Theodore as hero skirts either form of naked aggrandizement, it does mark a unique insertion into the Gothic novel to date. Neither the helpless mark for manipulation of the mid-to-late eighteenth century nor the sentimentalized idealization of the later Victorian period,[34] Theodore stands at the midway point in the developing concept of impoverished childhood. Theodore's protean nature is at once his strength and his weakness, his inheritance from his class position that will eventually enable him to rise but which prevents him from assuming the mantle of leadership as yet (139).

Graphic honor

Theodore's gleeful punishment of Cunegonde (163) matches the old-fashioned display of spectacular retribution which sits at the heart of Lewis's ballad, 'Alonzo the Brave and the Fair Imogine,' the poem to which contemporaries amateur and professional most responded.[35] This coarse vestige reveals rifts in social discourse, in this case about the correct modes of punishment, especially as this debate touches on aristocratic and sovereign power.[36] In *The Mysteries of Udolpho*, we have already seen how Montoni receives an invisible punishment at the hands of an authority represented as operating invisibly. Radcliffe's descriptions of desecrated bodies, as of those soldiers killed in Montoni's incursions and in-fighting, are notoriously coy, in comparison to the prolixity of her nature descriptions.[37] Far from coy, Lewis lavishes lingering gazes on physical corruption, thereby connecting his narratorial procedure with his thematic preference for spectacular honor.

Lewis's fascination with the body transcends its devolution to consider its re-volution as well. Though materially weakened by physical harm and psychological distress, the aristocratic body recovers with an ease and rapidity said to amaze all beholders (382). Raymond is but a metonym for that body. Attacked by Baptiste while unarmed, Raymond rises to the moment: 'I sprang from my seat, darted suddenly upon Baptiste, and, clasping my hands round his throat, pressed it so forcibly as to prevent his uttering a single cry. You may remember, that I was remarkable at Salamanca for the power of my arm. It now rendered me an essential service' (133). Essential service can be rendered because that body, as a collective force, proves trustworthy.

Collectivity multiplies observers; the gathering of empirical evidence can be parceled out to surveillance (124–7). Spectacularized and spectatorial, his heroes marshal themselves into the force of authority. Lorenzo convenes the Duke de Medina, Don Ramirez de Mello, chief of the Inquisitional forces, a 'troop of attendants' and a 'party of chosen archers' (333–4) to bring a justice underwritten by the Grand Inquisitor and Raymond's uncle, the Cardinal-Duke. In this troop, we see the representation of the aristocracy as public servants, selflessly gathering themselves into a voluntary corps like those assembling in the years 1793–97 as a non-autocratic means on the part of the British government to supplement manpower shortages in the teeth of invasion fears (Colley, 1992, 287–8).[38] Like good public servants, Lorenzo's 'party' arrests those whom they cannot save from mob vengeance and relinquishes the criminals to the institutional authority of the Inquisition, just as Raymond had earlier permitted soldiers to arrest and punish the banditti who had attacked him and murdered his servant. And like the ideal soldiers they are, none needs fire a single shot to achieve their united ends.

We should not blind ourselves to the inconsistencies in Lewis's portrait. To some extent, authority figures as nightmare: Raymond's familial obligations subject him to the possession of the Bleeding Nun. Once again, progressive and conservative doctrines clash, this time in the guise of chance and fate. On the one hand, Raymond encounters the Bleeding Nun accidentally, when he attempts to abduct Agnes; on the other hand, her ghost has awaited his birth for a hundred years (184, 186). Still, neither all authority nor all institutions are evil. The church at Rome grants the Papal Bull necessary to free Agnes from her vows, thereby recognizing an individual's right to happiness over the claims of the institution, a message more usually allied with middle-class Protestantism than it is with either an aristocratic bias or a Catholic persuasion. Likewise, the Inquisition's plan to pardon Ambrosio bespeaks a dewy individualism beneath the collective threats of auto-da-fé. At the same time, the fact that Raymond's uncle, a cardinal-*duke*, pulls the strings necessary to obtain the Bull, and to arrest the religious malefactors, suggests that we cannot read the novel as advocating either a traditional conservatism or a conventional subversion. In other words, we see again the melding of characteristics in a fantasy of the new leader, part middle-class, part aristocrat, who will head up the imagined post-Revolutionary community.

Spectral honor in *The Italian*

With British naval power once again in 1797 responsible for thwarting the French (Hobsbawm, 1996, 86), it comes as little surprise that Ann

Radcliffe's next novel should refer not only to *The Monk* but also to Walpole's *Otranto* and the naval glory days of the Seven Years' War.[39] Harking back to a less complicated time in its opening setting, the novel very quickly restores a sense of its more immediate quandaries. In so doing, *The Italian* 'presents itself as both a modern project that melts and transforms traditional attachments in favor of new identities and as a reaffirmation of authentic cultural values culled from the depths of a presumed communal past' (Kandiyoti, 1994, 378). Setting lower sights than her previous 'progressive' narratives, in *The Italian* Radcliffe dilutes class mobility, dams up independence, shrinks the manly ideal.[40] In the conflicts between public and private, virtue and honor alike bend to more desperate exigencies.

Mechanization and militarization at home

Domestic relations reveal the entanglement of public and private, honor and virtue:

> the imaginary honours of so noble an alliance vanished, when the terms of obtaining them were considered; and now, that the sound mind of Ellena was left to its own judgment [in contrast to the prudent persuasions of her aunt], she looked with infinitely more pride and preference upon the industrious means, which had hitherto rendered her independent, than on all distinction which might be reluctantly conferred.
>
> (1981, 69)

Virtuous industry provides a deadly independence because it will pain Vivaldi and extinguish the honor of Ellena's vows to him as sanctioned by her now-dead aunt. Conversely, Vivaldi's anguished response to his father's order to renounce Ellena enunciates a false 'heroics' (84) and a misplaced chivalry. Unable to 'reconcile' his filial and affective duties, Vivaldi vows to 'defend the oppressed, and glory in the virtue, which teaches me, that it is the first duty of humanity to do so.' Hierarchizing filial duties as 'inferior' as compared to 'the grandeur of a principle, which ought to expand all hearts and impel all actions,' Vivaldi thinks he supports the 'honour' of his house. His father scorns to treat disobedience as honor or 'degradation' of bloodlines as virtue. Vivaldi insists that no degradation can exist 'where there is no vice,' but that 'there are some few instances in which it is virtuous to disobey.' Conflating 'paradoxical morality' and 'romantic language,' his father concludes by warning Vivaldi that 'you belong to your family, not your family to you; … you are only a guardian of its honour, and not at liberty to dispose of your self' (30–1). This long passage telescopes the terms of debate over virtue as far as Radcliffe is concerned: no individualism, no matter how nobly prompted.

Asserting an almost monarchical precedence, the Marchese reveals correspondences between the familial and the political that had long formed a staple of British political theory. Romance had also long featured this connection.[41] But even in the domestic sphere, we realize that resemblances between victim and oppressor prevent our distinguishing and taking sides. Ellena's 'jealousy of propriety' mirrors that of the Marchese; the Vivaldi family repugnance to her marriage with their son inspires in her the same feelings of pride, disguised as 'delicacy [and] good sense … against a conduct so humiliating and vexatious,' which exhort her to 'preserve her own dignity by independence' (122).[42] Nor can we finally distinguish the private from the public: treachery leaks out from the familial to the socio-political realm.

Scenes of treachery, scenes of instruction

Nothing in the novel torques those firm notions of honor and virtue, of duty versus a culpable complicity, prudence versus timidity (121), more than the Inquisition. In the popular imagination, the Inquisition stood for the marriage of political and religious tyranny. Underscoring the seriousness with which the topic was greeted, the *Monthly Review* devoted two full pages in 1798 to reviewing a *Letter from Citizen Gregoire, Bishop of Blois, to Don Raymond Joseph d'Arce, Archbishop of Burgos, Chief Judge of the Inquisition in Spain, upon the Necessity and Advantage of Suppressing that Tribunal*. Even though his new constitution forbids interfering with other governments, the Bishop objects that 'the maiming of men, the traffic in negroes, slavery, and the inquisition' break 'the code of the rights of nations,' a metonymic reflection with dangerous implications for the *Monthly Review* in the climate of censorship. The reviewer seems unconcerned, conceding only that 'little danger is likely to accrue to these kingdoms from the tribunal of the holy inquisition, yet … we see no certainty that bigotry and superstition may not again have their day' (1798, 455). Further, by implication he casts the Cromwellian interlude as a reign of 'bigotry and superstition,' against the likes of which, from any direction, the British must arm by adopting vigilant allies. British troops may now need to combat the Citizen's flesh and blood, but the 'spiritual' threat of an invading Inquisition can submerge those differences and forge an imaginative alliance in print. The *Review* or its reviewer seem to agree with the Bishop that 'National egotism' constitutes a crime against humanity, and to join with him, however momentarily, in imagining a nationhood at once particular and universalist (455).

Unlike their representation in *The Monk*, in *The Italian* the powers exercised by the Inquisition exceed those of religion; no state body exists to counter its demands. Thus the Inquisition swells within the novel to represent statehood itself. Circulation in this novel occurs through its secret doors, giving access to manipulation and obfuscation (1981, 400–1), shuffling identity of prisoner and guard (387). Active intervention is pinioned; courage, justice, malice, and foolhardiness dance so madly together as to become hopelessly entangled.[43] Martial prowess disappears. A mild temper and gentle manners are only the 'pleasing merits of easy times' (121). No wonder that poetry disappears from this world. Neither poetry nor chivalry can cure a world mechanized and militarized (122).

Instead, the Inquisition is both disease and cure. The Inquisition teaches aristocrats to adopt a lower-class flexibility as one measure of their necessary reform.[44] To that end, Radcliffe tropes the need for sympathy, which exalts human relations. Sympathy levels both gender and class, since the narrator characterizes it as a 'delicate' honor (160), and distributes it equally among Vivaldi, Ellena, and Paolo (79, 220). Radcliffe uses the Inquisition as governing body, educational institution, and, above all, facilitator of a sympathy perhaps devoid of its patronizing associations with benevolence but all the more bracing for its even-handed distribution of terror.

In the countryside, poverty has strained sympathy, hardening hearts as it renders flesh: 'The lean and sallow countenance of poverty stared over their gaunt bones, and habitual discontent had fixed the furrows of their cheeks. They regarded Ellena with only a feeble curiosity, though the affliction in her looks might have interested almost any heart that was not corroded by its own sufferings; nor did the masked faces of her companions excite a much stronger attention' (62). This description marks a significant shift from Radcliffe's other picturesque descriptions of the rural poor, even in countries as torn by civil broil as *Udolpho*'s Italy. We do wrong to read this notice of poverty as just another, perhaps more sublime pictorial effect rather than the social commentary it strives to make. Radcliffe had demonstrated her thoroughgoing interest in the connection between 'political happiness' and 'civil character' in her 1795 *Journey* (1975, 33), a sensitivity possibly sharpened by the crop failures in England of 1795 (1975, 188–216, 206). Sublime nature linked in the public mind with the details of terrible human tragedy. As Anna Seward observed in a letter to the Right Honorable Lady Eleanor Butler, Radcliffe in the *Journey* rendered her tour of the Lake country as impressive as 'the descriptions of the waste desolation this ruinous war has produced in Germany. The political observations are not many, but they are just and pointed' *(1811, 150)*. Giving those anonymous poor a habitation and a name, as Radcliffe does with Spalatro, makes those objects of pity available for our sympathy and for extended homiletic treatment, simultaneously subjectifying and objectifying them.

Discerning a villainy tempered by suffering in Spalatro, Ellena ceases to fear him (210). Sympathy enables Vivaldi to shake off a slavish adherence to reason – that watchword of the Revolution – as the apogee of human nature (198). At the beginning of the novel, trapped in the dungeon of Paluzzi, despair for himself negates Vivaldi's interest in strangers (82). As a result of this new-found flexibility towards strangers, Vivaldi can forgive both his parents (388–9). Conducing equally to spiritual and material credit, sympathy makes immanent the otherworldly tendency of the sentimental novel, at the same time that it makes imminent the arrival of the hero envisaged in the 1790 Prospectus to the *Anti-Jacobin*: he who exhibits 'exquisite DELICACY OF SENTIMENT' with a 'system of general TOLERATION, IMPARTIALITY, INDULGENCE, FORGIVENESS, CONCESSION, & ACCOMMODATION, which can alone render the OPERATION OF MORALITY certain, because it alone makes the practice of it easy.'

Educating virtue

Radcliffe makes concrete the call for '*system.*' Educating the body and mind at once, the Inquisition turns virtue and honor inside out. Marrying truth and secrecy, the Inquisition momentarily turns heroes into informers and spies.

Because Vivaldi has subscribed to the Inquisition's oath binding him to 'reveal the truth, and keep forever secret whatever he might see or hear in the apartment' of the Inquisitors (201), the monk di Zampari can enmesh Vivaldi in his plot to destroy Schedoni, forcing Vivaldi to act as an intermediary witness by summoning those whose testimony can more directly implicate Schedoni. Yet the novel does not exonerate Vivaldi from a duty to the system. Vivaldi's allegiance to the Inquisition's rules may have been extorted; nevertheless, it forms a genuine impediment to his freedom of choice, just as his position as son to a rank-jealous family complicates his ability to freely choose a mate or to live beyond the duties he has to the maintenance of that family. Now it grows impossible to discern degradation and vice, to locate those instances where 'it is virtuous to disobey' (312). Two hundred pages earlier, Ellena had teetered on the edge of a similar moral quicksand: 'If it were possible that I could consent to practise deceit... what could it avail me? ... I should be punished even for having sought to avoid injustice ... for such a chance of benefit, there would certainly be little policy in forfeiting one's integrity' (97). The Bishop of Blois had referred to the Inquisition as a 'passive instrument in the hands of policy,' reversing the agency Radcliffe attributes to it, but resonating rhetorically with the dilemma she imagines. Policy and common sense threaten to strangle rectitude and justice.

Vivaldi turns to a literal definition of knowledge to help him equivocate: if he does not *know* that he knows, he cannot bear false witness (326). Ellena receives the same advice from Olivia, forced to seek monastic shelter to escape the murderous Schedoni. Here again, the domestic or private spills over into the public. Retreat for women, the resort to a convent, only appears to be shelter. Rather, like Vivaldi's 'prison,' it demands either complicity with the rules or the strength to endure physical punishment. Consequently, while Ellena maintains the moral necessity of ingenuousness, Olivia urges that the need for self-defense makes deceit morally acceptable (97, 126–7). Fusing 'Natural' and 'supernatural' law, Olivia's advice introduces the idea that a kind of 'virtuous' temporizing relieves predicaments that hasty and inflexible resistance only exasperate.

If neither Ellena nor Vivaldi can oppose their bodies to the law, so their bodies fail to give them intellectual guidance. The Inquisition perplexes Vivaldi as to the right course of action because it removes from him the ability to make *empirical* observations. As we have seen, this talent has amounted to a necessity for all previous Gothic heroes and heroines. At the beginning of *The Italian*, empiricism saves Vivaldi from the imaginative pleasures and dangers of superstition (19, 48–9, 58, 79). In contrast, sheer courage shields Paulo from superstition. Both represent a kind of materiality. But in the Inquisition appearance is ghostly; it operates through silence and innuendo (193, 195). One figure stands as representative of this institutional power. He is the monk who warns Vivaldi in the ruins of Paluzzi, and who later shows up in the prison (305–25). He moves without sound, he remains invisible to the guards (306) – very like the officers in Rome who punish Montoni and restore Emily's patrimony from afar or off stage. Since this man implicates Vivaldi in the sequence of spying and informing, Vivaldi must establish the man's identity to realize his right course of action: complicity or refusal (313–49). If a supernatural being, Vivaldi might be licensed to obey. If a man, ironically, he might too literally become Vivaldi's 'familiar,' as the Inquisitorial officers responsible for torturing prisoners are called.

To maintain his integrity and rectitude while spying and informing, Vivaldi must learn to draw the correct inferences.[45] Hence, reflections upon motive multiply (346). These kinds of oscillating speculations occur over and over again as we proceed into the depths of the trial scenes, just as the narrative becomes increasingly qualified, through syntactic short-circuiting, interrupted periodicity, and the demurral of the conditional. The insistent problematizing of truth and lie, of fact versus appearance, underscores the need to rely on less material witnesses and to ascertain probability.

Having almost coopted the firm grounds upon which either characters or readers could base judgments, Radcliffe redresses the balance. But her reinsertions of hope seem less scrupulous about their fidelity to fact or probability than they do to wish-fulfillment. Secretive operation is suborned as necessary to the efficient workings of a juridical and legal body; neither courage nor patronage can effect liberty.[46] Heroism attains a clean conscience (321), an air 'calm and dignified,' and a countenance that expresses 'solemn energy' (336). And this heroism extends both to Vivaldi and the representatives of the Inquisition; the grand inquisitor, or vicar-general, as Radcliffe calls him, casting an aura of military valor over his conduct, attains a 'glorious candour' equally attributed to Vivaldi's equivocations (352, 337). Vivaldi's newly developed ratiocination not only helps him steer the inquisitorial course but also gives him private hope at a distance about his domestic affairs (367). His *learned* adeptness at sifting probability and fact makes him, *ex post facto*, a very 'common sense' hero, the attribute the British most appropriated to themselves as their national characteristic. And if empirical talent requires a disciplined use of leisure to acquire, making it supranormal, 'common sense' rewards those in 'normal' conditions: under pressure, unschooled in scientific principles, or isolated from centers of observation.

Moreover, imputations of spying and informing, or of a base humility and servitude in Vivaldi's position, get washed away as circumstance of time or person becomes the means of determining right from wrong. Giving vital information into the hands of those fit to use it wisely bleaches the stain of informing. Vivaldi can thereby assert an independence in the midst of dependence. His role in the trial enables him to assert his own rights (331, 343, 350); the Inquisition becomes Vivaldi's mouthpiece, in that they repeat and thus legitimize the questions and objections he enters (351). Finally, Vivaldi's role as private witness and judge of crimes in the final confrontation between Schedoni and di Zampari melds the individual and the institutional (389–405).

While not the martial hero of *The Castles of Athlin and Dunbayne* or *The Sicilian*, then, neither is he 'passive and inept' with 'unlined' face, an 'inferior version of the charming and benevolent heroine' (Todd, 1981, 264). Vivaldi is the representative figure of a fully mediated authority. Vivaldi's schooling in the submission of private interest to public duty, and the rewards he garners as a result, resemble the lessons being learned daily by men in the navy (Rodger, 1996, 314–27), a point that returns us circularly to the beginning. As Macherey exhorts us, '[W]e ought to be scrutinising what is there from the first rather than what we will know at the last, which will not be entirely mysterious... The time of the novel separates the founding moment of illusions from the irruption of a truth which is also a promise of safety' (1978, 29). With Macherey, I see the beginning as only 'initially incompatible' with the end (36). The 'English travelers' reading the manuscript encounter a restored humanity that has changed its Italian coloring for English.

Sympathetic nationalism

Paolo's intense reaction to his native land figures as the kind of 'Italian' response that must be Anglicized. Upon seeing Lake Celano spread before them, Paulo had exclaimed at its beauty. While the landscape resembles that of his home, Paulo declares that he could never love it as much as the area surrounding Naples, even if Celano were 'an hundred times finer' (158). Paulo's native enthusiasm, his 'stroke of nationality' as Vivaldi calls it (159), produces only amusement. Moreover, his very local patriotism qualifies him as a lower-class hero because he imagines his relation to his land as unmediated. If Radcliffe resembles pre-nationalist thinkers, in that she shows institutional obligations as only one among a range of ties emanating from religion and the family and erases any 'significant potential for conflict between these claims' (Kelly, 1995, 102), her dual use of representation, as narratively enforcing a willing submission to mediation, makes her ideas coextensive with a more fully developed nationalism. Like Vivaldi, Paolo must learn to accommodate mediation.

Paulo's nationalism is reborn as a sympathetic identification with Vivaldi: 'here I am, sure enough! Dancing by moonlight, in my own dear bay of Naples, with my own dear master and mistress, in safety, and as happy *almost* as myself' (413). Having justly linked 'his' land with 'his' master and mistress, Paolo can now enjoy full 'ownership.' The nation must be composed of an emotional affinity, deflected through authority, that substitutes for genuine class mobility.

The artificiality inherent in this affinity cannot be fully banished from the scene. When the Marchese 'condescended to give Paulo a hearty shake by the hand, and to thank him warmly for the bravery and fidelity he had displayed in his master's interest' (407), that condescending handshake affirms the close connection at the same time that its condescension reminds us of the social distance actually obtaining, as Bourdieu has argued (1990, 127). Vivaldi's response to Paolo forms an ironic commentary on this fiction of identity: 'I rejoice in your happiness, my good Paulo ... almost as much as in my own; though I do not entirely agree with you as to the comparative proportion of each' (414). Vivaldi's qualifying 'almost' undermines the equality evoked when, just previously, he had presented Paulo to the assembled noble company as his 'faithful friend, and chief deliverer' (407). But Ellena's speech that follows immediately sweeps the lingering doubt out of sight: '"Paulo!" said Ellena, "I am indebted to you beyond any ability to repay; for to your intrepid affection your master owes his present safety. I will not attempt to thank you for your attachment to him; my care of your welfare shall prove how well I know it"' (414). Ellena's public declaration of that obligation reasserts the traditional role of aristocracy, at the same time that it acknowledges obliquely the fragility of reciprocal ties.

Conversely, hero and heroine must begin their new life together avowing their sense of *noblesse oblige*. Wedding each other as well as their tenantry, Vivaldi and Ellena take up residence in land styled like 'that of England, and of the present day' (412). Ellena shines forth as the royal apex of this society; clothed as a 'queen,' she and Vivaldi also treat their subjects with royal liberality: 'this entertainment was not given to persons of distinction only, for both Vivaldi and Ellena had wished that all the tenants of the domain should partake of it, and share the abundant happiness which themselves possessed; so that the grounds, which were extensive enough to accommodate each rank, were relinquished to a general gaiety' (413). It is a hierarchical, not a republican, generality: Paulo may serve as a 'master of the revels,' yet he lords it over 'a party of his particular associates,' showing his full participation in the distinctions preserved in this idealized melding.[47]

Paulo has the last words in the novel. But his words prove how loyalty to an individual aristocrat stands as a metaphor for serving the interests of the state:

> Who, I say, would have guessed we should ever be let loose again! Who would have thought we should ever know what it is to be happy! Yet here we are all abroad once more! All at liberty! And may run, if we will, straight forward, from one end of the earth to the other, and back again without being stopped! May fly in the sea, or swim in the sky, or tumble head over heels into the moon! For remember, my good friends, we have no lead in our consciences to keep us down!
>
> (414)

The strength gained from having shored up the nation with these bands of affection will arm the extension of that nation. Paulo's repeated cries of 'O! *Giorno felíce!*' ring with the optimism of Britain triumphant, at home and abroad.

Possessive honor in *The Midnight Assassin*

Should Edmund Burke have taken up a copy of *The Midnight Assassin: or, Confession of the Monk Rinaldi* in 1802, he might have been struck by a horror as great as that he felt when contemplating imaginatively the desecration of Marie Antoinette. For the chapbook redaction turns Burke's 'midnight assassins' and 'wicked abettors' into Italian Catholics motivated by vengeance and greed. While preserving the 'high Rank, great Splendour of descent, great personal elegance and outward accomplishments' so cherished by Burke for its hero, the chapbook makes those ingredients the basis of an individualistic 'sensibility of politics,' to reverse the phrase used by W. J. T. Mitchell to characterize Burke's figural procedures. Institutional authority and constitutional tradition, the trenchant cornerstones of Burke's thought and the more tentative underpinnings of Radcliffe, have leached out. And unlike Radcliffe's *The Italian*, from which *The Midnight Assassin* borrows its persons, situations, and events, no community of ranks formed by the hero and heroine's marriage recrystallizes at the end (1802, 72). Nevertheless, enough Burkean or Radcliffean slag remains to make Burke's private comments function as an eerily prescient dust-jacket blurb, confirming Macherey's observation that 'there is no innocent work: the apparent spontaneity of the easy book pledged to an immediate consumption assumes the application of familiar methods which may often have been derived from the most subtle literature, and can be smuggled from one work to another' (1978, 27). Like Burke, *The Midnight Assassin* 'rewrites the sumptuous, public display of female beauty, which was the sign of an aristocratic culture, as a domesticated object of the male gaze that evokes pity and love but never admiration or fear' (Zerilli, 1992, 55). Like Radcliffe, the anonymous author privileges virtue as the hallmark of heroes and embeds a fictional British nation in the margins of the tale.

The text flaunts its participation in the transmission of ideas of nationalism in its opening frame: 'strange as it must seem to a British reader, [the English gentleman] was told that the superstitious crowd brought him food, for the church laws protected him' (1802, 3). Informed that the assassin has received shelter within the church, the English traveler exclaims against the lack of punitive justice. His Italian friends remark, 'If these crimes were to be punished *as with you* ... the country would suffer much in its population' (A2, emphasis added). Drawing a firm distinction between the respective countries' legal systems, the text at first seems to operate in line with Linda Colley's 1995 analysis of nationalism as a construct that occurs in opposition to an Other. But if Otherness forms the acid etching, a more positive image also emerges on the plate. While the reader invoked is 'British,' Englishness quickly takes over as a synecdochic displacement of Britishness. These English travelers feel no curiosity about or interest in the architecture of the church, whose convent name changes from that of the 'Black Penitents' to that of the 'Black Crucifix,' underscoring the Catholicism of the tale; they only desire information about the mysterious man. The Church itself becomes a metaphor for the exotic terror of its inhabitants; the gloominess of the confessional provokes the travelers' horrified reaction, much as does the assassin. In Radcliffe, the English travelers' journey is innocent tourism. Here, it has a darker purpose; the travelers 'make an excursion' whose mode resembles a fact-finding mission by human rights activists such as Howard. Their guide exists solely to answer 'the questions of inquisitive strangers,' perhaps a play on the 'inquisitorial strangers' we will meet in the prisons at Rome.

Whether framing that reader as English or British, the subject position occupied is relentlessly male. No longer is our approach to the heroine mediated through the sensibility of the hero. Instead the

Ellena character, here called Amanda Lusigni, is exhibited to our inspection:

> Of all the modest, dignified, and enchanting females who paid their devotion in the church of San Lorenzo, at Naples, Amanda Lusigni was the most attracting. The melody of her voice corresponded with the grace and delicacy of her figure, and the tones, which with exquisite expression she uttered, led to a farther anxiety to inspect the countenance whence they proceeded.
>
> (4)

'Farther' opportunities arise for us and for Giovanni when he spies her through a window of her home. The shorthand description combines spirituality and sensuality; we see at once 'her devotional look, her loose tresses, her unveiled countenance, and elegant drapery' (7). Proclaiming her modestly clothed, the passage simultaneously strips her of individual personality, turning her into an object for our delectation.[48] The 'elegant drapery' she wears belongs to no discernible fashion; it serves only to adorn a body invoked in adjectives of abandon. In contrast, Radcliffe's description coyly preserves decorum through its aestheticization, a subliming that rationally permits a few tresses to escape from the confines of a loose net around her hair while it allusively compares her appearance to Greek models (12).

Radcliffe's representation of Ellena and Olivia also hews to Greek models of womanhood in that her women participate as thinking and acting human beings. Her representation conforms more closely than does the chapbook to women's actual circumstances at the time.[49] In contrast, Amanda loses all depth of intelligence, compassion, or ethics. Imprisoned at San Stefano, like her precursor, she quickly gives over the contest between pride and love: 'In short, Love triumphed, and she only feared that Di Sardo would remain forever ignorant of her monastic retreat' (20). Her willing immersion in the domestic sphere not only fosters the separation of the sexes but also rewrites that separation as voluntarily undergone.

Amanda's requisite transparency makes her vulnerable to misrepresentation and rumor. Since we know from the start of the tale that Amanda comes of a 'deceased but illustrious house' (6), it seems that parental objections to the marriage rest solely on the calumny which has been spread against her (12): 'the Marquis then informed his son, that his opposition arose from the most correct and convincing proofs of her baseness' (14). Details of this 'baseness' do not appear, but they implicitly embrace her unseemly eagerness to wed Giovanni, a species of striving after class mobility; she is compared metaphorically to a spider or to a con artist who has 'inveigled' Giovanni through her 'artifices' (12). Not surprisingly, Helena's (Olivia) advice to temporize draws no objection from Amanda (25). The text betrays its confusion and its ideology in these deviations from the Radcliffean model. When the 'resolution' to thwarted love comes from the disclosure of the very same information respecting Amanda's family that the Marquis had always known (56), transparency is reasserted not as the possession of the female but as the gift of the male.[50]

If Giovanni, and by implication the male reader, securely owns the female, so he securely owns himself. Giovanni feels no conflict between his duties of succoring the innocent and submitting to parental authority. The Marquis predicates his opposition solely on Giovanni's intention to marry Amanda (the Ellena character). No hint leaks out that the Marquis might feel justified in protecting family honor. Giovanni responds to his father's ultimatum by calling him a 'Cruel dictator' and a 'rigid parent' (12), which indeed the chapbook makes him seem. Again, no sense of horror arises in Giovanni when he considers that his mother's confessor may be involved in calumniating Amanda or poisoning her aunt. Evil intentions or acts sunder family ties (15).

Vivaldi's conflict between filial duty and egalitarian principle vanishes in the flattened caricature of Giovanni. Giovanni's rational capacity for deduction, mentioned almost in the same breath, ratifies his calculations about where and when to distribute loyalty (15). In comparison with the chapbook's assertion of 'cause and effect,' Vivaldi's cogitations are characterized merely as 'surmise' (46). Security of opinion matches the sense Giovanni maintains of the security of his person. Whereas Paulo and Vivaldi spend the night in the dungeon of Paluzzi in despairing exhaustion, Giovanni and Lupo 'laid down and sunk to sleep' (23). Nothing batters Giovanni's confidence in his physical or intellectual abilities, despite the fact that he can neither fight his way to freedom nor penetrate Rinaldi's duplicity (16). Believing in the existence of a 'chain of cause and effect ... he determined to discover the truth, to meet the slanderer of Amanda, and compel the confessor, or his agent, to reveal the mystery of such conduct'(15). Thus he feels no qualms when called upon by the Inquisition to summon Amato (Ansaldo) and Rinaldi (62).

Giovanni's independence of thought and action corresponds to the privatization of authority throughout. This privatization colors the frame tale itself. Unlike the situation in Radcliffe's novel, where the possession of the manuscript recording the deeds of Schedoni resides in the hands of the Church, thereby confirming the impression that institutions preserve order, the chapbook places the manuscript in private Italian hands. In Radcliffe, the 'student of Padua' records the narrative 'partly as an exercise, and partly in return for some trifling services' rendered him by the friar (4); in *The Midnight Assassin*, the student writer acts upon commission to satisfy individual curiosity (4). Within the tale proper, privatization of authority diminishes the sense of pervasive evil. We no longer feel that the Inquisition seeks to entrap its victims; Giovanni suffers no visit from a man claiming to be likewise a victim of the Inquisition and offering him sympathy. Whereas in *The Italian*, private agency perverts institutional authority, as in di Zampari's using the cover of the Institution to effect personal revenge, in *The Midnight Assassin* the same character's actions receive full vindication (59–60, 63). By eliminating the trial scene in the Inquisition which demands questions of Rinaldi, the chapbook makes his 'confession,' so foregrounded by the title, seem alone the product of Giovanni's presence in his cell.

At the same time that individuals take center stage, class relations shrink to the bare necessities. Rural poverty once more disappears from view. Again, this shriveling affects both the narration and the narrative. We are spared any description of prolix peasants and servants (the shepherds, 37; Beatrice/Annetta, 65). Intradiegetically, the peasant guide to Rinaldi and Amanda can furnish only histories concerning total strangers and especially strangers of the same class as the auditors. Thus, the inset tale of the 'ruinated castle' belonging to the Baron di Lodi (Cambrusca in Radcliffe) prompts no objections from Rinaldi as to the circumlocution of the tale (50–1). True, the account is less circumstantial, but its unopposed appearance severs any implied connection between Rinaldi and di Lodi, a point that remains murky in Radcliffe. When connections do exist, as between Rinaldi and Lipari (Spalatro), Rinaldi refuses to hear of them (52). Relations between intradiegetic narrator and narratee here have so withered that the guide omits to make any veiled threats against Rinaldi. But the constricted intercourse between the classes does not emanate from the villain alone. The fishermen who ultimately furnish the hint as to the direction Amanda's abductors have taken 'take no notice of Giovanni'; he learns of their involvement by eavesdropping (27). In contrast, Vivaldi had already recruited the aid of the fishermen (107). Lupo no longer waxes poetic on the advantages of his native countryside at

Celano (37). He also fails to remonstrate against his separation from his master in the prisons of the Inquisition (41). Their reunion occupies three sentences, as opposed to the four pages the scene earns in Radcliffe.

Social relations seem to exist primarily to furnish contrasts. For instance, Giovanni's role as a covert 'British' hero rises most clearly to the surface in his interactions with Catholics and Catholicism. Radcliffe had also been careful to insure her hero from calumny as a Catholic.[51] The chapbook repeats the characterization of the hero as kneeling only to 'avoid singularity' when he visits the shrine of Our Lady of Mount Carmel (1802, 28; 1981, 117). This repetition where so much has been eliminated suggests the importance of portraying a supposedly Italian hero as a good British Protestant. A greater difference between Radcliffe and the chapbook version exists in the caves of the shrine, when Giovanni and Amanda attempt to escape. Like Radcliffe's version, they are betrayed by the brother supposedly bribed to aid them, and they, too, encounter an aged priest who eventually lends them his assistance (36). However, Giovanni does not threaten the priest, nor do we receive a warning about acting precipitously. This omitting to condemn a trait rebuked by Radcliffe makes sense, given that the whole thrust of chapbooks is precipitate; they compress and hurry a story to its end.

This compression maintains the multiplicity of events but removes any interiority or reflection on the meaning of those events. Eliminating the inner thoughts of the hero from our purview disables us from witnessing 'the private self being constituted narratively through isolated reflection on its relation to circumstances,' as John Bender says in a different context (1987, 77). Nevertheless, despite its many differences, notably the absence of psychological modeling, underlying similarities remain, this time to Lewis, Burke, and Radcliffe. These similarities help us see why Macherey held 'the more or less accurate fake... often the most characteristic of a genre or style. Here is to be found in a pure if not original state all that defines the type. The skilful imitation can be more revealing than the model' (1978, 28). If *The Midnight Assassin* renounces Radcliffe and Burke's fascination with the psychological, it does so to restore the corporeal to the center of Gothic. Originally conventional to medieval and Renaissance iconography of aristocracy, the corporeal still forms the heart of Burke's figural language and his gendering of politics, as his linking of birth and rank with 'great personal elegance and outward accomplishments' in the epigraph shows.[52] As Roger Horrocks and David Simpson have noted of the period, the 'emphasis on the physical in the cult of manliness' struck against French and German theorizing and fed into British self-representation as a nation of virile common sense (Horrocks, 1995, 151). Like Radcliffe, a paratactic structure, now grown almost impulsive, hurtles the tale along. Whether elongated or truncated, both Radcliffe and the anonymous author show an interest in the ability of narration to measure narrative duration.[53] In *The Italian*, the friar insists that he must provide a manuscript since the telling of events would 'occupy a week' (3), restoring a preoccupation with consumption to a novel that disguises its basis as a consumer artifact, as when we are told that the 'English travelers' read the manuscript in their hotel room.[54] In *The Midnight Assassin*, that scene of reading obliquely underscores the national utility of the tale for the 'British reader': the travelers receive the manuscript '[O]n returning home' (4). In *The Midnight Assassin*'s extreme compression and homogenization of events, 'home,' too, becomes homogeneous; the 'British reader' becomes English. An early version of Debord's 'consumable pseudo-cyclical time' (1970, 147–53), in this time and place we no longer need to aspire to the condition of citizens or aristocrats because the nation as a fantasy structure has already been realized. We do not need to assent to being represented because we are already representative.

6
No Child's Play: the Gothic Chapbooks

> It is impossible that anything should be universally tasted and
> approved by a multitude, though they are only the rabble of a
> nation, which hath not in it some peculiar aptness to please
> and gratify the mind of man.
>
> (Addison, *Spectator*, 70)

Obviously, those seeking political rights in the years spanning 1800 to
1820, the years in which the chapbooks under consideration here were
produced, knew that they were neither representative nor represented.
How much and in what manner the chapbooks spoke to them forms
the burden of speculation in this chapter. These uncertainties brush
against a raw nerve of literary history: *to what extent popular literature
serves radical or hegemonic desires* has been the question plaguing historians of reading and of the book. This question has two axes. First, it
requires knowledge of the content of the chapbooks. Second, it
depends upon some information concerning the actual makeup of the
audience.

Historians of reading and of the book have assumed that a natural fit
obtains between the two hinges: locate the audience and you will automatically understand the substance. When they admit perplexity, they
do so because the paucity of written records detailing either who wrote
these works or who read them has thwarted certainty about audience
profile. Nor does material history aid us very much. Even though eighteenth-century publishers' accounts show that chapbooks of various
generic types circulated in the thousands, we cannot break these
figures down into comparative sales by title or genre, or by class or
political persuasion of purchaser.[1] Writing polemics for their own
product rather than history, Coleridge and Wordsworth did not let the

want of facts prevent them from giving their opinion. To them, the chapbooks signified commodified consumption of low-brow stimulants as opposed to the 'symbolic "reception" of high-cultural artefacts' (Klancher, 1987, 17). As such, the Gothic chapbooks that interest us would mark out a measure of resistance to hegemonic influence.

But perhaps the search for a one-to-one correspondence between genre and class misleads us as fully as do Wordsworth's and Coleridge's comments. As James Raven warns, '[Q]uestions of readership and reading strategies ... can be blurred rather than clarified by the recon-struction of an imaginary reader, either as implied by the author's text or by isolated contemporary commentators' (1992, 6).[2] As I will argue in discussing the Gothic chapbooks below, two paradoxes emerge, each of which sheds light on histories of readership: first, readership did not confine itself to any one economic or status population (the first section); second, the chapbooks serve both radical and hegemonic desires (the second and third sections). Radical strains beckon in the seemingly open invitation to join chapbook heroes. But the chapbooks ultimately beg off from a fully imagined cross-class mobility. Heroic models whose social relations fix women and servants in a hierarchical order insinuate a more palpable conservatism. Accordingly, the third section details the radical illusion before revealing that radicalism to be a mirage. The fourth section returns to the problem of readerly identification. It posits that a hypostasized masculinity blurs the class retreat, and preserves the heroic appeal for male readers. Hence, this section considers the subject position of the reader by comparing rep-resentations of male and female characters. Subject position in the chapbooks is enforced not only through verbal but also through visual narrative. Branching off into a separate section, this latter topic will force us to consider the connection between visual desire, as captured by the illustrations, and an increasingly isolated individualism (the fifth section). Finally, at the end of this chapter, we will examine the chapbooks' nationalism and imperialism by reading heroic tales of colonialist adventure and Scottish deeds.

Circulating ownership

In his *Journal of a West India Proprietor*, Matthew Lewis provides evi-dence for the heterogeneity of reading matter and population aboard the ship carrying him to Jamaica:

> At ten o'clock yesterday evening little Jem Parsons [the cabin boy]... came on deck ... to read by the light of the moon. I looked at the

boy's book ... and found that it was 'The Sorrows of Werter.' I asked
who had lent him such a book, and whether it amused him? He said
that it had been made a present to him, and so he had read it
almost through, for he had got to Werter's dying; though, to be
sure, he did not understand it all, nor like very much what he
understood; for he thought the man a great fool for killing himself
for love. I told him I thought every man a great fool who killed
himself for love or for anything else: but had he no books but 'The
Sorrows of Werter?' – Oh dear, yes, he said, he had a great many
more; he had got 'The Adventures of a Louse', which was a very
curious book, indeed; and he had got besides 'The Recess', and
'Valentine and Orson', and 'Roslin Castle', and a book of Prayers,
just like the Bible; but he could not but say that he liked 'The
Adventures of a Louse' the best of any of them.

(1969, 25–6)

On a later Sunday, Lewis finds the crew all reading: the carpenter
engages a comedy; the second mate pours over 'The Six Princesses of
Babylon'; a third reads a tract 'On the Management of Bees'; while a
group gathers round to hear *The Sorrows of Werter* read aloud. Lewis
ponders: 'I was surprised to find that (except Edward's Fairy Tale) none
of them were reading works that were at all likely to amuse them
(Smollett or Fielding, for instance), or any which might interest them as
relating to their profession, such as voyages or travels; much less any
which had the slightest reference to the particular day' (34–5). Lewis's
assessment of what might 'amuse' members of the merchant marine, like
his assumption that none of the readers understands what he reads and
partakes of books only out of reverence for the printed word as an act of
'good work' (35), misses the most interesting details in his own account.
With the exception of the tract 'On the Management of Bees,' each reads
an exotic adventure tale – or romance – with a hero challenged by and
challenging the world. Detecting how truly unrepresentative of his own
personal station is each man's reading, Lewis's comments are a sketchy
but useful indicator not only of catholic reading tastes but also of the
attraction heroes held for readers at every level of the social scale.

Bibliographic evidence drawn from the Gothic chapbooks seconds
Lewis's impression. People of means read and circulated inexpensive
popular culture. For instance, in my first chapter I mentioned the
volume bound as *Tales and Romances*. Julia Nolyen names the book as
her possession on the flyleaf, calling it *Ghosts Spectres Apparitions* 1818.
The family or one of its members may not have purchased all the chapbooks outright. At the end of the fifth chapbook, on the reverse of the

illustration to number six, a different hand announces his rights; though the corner is torn off, we can just make out the name 'Thomas – Lucessa.' Perhaps trades were made. However the volume reached its final, collected form, the Nolyen children appear to have been proud of their editorial efforts. Each records his or her successive possession: Julia's brother T. (later in volume two we learn that he, too, is a Thomas) owned it in 1810; after him came John, who recorded not only the text's but also the family's peregrinations. First, Black Tinkers Hill is inscribed, then crossed out to be replaced by St Patrick Hill, only to give way to Woodston which is also eliminated, though no locale comes to stand in its stead.

The fluidity of the Gothic chapbooks represents a miniature version of the shift 'from pattern to systematic randomness' intrinsic to a society transitioning from agrarian to industrial, as Ernest Gellner has explained it:

> Industrial society is very different. Its territorial and work units are *ad hoc*: membership is fluid, has a great turnover, and does not generally engage or commit the loyalty and identity of members... The *nation* is now supremely important, thanks both to the erosion of sub-groupings and the vastly increased importance of a shared, literary-dependent culture.
>
> (1983, 63)[3]

As the Gothic chapbooks circulate from high to low and back again, they inscribe themselves as part of the 'shared, literary-dependent culture' Gellner describes. Moreover, the chapbooks prey on the authority preempted first by the romance revivalists for literary history, and subsequently by the full-length Gothic novelists, to elevate their own product onto an equivalent plane, in so doing systematizing the randomness of cultural production.

If the cross-class readership indicates exchange, the formal features of the chapbooks assert interchangeability. Whereas the allusive echoes of earlier Gothic novels found in each successive production, beginning with Clara Reeve's use of Walpole in her *Old English Baron*, spoke not only to Gothic's reliance upon repetition as generic formula but also demonstrated the way such repetition encodes the social nature of the genre, these allusive echoes diminish in the chapbooks, which likewise eliminate all sublime scenery, all frame tales, in fact all of the literary hallmarks thought to comprise the Gothic. In part, this may be due to their compression: most restrict themselves to thirty-six pages.

But repetition appears in a different, related guise: reiterated verbal formulae and reconstituted plot conventions, reduced to their barest essentials. More important, their reductive plots make them virtually interchangeable. And this interchangeability seems to have been as much a goal, if not of the authors, then of the publishers and readers, as it was an accident. For instance, *Raymond Castle; or, The Ungrateful Nephew*, published by W. Mason and collected in the Nolyen children's *Tales and Romances*, vol. I, reappears under the guise of *Glanville, A Romance*, with a different publisher, in *The Entertainer*. Frontispiece illustrations were often used for more than one story. Chapbook number eight in *Tales and Romances*, vol. I, purports to be *The Avenger, or, The Mysterious Assassin. A Terrific Tale*, a story set in the close of seventeenth-century Sweden, written by Harvey Belmont and printed for Dean and Munday. Yet it bears a frontispiece identical with that announcing Isaac Crookenden's *Horrible Revenge, or, The Monster of Italy!* published by Harrild in 1812, with its temporal setting during the reign of Henry IV of France.

What allusion does occur harkens back to the Gothic, because medieval, past of *literary* history. Another of those private volumes housed in the Sadleir-Black library, *The Entertainer*, containing collected ephemera transmuted into cultural artifacts, envelops a series within the series. Denominated *Canterbury Tales*, the Gothic mock-medieval epic includes not *The Prioress's Tale*, *The Nun's Priest's Tale*, nor any of the other familiar Chaucerian titles, but chapbook stories called *The Great Devil's Tale; or, the Castle of Morbano*; *The Old Abbey Tale; or, Village Terrors*; *The British Sailor's Tale*; and, in the only nod to Chaucer, *The Knight's Tale*. In so doing, the chapbook title suggests an equivalence between high and low forms of literary culture. This spurious equivalence appears in tiny details, like the use of 'chapter' divisions by the anonymous author of *The Spectre Mother*. The seemingly parodic repetition of the Gothic evinces what Gerard Genette characterizes as the message behind such repetition: that it asserts such qualities as fundamental, as already there, at the same time that it betrays the anxiety that such a claim is not true. Like Johnson's stone, it functions as a kind of heuristic wish-fulfillment.

Encircling time

Drawing on the national value assigned to literary medievalism, Gothic chapbooks likewise assert their national significance by inviting their readers into a space and time that collapses past and present, foreign and domestic, thereby rehearsing the full-length Gothic novels. *The Three Ghosts of the Forest, A Tale of Horror*, from 1803, betrays a fascination with bourgeois detail that reminds us of Clara Reeve: Isabella can escape from her medieval prison because a servant leaves the door open, while he goes to 'clear away some weeds, which the heavy fall of rain had driven and stopped up a drain, which was in danger of overflowing the Castle' (16). England lurks behind the foreign disguise of 1806's *Fatal Secrets, or Etherlinda di Salmoni*. Supposedly set in Sicily, one castle is called Boswell Banks while another bears the name Water Beach. More overt comparisons appear: Sicilians and English are said to be identical in dress, and the two countries' political organizations to resemble one another (28). In *Adolphus and Louisa,* an anonymous entry bound with a redaction of Radcliffe's *The Mysteries of Udolpho*, the hero and heroine flee her father by leaving Italy for England. On board, they are befriended by the captain and a merchant and his wife, passengers who introduce them, upon arrival, to 'the best circles of fashion', and who shelter them until their marriage can be consummated (n.d., 32). For their honeymoon, they travel to Brighton, which receives praise.

Narratorial admonishment frequently reveals the current events lurking behind the antique costumes. For instance, in *Adolphus and Louisa* the narrator interjects the message that parents have a duty to warn off unworthy suitors but not to ruin their own or their children's lives by obstinate refusal in cases that are unconquerable (31). Conversely, past attitudes towards marriage supposedly resonate more with the Golden Rule than with the greed for gold, unlike the way the chapbook redaction of *The Mysteries of Udolpho* characterizes the debased temper of the present, as when we are told that St Aubert could have repaired his fortunes by marriage, but 'in those days, marriage was not, as at present, a business of interest or convenience' (n.d., 5). The titular précis advertises the importance of money by foregrounding 'the Attempt of Count Morano to forcibly carry her off, AND OBTAIN POSSESSION OF HER INHERITANCE.' Yet the explicitly egalitarian attitude taken towards love and marriage voids this interest. In *The Three Ghosts of the Forest,* the narrator blames the villain's depredations on an indulged childhood and irreligiousness, 'the use of the present day' (1803, 23), and declaims against riches as having too much influence, blinding the good as to the faults of the wicked (27).

Even when authors eschew explicit commentary, they draw their morals with a heavy hand. A Baron de Hainthal promotes the happiness of the young and grants his daughter the right to make a marriage beneath her socially in 'The Family Portraits,' the first of Sarah Elizabeth Brown Utterson's *Tales of the Dead* (1813). Utterson's third tale, 'The Death's Head,' underscores the link between paternalistic guidance and social welfare. A Colonel Kielholm, having newly purchased a chateau, acquires as accoutrements a tenantry and position as justice of the peace. When a troupe of rope-dancers arrive, he forces them to produce passports and warns them to behave. The chief of the troupe reassures him that they keep 'an extremely severe discipline' which 'has the effect of a secret police among ourselves: all can answer for one, and one can answer for all. Each is bound to communicate any misconduct on the part of another to me, and is always rewarded for such communication; but, on the contrary, if he omits so to do, he is punished' (181, 97–8). Whether men govern a land-based, traditional economy or more fluid and spectacular forms of commerce, the tale urges the necessity for the kind of claustrophobic surveillance we have seen in the private committees reported by William Radcliffe and discussed in Chapter 4.

The Midnight Groan or the Spectre of the Chapel (1808) elevates domestic affairs onto a plane relevant to current national concerns more insidiously. Horatio, raised by Lord Manfredoni, alias Sarpedoski, takes shelter from a midnight storm in a deserted castle. Tempted by a supernatural figure into the dungeon, he bursts through a rotting wooden door only to enter a large vaulted hall, lit by numerous candles and attended by a company seated on a dais hung with black velvet palls, surrounded by 24 armored men. At the head of the table is Manfredoni, who leads the company in a ceremonial dipping of their daggers into a huge bowl of blood that sits atop the table. Horatio is imprisoned for two months, after which time he is given the choice of becoming a member of the Assembly or of being stretched on the rack. To join he must drink a bowl of blood, swear 'an eternal hatred to mankind, ... and assist us in our tragical designs against those who have excited our enmity' (22). Unlike *Udolpho*, Manfredoni's organized enmity and villainy remains unmotivated by any precise political or military maneuvering. This ephemeral cause of enmity resembles the workings of the secret sect posited by the Abbé Barruel as the source of the French Revolution.[4] Reviewing the translation of his work into English, the *Monthly Review* reports Barruel's discovery of a 'three-fold conspiracy... sworn to effect the ruin of the altar, the throne, and all civil society' (1797, 530). Although he qualifies his acceptance, the reviewer cannot muster enough skepticism to make him reject

Barruel's theory: 'That, in the opinion of many, the author will be thought, in some instances, to indulge his imagination too much, and to have been hasty in his conclusions, it is easy to foresee: – but, after every deduction is made on this account, more than sufficient both of his fact and argument will remain, to establish his assertion of the existence of an antichristian conspiracy' (532). The reviewer only demurs to assure himself and his readers that England is free from such contamination, since Barruel names the Free Masons as part of the conspiracy (531). First invoking and then revoking the danger by distancing it and keeping it a foreign aberration, the reviewer's logic resembles that of the chapbook author. *The Midnight Groan* makes Horatio and his family the only victims of enmity and villainy to appear in the chapbook; it reduces the gain from such evil to a momentary financial aggrandizement. Nevertheless, in its Shakespearean setting and theatrical details – the skull, the bowl of blood, the daggers, and the oath all recalling *Macbeth*, – *The Midnight Groan* foreshadows what will happen when such societies come to roost on Gothic soil.

Contrasting the chapbooks' formal circulation with their vision of social circulation reveals similar gymnastics. Formally, the chapbooks imagine a radical egalitarianism; substantively, the chapbooks foreclose the possibility for egalitarian mobility, aligning them with a more conservative rhetoric. One chapbook in particular mirrors this reverse: the anonymous *The Life and Horrid Adventures of The Celebrated Dr. Faustus of 1810.* Although only 14 years separate this chapbook from Lewis's *The Monk,* in which a similar Faustian bargain is struck, the two representations are worlds apart.

Instead of verbal and typographical characteristics, Lewis concretely renders a Devil in 'native' form, having shed the guise of a beautiful boy with which he first enticed Ambrosio. The nature of that nativeness is racialized:

> He appeared in all that ugliness which since his fall from heaven had been his portion. His blasted limbs still bore marks of the Almighty's thunder. A swarthy darkness spread itself over his gigantic form: his arms and feet were armed with long talons. Fury glared in his eyes… Over his huge shoulders waved two enormous sable wings: and his hair was supplied with living snakes, which twined themselves round his brows with frightful hissing.
>
> (1952, 412)

Beyond the obvious attribute of swarthy skin, the Devil's physical traits compound aspects of racial and sexual depravity, categories never firmly sundered in representations of the Other. The Devil's gigantic form derives from physiological accounts of the various African tribes; his Medusa-like locks instance a conflation of generalized female depravity, particularly inverted maternal appetites, with the hypothesized Amazonian tribes said to hide in African jungles; his talons reflect the fear that cannibalism was an atavistic return to more primitive origins, here figured as animalistic, a reversion that threatened to contaminate even whites by contagion. The crossing of these categories, human and animal, male and female, black and white, is captured by the illustrator to the 1845 New York edition, where the Devil has leathern wings, animal claws and nails but not cloven hooves, and a beard and moustache (see illustration).

In the chapbook, our sympathy shifts to the side of the Devil. Our initial admiration for Faustus as hero evaporates as he barters with the Devil. Their negotiations rest on the distinctions between legalism, urged by Faust, and legality, upheld by the Devil. This portrait of devils and devil-worshippers as devotees of an infernal legal system prefigures Dickens's treatments of the law. Faustus willingly participates in a metaphorical cannibalism; the skin of his ancestor furnishes the canvas on which to gorge his own desires.[5] This metaphoric cannibalism merely extends the actual scavenging Faustus has committed on his uncle's fortune and on the world's expectations. 'Careless of his own reputation' (89), Faustus betrays his selfish individualism, his desire to get something for nothing. The narrator's condemnation of Faustus as a 'speculator,' a word trailing a whole history in eighteenth-century discourse, reveals the economics of Faustus's desire, as its typographical rendering in italics underlines the demonic nature of Faust's economic thirst.[6] If Lewis's work represents the 'reproduction and circulation of mimetic capital' that drew upon a 'stockpile of representations' of the cannibal Other (Greenblatt, 1992, 6), the chapbook author redeploys those images domestically. The radical implications of his deployment appear in the critique of the legal and medical professions that preyed upon the poor;[7] the conservative valence weighs in against the desire for exorbitant mobility.

Restricting circulation

Less delicate than their novelistic colleagues, the chapbook authors parade their heroes emphatically. Frequently, our attention is directed in the very first paragraphs. For instance, Isaac Crookenden begins his 1802 *The Vindictive Monk; Or, The Fatal Ring* with the following introduction:

The Monk. New York: Moore & Jackson, 1845.

The young Calini was descended of a good family and heir to great and still-increasing wealth. He was the last representative of an honourable house, and the delight and admiration not only of his doting parents, but of everybody who knew him. He possessed every grace of mental perfection; for his education had been conducted on so liberal a plan, that a clear, just, and accurate perception had been the happy result of his juvenile studies. His person was in every way answerable to the above delineation of his mind. His make exhibited the truest symmetry; and his countenance beamed with masculine dignity, corrected with a gracious condescension.

Although Calini was reared in the principles of the Romanist Church, that did not hinder him from seeing some of its absurdities; and therefore, while some of the votaries placed the essence of their religion in a gaudy exhibition of pompous ceremonies, his consisted in a steady, uniform system of good actions; an undeviating rectitude of conduct, prompted by the motive of his present and everlasting interest, as well as by the intrinsic beauty of benevolence. Such was the youth, whom we have selected for *the hero* for these memoirs.

(16, emphasis added)

The phrase 'our hero' recurs eight times in the short tale, six of them in the final two pages. Putatively foreign, as exemplified by his own and his companions' names, and antique, as evidenced by the feudal organization of his society, Calini's virtues reflect contemporary Protestant and British values. His education has enabled him to penetrate the artifices of his religion, and to renounce show for worth. In keeping with Evangelical principles, he favors good works over faith, simplicity over pomp. Although he preserves a keen sense of his worldly interest, in keeping with eighteenth-century Christian conduct-books on prudence, he never loses sight of an interest that will yield less mundane rewards. As if to ensure that we focus on the selflessness of his 'interest,' Calini exhibits an eighteenth-century devotion to benevolence for its own sake.

In his intellectual, moral, and physical qualifications, then, Calini is heir to the heroes of the Gothic novels. But his blazoning reverses the sequence of heroic attributes ascribed by fuller-length versions. There, nature takes precedence over nurture. Physical beauty and prowess head the list, followed by accomplishments. In this chapbook, fungible qualities come first. Birth and money enable the nurture that takes shape in education; genetics closes off the list. This reversal implies the possibility of progress: even Calini's inheritance is 'still-increasing.'

If wealth ceases to be static but participates in circulation, so the emphasis upon education that we find throughout the chapbooks initially correlates with a radical outlook. Education, or self-education, came to dominate the thoughts of those striving to better their conditions, causing some historians to see the culture of secular radicalism as melding the creeds of self-help and protest.[8] Attempts to regulate private schools, debated in the pages of journals like the *Gentleman's Magazine*, admit with anxiety the potential of education to furnish the means for social mobility. At the time, it cost a mere 6d. (ironically, the same price as a chapbook) to license a school. Too open to all 'talents,' schools require homogeneity to better monitor the acquisition of 'our mother-tongue,' protecting it from 'false spelling, false pronouncing, ... and even Scotch and Welsh,' preserving 'our labourers from illiteracy,' and preventing 'our mechanics from the affectation of fine words with all the weakness of slip-slops' (1804, 22). 'Illiteracy' manifests itself not through contact with the written word but by inability to select and pronounce the proper, because English, word. Yet mechanics, who seem by their very affectation to be rather more literate than is commonly held, are feminized for their attraction to 'fine words,' like fine clothing, a euphemism usually signaling an over-reliance on Latinate or French constructions.[9] In contrast, *The Great Devil's Tale* gives us a trusty servant and his peasant mother who writes poetry; no revelation that these peasants are disguised or disowned nobility occurs. Seldom do parents of any status in the chapbooks fail to give their children the education that will enable them to better themselves.[10]

Education serves the ability to apply empirical observation, even if retroactively, a trait associated by the full-length novels with heroism. Learning that his beloved Alexa has been abducted, Calini gives short shrift to rage. Instead, 'he vowed to discover her, if it was within the verge of possibility' (1802, 23). Thinking back over scenes shared with Alexa, Calini recalls a previously unrecognized rival for her affections in the nobleman Holbruzi, who 'was always exceedingly discourteous to himself, the occasion of which he had in vain attempted to unravel; but now it appeared plain enough' (23). Deducing the motive, Calini can equally well fathom Alexa's hidden location (24). Educated away from impulsive behavior, Calini plans not revenge but a fact-finding mission. He employs spies to confirm his suppositions; only their report is 'sufficient to stimulate our hero to instant exertion' (ibid.). Acting as the agent of the law, even in the absence of a legal tribunal,

Calini waits until he has evidence before prosecuting his claim with the sword.

In *The Captive of the Banditti*, Nathan Drake also furnishes an empiricist hero, who marries cool calculation to impetuous chivalry in defense of unfortunates unknown to him, thus widening the scope of action usually obtaining to the chapbook hero. Literally suspended at the brink of death, after having watched his companions be hurled into the abyss below, Montmorency recovers from a faint. A tripartite series of responses indicate his growing restoration and fitness to succeed. First, he prays; next he cringes in horror; finally, he puts observation, courage, and perseverance to work:

> His hands, which were bound behind him, he endeavoured to disentangle, and, to his inexpressible joy, after many painful efforts, he succeeded so far as to loosen the cord, and by a little more perseverance, effected his liberty. He then sought around for a place to escape through, but without success; at length, as he was passing on the other side of the chasm, he observed a part of its craggy side, as he thought, illuminated, and, advancing a little nearer, he found that it proceeded from the moon's rays shining though a large cleft of the rock, and at a very considerable depth below the surface. A gleam of hope now broke in upon his despair; and gathering up the ropes which had been used for himself and his associates, he tied them together, and fastening one end to the bole of a tree, and the other to his waist, he determined to descend as far as the illuminated spot.
>
> (1801, 59)

The concrete description of actions, emotions, and materials compounds the vividness of his heroism. We lack only a detailed explanation of how to escape from bonds, a detail which might seem too subversive of the law.

Heroes wedding reasoning and action can produce miniature repetitions of themselves in their servants. Thus the chapbooks stage the message about the necessity for an educated discrimination as a double scene of instruction: presented explicitly, the servant acquires the lesson at the feet of his master; related implicitly, the hero with whom servants and higher ranks alike identify similarly receives schooling, as in Sarah Wilkinson's *The Mysterious Novice; Or, Convent of the Grey Penitents* (1800).[11] The equal necessity to learn softens any imputations of a demeaning patronization and artificially levels the playing field, though servants never roam Eton or Oxbridge.

Philip, the servant of the anonymous *The Gothic Story of De Courville Castle* (1810), exhibits the most need to improve. Returning home to find his place of servitude empty, Philip assumes that the owner's death would produce such an effect. The hero, Alphonso, knows better. Philip's perspective indicates the insularity of his life; absent an employer, and the world itself becomes empty. Alphonso's rejoinder indicates his awareness of the requirements of hospitality and the responsibilities of the aristocracy. Death does not dissolve those responsibilities; the life of aristocracy throbs on, though the individual aristocrat's pulse may be still. One of those responsibilities concerns the proper education of servants, even if authoritarianism must be employed. Alphonso wields authority through ridicule rather than blows, spurring Philip to overcome his cowardice. Alphonso's trust, and his earlier example of empirical deduction, are not lost on Philip. After conducting Julia safely back to her father, Philip remounts to rejoin his master. He gets lost in the forest; spotting a distant light, he vows to discover its source. His pursuit leads him to the mouth of a cavern. At first Philip fears it to be the haunt of banditti, but he has acquired sufficient courage to persist. Coming closer, he hears 'a low murmuring voice, seemingly in prayer' (27). Reasoning that banditti don't pray, he enters and learns the whereabouts of Alphonso's long-missing mother.

In this way, the chapbook servants offer a portrait of nobility realized, in the sense of being cultivated. Only infrequently do the chapbooks preserve the topos of discovered birth, whereby 'peasants' or servants, whose identity has been unwillingly disguised or hidden from them, inherently exhibit their nobility. Beltoni in Crookenden's *The Mysterious Murder* (1806), is one such exception; a peasant, he hints his noble birth by the fact that he refrains from drinking to excess, the only one to show such restraint (6). But the illustrations to the chapbooks sometimes show that the division between such categories is not firmly fixed, in the process betraying a radical egalitarianism. The illustration to *De Courville Castle* adverts to page 12. There, Alphonso and Philip discover a chest containing skeletal remains; this discovery occurs just after Alphonso has chastised Philip for his cowardice, and before Philip has evinced the ability to learn noble behavior. Yet the illustration foreshadows his ennoblement. It depicts an older male figure in the upper left-hand corner of the picture, kneeling by the side of a casket whose open top reveals a skeleton reposing inside. The skeleton is swathed in a green cloth, so that only the head (with a gruesome frown on the upturned face) is visible. No hair remains on the skeleton, so no gender attribute can be made as to its identity. This inability to fix the identity of the skeleton spills over into our inability to fix the identity of either of the two men, given what we have read to this page, or to locate the temporal setting of the tale. The kneeling man looks about forty years of age; he is dressed in a red Elizabethan costume, with a white ruff and a hat plumed with red feathers. By his side and to the right stands another, younger male figure, holding aloft a flaming torch over the inside of the casket. The second man wears a costume that, at first, resembles a short toga, due to the red, skirted bottom. On closer examination, the skirt attaches to a blue tunic jacket, trimmed in gold piping, that gathers into a capelet over his back. He is clean-shaven; the older figure has curly hair and a beard. Since Alphonso is the young hero of the tale, we hesitate to identify him with the older figure in Elizabethan costume.[12] While the seeming nobility of the second man's appearance belies his association with Philip, the text alluded to makes clear that he can be no other, thereby encouraging us to picture Philip as the near-equal to Alphonso he eventually becomes.

Underscoring the contributions of heroic servants and peasants enables the chapbooks to stress their similarities with the full-length Gothic novels, at the same time that they differentiate themselves from the limited vision of public opinion. The *Analytic Review* fails to mention Ludovico's presence at all, substituting Du Pont as the actor for all actions undertaken by Ludovico (1794, 144). The *British Critic* acknowledges his presence in the narrative, but complains about his character as representing narrative faults. For example, his watching in the chamber too nearly resembles the episode in *The Old English Baron*, and his strange removal and later restoration seem 'improbable' (1794, 121). Flaunting difference, the chapbook redaction of *The Mysteries of Udolpho* restores Ludovico's importance, ignored by reviewers, in its title-page précis:

A Romance, Founded on Facts; comprising The Adventures and Misfortunes of Emily St. Aubert, who, being left an orphan, was placed under the care of an Unfeeling Aunt, who treated her with the greatest unkindness; Her Attachment to Monsieur Valancourt, and the Particular Circumstances that so long prevented their Union; Her Confinement and Adventures in the Castle of Udolpho; the Attempt of Count Morano to forcibly carry her off, AND

OBTAIN POSSESSION OF HER INHERITANCE; AND HOW SHE escaped from thence through the Bravery of LUDOVICO, SERVANT OF COUNT DE VILLEFORT.

Typographically, the précis equates Ludovico's bravery with the preservation of capital, something that only older men can usually effect.

The chapbook Ludovico follows the pattern set by Radcliffe; his bravery is the great exception in the chapbooks. By and large, the 'heroism' of the servants pales in comparison with that of the heroes. Philip's 'heroism' consists of his willingness to come close enough to the cavern to hear the hermit praying. He never has to confront banditti. Montmorency's servants ride in a body to aid his rescue; outnumbered, the banditti flee. But Ludovico's role as preserver of the family fortune reveals the more conservative function of the chapbooks' treatment of servants in particular and social relations in general. Because they virtually eliminate the topos of discovered birth, the chapbooks imply that, for servants, noble behavior is its own reward. Servants who crave material reward find masters who make them the instruments of an endless series of demonic exchanges that produce no new goods, thus thwarting both social and moral mobility. An example occurs in *The Gothic Story of De Courville Castle*: when the wife of the peasant Felix remonstrates with him, importuning him to repent and citing his apparent bad conscience as evidence of his guilt, he feels no compunction at murdering her, too. The cost to those who attempt ill-gotten gain is either the murder of their body or the alienation of their soul and reason (1810, 26). Accordingly, Philip disdains any honors. His reaction provokes smiling disbelief from Alphonso: '"sure you are very regardless of your own interest, to be so little elated at the prospect of your preferment." "Hang preferment!" replied he, "I would rather follow you, was it to the end of the world, than — "' (29). Philip's expression of extreme loyalty is cut off by a plot distraction, but its interruption only underscores the magnitude of his commitment, by refusing to limit it. His identification with his master's happiness inspires not only fidelity and protectiveness but also the desire to participate vicariously in his master's private emotion. His willingness to sacrifice his 'very best doublet' for the privilege of witnessing Alphonso's reunion with his mother suggests that aesthetic satisfaction is a better compensation than material gain, an *internalization* and *deflection* of value and status.

The aesthetic compensation of the chapbooks argues that the proper acknowledgment of social bonds will preserve members of all the social classes from direct consequences of corruption or usurpation, provided that those bonds remain in proper hierarchical order. Exiled, the disguised father of *De Courville Castle* encounters peasants who take him in, feeding him with 'the produce of their honest labour' (31) and nursing his fever. His illness consumes their little store, yet they make no complaint, and he reimburses them to the small extent he is able. Once recovered, he undertakes a pilgrimage to ease his suffering mind; his body is cared for by the generosity of goatherds. In his wanderings, he discovers an injured hermit, whom he helps back to his cave, and with whom he takes up his abode. Their physical existence is supported by donations from a neighboring village; their mental, emotional, and spiritual economy finds sustenance in each other's company (32).

Through this social interchange, especially when it depends more on benevolence than on biology, we see the bonds of communal identity being woven. Good fathers appear, replacing the predominance of paternal villains in the full-length novels and extending the definition of fatherhood. In addition to the Baron de Hainthal, Signor Calini of Crookenden's *The Vindictive Monk* heads the list for his paternal feeling. Although he informs the young Calini that he is not the youth's biological father, his assumption of responsibility only indicates further his humanitarianism: 'I resolved that the direful intentions of those who left you should not only be frustrated, but I would adopt you as my son, two of mine having recently died... . be assured, my dear boy, although you are not the natural issue of my own loins, yet I shall always feel for you a father's tenderness' (Haining, 1978, 16–17). Even the villain in this tale, the 'vindictive monk' of the title, admits his paternity of Calini and forgoes his revenge. While this part of the plot resembles *The Italian*, Crookenden's monk refuses to capitalize on the discovery, in contrast to Schedoni's action; instead, he disappears and is said to have 'passed his life in the most rigorous penance' (24).

While characters circulate within this affective economy, their status changes little. The De Courvilles reunite; they expand when Alphonso marries Julia and incorporates her father into the household. A society both circulating and enclosed finds its perfect figure in the portrait of Philip that closes the chapbook: 'Philip, become respectable from his recent services and advanced age, was rewarded by Alphonso with a handsome independence, yet chose to continue with his master and mistress... till his death' (1810, 36). Philip is not the only character to attain the status of grown child in that household. Converting the domestic to the social, we learn that the count and countess have 'the satisfaction to leave behind them children such as the fondest parents could desire – a family united among themselves by the strongest ties of duty and affection' (36). The invocation of duty and affection clarifies that these 'children' exceed biological limits and metonymically encompass the 'family' of the broader estate, now expanded through the inheritance to Alphonso of Julia's paternal lands:[13] 'peaceful prospects were once again restored to the poor tenantry of the count, who had been so long neglected; the rents were collected, and the grounds cultivated; and, in the happiness of his dependants, the count beheld the reward of his attention' (36). Syntactically, it is unclear who has been so long neglected, the peasantry or the count. But perhaps the distinction is meant to seem a vicious one. While the collection of rents might benefit the count more than the peasantry, the cultivation of grounds and of happiness serves both equally.

Yet the final words underscore how constricted is this expansive embrace: 'Though education in great measure stamps the man, virtue is within the reach of all; and although the path may be rugged, the reward is sure.' In this epilogue, the sleight of hand performed by the chapbooks becomes apparent. Education is necessary to furnish out a hero, because it will teach him to make empirical deductions, to forestall hasty and dangerous judgments, to slide out of danger; servants can learn just like their masters; but, in the final analysis, education may not be within the reach of all, just as only heroes collect rents. Servants can attain virtue; they can cultivate the ground of their own, because subordinated to their master's, happiness.

Even though servants can play on the larger national stage, they must retreat to the shadows when their work is done. I close this section with a broadside ballad, 'The Duke of Shoreditch; or, Barlow's Ghost,' published in 1803 when England was expecting an invasion by the French under Bonaparte, because it exemplifies the logic I have been tracing out in the chapbooks: social interchange that keeps the players on a treadmill replaces social mobility. 'Barlow's Ghost' shows how peasant heroes can be trotted out to serve the national interest, only to be rewarded with empty praise and hollow applause. As the *Bibliotheca Lindesiana* records, 'Barlow was a shopkeeper in Shoreditch, and in the time of Henry VIII belonged to a company of volunteers called the Finsbury Archers. When reviewed by the King, Barlow was addressed thus: "My good fellow, you have handled your arms like a Duke: you shall be the Captain of this warlike band, and shall be called the Duke of Shoreditch"' (320). Henry's bestowal of monarchical patronage encodes the limitations it would illusively banish: class mobility occurs in name only; and, within that name, Barlow's territory contains the borders beyond which his authority cannot stray. The broadside recapitulates the logic of lore. Barlow addresses his countrymen in a patriotic strain, calling on them to defend Sovereign and country from the Corsican Usurper.[14] But he speaks to them from beyond the grave; status and morality converge to extinguish the need for heroic compensation. Instead, the broadside offers fictional compensation for present-day social unrest. The specter of an idealized egalitarian past flickers in the present, discoursing of a second chance for national unification.

Fragmenting circulation

Patriotic appeals frequently located heroism in the sacrifices of the nation's people. In the same year that 'Barlow's Ghost' appeared, the Reverend Robert Hodgson, MA, Rector of the Parish Church of St George, Hanover Square, and late Chaplain to the Bishop of London, preached a sermon on 19 October, praising the composite nature of the nation:

> a people bound together in a solemn compact of reciprocal protection – a people voluntarily enduring personal distress for public security – a people rushing from the lap of ease into all the hardships and privations of a private soldier – a people resolute and determined to resist oppression, and prepared to stand or fall by their King, their country, and their God! It is now substantially true, that the hearts of the inhabitants of this kingdom are as the heart of one man. The whole physical energies are concentrated in one point. They have but one end, one aim, one principle, and that is NATIONAL HONOUR.
>
> (*Gentleman's Magazine*, 1804, 46–7)

However, the rising tide of individualism fast washed away such cohesion. Waterloo marked a double defeat for Napoleonic aspirations: the representative hero of the French nation gave way imperially and symbolically, as new, British heroes replaced him in the public imagination. To celebrate their victory, parliamentarians in the House of Commons stepped over the bodies of the slain multitude invoked by Hodgson to concenter national honor in the figures of the representative individuals adorning the monuments still today punctuating

London's skyline. Not even these monumental figures arose unanimously; in the parliamentary debates over the type and nature of monuments to be erected celebrating army and navy battles, a Mr Dundas had objected to the elimination of Howe, St Vincent, and Duncan. Others favored combining navy and army victories into a single memorial, one that would record the efforts of 'little men.' But Castlereagh's proposal to honor Nelson and Trafalgar carried the day, and only as a compromising afterthought did the legislators add a separate monument to Wellington and Waterloo (*Gentleman's Magazine*, 1816, 164). The chapbooks function like those legislators, emphasizing the contributions of their representative heroes to the social welfare. Unlike institutions in the full-length Gothic novels, institutional forces neither collaborate with nor aid the heroes. Such a characterological and thematic preference for individualism matches trends under way in more public arenas.

For instance, in *The Mysterious Novice* Steinfort exhorts his heroic friend d'Erfeldt to address the prince, thereby teaching d'Erfeldt and readers alike the proper chain of command. Despite the seeming soundness of Steinfort's reasoning, d'Erfeldt objects that he had not felt such a preemptive appeal necessary, given that the Church had no legal control over Constance while she was still in her noviciate. Yet the Church had been able, legally or not, to sequester Constance from d'Erfeldt's access, and the written evidence upon which to base a demand for her release had disappeared. Having demonstrated the need for an appeal, the question remains as to the *mode* of the appeal. Again, Steinfort dissolves the knot, pointing out to Adolphus the obvious existence of an eyewitness to the transactions, who would obviate the lack of written testimony. Himself a member of the Church, this eyewitness can purge the Church's reliance on a legalism ill assorting with spiritual governance.

Steinfort's logic reveals a masculinist bias underlying the shift to an individualistic heroism. Steinfort offers no reason why the prince, as opposed to the Abbess, should be trusted. The eyewitness who can counter the depredations of a feminized Church, headed by a female villain, is male, Father Francis. While his name might evoke memories of the saint, Steinfort gives him a character as 'mild and intelligent, a *bon* Catholic, but no bigot,' i.e. no prey to irrational emotion (1800, 39). In defining their abbreviated heroism, the chapbooks omit a signal feature of the novelistic heroes, as described in the introduction. Despite Montmorency's swooning, cross-gender characteristics seldom dilute the portraits of heroic masculinity. Calini's perfections are qualified as 'masculine'; what softening they acquire comes only from an overlaid condescension. Unlike Radcliffe's heroes, he never gives way to rage or despair, but reins in his emotions. Alphonso has 'manly dignity'; boyish impatience acquires the reins of 'manly' control (1810, 2). His gentleness is contrasted with austerity, thus preserving it from imputations of femininity (3). Alphonso ridicules Philip by feminizing his fear: 'my resolution is fixed; and were all the old women in the village to come and assist you in your idle tales, they could never change my determination. I have told you my mind: look to it' (11).[15] Although Montmorency exhibits traits usually associated with the feminine, such as fainting and cringing, he quickly moves through these temporary responses in a teleological growth towards manly action, a trajectory referred to as 'recover[ing] his perfect recollection.'

Just as chapbook heroes renounce feminization, so they also abjure brute force, passivity, or self-sacrifice as heroic for men. Sarah Utterson develops an analogy between self-sacrifice and a pyrrhic victory that consumes the victor in her 'The Family Portraits.' Removing any traces of noble heroism from the sacrifice, she makes self-sacrifice resemble weak passivity, in contrast to Radcliffe's representation in *A Sicilian Romance* of wise passivity and self-sacrifice as heroic. In Drake's story, three different heroes combat the banditti; each uses a different strategy. Only Montmorency survives. The first to go attempts furious combat, relying on his 'astonishing strength' (1801, 58). This strength is quickly exhausted, though, and he convulses on the ground, making him easy to toss over the cliff. Drake captures the futility of such physical heroics in the picture of this knight going over the side: 'his armour striking upon the rock, there burst a sudden effulgence, and the repetition of the stroke was heard for many minutes as he descended down the rugged side' (58). The burst of armed struggle lasts but for a brief flash; the clang of arms is a hollow echo of despair. The second hero undertakes a kamikaze revenge:

> He gave no opposition, and, though despair sat upon his features, not a shriek, not a groan escaped him: but no sooner had he reached the brink, than making a sudden effort, he liberated an arm, and grasping one of the villains round the waist, sprang headlong with him into the interminable gulf. All was silent – but at length a dreadful plunge was heard, and the sullen deep howled fearfully over its prey.
>
> (58–9)

The failure of other strategies, even of self-sacrifice, underscores the importance of intellectual heroism.

Drake's emphasis upon calculated individual action in the service of the greater public good contradicts his non-fiction enthusiasm for the supernatural elements in Gothic as 'calculated to soothe and support the mind,' discussed in Chapter1. I there argued that Drake's insistence upon the Gothic as schooling us to divine dispensation masked a more quotidian interest in political providence. Interestingly, the supernatural appears nowhere in his fragment.[16] Orthodoxy makes a brief entry, in Montmorency's awakening prayer for mercy; but eternal faith is marred by the stubbornly temporal: Montmorency prays with 'the briny sweat trickling down his pallid features' (59). Montmorency's body makes a greater impression on us than the bodiless invocation of Christ, repeating the impression given in *The Mysterious Novice* that the male body produces social harmony.

In contrast to the men, women in the chapbooks are *enjoined* to self-sacrifice and demonized for their failures, especially when their refusal to sacrifice themselves involves their children. Bad mothers stand out against the good fathers. *The Great Devil's Tale*, which bears the byline C. F. Barrett, uses such logic to blame the victim. The evil Baron Rudolpho marries the oldest daughter of Count Berengoch, a rich German noble, in default of obtaining her younger but more wealthily endowed sister. Rudolpho incarcerates Matilda as her time of delivery draws near, threatening her with vengeance if she doesn't produce a male heir. 'Thus situated,' Barrett tells us, 'the Baroness spent the tedious hours of her captivity in a state of anxiety that can be better imagined than described; and the horror she conceived on that occasion was so great, as to make her bring forth a daughter some time before the expected period' (1802, 10). Barrett's language blurs the line separating the scientific and the spectacular. The formulaic phrase, 'that can be better imagined than described,' here licenses the omission of empirical evidence. But the language of reproduction invokes empirical knowledge of the process, at the same time that reproduction takes on a demonic face. Gestation is figured as conceiving horror; horror deforms the outcome of pregnancy both by foreshortening the necessary developmental time and by producing the female.

Female perfection requires that heroines walk a narrow tightrope. Much of Crookenden's moralizing aims at women in this vein. In *Fatal Secrets*, the Countess de Berlandi is blamed for having incited Ricardo's passion for her, merely because she innocently gazes at him with gratitude and squeezes his hand in thanks. The Marquess Salmoni is praised for her fidelity to a husband who has almost ruined the family by gaming:

She was a lady of much good sense, which she had improved by an accurate, as well as an extensive reading. She gave a strict regard to every conjugal duty, discharging those duties in a manner that perhaps was impossible to be exceeded. However this lady might have been grieved at the former folly of her husband, she never once forgot her place; she had taken an oath to act in every thing as a *wife*, and she preserved it inviolable, although the poor Marquis had broken his. If every female could say the same, what a delightful world we should have!

(1806, 18)

Crookenden's self-congratulatory tone about the benefits of an 'extensive reading' elevates his own place in the world at the same time that it reinforces the place of women.

Women do occasionally manifest agency. In Drake's *The Captive of the Banditti*, Dorothee harnesses diligence and perseverance to effect her own escape, after Montmorency has disappeared from the cave; and she and Montmorency converse as equals, each taking time out to tell his or her separate escapades with *longeur*. Yet this equality of action and language derives from the pen of 'A.N.,' not from Drake; it forms part of the afterthought of the story. Moreover, Dorothee seems unique in this regard. Alexa in *The Vindictive Monk* has 'suspicions' about Calini's fate (Haining, 1978, 18), but these go no further than cogitations. She doesn't even recognize Calini's voice when it calls to her from behind her barred prison door (22).

Instead, Alexa becomes a verbal icon of female distress:

But we must take leave of the monk and young Calini a little while to *look after* the lovely persecuted Alexa. That unfortunate maid was ready to abandon herself to despair. Torn away from her peaceful retreat by ruffians, at the dreadful, the horror-working hour of midnight, to fall a prey to the unbridled lust of a lewd barbarian! Separated from her dear aunt! Torn too from the fond, and protecting arms of the youth she sighed for! What can exceed her misery, wretched captive as she then was in the most hated mansion of the nefarious monster Holbruzi? For she as yet knew nothing of the sanguinary scenes which had been exhibited in the castle ruins. The savage Holbruzi, when he left his house at midnight, had consigned the wretched maid to one of his trusty servants, who executed with relentless rigour the confidence reposed in him.

(22)

Crookenden's invitation to the reader to 'look after' the wretched Alexa contains a double imperative, each of which empowers the reader. On one level, the reader's identification with Calini is invoked. The reader can wrap a protective gaze around Alexa's distress and imagine his gaze as effective as Calini's protective arms. On another level, the invocation to 'look after' is an invitation to lubricity, to vicariously enjoy the spectacle of female vulnerability, giving the reader a sense of power over that despair.

No sooner do we have Alexa spread before our eyes than another female takes her place:

> We now, for a short time, turn from the unhappy beauty, to see the mournful effect which her loss had upon her disconsolate aunt... While she was in the height of her lamentation, a knocking at the door was heard. For a considerable time she was afraid to open it, lest in so doing, she should let in those who ravished from her embraces her beloved niece, and thereby herself become a victim of their savage fury.
>
> (22)

The passage heightens the sense of impending doom, extending it to all females regardless of age, physical or financial desirability.

Females can help themselves only when that agency serves the domestic or the maternal. The murdered Julia of the anonymous *The Spectre Mother: Or, the Haunted Tower* has the power to rise from death to protect her threatened babe. Angela, the heroine of the tale, married to the murderer of Julia, has the courage to follow the specter when she appears to her, and to flee with the child to seek protection (1978, 75–9). Yet the language of Angela's inspiriting denies to her the same kind of manly fortitude experienced by heroes in similarly compromised positions: 'by degrees, the terrors that pervaded the mind of Angela subsided, a pious enthusiasm elevated her feelings, and revived her courage, and believing that she was selected as the humble agent of some important event, she resolved to obey and comply with the silent direction of the spirit' (76). Female courage here takes the form of compliance and obedience, key doctrines in a woman's marital duty. Angela need not employ mental effort to seek help; supernatural agents perform that work for her: 'A sudden stupor pressed on the senses of Angela, and without being conscious of the means by which she had been conducted, she found herself, on reviving, in the open air; and looking round, saw that she reclined on a small bank, a few paces distant from her house' (77). Only anxiety for the health of the child impels her on: 'here she would have remained (fearing to proceed), but the current of air was so strong, that she had too power-ful apprehensions for the comfort and health of the child, to allow her to continue; and cautiously proceeding to the end (for it was still too dark to see her way), she found herself at the foot of a staircase' (78).

The characters of Margaret in *The Bride of the Isles: A Tale Founded on the Popular Legend of the Vampire* (circa 1820), and of Vitoria Ursula, the Mother Abbess who dies in the opening of Sarah Wilkinson's *The Mysterious Novice*, reveal the springes which catch women who attempt to exercise dominion over their lives. The narrative validates Margaret's actions when she quests to know the identity of her future husband, even though that quest necessitates her repair to the cavern of a witch and her participation in magical rites (115, 122). Margaret must rely on tainted sources of information because she has access to no better; the narrator blames 'the narrow education then given to females, even of rank' (115). But she is also depicted as prey to a sexualized fascination, permitting the vampire to gain ascendence over her feelings. And his spell causes her increasingly to act the part of a defiant daughter (127–8). Vitoria initially seems the ideal hero: '[T]hough vested by the rules of the foundation with an almost despotic sway, she had tem-pered her authority with tenderness and benevolence. Her deportment, though mild and affable, had a dignity of expression, that prevented undue familiarity from those committed to her charge, and procured respect' (1978, 26). Her attributes of leadership match those accorded to Calini and Alphonso. Our admiration for this female paragon of 'manly' virtue grows when we learn that she has suffered the more common fate of females, that of persecution by her father, causing her to occupy the position she had. Her solicitude for the 'Mysterious Novice' of the title derived from her knowledge that the girl was her daughter, yet she never gave the other nuns cause to complain of favoritism. Just when we think we have found at last a heroine whose virtues transcend gender bounds, we learn that her virtues ascend in expiation of even greater sins. She gained her love by deceit, manipu-lating both the eventual father of her child and her best friend, his intended, to engineer herself into her friend's place (45–7). Not only has her crime required that she enter the convent, but she also forced her daughter to join her in taking the vows, 'as the late abbess would not suffer any application to be made to the marquis [her father], lest her child should be taken from her' (51).

This constriction of the heroine's role matches conduct-book rhetoric about female domesticity and the widening gap between male and female spheres. While a few chapbooks contain a pessimism so deeply imbrued as to kill off all the characters in a grand bloodbath finale (e.g., *The Mysterious Murder*), most of the chapbooks end with what would be a fairy-tale marriage, were it not for the carnage that has often preceded it. Sometimes, the plot allows a decent interval before reestablishing domestic happiness. After a year's mourning, *The Spectre Mother*'s Angela marries her first love, Di Montmorenci and retires with him and a 'splendid retinue' to Venice, 'where the amiable Angela was received with the respect and esteem due to her rank as the Marchioness di Montmorenci' (1978, 85).[17] Likewise, Constance of *The Mysterious Novice* takes time to recover under the shelter of the dowager baroness Steinfort, after having undergone torments similar to those suffered by Agnes in *The Monk*, 'till her marriage to Adolphus took place' (1978, 53). Despite the resemblance of crime, the social vision of the chapbook settles on a single family and their married bliss to come. *The Captive of the Banditti* most clearly shows the elision of events:

> The conflict was dreadful in the extreme, and for some time victory hung doubtful over the head of either. At length Edelbert falling by the hands of Montmorency, the day was declared in favour of the latter, who having secured the banditti, conducted them, and the lady, to his castle. Thereafter, following the careful burial of the remains of Dorothee's father, and a suitable period mourning, she became the lawful mistress of A–y Castle by giving her hand to her valiant protector; and together they lived a life of uninterrupted happiness for many years, surrounded by the admiration of all people.
>
> (1801, 63)

Beyond the dizzying paratactics of the narrative, the syntax equates the capture of banditti and a bride. In much the same way, the phrase 'the day was declared in favour of the latter' reduces a fight to the death against criminals to a chivalric tournament with no consequences for the well-being of the countryside. Once captured, both banditti and bride disappear into vague generalities. At other times, the chapbooks hurtle towards happiness: Floriela and Lopez's marriage occupies the final paragraph of *The Nocturnal Assassin* (1806); Albio and Julia of *Horrible Revenge* (1812) marry literally in the midst of paternal gore.

Resembling fairy tales in their insistence on the 'happily ever after,' the chapbooks offer a more insidious fantasy of attainment just out of reach and yet ever just at hand. And like fairy tales, the chapbooks enable their readers to work out the consequences for a grown-up national identity in occulted dreams and dangers. One chapbook from the middle years of production brings those national and imperial consequences to the surface: 1802's *Gothic Legends*. Like the other chapbooks we have just surveyed, *Gothic Legends* plays with elements of subversion but harnesses them to a more timid perspective. Female initiative and gender transgressions quickly resolve themselves into a brief for orthodox domestic piety.

In story outline, *Gothic Legends* reproduces Shakespeare's *A Winter's Tale*. The villain, Sir James Langland, verges on evil only insofar as he allows himself to become sexually attracted to the wrong woman, in this case not his daughter but his young, adventurous, widowed sister-in-law, Leonora. Because he so deeply repents his mistake, we pity rather than condemn him, much like the attitude we take towards Leontes and his sufferings. And the inspiration for his repentance comes most directly from Shakespeare's play: recognizing the alienation and redirection of his affections, his wife, Isabella, feigns her own death. When James's penitence is deep and full, she reveals herself to him.

This revelation scene takes on a 'Gothic' coloring, in the sense of medieval, in the illustration to the chapbook. On the battlements of a Gothic building, with two more towers visible in the distance and with treetops waving over the tops of the parapets, a cavalier stands, plumed hat on head, drawn sword in his right hand. Accosting him is a ghastly female apparition to the left. She wears a white gown with empire bodice; a chain ending in a large cross depends from her waist and her face is covered by a nun-like veil. She stands with left hand upraised, palm out; he recedes in horror, his left hand upraised, back side out. The illustration contrasts vividly with the scene as actually described within the tale. This takes place inside the bedroom of their home, whose origins may be antique, since they are paternal estates at Land's End, in Cornwall, descending to Sir James, but whose rooms and furniture as they are described resemble a late eighteenth-century manor house.

Yet this rupture between narrative and illustration only serves to point out the way in which the chapbook is even more 'Gothic,' in the sense that house and story contain details of contemporary reality disguised as a tale of older times, drawn from the 'Gothic' monuments of British literature, in this case Shakespeare, celebrated by the romance revivalists of the 1760s. Sir James Langland inhabits his paternal home because his gambling debts have eaten away his patrimony. He has retired to the country to 'restore his health and save his money' (1802, 5). Reunited with James, Isabella shows him the secret panel she has discovered in her 'interment,' behind which hides an iron chest full of gold, silver, and 'various other valuables.' This treasure, she tells him, will enable him to 'pay all your debts, and live where you like' (41). James replies that he has found so much contentment in 'sweet retirement' that he wants to stay there, a proposition to which she happily agrees.

The linkage of women and treasure, especially treasure discovered in hidden recesses, continues in the subplot of Leonora's adventures, the richest aspect of this chapbook for its vision of the 'Gothic' nation. The orphan of a military officer, Leonora first falls under the guardianship of a Colonel Brampton, father of the Isabella who has married Sir James. Both Isabella and, subsequently, Leonora seem to marry well. Heiress to £20 000 at age 19, Leonora marries an 'inland commercial trader' in Madras, India, who has amassed the identical sum in just a few short years. Here, Leonora carries within her a treasure, £20 000, conjoined to a hidden treasure discovered in the recesses of a country frequently figured as a female body, India.

Left behind in India while her husband oversees a shipment back to England, Leonora grows worried at her husband's failure to return. She takes sail for England, only to be shipwrecked on a desert island, where she is captured by savages. These savages leave Leonora for dead and never inquire where her body has disappeared. Still alive, Leonora surveys her island home. Despite being alone and beset by danger, Leonora's reaction marries aspects of a Robinson Crusoe-like courage and initiative, a Joseph Banks-like empirical investigation, and an eighteenth-century traveler's aesthetic curiosity: she notices the beautiful natural scenery; she eats the fruit of the trees; she discovers that one large tree has a 'kind of door which slid into the trunk – on removing it my eyes were delighted with the appearance of a room, sufficiently large to serve as a bedchamber' (20–1). She spends five months inside her hyper-natural domestic space, until rescued and taken aboard the *Mars* man-o'-war.

If Leonora's marriage, providential accidents, and recoveries unite her to colonial adventure, her experiences aboard the man-o'-war figure a different type of appropriation as salvation. The captain of the vessel advises her to exchange her deteriorating dress, which exposes dangerous portions of her anatomy, for a sailor's suit. She complies: 'taking the skirts of my own dress, I made some trowsers and a cloak, such as I had seen the actresses wear; and when thus equipped, the Captain told me I made a very respectable appearance, said I should be his secretary, and told the officers he would have me called Mr. Sorrell [her husband's name]' (23). Despite her allusion to the stage, Leonora's assumption of the breeches' part exceeds the simple substitution of one gender's dress for another's. Instead, Leonora applies industry to convert her prospects and reinvent her identity. As though the details of conversion were not sufficiently symbolic, the plot recapitulates them on a broader scale. The *Mars* heads to the Cape because the Cape has recently been taken from the Dutch.

Leonora returns to Madras and sets out once more for Calcutta, still in search of her husband and still in male dress. A young English lady, daughter of Sir Robert and Lady Desmond, falls in love with her. Leonora unveils herself, and wins Miss Desmond as a friend rather than a lover. However, Miss Desmond insists that she clothe herself once more as a lady. Leonora lives with the Desmonds for two years, before taking to sea again in the journey that shipwrecks her into the arms of her sister-in-law and brother-in-law. Leonora then stays with the Langlands. The narrative has come full circle, bringing us back to the point at which we began in our introduction to Leonora and preparing us for her role as seductress to Sir James.

This narrative of adventure tempts us to read Leonora as radical anomaly, a female hero in a chapbook world dominated by hegemonic domesticity for women. But as much as her scrapes open up the possibility of transgression, that opening is a mirage. Her actions receive sanctimonious justification because they occur always in company with or search for her husband. The industry involved in Leonora's gender conversion also helps eradicate any sexualized taint. Her seamstressing 'such as I had seen the actresses wear' feminizes and purifies a career identified in the public mind with whoring, in much the same manner that the public relations machinery and insistence on marital status of actresses like Mrs Bracegirdle helped set their activities off from the all-too 'common' run. Fresh bouquets attesting to Leonora's virtue arrive at the end of the tale, adding to her odor of convention, if not sanctity. The suitor she had rejected years ago, before her marriage to Sorrell, now grown elderly, dies, leaving her a legacy of £40 000 (29). In person, character, and pocket, Leonora becomes the supplement to the family hearth; she and Isabella's bachelor brother Brampton stay with the newly-sentimentalized aristocrats, the Langlands. Shutting down the very hopes for a subversive female space it has raised, the narrative ends by closing out its fantasies of class mobility occurring through any other means than colonial exploitation. The Langlands' daughter, Elvira, marries a young sailor who has accompanied Leonora back to her family. Always italicized as *Mister*

Hammond, we learn that the apparent commoner is in fact the son of Lord Titchfield, one of the Lords of the Admiralty. Leonora's tale contains very little 'mystery,' despite the advertisement of the title. Class mobility will accrue only to those active enough and male enough to set sail for India. Comprising both medium and object of exchange, Leonora's female body represents at once the wealth of foreign lands and the domestic benefits to those women whose English men bring (or send) it home to them.

Scopic circulation

If Gothic novels and chapbooks linked the nation imaginatively through the kind of shared literary culture posited by Gellner, they also titillated visual desire for that culture. The early nineteenth-century spurt of books on the costumes of earlier times, such as W. H. Pyne's *Costume of Great Britain* (1808), Charles Hamilton Smith's *Selections of the Ancient Costume of Great Britain and Ireland* (1814), or Smith's collaboration a year later with Samuel Rush Meyrick, *The Costume of the Original Inhabitants of the British Islands, from the Earliest Periods to the Sixth Century; to which is Added, that of the Gothic Nations in the Western Coasts of the Baltic, The Ancestors of the Anglo-Saxons and the Anglo-Danes*, form one response to that desire. Writing the Preface to his first work from aboard 'His Majesty's Ship *Horatio*, in the Room-Pot on the Coast of Zeeland, 6th December 1813,' Smith associates himself with a Britain regnant at sea and its most glorious hero, Nelson, even though he disclaims intellectual utility in favor of the aesthetic nourishment of his work (v–vii). In fact, he produces nothing more nor less than picture-book history, with representative heroes and heroines of the period decked out in costumes and attitudes that he freely admits to having manipulated from his sources in monumental effigies, brass plates, paintings on glass, seals and illuminations, by 'restor[ing] the mutilations, correct[ing] the drawing of the figures, and ... vary[ing] and animat[ing] the attitudes of recumbent and kneeling effigies' (vi). Samuel Rush Meyrick makes a more overtly materialist, if Horatian, argument for the utility or desirability of their 1815 work. The study of human society's progressive civilization instructs and interests as much as or more than travel literature and voyages:

> In investigations of this kind, the art and manufactures, the habits and customs, the religious and military characteristics constitute the principal points of examination, and all these are intimately

blended with COSTUME. In this point of view, the subject before us assumes its proper character, and rebuts the intemperate and hasty charge, of carrying with it the inferiority of not being worthy the consideration of a man of letters.

(1)

But, in both editions, the tinted plates have clearly been designed to be removed from the text, to decorate contemporary walls, tracing a growing movement from intellectual property to personal property as public display that mirrors the aristocratic attitude towards art described by John Berger.

The chapbook illustrations allowed another kind of ownership. Like the costume books, even those outside the literate loop could consume them. But the illustrations focalized a vicarious *participation*. Viewing Gothic costume permits a patronizing attitude because the scenes remain at a secure distance from the viewer. In this framed distance and insofar as each depends upon tableaux, the Gothic costume books and the illustrations to the full-length novels resemble the Gothic drama, which Paula Backscheider sees as also serving national cohesion and identity (1993, 186–7). Drama and illustration to novels may exercise and contain powerful feelings by alternating periods of intense activity with 'freeze-frames' (Backscheider, 1993, 169). Yet their very distancing and security, I would argue, moderates the amount of manipulation contained in the theatrical 'bombardment of the senses.' In contrast, the chapbook illustrations actualize their manipulation by eliminating any framing devices, by collapsing the distance between *male* viewer and participant. The repetitive tunnel vision invoked by the chapbook illustrations corresponds to the narrowly male perspective of the texts. Unlike the full-length portraits adorning works such as the 1837 Exeter, NH edition of *Udolpho*, where Emily, Montoni, and Valancourt successively head up the respective volumes, the chapbook illustrations either disembody women or turn them into pornographic objects of distress for our delight, thereby concretizing narrative praise for domesticity and the policing of sexuality. Our identification with the hero is simultaneously encouraged by his foregrounding as the only agent of action, and corralled to the danger immediately at hand.

That this manipulation takes on a pornographic cast can best be seen when contrasted with the illustrations to the full-length novels. Although no illustration accompanies the 1797 T. Cadell London edition of *The Italian*, the 1797 P. Wogan Dublin edition, or the Robert Campbell Philadelphia version of the same year, the French version yields a rich harvest. Vivaldi receives his warning not to approach the Villa Altieri because 'la mort y est' from the shadowy figure, but in place of the sublime mountain ruin drawn from Rosa, we have a domesticated Claudian scene: the caverns appear more like a shepherd's thatched hovel, with Romanesque-arched doorways the only hint of an ecclesiastical setting; atop the thatching, trees gaily wave over the turreted round towers of a medieval chateau (see illustration). The wedding of Vivaldi and Ellena is interrupted by officers remarkably Napoleonic in costume; over the heads of the terrified priest and lovers a full-sized Christ watches from the Cross. When the mysterious monk enters Vivaldi's prison to suborn him, the monk has all the tragic grandeur and classical beauty of a noble Roman. Each of these illustrations distances the viewer from the action, by the physical placement of the scene within the frame of the picture, by its perspectival elements, and by the elevated facial expressions of the actors. This distancing becomes even more pronounced in the illustrations to the fifth London edition of *Udolpho*. In the first of these, we see realized the scene when Emily throws herself at the feet of Montoni to beg his mercy to Madame Cheron.[18] Cheron sits demurely upright next to her niece, her hands calmly by the arms of the chair, her hair held back by a modest white cap such as Puritan women might have affected but certainly not the style attributed to the vain and modish Cheron of the text. Instead, the scene resembles the sentimental domestic paintings of Greuze, made more dramatic by the positioning of the bodies as self-conscious displays of attitude and by the plain wooden floorboards of the otherwise sumptuously appointed room, a hint perhaps of the illustrator's theatrical impetus. Drapes form the up-center backdrop; these are tied back to stage right, revealing a blank wall into which Montoni's outstretched arm and hand thrust (see illustration).[19] Whereas domesticity prevails in the portrait of the St Aubert family under the pines of their native La Vallée,[20] theatricality comes to the foreground in the depiction of Emily encountering the dead soldier in the tower.[21] Framed like a scene played in the inner below of a Renaissance theater, the borders of the room are truncated by the head of the bed and the edge of a curtain sweeping across the front. Emily stands downstage right center, with the body up left from her (see illustration). Like the Gothic drama, as described by Paula Backscheider, in these illustrations 'performers rarely touched each other, and suffering was picturesque as well as part of a ritual pattern' (1993, 200). Indeed, in the first illustration, Montoni's facial expression indicates more sorrow than it does anger.

N'allez point à Villa: Altieri, la mort y est.

Gaitte Sculp.

L'Italien, ou le confession des pénitents noirs. Paris: Jeune, Maradan, 1797.

The Mysteries of Udolpho. London: G. G. and J. Robinson, 1799, vol. 4, ch. 9, p. 382.

The Mysteries of Udolpho. London: G. G. and J. Robinson, 1799, vol. 3, ch. 1, p. 21.

Ritualized viewing gives way to collusion when the theatricalized positioning serves a pornographic purpose, as it does in the illustration to *The Midnight Assassin.* The latter illustration depicts Schedoni's incursion into Ellena's midnight chamber on the banks of the sea, with the intent of killing her. Schedoni appears apelike: beetle-browed and crook-backed, his animalistic nature is enhanced by the mysterious tumescence protruding from his midriff. Hunching over, he brandishes a knife blade, point down, in his right hand, the position of the blade suggesting perhaps his detumescence at the realization that Ellena is his daughter and that he cannot, therefore, penetrate her. Even though she is ostensibly asleep, Ellena has her legs up in the bed. Her rather chunky thighs invite our gaze up to their meeting point in a very suggestive V, darkly shaded by the artist (see illustration). The almost lewd invitation of Ellena's pose stands in stark opposition to the more decorous body of the soldier in the illustration from *Udolpho*. Holding aloft a smoking lantern in her right hand, which shines upon the scene from a distance, unlike the overhead glare of Schedoni's lantern above the head of Ellena, Emily reveals the body of a very beautiful male youth stretched out upon a couch.[22] A gash slices across his downstage pectoral muscle; several more wounded stripes cross his abdomen. Wrapped in a white sheet or shroud that cuts off exposure at the waist, the body combines aspects of a conventional pietà with Fuseli's painting of *The Nightmare,* in that a (rather muscular) arm torques from bed to floor, indicating both helplessness and the terrifying force that has twisted nature, at the same time that the comparatively beatific expression of the face, the whiteness of the flesh in contrast to the wounds, and the drops of blood splattering the floor near his hand indicate his heroic struggle against the forces of evil.

The contrast becomes more stark when we consider the viewer contained within each representation, a role that would correspond to Genette's narratee. In *The Midnight Assassin*, Schedoni is placed directly up stage center, looking down on the sleeping Ellena, who occupies the down center position. Thus, he faces us as well as her. In contrast, Emily holds the curtain back with her left hand, placing her body in profile to the audience. This positioning forces the viewer both to see with and through Emily at the same time, cementing our identification with her and preserving her from becoming a pornographic object of our interest. Schedoni's confrontational gaze, half up at us and half down at Ellena's body, leaves us in a very uncomfortable position. If, as his gaze seems to dare us to do, we identify with him, we must ravish Ellena with our eyes. If we refuse to side with evil, we are left no other

The Midnight Assassin; or, Confession of the Monk Rinaldi (1802). London: Printed for William Gilbert, *The Marvellous Magazine.*

position than to identify with the victim. The room itself offers a third, if equally pornographic, alternative: the small barred Romanesque window up left, through which light spills, enables us to imagine a hidden viewer, observing us observing Schedoni observing Ellena in an infinite regression or panopticon.

Illustrations like this one increase the reader's sense of isolation, as I earlier suggested. Other illustrations turn isolation into an advantage, permitting surveillance. Putatively more pious, the illustration to Isaac Crookenden's *The Distressed Nun* (1802) translates verbal iconography about the need to police females onto the visual plane. It depicts a languishing female, seated on the ground in a rude cell, into which has just burst a hero. She is draped in a toga; he wears late medieval garb. At the bottom foreground of the picture, a crucifix has become separated from the rosary beads with which it originally hung. The beads are tied into a knot and occupy the viewer's left-hand corner; the cross itself sits prominently in the right-hand foreground, next to a pitcher, presumably of water. Cleaving the beads from the cross casts off any imputations of Catholicism, while scrupulously preserving a Protestant character. The female's lax right hand curls around her lap, the index and middle fingers pointed downward as though to point our attention to the symbols beneath her. Above her head and off to stage left, a candle flames, representing the beacon of the inner light. Placed between these two icons of piety, the woman's slumped and defeated posture shows that she has become separated from ideals that are still meaningful to her. The cause of that falling-off does not appear overtly but is suggested by the breasts that her falling toga exposes. Again, in the illustration to *The Spectre Mother; or, The Haunted Tower*, the ghostly figure preserves her appeal. Her shroud slips down off her shoulders just far enough to silhouette her breasts and stomach in an inverted V. In both illustrations, since the hero faces the viewer in three-quarter profile, his glance down at the imprisoned female shares the same perspective as the viewer who also studies her form (although, in the *Spectre Mother*, we cannot tell whether he is more horrified by the fact or the fleshiness of that specter's appearance). A triangular circuit is drawn; our eyes move first to him, then with him to her, so that we identify with his impending liberation of her.

These pornographic tableaux bear close resemblance to the more explicitly erotic imaginings of other texts. In Crookenden's 1806 *The Mysterious Murder; or, The Usurper of Naples*, the Duke Savelli begins to ravish the captive Estaphona:

> He caught Estaphona in his arms; she screamed; her dress became deranged; he devoured her charms with his eyes, and violated the treasures of her bosom with his hand; her shrieks became fainter,

and Savelli had nearly obtained the conquest of a villain; when a new and unheard of event secured her honour: Jacquilina [the old servant] burst into the room, exclaiming, 'Forebear! She is your own daughter! It is Julia di Savelli.'

(21)

Savelli plunges his dagger into the breast of the servant before stabbing himself, declaring himself 'half a monster.' The vulnerability of females to penetration, whether sexual or violent, makes the villainy of men such as Savelli a gender perversion, since he, too, can fall victim to such piercing. While the reader may momentarily share with the villain the 'devouring' of the helpless female's 'charms,' he or she is preserved from complicity by also being able to witness the villain's self-destruction.

In the chapbooks' sensational techniques, we witness a closer relevance to eighteenth-century ideas about physical and social power as mediated through the eye. Opening a 'window to the soul,' the eye revealed the mesmerist or the mesmerized, total control or the total abandonment of madness.[23] This symbolic significance of the eye appears not only in the visual aspects of the chapbooks, but also in narrative components. For example, Isaac Crookenden's reiterated verbal formulae show this double aspect of the eye as containing both disease and cure. In Crookenden's *Fatal Secrets*, love and passion are conveyed by an involuntary stream of 'dewy light' emitted from the eyes (1806, 21, 23). 'The beaming moisture of their eyeballs shot into each other's breast reciprocal but indescribable emotions' (24). In *Horrible Revenge*, the 'crystal medium' of the eyes conducts sympathy and eyes are said to be able to 'touch each other' (1812, 5). Alternatively, a gaze exchanged can produce mutual contagion (*Fatal Secrets,* 1806, 28). Crookenden acknowledges as much in the anonymous dedication to a society lady which graces his *Fatal Secrets*. The 'virulent *matter* of inflammatory desires' can 'innoculate the heart for the admission of inflammatory desires'; the 'moral countenance may be so much *ruptured* as to require the nauceous, but wholesome *medicine* of legal discipline.' But like a homeopathic practitioner, he also insists that the same 'virulent *matter*' can inoculate in the other sense of inculcating virtue.

If, as Backscheider claims, the power of the eye connects to the power of the individual and the institution of surveillance as a form of social control, then the contagion of reading that breeds one possible source for this contagion of the eyes, so dreaded by Wordsworth and moralists, can also be harnessed by conduct- and chap-books as a source of higher control through the very appeal to the eyes. By making the space of Gothic intrigue immediate, the chapbook illustrations and their verbal counterparts continue the privatization and domestication of Gothic heroism we have seen in the characterological and thematic aspects of the tales. Creating a private fantasy realm to be consumed in the privacy of the home, the chapbooks foreshadow the Victorian conversion of a man's home into his castle.

Concentric circulation

Two chapbooks round off this chapter. Ranging in date from 1770's *Young Grigor's Ghost* to 1820's *The Bride of the Isles,* and thus bracketing the phenomenon, these are border tales. As such, they help us see the evolution of nationalism in a minority genre as it participates in the creation of a nationalist myth. This participation differs from the top-down version described by most theorists of nationalism. For instance, Gellner defines nationalism as a deceptive discrepancy between myth and actuality. On the one hand, the actuality consists of the 'general imposition of a high culture on society,' mediated by academic idioms and codified by bureaucratic regulations. On the other hand, the myth portrays nationalism as the conquest of a folk culture triumphant over the alien impositions (1983, 57). The chapbooks that follow illustrate a variation on Gellner's history. Not just a minority genre, they are also voices in a minority key, written from the perspective of colonial margins or of the Scottish borders of the kingdom. The first chapbook depicts the high culture as the alien oppression; it attempts resistance by a minority cultural revival and reaffirmation. In the second chapbook, we see the revival or invention of a local high culture maintaining links with the 'earlier folk styles and dialects,' as detected by Gellner, but bypassing his 'literate, specialist-transmitted culture' for a folk highway (57). Far from oppositional, the minority voices raised forgo urging separation or preparation for a war of liberation. Instead, they insist on the unique value their joining the alien high culture will give to the dominant structure.

Young Grigor's Ghost is a ballad chapbook, one of the few truly subversive examples we have. Rudimentarily or fully, it combines elements attributed to radical literature: folk genre (the ballad), dialect (Scottish pronunciation), open appeal to a reader imagined collectively, dramatized dialogue, covert criticism of hegemonic forces.

While it maintains the customary primitive woodcut as its frontispiece, the ballad's length (three parts, eight pages, duodecimo) exceeds the form of broadside ballads, indicating its greater importance. Set in the 'high mountains that stand beyond Forth,' it addresses itself to all 'young lovers in Scotland.'

As a cautionary tale, it operates on two levels. On the most obvious side, it warns that broken loyalties to the [English] King will cause broken hearts and lives. Young Grigor's father had rebelled against that king; exiled, he had forfeited his lands. Yet he had retained sufficient wealth to endow Grigor, whose care he left to a friend, fully expecting that friend to continue the fine Continental education Grigor had already received as preparation for an aristocratic existence. This friend betrays his trust, just as Grigor's father had betrayed his trust to the King. He keeps Grigor impoverished and ignorant, and uses him as a drudge.

So much for the first layer. More subtly, the ballad condemns the King's treatment of his subjects as equally traitorous. The false friend's treatment of Grigor is compared to the King's 'recruiting all hands' through the kingdom, only to enslave them to his will. Moreover, the King's need to police the territorial borders of his extended kingdom can work to satisfy private vengeance. When the false friend suspects that his daughter has fallen madly in love with Grigor, he confronts the pair and she vows her eternal fidelity to Grigor. In retaliation for the daughter's stubborn adherence to Grigor, her parents send a secret message to Inverness, 'Which brought out a party young Grigor to press.' Grigor appears either a pragmatist or a fatalist: 'Now Grigor considering his pitiful case, / Received the bounty and swore to the peace.' Sent off to 'America,' Grigor proves his valor and his loyalty and is promoted to serjeant. His valor accounts him nought: 'near Fort Niagara, in the year fifty-nine,' Grigor is slain by a party of Indians who encounter him while he keeps a habitual, solitary romantic communion with his absent lover in the forests of the New World. His ghost appears to his true love, who pines away and soon joins him in the afterlife, as does her mother, leaving the father alone to bemoan his losses. The final stanza compares the 'old Father' metaphorically to the old King, veiling a threat to such 'cruel parents' that they will have 'plenty of gold, no girls nor no boys.'

The 1770 resonance between the ballad's love story and political events emanates from the emphatic dating of Grigor's adventures, 1759. In that year, probably the most rousing in terms of victories, during what Tom Pocock has called 'the very first world war,' and certainly the most significant in terms of Britain's imperial status by the end of that war, British forces defeated the French at Minden, at Quiberon Bay, and at Quebec, captured Ticonderoga, re-solidified their position in India (successful naval battles off Pondicherry and Madras), and beat off a threatened invasion by crushing the French fleet off Portugal at Lagos Bay (Pocock, 1998, 10–11). In 1770, Scotsmen who had tried and failed to throw off the English yoke just 25 years earlier saw domination secure if bloated, as Britain swallowed India and Canada. Recirculated in 1779, the American section of the poem could take on new significance. Even though the poem specifically states that Grigor goes to America in 1759, events shaping up in and around Fort Niagara would align the rebellious colony with the daughter's rebellion against the father. By implication, Scotland, too, that rebellious colony now quiescent, becomes part of the family triangle, the chapbook's Scottish identity insisted upon in the poem's rhyming of 'case' with 'peace,' 'hair' with 'appear,' 'blood' with 'wood,' and 'sea' with 'eye.'

Appropriately to its domestic emphasis, 1802's *Gothic Legends* had metaphorized colonialism as a feast. In *The Bride of the Isles* of 1820, the colonies write back. At the same time, the chapbook extends the metaphor connecting alimentary and political absorption in interesting ways, beginning with the cannibalism of its publication history. John Polidori's *The Vampyre,* first published by *The New Monthly Magazine* in 1819, established the thirst for vampire tales, both at home and on the Continent.[24] The theatre rushed to slake this thirst. In 1820, London's English Opera House presented a play entitled *The Vampire; Or, The Bride of the Isles*. This play had been adapted by James Robinson Planché from Charles Nodier's French melodrama, *Le Vampire*. The chapbook is a 'sixpenny adaptation of the play complete with a dramatic hand-colored frontispiece' (Haining, 1978, 113).

As though meditating on its own conditions of being, the chapbook depicts two kinds of circulation, the demonic and the providential. The providential is endogamous and is represented by the last-minute appearance of Hildebrand, Lord Gowen; the demonic congeals in the figure of Montcalm/Marsden, the vampire, and represents an exogamous, external threat. Each of these types of relationship correlates with the nationalist twist the chapbook gives the play's setting. According to Peter Haining, Nodier had 'inexplicably set the play in Scotland, and although Planché rightly insisted to the theater proprietor, Samuel Arnold, that vampires were unknown there, he was told that Scottish music and dress had already been prepared and "the public will neither know nor care"' (1978, 113). The chapbook incorporates the play's Scottish costuming by decorating the tale with mentions of Scottish ritual and customs. Yet I would suggest that this 'dressing' of the chapbook goes beyond a fashioning of consumer appeal to assert Scotland's place as heroic contributor to the well-being of the recently formed United Kingdom. In so doing, this particular chapbook comes full cycle, returning to the roots established by the full-length Gothic novels in insisting that private identity only matters insofar as it affects the public good.

Not a direct copy of Polidori's novelette, the chapbook tale neverthe-less shares some interesting aspects. Unlike later, more omnivorous vampires, these two early types must drink the blood of a female once a year in order to be renewed. Each also features a character named Ruthven: in Polidori, Lord Ruthven is the villain/vampire; the chap-book recycles this name, making the heroic qualities of its Ruthven immediately apparent through his actions and his title, Earl of Marsden. This hero's 'rank and birth were unexceptionable but his fortune was very inadequate to support a title, which made him (added to the love of military glory) enter into the profession of arms, of which he was an ornament' (116). Ruthven is quickly killed in battle. Eschewing the 'disinheritance plot' of Gothic novels, as had Polidori's tale, the chapbook nonetheless refuses to join Polidori's lead by shift-ing our interest away from 'the earlier "hero", who was a passive suffer-ing figure, to the more dynamic, action-initiating "villain", ... simply one aspect of Byronism' (Bleiler, 1966, xxxix). Instead, the chapbook grinds that transition to a halt, restoring to our gaze not so much a passive, suffering hero as Robert, the 'action-initiating' servant.

Son to the steward of Lord Ronald, the Baron of the Isles, Robert's heroic qualities are both innate and learned, though once again with a difference from other chapbook heroes. His innate qualities take the form of intuition: seeing the reanimated body of Ruthven, now occu-pied by the vampire but posing as having recovered his health, Robert 'stood aghast, his hair bristled up and his joints trembled, and alto-gether he would have served as a good model of horror to a painter or statuary' (1978, 119). Here, the clichéd late eighteenth-century associa-tion of the lower classes with bodily functions and a coarse corporality is both invoked and overturned. Robert's reaction restores a nobility to material life, equal to the supernatural authority accorded to material evidence in the Middle Ages, when corpse-touching detected criminals. Robert's certainty derives not only from his bones; he is said to be 'much better read than the warrior, his master, in the traditional tales of his country, and its popular superstitions' (123). Robert becomes the butt of jests for his insistence that Marsden had died and that the living body they see must belong to a vampire (121). Ridicule cannot deter him. Despite the fact that 'Robert had courage to face a cannon, and never turned his back on the bravest foe, but ... felt daunted at the disclosure he meant to make to Lord Ronald,' he vows to follow his 'duty like an honest servant' and inform his master (124).

Robert's common sense is matched by the commonness of his appetite. He fortifies himself for his task by visiting the 'cellar-man' to procure 'a glass of cordial and a horn of ale to revive his spirits.' His appetite furnishes further evidence against the false Ruthven: Robert complains to the Baron that the Earl neither goes to mass or prayer nor takes salt on his trencher (124); to himself, he complains that the Earl 'eats and drinks voraciously, it makes me sick to see him as I stand in waiting, and no salt – faugh!' (127). Moreover, his former wild oats nourish Robert's heroism. When the Baron is declared insane and incarcerated for having accused Ruthven of vampirism, Robert can come to his aid because he has access to secret pathways, 'for which he had a key, having procured it some time before he went to the wars, for he was then a rakish youth, and loved to steal out to the village dance or festival, after he was supposed to retire to rest for the night; but now he was contracted to the languishing blue-eyed Effie he was reformed, and voluntarily relinquished all such stolen delights' (127). His status as reformed rake makes him correspond to the fictions of Richardson and Fielding; the effortless voluntarism of that reform makes him exceed models like Tom Jones and Mr B.

But an even greater distance separates him from those earlier eighteenth-century heroes than his sexual fidelity and his rank. Despite the passage's insistence upon privacy (his private return, the private door), Robert puts his treasure to the service of the public good. Questioned by the Baron as to whether he is friend or foe, Robert replies, 'Friend, ... and when I prove otherwise to my most noble master and commander, may I be seized by the foul fiend and made food for vulture' (127). Robert's loyalty arises from the traditions binding his family to that of the Baron: '"My father", said the honest fellow, "has lived with you from youth to age: I was born within these walls, and my deceased mother suckled your amiable heiress; treachery in me would be double guilt: no, I would die to serve the house of Ronald!"' (124–5). Bonds of fealty flow between the two houses, just as the mother's milk circulates among them, creating affinities that result in obligations and responsibilities rather than in mobility.[25]

In contrast, Robert's fiancée, Effie, proves vulnerable to the vampire's seduction precisely because she forgets her duty and aspires to social ennoblement. The vampire insinuates that 'nothing but dress and rank' lacks to 'level her with her mistress,' qualities he can bestow. The devilishness of the vampire's proposition comes from its equation of fungible traits like costume with birth. But Effie's response shows that she, too, locates rank in exterior trappings: '"But I am ignorant, and can neither play music, sing, dance, or do the honours of a table, like Lady Margaret." This reply pleased the vampire; it seemed one of a very yielding nature, if she had no scruples but what arose from a fear of her own demerits' (129–30). The narrator excuses Effie on several grounds. First, the vampire has supernatural powers and 'eyes that are described like the fascination of a basilisk,' once again troping the mesmerism of ocular authority we saw in Crookenden. Second, any girl might have succumbed to the temptation of having an Earl sighing for her love. But no sooner does the narrator exculpate Effie than he castigates her for double treachery. Effie's head is also said to 'run on nothing but the glare of thy expected coronet,' revealing that ambition overshadows sympathy for a lover, and this ambition causes Effie to betray both her lover Robert and her 'kind and generous mistress' (130).

Servants are not the only people with public duties in this chapbook. Margaret's duty belongs to her father. Initially, she fulfills this mission: the narrative praises her for her 'dutiful affection' both to biological and to heavenly father (116–17). Affianced to the true Ruthven, Margaret and he refuse to go forward with their wedding plans when the Baron falls suddenly ill, 'declaring their joys would be incomplete without his revered presence' (117). Fallen under the vampire's spell, Margaret casts off her reverence for custom and joins the false Ruthven in begging her father for the right to a private marriage: '"Ruthven and I are in unison with each other's sentiments; we seek not in pomp and glare for happiness; we place our prospects of future bliss in elegant retirement and domestic pleasures. Allow us to be now united, I entreat you, and you can afterwards treat your neighbours, retainers, and servants, as plenteously as you like, but I shrink from the idea of a public marriage"' (125). Margaret's desires for a private ceremony, like her vision of a life spent in retirement, breach laws of hospitality whose traditions the Baron enumerates earlier in the text (124).

Her subsequent attempt to marry in secret while her father is incarcerated underscores the selfishness of her actions, as do his very Lear-like ruminations: 'he who had so ardently strove not only to fulfill his own duties, but to supply the place as far as possible of the late lady Cassandra, his amiable wife, and he felt there was no sting so keen as a child's ingratitude. The barbed arrow seemed to touch his very vitals, and for the first time in his life the brave Ronald shed tears' (127–8).

Lack of duty allies the prodigal son or daughter with demonic forces. It also emasculates the brave patriarch whose strength comes from his secure sense of right. While Ronald's insistence on the proper mode of marriage might make him seem patriarchal, the narrative carefully distinguishes his demands from those of unreasonable fathers like the one in *Adolphus and Louisa*. Not only do we learn that Ronald has raised his daughter with paternal *and* maternal affection, to the best of his ability, but we also see him setting aside his 'very exalted views for the aggrandisement of his heiress' in favor of her happiness (117).

In its depiction of duty, the chapbook distributes its demands egalitarianly. The Baron owes duty beyond his immediate family to his King. Ruthven loses his life when war breaks out in Flanders, enemy not of Scotland per se but of Great Britain, to whose 'glory and success' the battle ends (118). Having served his King, the Baron still has no leisure to follow his own desires, which would include accompanying Ruthven's body to its proper burial and consoling his daughter. Instead, he must 'pay his duty in England to his sovereign before he repaired to the Isles. Unexpected events detained him two months at the British court, but he at last effected his departure to his long-wished-for home' (119). Rather than enforcing subservience, duty secures a measure of independence. The Baron holds sway over his own dominions, unlike the political situation of actual Scottish nobles after the Act of Union. Promised that they would maintain their customary authority in their own domains and gain an equivalent authority in the English Parliament after ceding their right to an independent Scottish Parliament, Scottish nobles in fact became pawns in English ministerial control.[26]

Natural and supernatural powers ratify attention to duty. The Baron subdues the threat to his family only because another hero rides to the rescue at the chapbook's conclusion. This hero is Hildebrand, son of the Baron's sister, who appears unexpectedly to 'pay respects and duty to him as becomes a nephew and godson' (134). Hildebrand shares with Robert a 'strong belief in the existence of vampires,' learned at his mother's knee. His embrace of 'superstition' simultaneously levels and ennobles such beliefs. Together, the Baron, Robert, and Hildebrand conquer the vampire just as he is poised to wed Margaret and devour her, forestalling his design just long enough to cause the vampire's tenure to expire (135). As his reward, Hildebrand conquers the heart of Margaret; they pass the rest of their lives in wedded happiness.

Ruthven's incursions into the Baron's family integrity teach the Baron to distinguish the claims of duty: one must carefully discriminate friend from foe, or one suffers the danger of incorporation, literally realized in the vampire's eating habits. Just so, the chapbook enables the distinction between feasting off the riches of an assimilated people to vampirizing the living. The chapbook presents the marrow of Scotland, without draining that source beyond its ability to reproduce. In this fictional preserve, minstrels still tune their harps in the great hall of the Baron, singing 'the deeds of Scottish chiefs, long since departed, amongst whom the heroic Wallace was not forgot' (117). When the Baron imagines Ruthven miraculously restored to them after the battle, he welcomes his designated heir with more Scottish song, to which 'the damsels, with their swains showed off their best reels *à la Caledonia*' (120). More importantly, MacPherson's imagined Scotland appears in the name given to the cave where Margaret resorts to learn her future, the Cave of Fingal (115). This cave unites Scottish and English literary history: Fingal houses the spirits of Merna, the Hag of the mountains; Una, 'the spirit of the storm'; and Ariel, 'the spirit of the Air' (115–6).

Beyond the obvious allusions to a corporate literary identity, the text contains two significant commentaries on relations between Scotland and England, hidden to our view today but more transparent to its contemporary audiences. The first appears in the very name Ruthven, which had a specifically Scottish association, one that keys to its use by the chapbook author to signify true and false heroes.[27] In 1600, then King James VI of Scotland, soon to take the throne of England as James I, caused to be murdered two Ruthven brothers at their family estate, Gowrie House. James owed the Ruthvens £80 000. Moreover, the elder brother, the Earl of Gowrie, had just opposed James's demand for 100 000 crowns with which to prosecute his claim to the English throne (Roughead, 1919, 5). Proclaiming the murders defense against a treasonous plot, James could confiscate Gowrie's estates, eliminate his debt, and eradicate the family in name and person by banishing the surviving members. This tale of monarchical intrigue alone might suffice to underscore the chapbook's theme of baronial/colonial relations. The title given to that chapbook hero, Earl of Marsden, furthers the emphasis by reminding us of a more abbreviated hero of Scottish resistance, the Earl of Mar, who suffered defeat at the battle of Sheriffmuir in the '15.

Not all battles took on such military splendor or such an exotic cast. More mundane battles raged between England and Scotland in the period between the '15 and the '45, as Bruce Lenham relates:

Though the Scottish aristocracy wanted free access to English markets for the goods and products which helped pay their rents, they by no means accepted the idea that they must resign themselves to potentially destructive English competition in their own domestic markets, especially in activities into which they had sunk a lot of irrecoverable capital. Coal mines and salt works were the prime, and normally linked examples, for Scottish salt pans were coal-fired. The Treaty of Union contained extremely complex provisions, notably the lengthy eighth article, which had the effect of giving Scottish coal a temporary, and Scottish salt a long-term fiscal advantage in the Scottish domestic market.

(1984, 74)

Quite literally the marrow of the earth in some locales, Scottish salt was mined from internal brine deposits. In this context, recall that Robert's suspicions about the false Ruthven had been aroused by his refusal to eat salt (*Bride*, 1978, 124, 127).

This curious attention to spices reflects more than Robert's culinary knowledge. While by 1820 such glamorous battles as those between Ruthven and Stuart, between Jacobite and Whig, might seem a thing of the past, in the negotiations over the dimensions of the united kingdom, Scottish salt crystallized as a national product, to be protected as such. Ultimately, though, because of its centrality to English manufacture and empire-building, salt becomes a manifestation of imperial cooperation. A 'pillar of the first industrial revolution,' as S. A. M. Adshead punningly calls salt (1992, 146), the Leblanc process, a prime foundry of which existed at Glasgow, substituted coal-firing for solar evaporation, thereby enabling Newcastle merchants to utilize not only the largecoal needed for heating but also its by-product, smallcoal. The type of salt produced seasoned not only table fare but also industrial production, contributing the artificial sodium carbonate necessary to manufacture glass, soap, and textiles (104–42). As Adshead further says of the salt manufacture's structural organization, 'it was an industry before the bourgeoisie or the proletariat' (146). Salt exportation opened up new sources of revenue and new markets for import goods. In the American South, salt was exchanged for cotton; the Baltic poured in its grain and wood to pay for salt; Australia proffered wool; Bengal gave jute for salt: 'with a total production in the early nineteenth century of around four million cwt, [Great Britain's] was the most dynamic salt industry in Europe and already played a world role' (106).

Giving a relish to British industry, then, salt also rubbed in the wounds of its poorer classes. Because of its dominance in British households, governments seeking to raise revenue for foreign wars frequently depended upon raising the salt tax.[28] The rates at which salt was taxed were raised in 1780, 1782, and again in 1798. These raises occurred despite almost half a century of argument against the taxation of necessaries as either unjust to or lacking compassion for the poor; or as unfair to or lacking compassion for manufacturers, who would have to bear the burden of increased taxes in increased wages to pay for them. However, according to William Kennedy, the 'freeholder view of society' that prevailed throughout the eighteenth century held that every man had a duty to pay some tax in order to be considered a citizen (1964, 180–1).[29] Robert's disgust at Ruthven's abstention, recorded in that fricative 'Faugh!,' indicates simultaneously that the vampire has triply renounced his rights to citizenship: as a Scotsman, for failing to partake of a home industry; as a Briton, for failing to help provide military revenue; and as a human being, for seeking his source of salt in the blood of his countrymen and women instead.[30]

The vampire feeds upon others, promoting in the process only his own circulation. In contrast, the author of *The Bride of the Isles* feeds upon John Polidori's tale in order to circulate what Hobsbawm in another context has called the 'invention of tradition' (1983). Polidori introduces his tale by giving its superstitions an exotic genealogy:

> The superstition upon which this tale is founded is very general in the East. Among the Arabians it appears to be common: it did not, however, extend itself to the Greeks until after the establishment of Christianity; and it has only assumed its present form since the division of the Latin and Greek churches... In the West it spread, with some slight variation, all over Hungary, Poland, Austria, and Lorraine...
>
> (1966, 261)

Just as Matthew Lewis had done with his tale of *The Monk*, Polidori incorporates modern sources with those more distant in time and place, lending literary justification to his admittedly ghoulish interest. He retails a story that had appeared in the '*London Journal*, of March, 1732,' which he calls 'a curious, and, of course, *credible* account of a particular case of vampyrism, which is stated to have occurred at Madreyga, in Hungary' (ibid.). To these examples he adds those of

Byron's *The Giaour*, Southey's *Thalaba*, the history of Tournefort, and the scholarly researches of Calmet (262–3). In contrast, the chapbook author asserts vampirism as the unique property of Scotland, '*still extant* in the southern isles..., but not with the same force as it was a century since' (1978, 114). *The Bride of the Isles* brings the exotic home to roost on the margins of the nation, wedding it to British ideals and aspirations, and infusing it with a new spirit and new blood.

7
From Innkeepers to Puppet Masters: Staging the (Heroic) Author

'Now, sir', said Oswald; 'I congratulate you as the son of Lord
and Lady Lovel; the proofs are strong and indisputable.'
'To us they are so', said Edmund; 'but how shall we make
them so to others? And what are we to think of the funeral of
Lady Lovel?'
'As of a fiction', said Oswald; 'the work of the present lord, to
secure his title and fortune.'

(Reeve, 1883, 91–2)

Except insofar as the roles of women are concerned, the Gothic novels
and chapbooks we have surveyed frustrate any 'progressive' narrative,
in the sense of a purely linear development, of the nation's growth to
an incarnated state. Embracing both a critique and a validation of circulation, of individual and institutional action, they demonstrate the
delicate flirtations of factions before union could be consummated in
the nineteenth century, a marriage of ideas signified by the emergence
of an autonomous realm for culture that collaborated with the interests
of that state.[1] This seesawing accommodation of ideas about the nation
and the state tallies with Eagleton's view of dominant ideologies as
lacking 'purity' and univocality, a lack that enables the necessarily continual negotiations, appropriations, and reinflections of subordinate
ideologies (1991, 45). Nevertheless, the survey of Gothic writings in
the period does show the centrality of place held by concepts of the
Gothic hero and Gothic heroism in the process of that development.

Gothic authors contributed doubly to that consensus: by creating
heroic characters and by representing *themselves* as heroes.[2] To a large
extent, such claims to authorial heroism depended upon the personal-
ization and personal authority of the author.[3] Like the heroes of their
tales, the authors develop social relations, with their readers as with
their societies, through their very public interventions.[4] Accordingly,

this chapter returns to my own 'Gothic myth of origins' to retrace the heroic role played by the author, either through her or his editorial or narratorial strategy. Beginning with Walpole and Reeve, we will find an authoritarian relationship established, as they advance their own claims and the claims of their newly founded genre. As modes of production geared up to reach more modern capacity, dragging with them a change in the modes of distribution, anonymity combated authorship for pride of place. From the highly personal, quasi-authoritarian author, we will move to that increasingly anonymous voice, seeking to uncover what connection, if any, exists between the heightened individualism of the Gothic hero and the collective role assumed by his author. Taking in debates over copyright law along the way, I will argue that a narratorial and editorial movement converse to the emphasis upon individualism occurs, whereby the chapbook authors' foregrounding of modes of production and dissemination gives them the function of the institution, invisibly controlling the circulation individuals only apparently direct.[5] As I hope to show, Gothic authors advocating a heightened role for themselves qua authors located individual freedom in organized authority, just as Gothic tales made the same identification possible.

Cryptic encounters; or, the nation as book

During the years between publication of Walpole's and Reeve's novels, the battles for 'individual freedom' and 'organized authority' took on new urgency, due to legislative changes in copyright. In 1709's Act of Anne, the limitation on copyright was set at 21 years for old books and 14 years for new ones, with a possible 14-year extension if the author still lived. Many authors took up discursive cudgels against what they saw as a usurpation of their property rights, arguing for perpetual copyright, among them Johnson, Boswell, Hume, Goldsmith, Southey, and Wordsworth.[6] Cases testing the law percolated through the courts, notably 1760's *Tonson* v. *Collins* and 1769's *Millar* v. *Taylor*. With the 1774 decision in *Donaldson* v. *Becket*, perpetual copyright suffered perpetual defeat.[7] Refusing to acquiesce easily, authors continued their agitation and won modest reprieves on the abrogation of their income and their rights: in 1814, rights were stretched to 28 years for new works; in 1842, limits once again elasticized to permit protection for 42 years. According to Terry Ross, the new laws represented a sea-change in conceptions of literary property from an 'older, static conception of literary property as the fruit of an author's intellectual labour' to emphasis on property as acquiring value only through 'exchange and circulation' (1992, 3, 8, 19, n. 42), or, as J. Pocock interprets it, as a movement from 'the object of ownership' to the 'subject of produc-tion' (1985, 115, 119, 121).[8] Activating the view of literary property so that its value could only be liberated within a dynamic system of exchange and circulation meant that literary influence ceased to be a case of civic virtue and instead became a test of civilizing virtue. As such, it matched evaluative upheavals in late-eighteenth century society whereby the utility of capital won for it a nationalist tribute superseding the awe felt and allegiance paid to land-based power.

Among the judges deciding the fate of perpetual copyright sat Lord Kames, who presided over a 1773 Scottish Court of Sessions decision. Kames held against perpetual copyright because he wanted to ensure that cheap copies of canonical works circulated among all the classes. As such, his decision coheres with his earlier 1762 position about the social benefits of art. But as I demonstrated in Chapter 1, Kames believed the 'common sense' of taste to be providentially restricted, permitting social discriminations. With the proliferation of genres and subforms of literature foreshadowing the logical development of the market into stratified versions of art, 'common sense,' in all its over-tones, could be preserved at the same time that the opened floodgates would not obliterate all distinctions necessary to the smooth working of society, as Kames saw it. Whereas in his 1762 *Elements of Criticism* he had privileged dramatic spectacle and the plastic arts for their ability to knit men of different classes together, by 1773 he judged that common knowledge of literature could both provide the 'support to the social affections' needful when divisions of class and experience threatened an imaginary connection and preserve that 'separation of men into dif-ferent classes, by birth, office, or occupation, *however necessary*' (1830, 443, emphasis added), as long as literature was produced so that it wore the distinctive literary garb of its status, as though sumptuary laws had migrated into the booksellers' stalls.

In Chapter 1, I mused that Kames's prescription for the type of litera-ture that could best effect this imaginary connection, whereby fablers were urged to borrow from history to foster the delusion of reality and 'the subject chosen must be distant in time, or at least in place' (1830, 394), sounded like a Gothic novel. Copyright law mired Gothic authors in conflicting aims.[9] On the one hand, as authors, they desired to reap the financial benefits of their labor in perpetuity. On the other hand, as *Gothic* authors, who chose their generic affiliation because it encoded a social vision and enabled social commentary, exchange was more than a prerequisite of remuneration; it was the precondition for success on less tangible grounds. Because of the rapidity and fluency with which Gothic ideals (and novels) eventually leached out into the public domain, Gothic authors could be assured that their fictional social visions would find a wide audience and contribute to the debate over heroic leadership. But because each new production would inevitably be viewed as 'intertextual,' in the untheoretical sense of borrowings, Gothic originality, one of the very grounds for copyright, would become an oxymoron.[10] After the 1774 decision, the way yawned for the very repetition, replication, de- and re-formation lying at the heart of Gothic modes of production. The elaboration of repetitive devices and the forms of production simultaneously thematized repetition as a modus vivendi. They thus produced the reassuring effect of homogeneity with a difference.[11] The eventuality that the *Critical Review's* writer shuddered over would become fact: fiction, especially Gothic fiction, would become a social event. Though the individual act of reading be performed in isolation, though the material read be a three-volume novel, a 72-page redaction, or a 36-page chapbook, knowledge about the content of that readerly act, if not the actual experience, helped bridge the divide.[12]

Editing and editorializing the nation: heroic Gothic 'editors'

Publishers and booksellers found ways to circumvent the restrictions of copyright law because critical editions gave the editor a form of proprietary interest over canonical or non-protected works. Thus Shakespeare enabled a kind of commercial as well as literary and national appropriation, as I suggested in Chapter 1. While Gothic novels are not critical editions, they often exhibit critical mass in their reliance on Shakespeare, either for prefatorial defenses, for plot situations and allusions (Walpole, Reeve, the chapbooks), or, in company with Blair, Young, and Milton, as fodder for epigraphs (Radcliffe). As we will see, this appropriation of literary authority and tradition as constituting proprietorship found sanction in reviews of Gothic novels like *The Monk*, requiring us to moderate claims about the pressures for originality.[13] Just as Blackstone analogized literary and real property, so Gothic authors acquired a 'virtue' in each of the dual senses outlined in Chapter 5: as part of a circulating economy and as part of a hereditary status. In this section, we will look at the editorial strategies that, while allowing their ideas to circulate, nonetheless lent their voices a hereditary status.

Walpole's Theodore may have been hailed as a new national type, if the Gothic novels that followed and the conduct books celebrating Walpole's characters by name are any indication. But Walpole's impact was doubled by the inclusion of a second hero behind his tale. This hero is the author himself, first in the guise of 'editor,' finally *in propria persona.*[14]

Antiquarian *sprezzatura* places the accomplishments of Walpole's 'editor' out of the reach of many. The title page to the first edition trumpets two principal attributes for editorial work: William Marshall translates, and he is a gentleman. These claims could be self-reinforcing. Before the nineteenth-century professionalization of education, scholarly achievement and status were relatively synonymous. Yet, at times, Marshall's scholarship seems almost too excessive to be genteel. He is a historian, who notices the typography employed and its provenance, and who can delimit the possible date of composition by the use of Spanish names for the domestics, since the establishment of Arragonian kings resulted in familiarity with such appellations. Aesthetic appreciation tempers this tendency to be 'Dry-as-Dust.' As a grammarian ('The style is purest Italian' (1963, 3) and a connoisseur of Italian literature, the 'beauty of the diction' leads him to believe that the story has been penned near in time to its date of printing, because '[l]etters were then in their most flourishing state in Italy... ' (ibid.).

Lest his antiquarian tendencies make him seem *démodé* and hence *déclassé,* the standards by which he judges this manuscript as fit to be offered to the public are distinctly modern. No bombast, similes, flowers, digressions, or unnecessary descriptions, brags the editor, detract from the story's thrust towards catastrophe: 'Never is the reader's attention relaxed. The rules of the drama are almost observed throughout the conduct of the piece. The characters are well drawn, and still better maintained. Terror, the author's principal engine, prevents the story from ever languishing; and it is so often contrasted by pity, that the mind is kept up in a constant vicissitude of interesting passions' (4). The eighteenth-century aesthetic standards of artistic decorum in which 'Marshall' judges the novel would be calculated to lull a sophisticated audience who might have greeted his claims about the historicity of his 'discovered manuscript' with dubiety, but who would credit the familiar litany of categories, in descending order of importance, by which men could know art.[15]

And yet the litany does more than merely lull. It subtly reinforces the identity between knowing art and knowing how to run the nation, an identity that would become even more pronounced in the mid-nineteenth-century battles over extension of the franchise. This collapsing of civic and civil recurs when 'Marshall' insists that the story has value for a modern audience: the 'piety that reigns throughout, the lessons of virtue that are inculcated, and the rigid purity of the sentiments, exempt this work from the censure to which romances are but too liable' (5). An interesting ambiguity arises in this sentence of praise. The 'rigid purity' of the sentiments could bespeak the 'piety' with which the sentence begins. But the syntactic separation opens up the possibility that the rigid purity refers equally well to the diction of the piece. 'Marshall' yokes the values by sliding metonymically from content to form, a dexterity for which he also praises the 'author.'[16]

Neither the language nor the conduct have anything that 'savours of barbarism,' he tells us, a comment that mirrors the linguistic class biases present in the text's dialogics, as I argued in Chapter 2. Now, the 'editor' trains his critical eye and ear on his own century and class. According to him, neither contemporary manners nor linguistic skills can bear comparison with those depicted. The 'editor' fears his 'translation' falls short of the original because so 'little care is taken to speak pure language in common conversation. Every Italian or Frenchman of any rank piques himself on speaking his own tongue correctly and with choice' (5). The 'editor' of the first Preface presents himself, then, as a reformer of British national standards. He intends to resurrect linguistic morality through the reimportation of foreign models, at the same time that he draws attention to the difficulty of his endeavor. 'Common conversation' has debased the nation's ability to speak with propriety, both in the overt sense of correctness and the covert sense of class distinction ('choice'). Instead of granting audiences the right to censure his product, he reserves the right to censure modern English audiences. And the message of the tale reinforces this chastisement by showing the political consequences of a want of discrimination.

To some extent, the first Preface's playful 'editorializing' of Nicholas Murano in the persona of William Marshall enacts Walpole's 1747 definition of literature as inevitably intertextual, the grounds upon which he had ridiculed perpetual copyright: 'Poet would commence Action against Poet, and Historian against Historian, complaining of literary Trespasses.'[17] Yet, in his attack on Voltaire in the second Preface, Walpole proceeds in the very manner he had satirized.

Walpole's action against Voltaire reverses the language politics of the first preface and demonstrates the concern to defend national interests as he defined them that I have previously argued motivated his creation of *Otranto* in the first place. Because Walpole now speaks out in his own voice, and because the fame of *Otranto* has furnished him a national pulpit, he can now speak as the Voice *of* the Nation, instead of as a voice *to* the nation. Within the novel proper, Walpole's desire to proffer a national model for British identity, despite the flimsiness of his vehicle, had appeared most readily in his invocations of Shakespeare's ghost.[18] Echoes of Shakespeare's plays occur at key moments in the tale. But the loudest notes sound in the second Preface, where Walpole claims to 'shelter my daring under the canon of the brightest genius this country, at least, has produced' (14). Using that Shakespearean canon as a weapon, Walpole defends Shakespeare against the depredations of Voltaire by deriding Voltaire's imperfect command of English history, agitating in the process the lull in Anglo-French relations:

> May not the critic's skill in the force and power of our language have been as incorrect and incompetent as his knowledge of our history? Of the latter his own pen has dropped glaring evidence. In his preface to Thomas Corneille's Earl of Essex, monsieur de Voltaire allows that the truth of history has been grossly perverted in that piece... he undertakes from the overflowing of his own reading to give the nobility of his own country a detail of queen Elizabeth's favourites – of whom, he says, Robert Dudley was the first, and the earl of Leicester the second.
>
> (11)

Walpole's language games in this passage contribute to the fun. Characterizing Voltaire's efforts as 'undertaking' from his 'overflowing' subtly empties out his achievement, suggesting both that Voltaire has culled from the dregs of knowledge and that his ill-informed hubris buries him in the attempt. Walpole's attack on Voltaire stands alone in the period's deification of the French author in the service of cosmopolitanism as an aristocratic ideal, urged by Newman (1997, 1–16). Moreover, as an example of the nascent British nationalism Newman charts, it is anomalous in class origin as well as time, thereby bolstering my contention that the Gothic novel furnished the best and earliest resting-place for nationalist ideology. Far from the worship of a

Francophonic and Francophiliac cosmopolitanism, Walpole's appropriation of French in the body of the Preface demonstrates his linguistic
superiority. His allusions to Greek theater, to the Elizabethan stage,
and to classical French dramatists attest to the preeminent breadth of
his learning. And all these accomplishments, he insists, belong to
'English ears' (1963, 14).

Speaking corporately, Walpole calls his audience's attention to such
Englishness. To the traditional institutions of government as the guar-
antors of British liberty, he adds the author as institutional force for
good, making the social agenda of Walpole's novel and his editorial
polemics congruent. Yet this force utters a two-sided message of cajol-
ery and threat; it opposes generic, characterological, and narratorial
registers of tragedy and farce, of identification and distancing, of spurious authenticity and confessed fictionality. Historical detail – the
authentic particulars of chivalric pomp and feudal codes of hospitality
strewn throughout the novel – works to enforce an authority with
control over our intellectual *and* material lives. The long description of
the Knight's procession with his retinue into the courtyard of Otranto,
which so impressed Scott with its historical accuracy (Edinburgh
edition, 1811, xix), drew on Segar's 1602 *Honour, Military and Civil* and
Morgan's 1661 *Sphere of Gentry* (Lewis, *Otranto*, 1963, x). But the scene
impresses literally with a concrete quantification that approaches the
formal grotesque (64), and that matches Walpole's descriptions of
criminal spectacles abroad in London.[19] In Walpole's hands, historical
research and criminal spectacles furnished equal opportunities to
impact the popular imagination: both spatialized the power relations
of society; in both, processions reenacted those power relations.[20] An
aristocrat by habit if only lately by birth, Walpole clings to traditional
methods of enforcement as rank matters less and power evaporates.

Clara Reeve has new battles to wage as a *woman* author. She bolsters
Walpole's title to Shakespearean pretensions: advertising her effort to
improve on Walpole, she fears her revision may spoil the 'original'
manuscript she employs for that purpose in the like manner that translators and imitators of Shakespeare destroy his spirit (1883, 5). At the
same time, she scavenges on that title by implanting Shakespearean
echoes of her own. Edmund responds like Hamlet to a sudden din from
below during a vigil: '"I am called", said he; "I obey the call!"' (77).
Tracing the noise to a closet, Edmund discovers a collapsed suit of
armor, whose inner breastplate is stained with blood. In further echoes
of *Hamlet*, this time deriving as much from staged performance as from
the play's text, hollow groans rise from beneath the floorboards where

the armor lies collapsed. Fear, loathing, and desire alternate as Reeve's claims to or appropriations of literary authority explode social and gender boundaries.

Foreshadowing the claims made explicitly in her treatise *The Progress of Romance*, Reeve's editorial interventions in *The Old English Baron* promote authorial status and influence under the guise of public service.[21] She claims to obtrude herself solely in the service of the reader, to instill the discipline that will earn the merit of a greater status. This humble portrait of literature as handmaiden to the reader keeps company with the novelistic detail of Edmund learning literature, manners, and policy at the feet of his preceptor, Edwin. Yet clearly, in practice, Reeve envisions merit accruing more readily to her than to her reader. Merit veers alarmingly in the opening gambit of the Preface to the first edition. With barely veiled condescension, she asserts that her elucidation of the design aims at enabling the reader to make a 'right' judgment of the work (i). But what begins as conference quickly modulates into confrontation, when she immediately challenges the reader's fitness to enter her world. Prior reading experience could constitute the audience's bona fides; but no presentation of such accreditation is possible in the structure of Reeve's interrogation. The illusion of dialogue camouflages the fact that she ventriloquizes responses from the reader that increasingly demean any pretense at readerly expertise. A passport into her fictive world will be granted only on condition that the reader accede to Reeve's valuations.[22] In designating herself as a fit guide, Reeve replaces masculine authority with the authority of the feminine, and she relentlessly insists on equal pay for equal status.

Reeve's personal ambitions intertwine with her thematic preoccupations. Although both her novel and her treatise postulate that access to authority can be gained by reading and writing, the proper modalities to enable such authority depend on performative transitivities of gender identification and on epistemological inquiry through and beyond the literal to the symbolic, since power requires the ability to discern disguises. Reeve's gendered authorial identification is slippery, moving as it does from the assumption of a mere translative editorship in the Preface to a specified coincidence with the figure of Oswald, who we learn has transcribed the family history for posterity.[23] Oswald's rehearsal of the past mimics in miniature the larger project of rehearsal conducted by Reeve (1883, 50–3, 55–63). The manner and matter of Father Oswald's clerical interventions seem inextricably tied to Reeve's self-representations, her notions of literary authorship, and the role she envisions for romance. The moralistic ending, which brings the story full circle by its introduction of the reader's posterity (153), makes the same point Reeve hammers home in her non-fiction editorializing: controlled circulation is the key to both social and literary health. The conflation of Reeve and the 'father' figure underscores the hermaphroditic nature of her enterprise, since Oswald is a man in skirts, and it lays claim to the sanction and authority of religion for the instantiation of a written word that empowers those who come into contact with, or more especially wield, it.

These twin acts of translation are encoded in the prefatory materials to the second edition of the novel. For that edition, Reeve owned her authorship; yet the language she adopts to speak of her novel conflates its situation with the circumstances of her nominal hero, Edmund. Adopting Walpole's pose of diffidence, she insists that her novel is published only through the approbation and encouragement of 'a circle of friends of approved judgment.' Dedicating this new edition to her friend Mrs Bridgen, the daughter of Samuel Richardson, she acknowledges the 'patronage and protection' the book has found at the hands of her friend, who 'cast an eye of favour upon his [the book's] first appearance, under all the disadvantages of an incorrect and very faulty impression' (1). Like Sir Philip Harclay, Edmund's champion, Mrs Bridgen has taken the book from this 'degrading dress, and encouraged him to assume a graceful and ornamental habit.' Moreover, Richardson's daughter revised and corrected the errors of the first impression, and 'gave him all the graces necessary to solicit and obtain the notice and approbation of the public.' Edmund's accession to social prestige fictively realizes the social (and financial) prestige Reeve demands for her literary work. The general diffusion of virtue in the novel consoles for the thwarted diffusion of literature, especially feminized (because romance) or female-authored works. Social institutions work to protect the rights of dependents, just as authors themselves are said to safeguard the populace through their work.

The masculine pronoun Reeve employs for her book further suggests that patronage can be the province of female, as well as male, mentors.[24] Perhaps more disturbingly, women can patronize men (or things characterized by the masculine pronoun). A double meaning attaches to the language I have quoted above, one that extends the implication of the novel's chivalric setting into the sphere of eighteenth-century book production. Patronage can mean both chivalric sponsorship and economic trade; a 'faulty impression' is both an insufficient evaluation and a poor edition of a book. Both meanings of the two words come together in the mind and works of Clara Reeve.

Like Walpole, Reeve frames her argument by temporal distancing and displacement; but, unlike her predecessor, she preserves spatial congruence by setting her story, not just the provenance of her manuscript, in the north of England. The familiarity of the geographical setting compensates somewhat for the disorientation of time. Reeve also makes the fiction of an editor work as a spatial and temporal bridge. She foregrounds her 'editorial' function by narratorial intrusions to explain the 'fragmentary' nature of the manuscript she supposedly proffers (22, 27). Both 'original' narrative breaks validate the necessity of her presence. The device occurs again four pages later. More important, such extradiegetic excursions remind the reader that the preservation of the material and the materiality of the manuscript from which she supposedly works depends upon the intervention of a person contemporary with them. Her editorial persona provides continuity, thwarting the potential of the rudimentary chapter (and thus temporal) divisions to segment experience.[25] Reeve's editorial interpolations contravene Tompkins's description of Gothic novels as set at a 'double remove' (338). Reeve employs the frame-tale topos of romance speciously to bathe both her message and her persona with the ambience of historical duration.

As we have seen in the discussions of individual novels, acknowledgment of fictionality wars with remnants of 'authenticity' preserved in framed tale and authoritarian narration. Lewis's and Radcliffe's novels are self-reflexive, sometimes almost parodically so. This self-reflexivity takes the form of frequent meditations about the act of reading or writing, or about transcribing putative oral traditions, either as an authorial intrusion or on the part of characters who are also authors. More oblique than the editorial manipulations, thematized scenes of reading and writing and allusive echoes of earlier Gothic novels gesture towards an encroachingly hegemonic insularity.[26]

Lewis's opening 'Advertisement' adverts to the transcriber's situation, at the same time that it lets us see the evolving importance of the literary marketplace:

> The first idea of this Romance was suggested by the story of the *Santon Barsisa*, related in The Guardian. – The *Bleeding Nun* is a tradition still credited in many parts of Germany; and I have been told, that the ruins of the castle of *Lauenstein*, which she is supposed to

haunt, may yet be seen upon the borders of *Thuringia*. – The *Water King*, from the third to the twelfth stanza, is the fragment of an orig-inal Danish ballad. – And *Belerma and Durandarte* is translated from some stanzas to be found in a collection of old Spanish poetry, which contains also the popular song of *Gayferos and Melesindra*, mentioned in Don Quixote. – I have now made a full avowal of all the plagiarisms of which I am aware myself; but I doubt not, many more may be found, of which I am at present totally unconscious.

(1952, 32)

Calling attention to itself as a consumer artifact, Lewis's 'advertise-ment' to *The Monk* announces the collapse of literary propriety: he refers his readers to a broad spectrum of geographical locations and lit-erary sources, ranging from rare scholarly manuscripts to widely dis-seminated newspapers, that stand in for historical dates and places. Typographical convention reinserts a new propriety: names of fictional characters and titles of epic romance poetry gain a status equivalent to place names, while published works, whether of fiction or of non-fiction, such as *Don Quixote* and *The Guardian*, lose their distinguishing factors. This interchange between the authentic and the ephemeral, the elite and the common, located within the novel in acts of reading and writing and at the novel's borders in its 'Advertisement,' finds its counterpart in the novel's meditation on the economics of desire, and its fears that novelistic consummation consumes the consumer, making any lasting fidelity or fame impossible.[27]

Lewis's ingenuousness serves to disarm accusations of plagiarism, while it disingenuously occludes the real source of inspiration, Ann Radcliffe's *Udolpho*. But his anxiety about plagiarism occurred for nought. The *Monthly Review* ratified his procedure. After enumerating all the sources and resemblances of the novel, the reviewer says:

This may be called plagiarism; yet it deserves some praise. The great art of writing consists of selecting what is most stimulant from the works of our predecessors, and in uniting the gathered beauties in a new whole, more interesting than the tributary models. This is the essential process of the imagination, and excellence is no otherwise attained. All invention is but new combination. To invent well is to combine the impressive.

(1797: 451)

Even when the *Monthly's* reviewer praises *Alonzo*, he compares it favor-ably with the *Lenardo* and *Blondene* of Bürger. Assessing invention and originality on Lockean grounds, whereby labor alters and improves original objects and consequently creates a kind of property in them, the reviewer accepts the basis upon which Gothic authors will assert their heroic function. Coleridge's exertions in the *Biographia* to salvage for the imagination originality and authenticity must be read against its losses in the periodical press, in popular fiction, and in the courts.

In the novel, Theodore's poeticizing provides a double opportunity to meditate about the act of writing or reading (1952, 199–206). Raymond's reaction scythes away the pastoralism, punishing Theodore's narcissism by satirically holding the mirror up to it and by representing it as ineluctably entwined with the marketplace. Like Reeve had done in *The Progress of Romance*, Raymond warns Theodore that publication will expose him to the vagaries of 'partial and ill-humoured criticism,' since 'though all are not able to write books, all conceive themselves able to judge them' (204). According to Raymond, attacks will not be limited to the work but spill over to destroy the man, words prescient of Lewis's experience in publishing *The Monk*. On the one hand, this accusation of an *ad hominem* bias in critical circles speaks to the growing influence of the author as a hero, as does Raymond's ironic self-accusation about his own hypostasized impact as an author: 'you must not count my opinion for anything. I am no judge of verses, and for my own part never composed more than six lines in my life: those six produced so unlucky an effect, that I am fully resolved never to compose another.' On the other hand, the passage undermines the author's status by making it seem a figment of his own (diseased) imagination: 'But I am conscious that all these sage observations are thrown away upon you. Authorship is a mania, to conquer which no reasons are sufficiently strong' (204). Mania or not, in order to test his skills an author must submit them to judgment. Consequently, like any other maniac, he must subject himself to the rules of the warders. Raymond advises Theodore of the world's critical strictures, such as the need to avoid mixed metaphors and to scan carefully for plagiarism. While these warnings may sound annoyingly familiar to students of composition, Raymond's words function as more than a pedantic reminder of literary values. In fact, the near relationship of the two faults in copyright law becomes apparent by their proximity in the passage: 'you are too apt to make the strength of your lines consist more in the words than sense; ... And most of your best ideas are borrowed from other poets, though possibly you are unconscious of the theft yourself' (205). This admonition about plagiarism reinforces the ingenuousness of Lewis's disclaimer in the 'Advertisement.' Raymond's familiarity with literary values, aesthetic and materialistic, makes him the perfectly literate British hero, able to navigate at once in the lecture halls of Oxbridge and the bookstalls of St Paul's.

While we might be tempted to identify young Theodore with Lewis, alike expatriate, alike writing for fame, Lewis carefully crafts his authorial self-representation to make it consonant with the greater wisdom and foresight we later descry in Raymond. Lewis's work begins with an apostrophe to his book, in imitation, as he tells us, of Horace's *Epistle* 20, Book I:

> Methinks, Oh! Vain, ill-judging book,
> I see thee cast a wishful look,
> Where reputations won and lost are
> In famous row called Paternoster,
> Incensed to find your precious olio
> Buried in unexplored portfolio,
> You scorn the prudent lock and key,
> And pant well bound and gilt to see
> Your volume in the window set
> Of Stockdale, Hookham, or Debrett.
>
> (ll. 1–10)

Lewis initially portrays his book as vain and social-climbing, feminine and masculine. Like the ungovernable passions obtaining in women, his book 'pants' to display itself; like women, the book may suffer the demise of reputation and seek to crawl back into the paternal fold. Like a lower-class man, the book aims to find itself enrolled among the company of Debrett's. Lewis's appropriation of Horatian authority, like his unacknowledged quotation from Shakespeare's *Hamlet* (ll. 11–12), covers him with not only literary but also social authority, as does his moralizing tone and his later characterization of himself as a 'conjuror' forecasting the book's fate.

Nevertheless, Lewis is willing if possible to gather his book's reflected glory. No sooner does he prophesy pessimistically about his book's encounters with the world (ll. 19–20) than he advises the book to advertise its connections should it meet with approval (ll. 29–56). To inquire about one's 'condition' indicates interest in both economic and social status. This latter attribute Lewis then elides, shifting instead to paint his character in the sense of personal and emotional traits. Like his heroes, he portrays himself as rash but loyal, idealistic and realistic about human nature; unlike them, he insists upon his physical debilities, perhaps in order to provoke sympathy and/or amazement at his ability to transcend them, a ploy extended in his underlining of his youth. Though possessed of 'full leisure to polish his composition' (205), Lewis frequently called attention to the white-hot speed with which he composed, another means by which he stressed his youth, impetuosity, and inspiration. At the same time, the personal deficiencies of the author make the potential success of the book seem to occur all the more in the kind of society Lewis envisions in the novel, one open 'to all the talents.'

Lewis's authorial self-representations waver between dominance and solicitation, between arrogant authority and a more genial collaboration. His demonstrations of punitive authority are tempered by his invitations to the reader to become a party to that authority, thus conforming to notions of hegemony as theorized by Gramsci and Bhabha. We see that invitation in his poetic preface, which personifies his book as his agent venturing out into the world. The vulnerability he feels as an author in the teeth of that reader's power appears in the dialogue about publication between Theodore and Raymond. Lewis's strategy of calling attention to his position as literary producer seeks to compensate for that vulnerability by making the reader his partner rather than his judge.

Radcliffe's personal reticence prevents her from making any *ex cathedra* pronouncements in her early novels; but her editorial strategies permit us to infer her opinions about literary production and provisions.[28] With a false decorum, Radcliffe only appears to maintain literary propriety more than does Lewis. Her use of conventions, such as the interpolated narrative of *The Provençal Tale* read by Ludovico in *The Mysteries of Udolpho*, simultaneously mirrors and deflects pure nostalgia. The tale's setting in Bretagne connects it with a lost British glory that is also a land of myth. While the interpolated narrative appears to honor conventional romance, it calls those conventions into question as much as does Lewis's mingling of literary forms, making the Baron regret 'the comforts of his warm chamber, rendered cheerful by the blaze of wood' (1970, 555) just as he leaves to aid the mysterious Sir Bevys of Lancaster (of chapbook fame). The intradiegetic tale distances us from its consumption; at the same time, the intradiegetic framing reproduces the inset as a fictional simulacrum of the past. Radcliffe brings the analogy home to us with force, making Ludovico pause at that instant in his reading to stir his own fire. If the Baron of the interpolated tale and Ludovico share a relish for domestic comfort, we also remember that Ludovico inhabits the haunted chamber not because a spirit has requested his aid, but because the Count de Villefort, like them, longs for domestic comfort and security, and has employed Ludovico to secure these for him, instead of taking up the quest himself. In *The Italian,* she returns to a frame tale, last employed for *A Sicilian Romance,* thereby installing the institutional resource of the holy manuscript as a counter against Lewis's advertisement. But the 'holy manuscript' sits in a frame that resembles Walpole's novel more than it does an antiphonal. Returning us to 1764, the year Walpole wrote *The Castle of Otranto,* some 'English travellers' find themselves in 'the environs of Naples,' the very setting of Walpole's novel. The story that follows appears in a volume, written by a young student/antiquarian scholar from Padua. And the first epigraph to chapter one comes from Walpole's *The Mysterious Mother.* Finally, in the recital of the murder enjoined by Schedoni, we learn that the victim, his brother, is attacked when he has crossed the Adriatic 'from Ragusi to Manfredonia' (1981, 361). Radcliffe's preference for traditionary forms of literary authenticity initially instances allegiance to conventional notions of honor, but her fudging of the techniques of production, her fidelity to an honorable, *because disguised,* machinery will correlate with the thematic values propounded by Radcliffe's heroes.

Just as we cannot discern the truth value of a story because it is manifestly fiction or ascertain reality by the evidence of our eyes, so we must not make the opposite mistake of ennobling 'primitive' accounts as automatically authentic.[29] What we require instead is a mediated fiction, guided by the controlling voice and misdirecting hand of the narrator. Radcliffe's technique of mediated narration corresponds with her representation of Vivaldi as the representative figure of a fully mediated authority, as I argued in Chapter 5. Once in a position to mediate between expectations and reality, Radcliffe uses her narratorial interventions either to inflect class relations, as in the scene between the peasant guide and Schedoni (volume 3, chapter 1), or to govern our moral growth. The 'progress' of moral and emotional sympathies is painted for us in present-tense description à la Hogarth (*Castles,* 1995, 7); inner moral landscape becomes a prospect view just like those of the natural landscape Radcliffe has already so lavishly described.[30]

Distracting and displacing terror like the English poets, Radcliffe's sublime narration installs a national authority akin to the new scopophiliac regime inaugurated by criminal reform, whose logic reflected 'the deepest anxiety of the modernizing state ... that the unleashed passions of the scaffold crowd mirrored the state's violence too candidly ... The crowd gave the lie to the great world's representation of itself as civil, benign, and humane' (Gattrell, 1994, 23). Like the new criminal regimen, Radcliffe held the socio-moral purpose of the sublime to blush with a nationalist tinge, 'powerful, yet silent in its power.'[31]

Radcliffe's preference for a silent power contrasts with Lewis's noisy displays. Born as much out of the skirmishes over authorial rights as they emerge from social theory about the state's power, denominating either of these solutions 'Male' or 'Female' does an injustice to the historical complexities out of which they emerge. For that very reason recurrent and oscillating, these solutions will cast long shadows over the narratorial strategies of the chapbook authors and of Maturin and Hogg, with whom this chapter ends.

Corporate heroism

Thus far we have considered the consequences of copyright law and literary commodification for narration and authorial self-representation in the full-length Gothic novels. But just as we had to include the Gothic chapbooks for a full survey of emergent Gothic nationalism, so equally must we attend to changes in narration and authorial self-representation introduced by those producers of commodified literature. Deleuze and Guattari's definitions of a minor literature might help frame the terms: 'The three characteristics of minor literature are the deterritorialization of language, the connection of the individual to a political immediacy, and the collective assemblage of enunciation' (1994, 168). In their eyes, this last trait emerges from the very lack of talent in a minor literature, which voids the possibility for 'an individuated enunciation that would belong to this or that "master" and that could be separated from a collective enunciation ... what each author says individually already constitutes a common action, and what he or she says and does is necessarily political, even if others aren't in agreement' (167). While I would stipulate that the politicized collectivity they envision does not always and necessarily lead to a revolutionary consciousness, their account has value insofar as it is borne out by the paradox of the Gothic chapbooks: at the same time that community in the chapbooks' endings etiolates, community between author and reader enlarges.

The Midnight Assassin offers a good example of this very different melding of old and new. It appeared in the *Marvellous Magazine and Compendium of Prodigies* (1802–4), a publication that, like the *Tell-Tale*, obeyed the letter of copyright law by disguising the authorship of classic Gothic novels, redacting them as 72-page chapbooks, then collecting them into volumes. The transformations worked on Radcliffe exceeded even copyright requirements. Yet this excess signifies more than a disregard for 'received opinion and the approved monuments of the past,' 'a new age … in which a large popular audience could now interest itself in sensational fiction divested of its genteel trappings' (Mayo, 1962, 369). Instead, *Midnight Assassin* jauntily transforms loss of innocence into 'genteel' candor.

No longer can the travelers to Italy be mentioned without justification. Instead, we immediately encounter an anxiety about veracity and authenticity: 'Before entering at large into our history, it will be necessary to say a few words on the manner by which it was obtained' (1802, A2, p. 3). While the caveat acknowledges a heightened attention to empirical evidence, it also exhibits a nervousness about such evidence. One reason the tale fidgets thus concerns the issue of plagiarism; redactions necessitate justifying how the present author has come across a tale published just a few short years before. To rub away the imputation, dates get erased. No longer do we learn that it is 1764. Instead, the events occur 'about forty years ago.' However, instead of substituting an open embrace of fictionality, as McKeon might argue, the author blazons the actual circumstances of production and transmission, invoking the 'reader' on the very first page, inciting and simultaneously forestalling that reader's skepticism and/or surprise. The absence of narratorial mediation facilitates a greater fiction of equality between readers and noble heroes. This overt turn to the reader resembles Burke's procedure, as we see not only in his letter but also in the framing of his *Reflections as* a letter.

The anonymous author of *Vildac, or, The Horrid Discovery* invokes an intimacy amounting to complicity: 'The adventure which I am going to relate to you, my dear friend, is of so strange and dreadful a nature, that you are the only person to whom I must ever disclose the secret' (1800, 33).[32] The narrator of *Adolphus and Louisa, or The Fatal Attachment, A Tale of Truth* begs the reader's belief:

> The improbability, and extreme singularity of the incident which I am about to relate, will, no doubt, tempt the reader to consider it as nothing more than a romance: but strange and inconsistent as it may appear, it certainly is not an imaginary event, formed by the illusive contrivance of premeditated fiction, but a real fact, which actually transpired in the same extraordinary manner as is here recited.

(1)

The greater the amount of space preserved within the fictional world for the reader's presence, the more openly that reader's identification is solicited.

This 'literary' relationship, this heightened community, contradicts the isolated adventures of the later Gothics. More importantly, it signals a change from the authoritarian relationship established by the early Gothic authors, as they advanced their own claims to heroism along with those of their heroes. In the Gothic chapbooks, narrator and reader collaborate. But the collaboration takes a different form from that fostered by the later author of radical texts who, according to Jon Klancher, represents the crowd by inhabiting the 'dramatized voices of others that displace his own presence to the reader' (1984, 84). Radical representation is said to eviscerate the individual 'implied reader'; instead, readers were envisioned and addressed as collectives, in an attempt to bind them to each other. *The Midnight Assassin* shows us how the chapbooks both follow and modify this mold. While the author addresses his audience as the collective 'British reader,' he also dramatizes his own presence in the text. Of the chapbooks I have covered, those written by Isaac Crookenden most openly advert to his own presence and that of his readers. In *Fatal Secrets,* the narrator uses the plural pronoun while addressing readers, but claims personally to know the characters whose history he relates (1806, 21).

As a result, the chapbooks inspired more than a desire for possession; they spurred authorial emulation. Despite the avidity with which the Nolyen children consumed and carted their possession around, their talent for this kind of work seems limited, even though the 'spirit,' so to speak, was willing. T. tried to compose but could only manage 'what is this secret [something illegible above the word secret] / This – old tale / What art our passions – [illegible] / whose curiosity ...' Other owners had better success. Running vertically up the end page to number five is yet another owner's mark, this time more indelibly engraving his inspiration as the result of his reading: 'Awful and melancholy is the / Tale of other times. Thomas Thompson. / When this you see remember me / And keep it in your mind / Let all the world / Say what the [*sic*] will speak of as you find / By diligence and care you may learn to write fair.' Of course, the most famous consumers inspired by chapbook material would have to be the Shelley and Byron circle at the villa Diodati in the summer of 1816, where they read Sarah Brown Utterson's *Tales of the Dead* before launching their own ghost-story writing competition.

Thomas Thompson's admonition about 'learning to write fair' encodes some of the more 'radical' principles discernible in the Gothic chapbooks.[33] Thompson's comment marks two parallel roads to progress. Education, or self-education, 'writes oneself fair,' as I discussed in the previous chapter. Furthermore, the eighteenth-century circulation of written and printed texts kept pace with and responded to the expansion of education and literacy, at the same time that it depended on the extension of roads. Greg Laugero has drawn our attention to this connection between roads and texts. According to him, '[B]oth roads and writing... function as the architecture for a society organized in terms of the productive interaction of individuals, objects, and information' (1995, 48). By their very nature, Gothic chapbooks illustrate one facet of this 'productive interaction.' Whether read by an audience well-provided for economically and politically or by those struggling to attain a measure of economic and political self-determination, the Gothic chapbooks offer a means of writing oneself imaginatively into the heart and head of the nation, thereby participating in a Gramscian consensus.

Maturin and Hogg make their authorial presences abundantly clear, at times addressing their readers directly, as do the chapbook authors. At the same time, they wrap those presences behind mystifying layers like those muffling Radcliffe's identity in *Gaston*. In their narrative innovations, these novels manage not only to occupy the end-point of our history, but also to demonstrate a kind of teleological growth.[34] Written from the uneasy outer rings of the nation, they nevertheless testify to national longings and concerns as much as they bespeak the Gothic author's emergence into corporate spokesperson for those issues.

Engulfing national borders, Charles Robert Maturin's *Melmoth the Wanderer* (1820) makes all places bow to its encompassing perspective. Insistently positioning the narrative in a specific place that is simultaneously no place and every place, the narrator recapitulates the powers of his eponymous anti-hero, like him transgressing barriers of time and space, moving through seemingly impermeable boundaries that melt under his penetrating gaze.[35] The image of the juggernaut, which Maturin uses to characterize vain superstition, also figures his artistic procedure, whereby distinctions of art, of verisimilitude and truth, are obliterated. No longer confining these sources to the eipiphenomenal margin of epigraph, Maturin continuously draws in examples from drama, poetry, novels, or the plastic arts to validate the narrative's truthfulness.[36] A counterweight of footnotes offering official and anecdotal histories further introduces 'dimensions beyond the novel' (Bayer-

Berenbaum, 1982, 88–9). Although not original with Maturin (Byron had employed empiricizing footnotes to authorize the romance improbabilities of his Eastern Tales), Maturin's notes extend his empire of 'truth.' Even music enters the sway of literary power, its melancholy notes captured on a staff footnoted at the bottom of page 489. If Romantic poets like Keats and Coleridge prize synaesthesia as a means to indicate the organic interwovenness of spirit and matter, Maturin uses Romantic synaesthesia to the end of swallowing all other forms of art.

The new literature of parts stands on the thresholds of two worlds, a fact it signals through its hybridizing of high and mass culture, represented alternatively as dematerialized 'reification' and increasing materialization, but which Jameson argues, and Maturin seems to foreshadow, are one and the same phenomenon (1992, 16–17). Maturin's depiction of successive authorship, moving from Jew to Protestant to Catholic, dovetails with the catholicity of its heroes and heroines. Despite the successive acts of dispossession committed by the parents of characters in *Melmoth*, each victim/hero refuses the ultimate dispossession offered by Melmoth's bargain. Instead, the nation produces itself anew through their stand, justifying their tenure on the new grounds of sectarian liberality, geographical identification, and British union.

Robert Wringhim in James Hogg's *The Private Memoirs and Confessions of a Justified Sinner* (1824) may fail his promise to provide readers with 'a key to the process, management, and winding up of the whole matter' (1986, 215); Hogg very carefully implants just such a key to guide us. Turning it, we find expressed the way contemporary Scotsmen still experience their haunted possession by an alien force.[37] Fittingly, Hogg's keys dematerialize the concrete specificity of Maturin's footnotes. Instead, even the 'editor's' veracity must be questioned. Although he disclaims any intervention in the manuscript he proffers, and promises to leave 'every one to judge for himself' (106), he also shares the plans he entertained for making additions and alterations to it: he planned to change the title to 'Self-Justified Sinner,' but was prevented by his publisher; he promises to add samples of Robert's handwriting, which, of course, he has omitted, in order to further 'justify' his narrative (241). Such doublings and denials have tempted critics to read Hogg's novel as a metanarrative commentary on 'writing's uncanny powers and reading's strange effects' (Botting, 1996, 111–12). I would like to tether the commentary to a more immediate reality, to suggest that writing's duplicity served the turn of aspiring authorial heroism. Hogg's career demonstrates the perceived gulf opening between high and low culture, and the opportunity furnished by such a gulf for authorial self-aggrandizement.

Hogg blamed the failure of his weekly paper, *The Spy*, in 1811 after only 52 numbers on just that form of snobbism: 'The learned, the enlightened, and polite circles of this flourishing metropolis, disdained to be either amused or instructed by the ebullitions of humble genius.'[38] Scottishness also cleft him. As he claimed in the autobiography he reworked and reissued four times, from 1807 through 1832, in which he emphasized his background as a self-taught shepherd to stimulate sales (Smith, 1980, 32–3), his position entailed upon him the necessity of keeping 'history and tradition alive' to secure the survival of his nation, threatened as it was by 'a more powerful and less tolerant neighbor' (Smith, 1980, 77). Resituated as part of a more elaborate meditation on national prosperity and harmony, as a comment on the role of national literatures and as a bridge between the increasingly divided cultural worlds of magazine and book publishing, the divided or doubled nature of the *Memoirs'* protagonist, like that of its narrative structure, takes on a new significance.

If doubling and deception occupy the heart of the novel's content and form, they also made up a large portion of the entertainment furnished to readers of *Blackwood's Edinburgh Magazine*. Returning novel and author to their original contexts will help us fathom the position Hogg's novel occupies vis-à-vis authorial heroism. The first inklings of the story appeared in *Blackwood's Edinburgh Magazine* for August 1823, where it took the form of a 'letter' to the editor, 'Christopher North,' from the 'Ettrick Shepherd.' The Shepherd claims to be fulfilling a promise made to North to furnish a panegyric on 'the phenomena of nature.' By such a request, North had ostensibly meant a Romantic celebration of nature personified as a power transcendent over man. The Shepherd complains early in the piece that these natural beauties were so familiar to inhabitants of the Scottish glens that they forbore remarking: 'I could not persuade myself that any of these was the particular thing, a description of which you wanted; because they were, in fact, no phenomenons, if I understand that French word properly, nor were ever viewed as such by any of our country people' (1823, 188). The phenomenon he provides instead is the natural preservation of a suicide's corpse from over a century ago, in a tale he titles 'A Scots Mummy.' Ending his brief tale with a (for Hogg and the writers of *Maga* in general) customary acerbity, the Shepherd declares the Romantic immersion in the 'mossy cell,' the cloud and storm, a 'very valuable receipt' for ' the preservation of dead bodies,' an experiment he urges North to undertake on his own hide (190).

Hogg's doubling in *Maga* plays not only on Romantic but also on linguistic posturing. In addition to the glancing reference at 'North's' erudition – the demonization of classical education ('phenomena') through association with the French – Hogg volleys back the disdain to which English speakers treated Scots by shifting with lightning rapidity between them. In the original piece, after relating the events leading up to and following the suicide, he tries to date the events with empirical precision, in a slight mockery of antiquarian reporting (189-90). But no sooner does he invoke historical authority than he breaks into its opposite, the authority of local tradition and vernacular wisdom, articulated through a broad Scots dialect:

> Well, you will be saying, that, excepting the small ornamental part of the devil and the hayrope, there is nothing at all of what you wanted in this ugly traditional tale. Stop a wee bit, my dear Sir Christy. Dinna just cut afore the point. Ye ken auld fools an' young bairns shouldna see things that are half done. Stop just a wee bit, ye auld crusty, crippled, crabbit, editor body, an' I'll let ye see that the grand *phenomena of Nature's* a' to come to yet.
>
> (190)

Neither a straightforward contrast between English and Scots, between natural and artificial intellect, Hogg's persona weaves these positions into a melange of styles that he wields with dexterity.[39] No sooner does 'the Shepherd' enter the narrative than the language reverts to the polished prose of magazine correspondents: 'It so happened, Sir...'

Hogg tropes the fictionality of journalistic representations of Scottish reality by turning his real-life colleagues into characters in his novel.[40] The 'Editor' of the *Memoirs* offers the *Maga* piece as evidence, at the same time that he questions *Maga's* authenticity:

> The letter, from which the above is an extract, is signed JAMES HOGG, and dated from Altrive Lake, *August 1st, 1823*. It bears the stamp of authenticity in every line; yet, so often had I been hoaxed by the ingenious fancies displayed in that Magazine, that when this relation met my eye, I did not believe it; but from the moment that I perused it, I half formed the resolution of investigating these wonderful remains personally, if any such existed; for, in the immediate

vicinity of the scene, as I supposed, I knew of more attractive metal than the dilapidated remains of mouldering suicides.

(1986, 234)

Traveling to Edinburgh, the 'editor' enlists on his expedition John Gibson Lockhart, Scott's son-in-law, who admits to half believing the tale but also to skepticism since, 'G–d knows! Hogg has imposed as ingenious lies on the public ere now' (235).

Although the narrative in the longer book treatment omits all the Scots jocularity quoted above, as it leaves out the frame encounter with 'North' in which 'North' asks 'Hogg' for a tale of natural phenomena, it nevertheless reflects its genesis in the literary and political climate of the magazine. Preceding 'A Scot's Mummy' is an article called 'The Tory. No. II,' which celebrates the immediate condition of England:

> England has at length fully reverted to her old state of peace. War is at an end, and even the spirit of war is laid; ...the fluctuations that followed the pause of hostilities, and made it more uneasy than ever, has gone down; manufactures and agriculture have put on a face of activity, cheerfulness, and profit; the restoration of cash payments has gone through its round, and entered into the healthful and quiet system of the national prosperity, which it is to disturb no more. The reductions of the national expenditure, painful and anxious operations at best, have now completed their course of difficulty, and they are henceforth to be felt only in lightening the public burthens. At this hour, England stands in a more vigourous and loftier position, with veins filled with a richer plenitude of health and spirits, and her eye commanding a larger horizon, than in the most prosperous days of our forefathers.
>
> (1823, 184–5)[41]

In the novel's editorial frame, the unnamed editor encounters the Ettrick Shepherd, whom he tries to hire away from a market fair to act as his guide to the district's 'phenomena.' Instead, 'Hogg' castigates the 'editor,' proclaiming inquisitive jaunts into local history a waste of time, expense, and spirit (1986, 235–6). His scowling face contradicts the smiling face of agricultural prosperity conjured up by 'The Tory'; the turbulent noise and dirt of the ewe fair at Thirlestane bursts the article's 'quiet system of the national prosperity'; and, of course, the 'Scot's mummy' itself, its veins filled with the dust and peat of the exhausted land, and its bones mashed, despite the reportedly miraculous preservation which instigated the tale, mock the Tory portrait of England's 'vigourous and loftier position, with veins filled with a richer plenitude of health and spirits' (237–8).

If the 'Hogg' of *Blackwood's* contaminates his reliability by his particuipation in the magazine, the Hogg of book publishing cures that distemper by reverting to an authorial heroism that of necessity maintains a doubled perspective.[42] James Hogg adopts a Border identity, if not a Border name, to instance a different type of heroism.[43] Gil-Martin persuades Robert that 'self-destruction was the act of a hero' (225). Read ironically, self-preservation becomes heroic. Hogg's novel thus counterposes the vision offered by Maturin in which suffering is reified. In order to survive union without losing one's soul, one must preserve a native enthusiasm for nature, but temper that enthusiasm with a saving knowledge (62). To further that work, not the work of division, is the task of the hero.

8
The Afterlife of the Gothic Nation

> Sir, I have often said, that *History in general is a Romance that is believed, and that Romance is a History that is not believed*; and that I do not see much other difference between them –.
>
> (Horace Walpole to Robert Henry, in Lewis, 1973, 15: 173)

Gothic tints linger long in the cultures of the nineteenth century. Again we have cross-class and cross-domain evidence for such influences. Politically, demotic broadsides against Napoleon sparked by 1803 fears of invasion reproduce the typological extremes of Gothic villain and hero. Philosophically, Gothic ideas and ideals shape up later in the period as Christian Socialism, the radical romantics of Carlyle and Ruskin, and the muscular Christianity of Charles Reade. The chapbook illustrations record the new directions of this spreading appeal: in the 1837 edition of *Udolpho*, Volume Three's frontispiece portrait of Valancourt indicates a shift in focus from Emily to Valancourt as hero, even though he plays virtually no role in the solution to the 'mystery' and only appears in the last chapters; in the Victorian edition of *The Old English Baron*, Edmund grows to a middle-aged man; in *The Castle of Otranto*, Isabella guides Theodore, her exposed arms bulging with the muscularity of a washerwoman.

Higher realms of art also chronicle Gothic influence. In 1771, when Benjamin West wanted to glorify General Wolfe as a hero because he gave his life to secure a foreign British possession, he painted Wolfe surrounded by the symbols of that nation. His officers hover round him, showing the affection and esteem in which he is held by his men and implying consequently his fitness as a great leader. Like any true British hero, he displays the insignia of his Christianity, even or especially in his death. Three men support his limp body on the ground, cradling it as the Virgin Mary cradles the dying Jesus in Michaelangelo's Pietà; Wolfe's eyes gaze heavenward as one of the group cradling him tries to stanch the flow from his wounded *left* side; a furled British flag flies over him, symbolically pointing to his pending path into the lowering sky; while a noble savage sits at the left edge of the spectator's view, pondering the significance of this imminent translation, and perhaps pointing to the missionary effect of Wolfe's sacrifice. Such iconographic deification was not lost on another aspiring hero. Meeting West at a dinner after his early naval victories, Nelson lamented to the artist his lack of knowledgeable appreciation of art, but confessed that he had always been struck by reproductions of the *Death of Wolfe*. When West opined that Nelson's actions furnished the first opportunity for a heroic subject since the death of Wolfe, Nelson eagerly grabbed at his implied promise to paint him, offering to die in his next engagement to hurry the process (Hibbert, 1996, 383–4). After Trafalgar, West kept his promise. But his treatment of Nelson's apotheosis forms a startling contrast to the depiction of Wolfe. There, West had showed Wolfe and his British officers in contemporary military uniforms, in a sanitized and idealized rendering of their appearance on the battlefield. As Linda Colley notes, '[I]nstead of clothing his subjects in timeless togas or chivalric armour, West ... took classical and Biblical poses of sacrifice and heroism and brought them into the here and now' (1992, 179). Nelson's pictured death illustrates the increasing prevalence of Gothic ideals. The canvas, crowded with scenes from Nelson's career and life, echoes medieval representations of temporality captured by dispersal across perspectival planes. At the center, the tiny, marmoreal figure of Nelson, wrapped in linen drapery, rises to heaven in the arms of a Neptune-like character, his naked muscular torso, long hair topped with a golden coronet, and flowing beard all fixing him firmly as a primitive god. Beneath the giant's right arm, we see the burning ship and sea, with figures mourning on its banks, thereby cementing the connection between the giant and Neptune, and turning Neptune into a figure for British naval power. At Nelson's head, the winged figure of Victory simultaneously cradles him and offers him with one arm to Britannia, regnant over heaven, while the other hand temporarily holds Britannia's trident so that she can reach for the fallen hero. Most Gothic of all, Britannia is represented as a warrior clad in a long gown with mail bodice and heavy skirt, her hair held back by a medieval helmet topped with a plumed feather, such as might have been worn by chivalric knights on the tournament field.[1]

Chivalric display might have ennobled the otherwise sordid reality of warfare and reaffirmed 'the paramount importance of custom, hierarchy, and inherited rank' (Colley, 1992, 147), but Gothic was also transfused into dissent and spectacle. As I suggested in Chapter 1, aristocrats tailgated on the taste for heroes by adopting Gothic garb and trappings in both their private and public displays, for example, William Beckford's entertainment for Nelson and Lady Hamilton at Fonthill, Christmas 1801; George IV's coronation; and Victoria and Albert's costume ball in 1842, which fused monarchical and domestic Gothic ideology.[2] Public and private converged in the new castles built throughout the latter half of the eighteenth century and into the nineteenth, appearing at the highest levels in the interior and exterior redesigns of the state apartments at Windsor by George III between 1800 and 1814, and the same monarch's unfinished Gothic project at Kew, as well as in Lord Eglinton's disastrous tournament of 1838.[3] Nor did Gothic display as political symbolism confine itself to the aristocracy.[4] Gothic ideals circulated in the economy when British merchants characterized trade as chivalrous.[5]

In literary history, the success of Gothicism appears in its diffusion and adoption into other genres.[6] Novels of manners like Selina Davenport's 1828 *Italian Vengeance and English Forbearance* use Gothic tropes to sensationalize a domestic novel of manners.[7] George Croly attaches the Gothic persona of the Wandering Jew to a contemporary moralizing over religion in *Salathiel*, as does Coleridge in *The Rime of the Ancient Mariner* and 'The Wanderings of Cain.' And, of course, Sir Walter Scott detaches the Gothic fascination with the past to annex it to his own creations, the ballad romance and the historical novel.[8] By reverse implication, Scott's critique of supernatural fictions in 'On the Supernatural in Fictitious Composition' (1887) portrays the Gothic novel as poetical and as conveying a seeming authenticity, a position he admits in the 'Introductory' to *Waverley*, where he testifies to its 'excellent effect in fictitious description' (1985, 33–5).

Like the Gothic authors, Scott contributes to the Gothic legacy both through his narratorial and his editorial procedures. In concert with Anna Barbauld's *British Novelists* series (1810), the *Ballantyne Novelist's Library* of 1824 codifies the status of the author and selectively canonizes literary texts. Reifying the productions of a literary marketplace, Scott's and Barbauld's efforts cannot escape the very conditions they seek to surmount. As they ruefully acknowledge, their principles of selection included not only variety, popularity, and public taste, but also financial considerations: 'Copyright also was not to be intruded on, and the number of volumes was determined by the booksellers' (Barbauld, 1820, 58–9).[9] Nonetheless, these collections represent a final bulwark in the reputation of literature. Among the novels canonized, Barbauld and Scott nominate the Gothic novels of Walpole, Reeve, and Radcliffe. In discussing those particular novels and in analyzing the place of the novel in general, Barbauld and Scott confirm several strands in the argument that I have been elaborating: that novelists imaginatively participated in the public events of the day; that their participation took the form of analyzing and, in some cases, idealizing earlier social organizations as a means to reforming contemporary reality; that the hero concentrated that temporally hybrid ideal; that readerly identification with the characters and viewpoints expressed in novels colored the reader's own existence; and that readerly identification accompanied a recognition that authors imaginatively participated in the public events of the day.

Barbauld opens Volume I of the *British Novelists* series with an introductory essay, 'On the Origin and Progress of Novel-Writing.' Conceived as a defense against the detraction novels have long suffered, her essay exhorts respect not on the grounds of an autonomous liberty for the aesthetic realm, but on the basis of their immersion in social and civil life: 'They take a tincture from the learning and politics of the times, and are made use of successfully to attack or recommend the prevailing systems of the day' (1820, 2). While novels provide a temporary exemption from daily travails (44–5), they also 'infuse principles and moral feelings' (46). Generous heroes and heroic sentiments 'counteract the spirit of the world, where selfish considerations have always more than their due weight' (47). Readers can draw heroic actions and circumstances into their own more modest circumstances precisely because literature furnishes examples of governance either to avoid or emulate. Reeve's *Old English Baron* is judged to inspire 'none but noble and proper sentiments' (XXII: 1). Radcliffe contributes not only novel but also poetic inspiration: Barbauld praises the 'elegant pieces of poetry interspersed,' among which she distinguishes the 'Song to a Spirit' and 'The Sea Nymph,' poems whose significance for a nationalist vision I have analyzed in Chapter 4.

Scott thinks that no one has approached the excellencies of Radcliffe except 'the author of *The Family of Montorio*,' i.e. Maturin (1827, xviii). He proposes Gothic romances as the one species of fiction capable of gratifying 'the learned and the unlearned, the grave and gay, the gentleman and the clown' (ibid.). Moreover, since its inception Gothic fiction has furnished models for living, in the architectural and decorative patterns derived from Walpole's experiments at Strawberry Hill,

and in the linguistic refinements which his *Castle of Otranto* introduced: 'The style of the Castle of Otranto is pure and correct English of
the earlier and more classical standard. Mr. Walpole rejected, upon
taste and principle, those heavy though powerful auxiliaries which
Dr. Johnson imported from the Latin language; and which have since
proved to many a luckless wight, who has essayed to use them, as
unmanageable as the gauntlets of Eryx' (867, I. 310)

Having begun this saga of Gothic fictional influence with *The North
Briton*, it seems but fitting that we close with the example of another
North Briton, Thomas Carlyle, and his published series of essays, *On
Heroes, Hero-Worship, and the Heroic in History* (1840). As defined by
J. G. A. Pocock, a 'North Briton' was 'a Scotsman committed to a
restatement of English culture in such terms that it would become
British and that Scotsmen would make their own way in it' (1985,
128). In other words, Scotsmen who criticized English culture for its
exclusionary practices mastered that culture sufficiently to elevate their
own authority; their appropriation of that culture furthered their critique both by illustrating the unfairness of their exclusion and by
marking the dominant culture with Scottish values. *On Heroes*
magnifies the range of appropriation. Carlyle's cosmopolitan perspective surveys divine, hieratic, monarchical, and literary heroism, and
rambles from pagan to present times. But the match between his principal heroic inspirations and those cited by the nationalist historians of
Gothic greatness we have already encountered reveals that his universalism serves a more narrow cultural aim.[10] Like those earlier theorists
from Sir William Temple onward, Carlyle traces heroism from the
Scandinavian mistiness of Odin's time to Shakespeare.[11] His major contribution to the Gothic dialogue, his move beyond the Renaissance to
the harsh light of Grub Street in the 'The Hero as Man of Letters,'
seconds my claim that Gothic authors attributed heroic status to their
literary labors.

Lecture III of *On Heroes*, 'The Hero as Poet,' validates Pocock's analysis, showing Carlyle conflating his own very Scottish voice and personality with Englishness to sing the national value of Shakespeare.

In spite of the sad state Hero-worship now lies in, consider what this
Shakspeare *[sic]* has actually become among us. Which Englishman
we ever made, in this land of ours, which million of Englishmen,
would we not give-up rather than the Stratford peasant? There is no
regiment of highest Dignitaries that we would sell him for... For our
honour among foreign nations, as an ornament to our English

Household, what item is there that we would not surrender rather than him? Consider now, if they asked us, Will you give up your Indian Empire or your Shakspeare, you English; never have had any Indian Empire, or never have had any Shakspeare? ... Official persons would answer doubtless in official language; but we, for our part too, should not we be forced to answer: Indian Empire, or no Indian Empire; we cannot do without Shakspeare! Indian empire will go, at any rate, some day; but this Shakspeare does not go, he lasts forever with us; we cannot give up our Shakspeare!

(104–5)

Shakespeare's value lies not merely in his personality but also in his ability as reified text to extend British empire. Carlyle's argument thus inherently embraces the two poles of copyrightable property:

Nay, apart from spiritualities; and considering him merely as a real, marketable, tangibly-useful possession. England, before long, this Island of ours, will hold but a small fraction of the English: in America, in New Holland, east and west to the very Antipodes, there will be a Saxondom covering great spaces of the Globe. And now, what is it that can keep all these together into virtually one Nation, so that they do not fall-out and fight, but live at peace, in brother-like intercourse, helping one another? This is justly regarded as the greatest practical problem, the thing all manner of sovereignties and governments are here to accomplish: ... Acts of Parliament, administrative prime-ministers cannot... Here, I say, is an English King, whom no time or chance, Parliament or combination of Parliaments, can dethrone! This King Shakspeare, does he not shine, in crowned sovereignty, over us all ... We can fancy him as radiant aloft over all the Nations of Englishmen, a thousand years hence.

(105)

More than a backward glance at England's greatness, in *On Heroes* Carlyle envisions a teleological destiny for 'his' kingdom in the arrival of 'The Hero as Man of Letters.' This penultimate lecture takes as its examples Johnson, Rousseau, and Burns, thereby dousing in one breath ancient rivalries, French and Scottish:

Much has been sold and bought, and left to make its own bargain in the marketplace; but the inspired wisdom of a Heroic Soul never till then, in that naked manner. He, with his copy-rights and copy-wrongs, in his squalid garret, in his rusty coat; ruling (for this is what he does), from his grave, after death, whole nations and generations who would, or would not, give him bread while living, – is a rather curious spectacle! Few shapes of heroism can be more unexpected.

(143)

This modern form of heroism, 'altogether a product of these new ages,' is also the future of heroism (143). The man of letters can be a hero to his time because he encompasses past, present, and future. Like Odin, whose runes Carlyle calls the first heroic writing, authors of books have the power to shape the actions of even the most naive of readers. And this power accrues not only to works of philosophy, religion, or political science but also to the form most feared by aesthetic sociologists of the eighteenth century like Kames and Monboddo, novels: 'Not the wretchedest circulating-library novel, which foolish girls thumb and con in remote villages, but will help to regulate the actual practical weddings and households of those foolish girls. So "Celia" felt, so "Clifford" acted: the foolish theorem of Life, stamped into those young brains, comes out as solid Practice one day' (148–9). Books usurp the functions of university, church, and Parliament, while printing is a synecdoche for democracy (151–2).

Carlyle concludes with the hope that '[I]f Men of Letters are so incalculably influential, actually performing such work for us from age to age, and even from day to day,' then perhaps they will not 'always wander like unrecognised unregulated Ishmaelites among us' (153). I have told again this Gothic story in order to domicile its authors and texts in their original contexts: an eighteenth-century fold where they were cherished for more material contributions than their phantasms, and from which they have strayed in the critical understanding of the intervening years. Neither banal nor subversive, Gothic novels and chapbooks were nonetheless *popular* literature in the fullest sense, their cryptic encounters the British rendezvous with its own national spirit.[12] If I have contributed at all to decoding those encounters, I shall consider it a debt to ancestors well paid.

Notes

Introduction: Punctuating Disequilibrium

1. The phrase is Herzfeld's (1997).
2. See also Dunlop (1814), 576–77. On the giddy proliferation of the culture industry in eighteenth-century England, see Brewer ('Polite', 1995).
3. Benedict Anderson's work has been instrumental in this conception (1991). See also Hobsbawm (1992), and Wilson (1995); Wilson and I differ as to the scope allowed women in this imagining and the degree of contiguity between eighteenth and late-twentieth century manifestations. Lawrence Klein (1995) furnishes a useful corrective.
4. See Martin (1998), 70. Important differences about the role played by the economy exist between Gramsci (1971) and Habermas (1992). In Hobsbawm's account, top-down mechanisms predominate; the only medium for upward nationalism seems to be xenophobia (1992, 92 and *passim*). Nairn (1997) offers a more dialogic picture, as do Gellner (1983), Pickett (1996), and Colley (1992). For Nairn, nationalism arises equally from all classes in response to an uneven distribution of the modes and fruits of production in modernity. Balibar agrees with Nairn that nationalism is dialectical and the ultimate response to class warfare; however, he takes nationalism as the successful imposition on the peasantry of internal and external subjugation (1991, 90), even though this imposition does not derive from centralized state functions, as Hobsbawm had argued (1992, 88–90).
5. Contributors to the development of this topic include Raymond Williams (1958), Lloyd and Thomas (1998), Woodmansee (1994), and the articles collected in Mattick (1993).
6. See, for example, Habermas (1992), 23–4, 29, 59, 182; Hobsbawm (1992), and Nairn (1997), where it connects with linguistic nationalism, *passim*; Balibar (1991), 86–7, 96–8; Brewer ('This', 1995), 4; and Klein on the use of 'dialogues' in moral and genteel manuals for the lower classes ('Politeness', 1995, 370). La Vopa redefines Habermas's public sphere as a professional sphere able to bridge the private and the public, among whom he counts educators and writers (1992, 109–12). As Alan Bray and Michel Rey put the case for the seventeenth century, representation 'was constitutive and not merely mimetic' (1999, 70).
7. See also Herzfeld (1997), 21–6, 39. D. A. Smith also gives a concise résumé of nationalist concepts (1991, 9–11).
8. John C. Stephens, editor of *Longsword,* makes the ascription (1957, xviii). His impression seems confirmed by Leland's sudden modal shifts in the passage, first into the subjunctive mood as though he were conjuring up a vision of the future reign of the newly installed king, and then into the imperative mood as he demands assent for that vision.

9. Despite current attempts to place Godwin in the Gothic camp, Godwin's contemporaries did not share that view. Dunlop's criticism of Godwin's *St. Leon* confirms the distinction.
10. The phrase is Walter Reed's (1981); qtd by Robertson (1994, 15, n. 23).
11. Cf. Hoagwood (1996), esp. 6–7.
12. Rose (1988), 56.
13. See Varey (1990), 163, 166.
14. Even Baudrillard must depend upon a linear narrative of that vortex 'where linear continuity and dialectical polarity no longer exist' (1993, 31).
15. Post-structuralist interpretations have contributed usefully to Gothic's reevaluation. Yet I would urge that work remains because, to a large extent, these new readings of the Gothic have combed the Gothic more for the message it has to deliver to us, in our immediate moment, than to seek the meaning Gothic carried for *its* moment. See, for example, Samara (1996), 243. We run the risk of missing other outlines when we insist upon seeing only those shapes that resemble ourselves.
16. While the neglect of nationalism that Raphael Samuel bemoaned in 1989 has been mended, studies still largely concentrate on nationalism as an institutional force or as a reactive measure against some perceived threat. Samuel's other point, the role of the hero as a focalizing element, remains underrated. Even so, Samuel himself restricts the significance of the Gothic to its provision of 'counter-image' villains (xxvii), despite the fact that he notes '[T]he discovery (or rediscovery, or invention) of national heroes seems to be a feature of patriotic moments in British history' (xxiii).
17. Cf. Schmitt (1997); he follows Spacks in seeing national identity fostered through the victimized female, and equates Englishness with paranoia (28); Spacks (1976), 169.
18. For a debate over the 'heroics' of Byron's poem, see La Chance (1998) and Christensen (1993).
19. In discussing the need for credit and the credentials by which a man signified himself creditworthy, John Brewer lists the following attributes: 'reliability... candour and affability... piety, good humour... a plain dealer, – and, above all, fairness and generosity' (1982, 214), a list that reproduces many of the qualities of the Gothic hero, where they appear colored as romantically chivalric.
20. Virtuosi collected curiosities ordered by fanciful rhetorical tropes; connoisseurs employed empirical judgment to construct scientific classifications. On direct commercial applications for connoisseurship, see Bermingham (1995), 504.
21. See, for example, Clery: dismissing Theodore as 'bland' (1996, xviii), she celebrates Manfred as 'developed,' a 'draft version of the fascinating anti-hero which Byron would later perfect' (xix).
22. Robert Darnton's call to 'make contact with the otherness in other cultures' has been my siren-song (1984, 261).
23. Thus, while Newman persuasively connects English nationalism with other European experiences (1997, xxi–xxii), I urge the uniqueness of the Gothic's contribution to that evolving nationalism, since, as I argue in Chapter 1, Gothic discourse took on a decidedly English, and later British, cast.

24. On a new, middle-class masculine virtue, see Kuchta (1996), 71. For the political role played by the term 'masculinity', see 63–4.
25. Terry Castle (1987) and Catherine Craft-Fairchild (1993) represent the hero as feminized; Janet Todd (1989) stands in for the opposite camp. Still, as Craft-Fairchild rightly acknowledges, just because the hero is feminized doesn't mean that the masculine disappears as a category (13).
26. For example, Cawelti (1976), Miles (1993), Williams (1995), Robertson (1994). Ian Duncan splits Radcliffe's narration into two, gendered halves (1992, 46–50).
27. An internalization made external when the qualifications necessary to be a 'gentleman' were redefined. See Corfield (1992), *passim*.
28. See Shell (1978), 71–7.
29. For the archetypalist school, see Hume (1969), Railo (1927), and Nelson (1963).
30. Unlike Richardson's Clarissa, even when Gothic heroines are helpless victims, they do not solely have to defend their virtue from attack. Instead, even in cases where concupiscence appears to be the motive, cupidity for power and money lies at the heart of the matter.
31. I owe this distinction to Spacks (*Imagining*, 1976, 78); however, she sees this perspective as pertaining solely to women writers.
32. Howe served the Army; Jervis and Duncan represented the Navy. As the drumbeats of war pulse more loudly, the poetry in the *Anti-Jacobin* becomes increasingly martial and nationalistic (21 May, 1798, 219–20). These verses sing 'matchless heroes' from Elizabeth's time forward: William III, Blenheim, Chatham, Wolf, Rodney, Lord Heathfield; each steps forth for his share of praise.
33. An earlier article in the *Critical Review* combines those qualities. Writing of Cornwallis's capture in the American War, a poem entitles him 'The British hero in Captivity' (March 1782, 229).
34. Marilyn Butler (1993) assigns these political designations while giving a necessary overview of the periodicals' investments in literature and politics.
35. Hence, I would have to join La Vopa in questioning Habermas's separation of the two categories (1992, 103).
36. The couplings are not the mere result of revolutionary fever. In 1780, the *Critical Review* assessed *The History of a French Louse* as a 'pamphlet written in favour of administration, and with a view of turning into ridicule the Ministers of France, the American Congress, and the patriots of England' (51).
37. To date, the mass-market versions of Gothic have been studied only when the novels in question can be shown to be part of the 'Northanger' set that influenced Jane Austen. Tracy (1981) includes the chapbooks in her descriptive catalogue indexed by literary motif, but her index contains references neither to nationalism nor to heroes, each of which is key to the argument I will be developing here.
38. On the nexus between gender and geography, see Williams and Chrisman (1994), 374.
39. Terry Lovell pries apart the lumping of feminism with a culture of victimization (1995, 37). Poovey (1988), Rogers (1982), and Howard (1994, 72, 98) have concluded that women authors of the Sentimental novel and the cult

of sensibility adopted an insistence on the inherent nature of female sensibility as a strategy for empowerment.

40. As well-educated women, Reeve and Radcliffe were actively involved with the political and social issues of their day. Both came of families well-connected in royal, medical, ecclesiastical, and financial circles, and were educated by those families beyond the level usually available to women.

41. For one form this nationalism takes in a later period, see P. Kelly (1995), 43. More extended discussions of Romantic nationalism occur in Eagleton (1990), 23–39; and Ross (1991).

42. On literature as contributing to 'the formation of a national culture,' measured not by its impact on individual readers but by its pervading the 'fabric of a culture', see Ross (1992), 9–10.

43. See Darnton's call for a verifiable account of the way diverse people read (1996).

44. Park joins earlier critics like Mary Douglas in asserting the social iconographics of the human body (1987, 11).

45. Byars (1991), 141; qtd in Horrocks (1995), 52.

Chapter 1   Tailoring the Gothic Myth

1. The 'great financier' Robert Morris was also a signer of America's Declaration of Independence because his financial aid, whether borrowed from France, requisitioned from the states, or dug out of his own coffers, made possible the transfer of Washington's army from Dobbs Ferry to Yorktown in 1781 (*Encyclopedia Britannica*, 1911, 871). So the speaker of this footnote to history who refers to Morris as 'our' must clearly be an American, yet the fact that the financier's son has returned to or retained an English estate suggests a renewed current of business between the recent enemies.

2. Cf. Mayo (1962), 349.

3. These private productions ape the serial chapbooks such as *The Marvellous Magazine and Compendium of Prodigies* (1802–4) and the *Tell-Tale, or Universal Magazine* (1803–5), q.v., chapters 6 and 7.

4. For Gary Kelly, the novel of manners thematizes the 'authentic self' as a passionate lover inhibited by lack of social standing; the Gothic novel transposes the setting, time, and place of the conflict, and the hero becomes imprisoned in a 'false social self ... The novel of manners is in effect the novel of social emulation' (1989, 42–4). Cf. also Wiesenfarth (1988).

5. The plot and characters of this novel echo in some respects *The Old English Baron*, a point I develop further in Chapter 3.

6. But cf. Donoghue (1995), who claims that the *Monthly Review* and the *Critical Review* had converged with respect to the social purpose of reading by the latter decades of the eighteenth century.

7. Cf. Richter (1996), 121.

8. Bunn-Heidler charts the gradual movement from neoclassical doctrines of fable or plot, characters, sentiments, and diction, in that order of importance, to a discussion of the beauties and defects of the piece, and on to the mid-century precedence given to characterization (1928, 47, 62). When plot structure resurfaced as a critical topic towards the close of the century, it

was newly prized as an adjunct to the kind of probability fostered by truthful characterization; reviewers of the 1770s held it necessary to aid the appeal to readers' sensibilities that would ensure the work's moral efficacy (112). See also Tompkins (1932), 17.

9. What changes is the scene of reading imagined. Whereas the *British Critic* envisions an aristocratic idyll, the reader under the shade of trees on his own domain after unspecified 'severe labours,' Dunlop's worker seems more a drone in the bureaucratic life, his 'severe and serious studies' indicating perhaps a clerkship or apprenticeship to the law, while the 'place at the chimney-corner' where he reads implies that he has not yet left the kitchen of a winter's night, that those 'severe studies' do not yet remunerate him sufficiently to provide a wing-back easy chair beside his own fireplace.

10. See also Nairn: 'through nationalism the dead are awakened' (1997, 4).

11. On taste in general, see Bourdieu, (1984), 174–5 and *passim*.

12. See Brewer ('This', 1995), 18. On the animus which especially targets women, see Pawlowicz (1995). Gadamer also sees 'taste' as socially mediated, but omits the contentiousness (1975, 34; cited by Habermas, 1992, 252, n. 17). For substantive agreement (but methodological variance), see the collection of essays assembled by Paul Mattick, especially those by D. Summers, Woodmansee, Mason, and Mattick himself (1993). See also Pocock (1985), 107, 114–15, 120–1, and 307.

13. Norton mentions Kames only in passing, but usefully reminds us that Schiller knew the *Elements of Criticism* and acknowledged his debt to Kames (1995, 228).

14. Kames's writings in general sparked numerous strictures by authors such as Hugh Blair (1756), Jonathan Edwards (1758, 1768, 1775, 1790, 1804, 1818, 1837, 1851), Samuel Stanhope Smith (1787, 1788, 1801, 1810), William Robertson (1759), and the pseudonymous Phileutherus (1751), as well as admiring treatises by William Smellie (1800), Mary Knowles (1804), and Woodhouselee (1807, 1809, 1814). Elphinstone (1771) specifically attacked *Elements*.

15. Martha Woodmansee makes the amusing observation that Wordsworth's first readers considered the *Lyrical Ballads* 'indistinguishable from the popular verse of the day – that literature of "outrageous stimulation" that Wordsworth is denouncing in the *Preface*' (1993, 114).

16. Such is the use made of Gothic origins and Gothic confusion by fifteenth-century speculative geographers at Uppsala University, headed by Olaus Magnus. They capitalized on the etymological confusion discussed below by using it as license to locate the home of the Gotti in Juteland or Sweden. The term 'Gothic' could then be raised as an umbrella to cover all the various successive waves of invading groups that swept through Europe and terminated the death throes of the Roman Empire. Thus the geographers were able to reconstrue their homeland as the 'hive' of modern nations, and to break reliance upon classical Rome as a model (Johannesson, 1991).

17. Jordanes, a sixth-century historian of the Goths, introduced the etymological conflation of Jutes with Goths. Bede is the first historian in England to develop the Gothic myth; the 'Alfredian' translation of Bede into Old English in the tenth century AD perpetuates the conflation and inaugurates the tradition of 'Gothic' origins in England (Kliger, 1952, 14–15). Englishmen like Sir

Henry Spelman, who as members of the first Society of Antiquaries, founded in 1572, preserved Bede's and Jordanes's collocation of Jutes and Goths, promulgated the tradition. Cf. Novak, who characterizes the attitude to the past in the Gothic novel as almost uniformly pejorative (1979, 55).

18. On *witenagemot* and its role in thwarting absolutist aspirations, see Pocock (1957), 30–56, 91–124; and Hill (1958), 58–126.

19. On Sir Henry Spelman's researches, see Parry (1995), 157–89. Parry argues that Spelman demonstrated the relative newness of Parliament; as a result, his researches ironically were favorable to Charles I in his battle against parliamentarians (177–8).

20. Cf. Kliger (1952) and Spector (1966), 269, 277, 292, 294, 340–1; Spector relies heavily on pejorative references by Whig writers to Gothic architecture.

21. Compare 'Of Heroic Virtue' with 'Of Poetry,' *Miscellanea the Second Part* (1690, 1963). In 1672's *An Essay upon the Original and Nature of Government* (1964), Temple identifies the Normans as a later and more civilized branch of the English Goths, to counter assertions that the Danish and Norman invasions had diluted the Gothic stock and that the British were now mixed and hence amenable to the absolutist aspirations of James II. This essay echoes the position taken by the Parliamentarians against Charles in the breath before the Stuarts are swept away by the Glorious Revolution, a transition to which Temple is accessory and which is foreshadowed in his numerous eulogistic references to William of Orange in the 1672 piece.

22. On the significance of generic constellations, see Simons and Aghazarian (1986), 7.

23. Introduction to his edition of *Bevis of Hamptoun*, sig A2.; quoted by Johnston (1964), 31.

24. I have condensed and paraphrased Shurley's prefatorial remarks to *Valentine and Orson*, *The Seven Champions*, and *Don Bellianis*.

25. Among this group should be included Horace Walpole, a member of the Society until disagreements over his interpretation of the events of Richard III's career caused him to resign.

26. Thus Percy translated and compiled Mallet's works as *Northern Antiquities* in 1770, using Mallet to stress the role played by the North (i.e. Britain) in producing imagination, and adverting to the Odin legends, like Temple before him. See also 'Essay on the ancient Metrical Romances' (1775). Locating literary antecedents on home territory was a species of the eighteenth-century's status-driven genealogical research; see Lewis (1973), I: xxxi.

27. Scholars failed to discriminate between genuinely medieval literature, Peninsular romances, and modern redactions or imitations, so that in the category were mingled such diverse authors as Tasso, Ariosto, Sidney, and Chaucer with the three above, and works from *Amadis de Gaul*, *Don Bellianis*, *Guy of Warwick*, *Bevis of Hamptoun*, to *Valentine and Orson*. Even so, their ambition required strenuous effort to succeed.

28. Such egalitarianism increasingly bleeds out when opponents attempted to decide whether or not Gothic rights applied to those without property. For a summary of the debate, see Kliger (1952), 120, 202, 205–7. Bolingbroke calls *Witanegemote* 'that original Sketch of a British Parliament', but limits membership to 'Kings, Lords, and Saxon Freemen' (*Craftsman* (1730): 51). Bolingbroke's championing of Gothic liberty was designed to break the

power of Sir Robert Walpole, a power gained by what Bolingbroke saw as the executive branch's meddling in Parliament. Bolingbroke's aspersions on Walpole for meddling are ironically reversed when Sir Robert's son writes his own version of Gothic liberty.

29. On conflicts over the respective value of novel versus romance, see Bunn-Heidler (1928), 137; Ioan Williams (1970), 1, 13–14; Connors (1986), 32.

30. Thomas Warton cites the idea in the second volume of his *The History of English Poetry* (1774–81); when reviewed by the *Critical Review,* the article's author uncritically retransmits it (1778, 422) .

31. Even if that status is not of longstanding. Henry Home was born at Kames, in the county of Berwick, in 1696 and did not ascend to the title 'Lord Kames' until he was made a judge of the court of session in 1752. In 1763, the year after he published *Elements of Criticism,* he was named a lord of the justiciary.

32. Hurd's career reflects the success of this myth: George III appointed him tutor to his son and heir, and exchanged visits with Hurd between Worcestershire and Windsor (Girouard, 1981, 22).

33. In denominating Spenser and Milton the successors of romance, Hurd follows Thomas Warton, whose *Observations on the Faerie Queene* (1754) had credited thematic and formal attributes of romance as sources for aspects of Spenser's and Milton's work.

34. Temple, *Works*, ii: 532; qtd by Johnston (1964), 18.

35. Interestingly, in the 1788 revised edition of his work, Hurd will drop the references to horror and Gothic magic.

36. The history of architectural criticism of Gothic is one of a continual see-saw of opinion. See Robson-Scott (1965), 4, 6; Germann (1972), 7–8, 51–2, 58, 66, points out that all these various Continental critiques of Gothic architecture derive from nationalistic impulses in their respective countries.

37. In this, Hurd is not greatly distant from Kames, who defends Gothic architecture on the grounds that its utility lends relative beauty to its form (1830, 96); on the grounds of beauty, see 150.

38. Another area of overlap between Hurd and Kames (390).

39. See Dowling (1981), esp.112–14.

40. Much has been written about the centrality of the Gothic setting to the intent of the form. See Botting (1996), 2–3; Railo (1927), 7, 11, 15–18; DeLamotte (1990), 15; and Fleenor (1983), 13–15.

41. Walpole and Reeve knew Hurd's work (although Walpole was contemptuous of Hurd's social pretensions), as well as that of Temple, Warburton, Warton, and Percy; Walpole read Mallet in the original and was greatly influenced by it.

42. Reeve's feminist inflections appear from the start of her career, when she justified her new translation of *Argenis* (1772). For evidence of Reeve's interest in politics there, see esp. A4. Her complaint about two previous seventeenth-century translations into English reverses conventional divisions between men as abstract and women as material thinkers: the previous (male) translators had followed Barclay's prolixity and had rendered the words, rather than the sense, of the author. This fidelity to surface forms had obscured the value of the content, making the translations 'only a caput mortuum, as Sir John Denham has expressed it' (A5) – the very

expression used by Walpole to dismiss Reeve's *The Old English Baron*. Reeve's comment takes on new coloration in the light of copyright debate, resting as it does on a tripod of aesthetic, legal, and economic underpinnings. For the copyright debate, see Chapter 7.

43. Despite invoking democratic principles, the actual structure Reeve evokes conforms most closely to an oligarchy whose ruling class is composed of authors.

44. But not too freely. See the strictures against the triple 'pilfering' represented by the 'swarm of imitators,' magazine reviewers, and the circulating libraries (*Progress*, 1930, I: 82–3, II: 5, 7).

45. To eighteenth-century critics, romance took its origin from the Greek. The writer in the *British Critic*, XII (1798) chastises Dr John Moore for beginning his *A View of the Commencement and Progress of Romance* with the Romans. For good discussions of the varieties of Greek romance, 'presophistic' texts like *Chaereas and Callirhoe*, and more familiar works like the later, 'sophistic' *Aethiopica*, see Williamson (1986) and McDermott (1989).

46. Cf. Bakhtin, (1986), 87–8. Perhaps another difference deserves mention here. In the Greek romances, from which Gothic novels in part derive, journeys typically move from barbarous or heathen realms to civilization or Christianity (Lynch, 1986, 39; see also 65). In the Gothic novel, the heroes and heroines begin in what appears to be an enlightened society, are exiled or transported from security to a sinister underworld, only to win their way back to a (reformed) civilization. But, as I have already suggested, the civilized status of that initial society is only apparent. Part of the function of the sojourn in the sinister underworld is to reveal to the hero/heroine the close links between that society and its underworld. The Gothic interpellates that corruption in order that reformation can occur.

47. Nevertheless, Coleridge's response to the Gothic has lasting significance, because it demonstrates the attempt to control the appetite for the Gothic by demonizing it, one result of which would be the demarcation of rank, the division of Gothic forms into high and low-culture manifestations. Thus, the impoverished forms of the 'low' side, represented by the chapbook versions of the Gothic, fittingly instance the lack of discrimination on the part of 'lowbrow' audiences, who cannot even advert to the 'highbrow' consolations of poetry, manners, and scenery that partially justified the taste for the now-canonical Gothics. But current criticism on the Gothic unwittingly repeats this discrimination, in the sense of bias, by focusing solely on those luxury editions.

Chapter 2   When Everything New is Old Again: Horace Walpole's Heroic Bequests

1. The epigraph to this work is taken from the *Histoire de l'Académie des Inscriptions*, volume X, the same society that had promulgated French theories of romance origins, and that had been so heavily relied upon by Hurd.

2. *Journal of the House of Commons*, xxix. 675, sub 24 Nov. To view the Wilkes event from the perspective of George III, see Pocock (1957), 81–2.

3. On the nexus between bourgeois social and economic aspirations, Wilkite politics, and an expanding market for politics and political artifacts as cultural commodities or products, a market of the sort which the Wilkite associations themselves approved, see Brewer (1982), 201. Walpole's familiarity with the *roman à clef* tradition was visceral: his father had been the demonized target of George Lyttelton's 1741 *The Court Secret: A Melancholy Truth* (Beasley, 1982, 14). This personal history, coupled with the deliberate obscuration of historical sources for Otranto and his characters, encourages us to read the work as encoded. On the accuracy of Walpole's 'accidental' details, see Alice M. Killen (1925) 10, 14–15; Wein (1998).

4. Walpole's employment of Bathoe and Lownds worked not only to protect his anonymity but also to free the novel from the exclusivity of his coterie productions. For a complete list of works issuing from the press, see Dobson's Appendix, 1890, 299–323.

5. For example, Anderson (1982) and Flint (1998), 253–71.

6. See Jones (1978).

7. For example, Lewis (1973), 30: 178. Spector attests that we cannot detach *Otranto* from 'the secondary material on the multiple aspects of his career' (1984, 84).

8. Cf. Paulson (1981), 537.

9. His father had early taught him the power of the pen. One of Sir Robert's first acts upon gaining the premiership was to secure as much control of the media as possible through patronage or outright hire. See Downie for a list of Sir Robert's preferments of journalists (1984, 174–5, 177), and Michael Harris on abuses of franking privileges to distribute these London papers to the country (1984, 192).

10. In the late 1740s, Horace wrote anonymous articles for his father's enemies, in an attempt to secure reversionary favors for himself upon Prince Frederick's accession. See Sedgwick (1967), 45, 54.

11. Cf. Nelson (1963), 238, and Ellis, who sees the novel as uniformly subversive (1989, 5).

12. Lewis (1973), 22: 53. Horace's remarks to Mann just after the publication of *Otranto* furnish a perhaps more telling example (22:276).

13. See Dole (1988), 33.

14. Allen T. Hazen's valuable *Catalogue of Horace Walpole's Library* (1969) records that Walpole owned numerous works by and about Henry VIII. See books listed under Press A, where Walpole shelved titles of royal and noble authors.

15. In Henry's case, the text applied was *Leviticus*, 20: 21, whereas Manfred cites *Exodus*, 20: 5–68. On religion in general as fad or fashion, see Lewis (1973), 20: 378; 25: 541, 584; 34: 170; as a commercial enterprise, 31: 269. When not taking a relatively lighthearted attitude towards the subject, Walpole could be even more critical. See 24.516 to Mann for the unnaturalness of religious doctrines of sin; on religion as a cloak for 'Gothic' villainy in the Gordon riots, see 35: 354.

16. For an excellent discussion of the legal proceedings against Wilkes, upon which I draw here, see Rudé (1965), 22–30. Cf. Samson (1986), esp. 145–50, 152.

17. See Lewis (1973), 22: 288 and Walpole (1845), ii: 91–2, 96–8.

18. See also his comments in *Historic Doubts*, published just three years later (1987, 128).
19. Walpole's complaint against politics masquerading as orthodoxy may mask a further possible target: Fielding, who is never mentioned other than derisively. See Lewis (1973), 9: 84; 15: 296; 16: 268–70; 28: 489; 33: 77; 35: 214 and 159.
20. Cf. Stevenson (1990), 94; he muddies gender and genealogical legitimacy, holding matriarchal transmission acceptable for Alfonso's line but forbidden in Manfred's case. Walpole's precise rendering of genealogy at the end of the novel (114–15) underlines the fact that the distinction between Alfonso's and Manfred's cases is purely a matter of class. For legitimacy read psychoanalytically as oedipal conflict, see Stevenson (1990), 108; Harfst (1980); and Karl (1974), *passim*.
21. *Encyclopedia Britannica*, 11th edn (1911), 1: 734.
22. The relationship between Walpole and his cousin had always been a close one, with Horace frequently dispensing solemn advice which Conway almost always heeded. W. S. Lewis avers that Walpole's 'main political purpose was advancing the career of his first cousin and closest friend, Henry Seymour Conway . . .' (1973, xi).
23. Letters from Walpole to Horace Mann, consul at Venice, indicate that he believed reason existed for caution, if not for outright alarm. When he writes to inform Mann of Conway's dismissal (14 May 1764), he warns Mann not to jeopardize his position by responding openly to the news in writing (Lewis, 1973, 22: 238). See also 22: 256. On his use of 'private hands' to circulate news, see 22: 294. Despite the fact that Horace postures in the above letter to Mann as careless of his own 'interest,' a loaded word in any event, on numerous occasions he does seem to have acted with circumspection.
24. Horace persuaded his cousin to support the Opposition when Bute was succeeded by Grenville in November 1763. Grenville then conspired with the King to remove Conway. On the link between politics and military advancement in general, see Brewer (1988), 45.
25. Lewis (1973), 39: appendix 6, p. 528. To Strafford, Walpole panegyrized the old Constitution 'exactly as it was in the last reign ... It made us *then* the first people in Europe – we have a vast deal of ground to recover – but can we take a better path than that which King William pointed out to us? I mean the system he left us at the Revolution. I am averse to *all* changes of it – it fitted us just as it was' (35: 355). The valorization of Constitution and King William in this letter connects with the defense of Conway in the 'Address' and in the novel, forming a trinity of ideals and goals.
26. Although usually mistaken as part of Walpole's fancifulness, the enslavement of sailors was a fact of life; the crew of the *Lichfield*, shipwrecked off the coast of Morocco in November 1758, endured more than a year of slavery (Rodger, 1996, 139). While the history of Theodore's adventures at sea is sketchily drawn (84–5), neither the corsairs nor the Christian sailors are portrayed as participating in the 'gothic' excesses of cannibalism or sodomy detailed by Malchow (1996, 96–123). As Malchow relates, contradictory images of sailors circulate during the eighteenth and nineteenth centuries. While it is surprising that Theodore's captors remain free from

imputation, his rescuers seem to foreshadow the 'Victorian need to senti-
mentalize the sailor as the white, Christian, and patriotic guardian of the
British nation' (Malchow, 1996, 104). The role played by the navy during
the Seven Years' War certainly contributed to this sentimentalizing tendency. But Theodore's association with the corsairs, lasting twelve years,
also indemnifies scavenging on mercantilist trade, making each enterprise
seem equivalently legitimate.

27. Introductory material to second edition of *Pamela* (1741), quoted by
Williams (1970), 115.

28. Walpole's colleague on *The World*, William Whitehead, distinguished the
ancient and the modern romance (novel) on class grounds, identifying the
novel with 'orphan-beggars, and *serving-men of low degree*' (*The World*, 19,
Thursday, 10 May 1753; reprinted in Williams, 1970, 207). According to
Whitehead, authors of novels reveal the debased class origins they share
with their characters when they attempt to install their heroes and heroines in genteel life at the novel's conclusion. Such ignorance of 'life'
makes novels more detrimental to readers than heroic romances
(Williams, 1970, 208–9).

29. For Theodore's appearance, see *Otranto*, 40 and 54. For Conway's physical
attributes, see Lewis (1973), 20: 49, 265, 309.

30. Orondates is the hero of La Calprénéde's *Cassandre*. He is marvellously
handsome, with a martial beauty, a demeanor majestic enough to
command love, fear, and respect simultaneously, and a stature that is tall
but well-proportioned and graceful. The letter goes on to tweak Conway
about women mourning his absence; the women are also paralleled as characters in *Cassandre* (Lewis, 1973, 37: 196—7).

Walpole's romanticization of this episode is marked when contrasted with
the actual events of that campaign, in which the British infantry unexpectedly
came face to face with the French enemy only thirty paces away at the crest of
a hill. For a description of that encounter, see McNeil (1990), 17.

31. On the early novel's fundamental investment in epistemological concerns,
see Hunter (1990), 44–7.

32. We come even closer in the first italicized section. There, the lack of verbal
markers makes the status of the statement's utterance ambiguous, so that
the passage can be read alternately as consonant psycho-narration or as one
of the first instances of indirect free style.

33. Frenchmen think duty superior to pity or humane feelings (1957, 39–40);
yet that sense of duty does not extend to the rules of chivalry, which in
their cowardice they flout.

34. For my remarks on melancholy, I draw on Sickels (1932), 13–17, 60–1, 70,
75–6, and the catalogue of titles on 356.

35. Despite their reservations, which varied in source among the two periodicals, both the *Monthly Review* and the *Critical Review* were united in their
approbation of the handling of character. The *Monthly Review* declared the
characters 'highly finished; and the disquisitions into human manners, passions, and pursuits, indicate the keenest penetration, and the most perfect
knowledge of mankind' (97). Less favorable than the *Monthly*, the *Critical
Review* yet proclaimed the characters 'well marked' (51). Though the story is

composed of 'rotten materials' and the 'monstrosities' render the work absurd, 'the narrative [is] kept up with surprising spirit and propriety' (ibid.).

Chapter 3　The Prince in the Pauper: Clara Reeve and *The Old English Baron*

1. Cf. Punter, who conjoins 'the feudal baron and the figure of antisocial power' (1980, 53). Instead, the anti-social threat emanates from a misappropriation of noble status.
2. These three categories may appear discrete; however, her later comments in *The Progress of Romance* as well as her practice in *The Old English Baron* reveal that she did not view them that way. See Chapter 1. Writing on Barclay, McKeon confirms the foresightedness of Reeve's critical acumen (1987, 59).
3. In contrast to the way she is usually depicted. See Scott (1827), xxxi; cf. Halimi (1985), 154.
4. Precise dates are never given; they can be worked out from the reference to the death of the Duke of Bedford, who is not a character in the work (1883, 26–7). While a critic of *The Gentleman's Magazine* opposed Reeve's denomination of the periods of Henry V and VI as Gothic, the iconography of Henry V historically coupled him with the Gothic leadership of Arthur and Godfrey: national kings who were also leaders of Christendom (*Encyclopedia Britannica* (1911), 11: 436).
5. Unlike the writer in the *Monthly Review* for April 1778, who urged that resentment over the colonial rebellion should be directed at the 'systematic deceit and perfidy of France' (313).
6. Even Edmund Burke, speaking in favor of conciliation with the colonies, accuses the colonists of having become 'suspicious, restless, and untractable' (1960, 123) and defines them as 'acute, inquisitive, dexterous, prompt in attack, ready in defence, full of resources' (127), anarchic 'monsters' (129).
7. *OED*. By the reign of Charles II, the inner committee of the Privy Council was being referred to as 'the Cabal,' especially the five ministers who signed the Treaty of Alliance with France for war against Holland in 1672. Hume's 1762 *History of England* contains the identification of the cabal with the French alliance, and George Canning puts it into a political parody of the current moment in a poem published with his collected works in 1767.
8. 'The Prophecy of Queen Emma, an ancient Ballad, lately discovered,' echoes Reeve's fictionalizing of the American war and repeats her character names; its review stresses the contemporary allusions (*Critical Review*, 53, 1782).
9. The conjunction of military with public administrative service measured out in Philip Harclay mirrors the reality known to Clara Reeve. Beginning in 1754, military men in both branches equaled 14.7 percent of the total number of MPs in the Commons. As such, they constituted the largest professional group (Brewer, 1988, 45). Moreover, the military's employment in the control of smuggling, during peacetime, necessarily involved them in the work of the Exchequer; and since Suffolk, Reeve's home, was one of the principal smuggling areas, she would have had first-hand experience of the horse regiments stationed there.

10. Sterne's *Sentimental Journey* is exemplary in this respect. For acts of random charity and a patronizing insistence upon merit in objects of sympathy, see also *The Man of Feeling* (1923, 405–6, 412).
11. For critics who conflate the Gothic and the sentimental, cf. Napier (1987), 23–6; MacAndrew (1979), *passim*.
12. I will return to the significance of character as writing later.
13. Rubin (1975), 199; cf. Stone (1977), 93–100.
14. Her representation of aristocratic children's right freely to choose their marital partners thus opposes Walpole's depiction of the duties pertaining to kinship demands. In this, Reeve demonstrates her allegiance to the more progressive ideas of her day. Emma's father allows her the power of veto over his marital arrangements. He offers the same freedom to his eldest son.
15. John Dunlop noticed the same insistence upon material minutiae (1970, 579).
16. To a large extent, Reeve's political economy resembles Baudrillard's description of the artisanal period, characterized by production control and 'the reciprocity of the group' (1975, 97). Whether such a mode actually existed, or whether each dreams a fiction of social relations, is a moot point here. Irony abounds, however, in the clash between Reeve's internal dream and the external reality of her publishing experience, a clash I address in Chapter 7.
17. A similarly homosocial, if not homosexual, bond reinforces the intellectual superiority of the character Euphrasia (the mouthpiece for Reeve) in *The Progress of Romance*.
18. The preservation of the villain distinguishes the Gothic novel from the syntagmatic taxonomy of the *Bildungsroman*, as described by Moretti (1987), 186.
19. For a discussion of literary circulation as strengthening national cohesion, see Klancher (1987), 31–2.
20. This imagined privatization of jurisprudence comports with the political structure Reeve articulates as ideal in *The Phoenix*; see vol. III, book 3, Chapter 22, p. 50; for complaints against the law, see p. 53.
21. Perhaps accounting for Reeve's change of title between the first and second editions. Cf. Scott (1827), lxxx. The blurring of agency and the conflation of heroes amplifies the portrait of virtue, championship, antiquity, and aristocratic duty that the novel furnishes.
22. While none of Reeve's reviewers complained of this valorization of private justice, critics a decade later were less cavalier about the consequences of such fictional representation, as the *Monthly Review*'s 1798 assessment of *Adeline de Courcy* records; see Chapter 1.
23. 'Convenience' resembles a domestication of climate theory in classical thought. For eighteenth-century 'convenience,' see Varey (1990), 10, 19–23, 101, 107, 110–11, 115, 168, 173–5, 181, 193; for 'convenience' as affecting literary characterization, especially as practiced by Fielding, see 156–80 and 203.
24. See Reeve (1883), 18, 22, 25, 37, 56, 58, 115, 121, 136.
25. The overdetermination of this 1778 assertion appears when we remember the notoriety of William Dodd's forgery the preceding year.
26. See Couturier on the problems for which anonymous publication was the solution (1991, 61). Reeve's use of anonymity seems slyly self-assertive. In *The Phoenix*, the attribution of the work to 'A lady' pretends to modesty at the same time that it trumpets that lady's unusual abilities (translating

252 *Notes*

Latin). When the anonymous *Champion of Virtue* proclaims itself the work
of the editor of *The Phoenix*, Reeve puts forward her credentials to be taken
seriously as an author, again under the guise of modesty or diffidence. The
title page of *The Progress of Romance* amplifies this accretive structure of
authority. I take these obfuscations as indicative of a covert aggression. For
romance as authoritarian, see Beer (1970).
27. On this practice, its causes, and its persistence into Reeve's time, see Bossy
(1975), 258.

Chapter 4   Radcliffe, Revolution, and the Romance of Heroism, 1789–94

1. *The Italian* (1981), 194. Critics who have complained of Radcliffe's pre-
dictable extremes seem to have mistaken plot devices for character. Cf.
Cottom (1985), 55–6, and Durant (1980), 28.
2. On the general existence of contention about defining masculinity, see
Hitchcock and Cohen (1999), 'Introduction.' On politeness, see Cohen
(1999), 'Manliness,' 50–7; Samuel (1989); Klein (1994). On sentiment and
the cult of sensibility, see Todd (1989) and Foyster (1999), esp. 164–5; on
violence, see Beattie (1986) and Shoemaker (1999); on active versus passive
duty, see Gregory (1999).
3. William C. Dowling aligns this latter group with the benevolist tradition,
stretching back to Shaftesbury, Butler, and Hutcheson (1981, 121).
4. On these changes of aristocratic behavior, see Colley (1992), 155–64,
167–70, 175–6, 191.
5. For instance, the edition of the 18th–21st carried a banner heading
announcing 'French Revolution!!!' and calling the outbreak of hostilities
'great and glorious,' despite the news of beheadings, the murder of the
Mayor of Paris, and the 500 000 sous price on Marie's head, all reported on
in the same issue. Surprisingly, given the tone of support, the *Chronicle*
informs us that this latest news was gleaned from 'the Duke of
Luxembourg, late President of the Noblesse, one of the first wave of royalist
escapees to arrive in London.' The 'English Gentleman's' report which
follows puts an even better face on events. He praises the sublime yet
orderly and peaceful transition. Though the summary trial of the Governor
of the Bastille et al. resulted in execution by gunfire, then beheading, such
steps were 'sad but necessary... conducted with a decency, a firmness, a
solemnity worthy of the highest admiration' (2).
    On the personal intellectual investment of proprietors in their publica-
tions during the period, see P. Anderson (1991), 11. The lack of ascription
in these 'reports' and 'letters' makes it impossible to decide who speaks. I
have seized upon congruences in attitude between these reports and the
explicit editorials as license for my belief that William held veto power over
the newspaper's content, thereby making him implicitly responsible for the
beliefs uttered pseudonymously.
6. William is not so besotted with the Revolution as to forgo sanguinary fears,
predicated not only on external opposition but also on the threat of civil
war (editorial, 30 July–1 August 1789). In 'Thoughts on the Present State of

France' of the same date, William compares the situation with that of England's Civil War, when an army feeling its power disbanded Parliament and the Constitution. His reaction to the potential threat goes beyond traditional English reluctance to maintain standing armies; it betrays his class fear, as well. If anything, the events of the fall intensify his fears of the lower classes, whom he denominates a 'mob' in the report of 7 October about Louis's incarceration.

7. See Brewer (1982), 199.

8. Adeline succeeds at mustering empirical evidence, at corralling medical knowledge on Theodore's behalf, and at (occasionally) commanding her emotions (*Romance*, 1986, 183–9, 310). Like most Gothic heroes, Emily has the empirical wits to discern the sound of rusty bolts being drawn back, and to determine the direction of footsteps (*Udolpho*, 1970, 243–4, 347). Those same empirical talents fail her in human discovery, though (217–19, 258, 533), subsequently weakening her faith in the law and rendering her resistless to Montoni's imprecations, so that she signs away what Cheron has preserved at the cost of her life (393–4, 436).

9. The *Critical Review* responds huffily to this attempt to render Scotland British (1789, 251). What the reviewer envisioned as the 'manners of the Highlands' can be glimpsed in the preceding issue's review of Richard Hole's *Arthur* (85–6). Ironically, the very absence of the supernatural prevents the *Castles* from seeming Scottish, underscoring Radcliffe's incorporation of things Scottish into things British.

10. On the significance of those titles Earl and Baron as representing the 'order of emerging statehood' versus the 'local despotism of the clan system' respectively, see Milbank (1995), 114, n. 3.

11. In contrast, Mary's mother, otherwise admirable in her parental love, is less scrupulous about promoting her own version of happiness for her daughter's future (83).

12. As late as the American war, Scottish gentry carried their tenantry to war with them (Rodger, 1996, 156–7).

13. Here we have an echo of *Hamlet*. Although the ghostly figure resembles the women in his silence and vulnerability, the figure of Shakespeare *behind* the figure stamps it with a masculine energy and authority, a crossing of gender authority to whose relevance I return in my Chapter 7.

14. Structure calls our attention to the significance of these two men as a pair. As the novel begins, we get alternating chapters of the two heroes. Later in the novel, once we have been introduced to the two heroes, the alternations speed up to become juxtaposed paragraphs, as on page 50.

15. See Gallagher (1985), 187.

16. On 'interest' as economically-motivated, see Mattick (1993), 173.

17. The same awarding of a name to virtue occurs with the guard inspired by Alleyn's conduct to free him (25).

18. Ultimately, though, the scheme requires Osbert's input, thereby demonstrating that the underclasses will not manage alone to free themselves (58).

19. The narrative is ambivalent, in that it preserves a more conventionally gendered version of this belief. Louisa and Laura have transparent bodies that signal their rank and beauty, even though their features are half or completely obscured by veils (34).

20. In the dilemma faced by Louisa's father, the Marquis de St Claire, the novel extends and nationalizes the generational conflict of divided loyalties (61).
21. Demographics may have contributed weight. Over half the population was under the age of 25 in these years.
22. Radcliffe's insistence on active duty is part of her efforts to redefine the sentimental hero as he had taken shape by the end of the eighteenth century, at the same time that her habitual employment of hyperbolic adjectives to describe her heroes indicates her schooling in the sentimental. For example, see *Castles* (1995), 7, 36, 39–40.
23. This view represents the theory of gender provided by social anthropologists. See Horrocks (1995), 14, and Gilmore (1990), *passim.*
24. For Adeline as heroic, see 104–6, 122–3, 129, 136, 163.
25. For Peter, see 145–8; for Jacques, see 169–70. Jacques seems to perform better when his reports can be delivered orally instead of in writing. If this reflects a residual linguistic class bias on Radcliffe's part, it also forms a democratic encouragement to seek for one's native strength in order to discover one's innate nobility. Dunlop's comments instance contemporary appreciation of this cross-class heroism (1970, 582–5).
26. The one representative of a beneficent patriarchy, Adeline's dead father Henry, partakes of the virtues and heroics of each of the men we meet in the novel. Like La Luc, he studies science and literature, and practices benevolence and virtue (1986, 343); his contemplativeness resembles that of Verneuil and Amand. Strangely, though, the energy which typifies Theodore's heroism seems to be an inheritance from Henry's half-brother, Philippe, the present Marquis de Montalt. The vestigial traces of heroism that remain contrast sharply with *Fontainville Forest* (1794), the dramatization of the novel by James Boaden, who compresses all heroes into one, Louis, eliminating entirely the Swiss episodes and characters.
27. A fact also noted by Howard Anderson (1982), 206.
28. However, Verneuil and Amand are distant, unknown relations (1986, 349, 354). When Verneuil accompanies officers to the Abbey to recover Henry's body and the manuscript, he is robbed of his name in these services, becoming no more than an initialed dash (354–5)
29. In *Fontainville Forest*, Nemours, the lawyer responsible for spiriting La Motte out of Paris and away from his creditors, becomes the deus ex machina as the 'delegate express' from the Sovereign (1794, 64). His representative status suffices to effect an individualized justice: Montalt stabs himself, refusing the 'slavery' of the law (66). In the novel, the very idea of the court buoys Adeline (1986, 335). For the King's exemplary behavior, see 324–5, 353. Like Peter and Jacques, the servants of La Motte and the Marquis, respectively, the King as servant of his people must learn to set aside misplaced loyalty and to exert justice in their stead. The courts aid him in that endeavor. But when the rigors of the law provoke the Parliament to harshness (338), the King, like Adeline and her father before her, must learn to temper that justice with clemency. For a more extended treatment of the role of the law, see Wein (1997).
30. See Kuchta (1996), 64, 75, n. 33. Obviously, Gibbon stands as the great skeptical example.
31. On Roman decor, see Schama (1989), 169–74; cf. Chard (1986), 379.

32. While Montalt undermines language's basis in truth, Radcliffe wants us to see the glitter of Montalt's words as mere veneer. When irritated with rage, he resorts to terms of 'coarseness and vehemence... To invent and express these terms seemed to give him not only relief, but delight' (238).

33. Nevertheless, La Luc's educational schemes for his son sound more pointedly studied than those in *Emile* (253–4).

34. The unseen circulation of wealth explains why Clara's belief that inherent nobility wears itself on the physiognomy of the possessor is deemed a 'romantic notion' by her aunt (256). Like a supernatural visitation, money can spur moral reform (353–4).

35. Cf. *Critical Review*, 53 and 54 (March and May 1782).

36. The phrase is Jameson's (1981).

37. See Walvin (1997), *passim*. Moira Ferguson (1992) discusses the appearance of 'greengrocer's' items in the fiction of Wollstonecraft and its significance as indicating an unconscious colonialism. Adeline's 'activity,' and the novel's valorization of a gendered equality, contrasts with Wilson's characterization of colonial empire as simultaneously establishing 'exclusive, gendered definitions' of domestic citizenship limited to an 'aggressive masculinity' (Bermingham and Brewer, 1995, 238).

38. See also 361.

39. See Newman (1997), esp. 239, 241–2, for a description of similar splitting by Romantic poets. Cunningham notes that such ambivalence was common; desire for peace overrode militaristic enthusiasm such that 'bursts' of martial patriotism punctuated a dominant attitude of apathy or hostility (1989, 63).

40. On the volunteer militias, see Colley (1992), 288–91. In her ambivalence, Radcliffe resembles her contemporary countrymen.

41. The nexus of trade, political, intellectual, and social leadership in the period can be viewed in the few 'captains of industry,' such as Wedgwood, Watt, his partner Matthew Boulton, Priestley, Erasmus Darwin, the printer Baskerville, and Erasmus Darwin, founders of the Lunar Society of Birmingham. Eric Hobsbawm stresses how anomalous such men were, in that most 'industrialists' were 'petty operators' (1996, 20–1). Radcliffe's family was closely allied to the Wedgwood phenomenon.

42. War meant a civil competition for goods and money and led to the creation and widespread introduction of untethered paper currency. See Hobsbawm (1996), 94–7.

43. See also St Foix's sublime ruminations on the conjunction of land and sea, echoed by a fragment from Beattie's 'The Minstrel' (1970, 601–2).

44. In keeping with his editorial responsibilities, William reports a movement sweeping London parishes to create committees of voluntary spies. Joseph Banks heads one such, convened at Jack's Coffee-house, Dean Street, in St Anne's parish, Westminster. Banks's committee resolves to 'collect the names, business, and way of life' of all foreigners newly arrived to the parish and to question anyone giving shelter to such foreigners; to request Publicans to forbid meetings of clubs, societies, or persons 'disaffected to our happy Constitution,' and to frustrate the circulating of petitions or exciting of disturbances; to apply to the magistrates to have the licenses of uncooperative publicans revoked; to have beadles, constables, patrols, and

watchmen seize all persons circulating handbills and haul them before the law. To further such noble aims, the committee agrees to defray the expense of arrests by subscription. Meeting every Tuesday, they request all secret communications be directed to W. R. H. Brown, secretary, at Jack's. Other like committees exist in the City and in Cornhill wards.

The very fullness of the report lends it credence and apparent approval. Yet a poem called 'National Alarm' that heads a new feature, the 'Parnassian Corner,' subverts the nobility of these endeavors: 'there can be no harm in giving alarm / and fearing the People with strange Apprehensions/by brewing this Storm, we avoid a Reform / and securely enjoy all our Places and Pensions' (*English Chronicle*, no. 2123, 6–8, December 1792). Like the poet, Radcliffe appears here to disagree with Austen about the value of a neighborhood of voluntary spies. (The comment is Henry's justification for Catherine's security in *Northanger Abbey*; of course, Austen's customary irony makes the proposition unstable and open to interpretation.)

45. For example (1970), 444–9, 469, 536, 573.
46. Despite the aptness of the phrase for the argument I am making, I demur from Hobsbawm's other characterizations of the Gothic movement, which he sees as merely the 'romanticism of reaction'; see (1996), 264–5.

Chapter 5   Speaking Shadows

1. Marlon Ross (1991) discusses the pervasiveness of this problematic in the period, and its local consequences for the work of Wordsworth, Hazlitt, and Scott. Cf. Hunter (1990), 37–8. Although this question underlay the analyses of political power in Walpole and Reeves's fictional worlds, there a complacency reigned: minor adjustments could regulate imbalances. Once individuals had been restored to their proper places as rulers, no further structural realignment was necessary. As a result, individuals themselves experienced no pull from competing demands and duties.
2. Parreaux (1960), 84–6.
3. However, the initial objection was not to 'property in exchangeable commodities – they called this trade and greeted it as a means to independence and virtue' but to mobile property in the form of public credit, which fueled the patronage coffers and increased governmental corruption (Pocock, 1985, 68–9). Investment in public credit led to the mania for speculation, that dirty term in Swift's world and the basis for Radcliffe's critique of Quesnell in *Udolpho*, who not only speculates in the paternal lands but also delights in courtly gossip and scandal.
4. See Hitchcock and Cohen (1999), Introduction, esp. p. 14; Deane (1995), 275–95; Rodger (1996), 248, 340–1; and Tosh (1999), 219; cf. Dabhoiwala (1996), 204, 211. Evidence of an increasing distaste for physical violence and a corresponding recourse to the verbal violence of the law fuels Foyster's argument (1999, 158, 161). In contrast, Pocock uses honor and virtue interchangeably.
5. A usage confirmed by 'Muceus' in the *Anti-Jacobin* (1791), quoted in the introduction.

6. On the presence of a similar paradox in the rhetoric of the London Revolution Society and its spokesman, Richard Price, see Fitzpatrick (1995), 213, 220. However, he sees this blended rhetoric as breaking apart and disappearing in 1794 (226–7). Both the reviews cited here and the novels to be discussed indicate that the tendency for a confused melding or for contradictory sentiments, especially those that combine local and universal patriotism or cosmopolitanism, persisted long past England's entry into war with France.

7. Lewis's influencing by Radcliffe is well documented. His differences from her have also been marked, chiefly as these regard narrative style. Drawing on a distinction Radcliffe herself popularized, critics have assigned these differences the stylistic terms of terror and horror, respectively. Ascribed gender characteristics, less consideration has attended the political significance of these differences.

8. Lewis's attitude may constitute an ostrich-like response to strain he felt on his own pulses, not only in the domain of sexuality but also in his commercial position as landholder in Jamaica .

9. *Esprits des Lois*; qtd by Hughes (1982), 184.

10. For a useful survey, see P. Anderson (1991), 4–5.

11. In *The Castles of Athlin and Dunbayne*, class mobility had been mediated by the topos of discovered birth, which punctured any sense of class competition and drained away any corresponding tension. That trope soon all but vanishes for men; it recurs with Adeline in *Romance* and with Ellena in *The Italian*. By redirecting the trope from male servants onto ambiguously stationed females, discovered birth functions more to solidify the domestic than the social realm.

    Radcliffe uses it once more for a male character, this time obversely, in her posthumous *Gaston de Blondville*. Lewis picks up the trope for his *Castle Spectre*, after parodying it in *The Monk* as part of a gentleman's 'education,' but he, too, uses it for his heroine. Birth holds virtually no mystery for the chapbooks.

12. Thus defusing pamphlet literature's direct address to the reader operating as a political call to arms.

13. Cf. the *Analytical Review* (1796): 403–4.

14. Foucault (1979), 9, 23, 34, 48–9.

15. The remarks represent some of the skirmishes provoked by Lewis's novel and Matthias's condemnation. Earlier, reviewing Matthias's poem, the same journal admitted to having limited their initial remarks on *The Monk* for fear that attention paid to the work by them would encourage sales. They now conclude that 'whoever points out its turpitude and seductive tendency, pays a homage to virtue and religion' (1798, 306).

16. Madrid's venality, evenly distributed among the sexes and the classes, proves Ambrosio no anomaly (1952, 35, 334–5, 360). Neither does religious virtue extend beyond the borders of Spain (138).

17. On the Grand Tour, see Newman (1997), 42–7.

18. The scene in which Ambrosio shudders to draw back the curtain of the bed, where he imagines a ghost lurks (1952, 328), fittingly echoes Emily's adventures in the Marchioness's bedroom at Chateau-le-Blanc.

19. Mockery of education collides with the satire of superstition when Theodore relates to the 'credulous' nuns that 'he was born in Terra

Incognita, was educated at an Hottentot university, had passed two years among the Americans of Silesia' (281). Their colloquy respecting the color of the Danish people shows how easily superstition and ignorance combine to produce racism (282).

20. Daniel Watkins struggles manfully to overcome the implications of Lewis's position vis-à-vis women (1986, 119–29).

21. *Henry II*, III.178; qtd in the *OED*, V, 367.

22. Despite this treatment, Agnes foolishly believes in parental goodness (1952, 146).

23. Reaching back to Greek idealism, this phrase originally placed man in a concentric series of radiating affinities: his own body and physical needs; his immediate biological and acquired nuclear family; more distant relations; his city, state and, ultimately, the entire human race (Fitzpatrick, 1995, 224, n. 40). In revolutionary times, the phrase came to mean an 'enlightened form of patriotism, updated Christian stoicism, which united love of country and love of mankind, state and world citizenship' (ibid.). Lewis seems to reinsert the biological in his emphasis upon families while retaining the political and social implications of the idea.

24. Even the most severe critics of the novel praised 'The Exile.' For example, see Coleridge's letter to Wordsworth, January 1798, I: 237; cited in Parreaux (1960), 49.

25. See Lewis's footnote to the provenance of the cientipedoro that attacks Ambrosio (1952, 93).

26. Kilgour calls Lewis a 'member of the colonial nouveau riche, he tried to ally himself with those of aristocratic birth' (1995, 166). Scott was the first to accuse Lewis of being 'a good deal too fond of the nobility' (*DNB*, 1921, XII: 1071), a good case of kettles and pots. Lewis's lineage had been ennobled by mid-century. His maternal grandfather, Thomas Sewell, was knighted in 1764, after his participation in the Wilkes debate and just prior to being offered the position as Master of the Rolls that he held until 1784 (*DNB*, XVII). His father was deputy Secretary-at-War.

27. Raymond should have filled that role for Antonia; he repents his lapse and the novel justifies it with every excuse from illness to supernatural possession. Lorenzo, her lover, is no more successful at ensuring that her needs are met and her dangers deflected.

28. During the French Revolution, orphans were moved from 'Houses of God' to 'Houses of the Nation' and the nation took over the charge of adopting those it had caused to be abandoned, as when public rituals of adoption were staged for the children of those executed (Shell, 1993, 144). Rousseau and Sade each express the idea that republicanism requires a transcendence of the ordinary family unit; Rousseau would accomplish this through orphaning everyone, while Sade wanted universal incest.

29. This repetition of class miscegenation has led Watkin to deem Lewis 'extremely conservative' (1986, 117–18, 121–2). Lewis could never avoid political labeling as a kind of name-calling. See his note appended to the published (1798) version of *The Castle Spectre*, where he attempts to counter assertions that he was a leveling radical (184). Yet the play includes a similar scene with heightened republican sentiments, eliminating the hero's awareness of Angela's noble blood (157). See also the *Monthly Magazine*, 1798, 508.

30. On the 'new family' which freed itself from both biology and the law to become a value, a theme of expression, an occasion of emotion', see Ariès (1962), 10 and *passim*.
31. The less obviously self-interested representation of adoption perhaps arises from the cult of domesticity now part of the public relations of the King.
32. Percy's servant Motley has been 'brought up' with Percy, in the same manner practiced by seventeenth-century families. See Lewis (1992), 156; Ariès (1962), 396–8.
33. As examples, Linda Colley notes 'the foundation in London of a spate of maternity hospitals' (1992, 87) and projects like Coram's Foundling Hospital. Speaking to the other side of the equation, Ariès notes that '[F]ront-line troops, those most exposed to danger, were called the "lost children"' (1962, 27).
34. On childhood disease and death, see Walvin (1987), 255, and (1982), chs. 1–2.
35. See *The Monthly Review* (1797): 451. Recall, also, that Hester Thrale Piozzi's praise for 'Alonzo the Brave' overlapped with her desire that mutinies be ruthlessly suppressed and their leaders executed (chapter 1); see also her letter to Penelope Pennington, 21 December 1796 (1989, 411).
36. Gattrell contrasts the discourse and the practice, arguing that 'culturally dominant groups most deplore brutality when the state's authority or their own is strong enough to obviate the need for its outward display' (1994, 12). Obviously, in the revolutionary climate, the state's actions vis-à-vis censorship, spying, and sedition trials bespeaks a distinct lack of comfort or security. For the emphasis upon 'humane' movement, see Bender (1987).
37. For the correspondence between attitudes to punishment and the reader relations variously constructed by Radcliffe and Lewis, see Chapter 7.
38. They also resemble the voluntary associations mounted by men of property to prosecute offenders and underwrite the costs of prosecution, both of which were left to private initiative until the middle of the nineteenth century. See Beattie (1986), 35, 49.
39. Vincentio first sees Ellena in church; he hears her expressive voice, but is prevented from seeing her face by the long veil which covers it. She leaves the church with an elderly lady leaning on her arm. He follows them. So here we have the exact situation of the opening of *The Monk*.
40. Once again, the novel displays a belief in gender equality. Ellena displays a less dithering courage than Emily had: fear for her own safety doesn't prevent her from running to the assistance of Beatrice. Conversely, Vivaldi must subdue the 'wilder energy' of his passions (116, 138–40, 198–99). Greater composure permits him a more feminist sensitivity to Ellena; he learns to allow her the time she needs and the security she craves before pressing his own needs (160). For class mobility and its representation in Paolo, see below.
41. The Marchese's dictum about ownership reverses the progressive statement, issued by Fénelon in his *Télémaque* and prized by later political revolutionaries, that 'kings exist for the sake of their subjects, and not subjects for the sake of kings.' Quoted by Fitzpatrick (1995), n. 215.15, . The currency of *Télémaque* in the late 1780s speaks not only to the enduring influence of romance but also to its involvement with politics, as I have argued throughout.

42. For the Marchese's pride, see (1981), 7, 385. Vivaldi's jealous pride also partakes too much of his father's and mother's to comfortably distinguish him as hero on grounds of humility alone, a regard that initiates the long series of differences between Vivaldi and Radcliffe's other heroes (7–8).
43. On active versus passive virtue, see Gregory (1999), 92–3.
44. Peasants routinely make the best of circumstances. Paulo's reaction to getting lost exemplifies this kind of labile optimism (1981, 113–14).
45. Like Vivaldi, Olivia must use inference and probability to secure her person and her integrity (1981, 370).
46. The Marchese attempts to use influence both political and religious to extricate Vivaldi, but this drags on for more than three weeks. Conversely, Paulo uses courage to escape, but escape only enables him to learn Vivaldi's whereabouts, with the above delay attendant. Only Schedoni's confession enables the institution to work in its own way, through its own channels.
47. Yet class antipathies, especially in the Navy, had riven the calm by 1797 (Rodger, 1996, 206).
48. On the link between the specularized female body and female powerlessness, see Scarry (1992), 207 and 361, n.20.
49. See Colley (1992), 237–81, and Klein (1995).
50. The consequences of such ownership are occulted in Amato's (Ansaldo's) report of the confession: Olivia is not raped, merely threatened verbally (1802, 61).
51. Increasing moderation in portraits of Catholics and Catholicism may reflect contemporary political realities. As Thomas Bartlett observes, British ministers began from the early 1770s onward to cultivate better relations with Irish Catholics to counter independent leanings by Irish Protestants, and to satisfy the need for navy and army manpower (1995, 86–7). On the divorce of Catholic ceremonial and practice from dogma, see Tarr (1946), 21, 43.
52. On the psychological versus the corporeal, cf. Schmitt (1997), 28; on Burke's gendering of politics, see Zerilli (1992).
53. Something Genette finds an impossibility (1980, 87–8).
54. Another eruption of consumer reproduction occurs in Radcliffe's description of Ellena as artist. Vivaldi sees in her home copies of prints from Herculaneum, 'thought to be the only copies permitted from the originals in the royal museum' (1981, 24). He realizes with a shock that Ellena has made these copies. Ellena's art thus earns simultaneously a stamp of authority and of a specious authenticity. *The Midnight Assassin* repeats this mini-episode verbatim (1802, 10).

Chapter 6   No Child's Play: the Gothic Chapbooks

1. See P. Anderson (1991), 27-35.
2. See also Feather (1984), 417, and Plumb (1973), 4. Spufford (1981) and Neuberg (1969) argue that the extensive number of titles and surviving copies of chapbooks explode the myth that the poor were almost entirely unlettered until the mid-Victorian period. Cf. Altick (1989); Newman (1997), 31.
3. Gellner distinguishes between the term 'culture' in its anthropological sense of a 'distinctive style of conduct and communication of a given commu-

nity,' as opposed to the term *Kultur*, meaning 'high culture or great tradition, ... endorsed by the speaker as superior ... the rules of which are usually codified by a set of respected, norm-giving specialists within the society' (1983, 92).

4. Barruel was not alone in positing the existence of secret societies, although his 1797 work was probably the most famous of those connecting the activities of the Revolutionaries in France to the existence of secret societies. Later in England, as revolutionary fears subsided under the guns of Wellington, 'secret histories,' published from 1816–19, would focus on corrupt societies of graft in government among British elite.

5. H. L. Malchow's bracing discussion of cannibalism locates such anthropophagic elements in Gothic literature as 'severing of body parts, drinking of blood, desecration of the dead, and handling, smelling, and ingesting the putrefied and unclean' (1996, 45). My discussion of cannibalism, whether recorded fictionally or in the 'scientific' accounts of ethnographers, explorers, and missionaries, draws on his research. See especially his chapter two.

6. Italics signal duplicity in part through association with Latin Roman Catholicism. The 1818 science-fiction newspaper tale, 'Five Hundred Years Hence!' (Haining, 1978), offers as one of its examples of human progress the abolishment of italic type.

7. Despite the benevolence of Faustus's medical practice, he dabbles in medicine to 'the great mortification of his uncle,' and his interest in treating disease syntactically appears as the first example of his 'most dissolute and ungodly life' (1810, 89).

8. P. Anderson (1991), 19; see also Cunningham (1980), 37–41; Lloyd and Thomas (1998). Cf. E. P. Thompson (1978).

9. Scottish schools have a Quixotic champion in the February issue: J. G. Mete defends Scotsmen by insisting they have the good sense always to employ Englishmen to teach the English language (1804, 128).

10. The chapbooks thus revise the full-length Gothics' taxonomic assignment of linguistic style, mentioned in Chapter 2.

11. Wilkinson was 'curator' as well as chief redactor for the *Tell-Tale, or Universal Magazine* (1803–5), a serial anthology of Gothic novels which 'made a regular practice of butchering the classics of Gothic romance, compressing them to a fraction of their original length, intensifying (if possible) their melodrama, and subjecting them to a general rechristening' (Mayo, 1962, 367–8).

12. The architectural details continue the blurring of specificity. A Norman window, with rounded arches and mullioned panes, fills the upper right-hand corner of the drawing; the vault itself has gently rounded arches supported by Ionian capitals.

13. Women's rights, at least in terms of marital property, make a brief, potentially divisive appearance. The Baron bequeaths 'one-third of his estate to Julia; the remainder, with his title, to Alphonso and his male issue for ever.' The tangle of inheritance law is brushed away with the objection '[T]he acquisition of fortune or title was not in their eyes a compensation for the loss of such an indulgent parent, and they regretted his death with unfeigned sorrow' (1810, 36).

14. Napoleon mirrors Gothic villains in the broadsides and cartoons of the day, which variously depict him as 'the Corsican Monster, *alias* the Poisoner,' a

bad actor (with the invasion a theatrical force), a vagrant, and a usurper with a band of Assassins. See numbers 1494 (June 3, 1803), 1499, 1515, 1516, 1520, and 1543.

15. Philip's submission earns him renewed respect, such that Alphonso ultimately trusts him to accompany and chaperone his beloved, although Philip's feminization may also make him a worthy companion (1810, 21).

16. Only in the continuation by 'A.N. Other' do we briefly glimpse the supernatural, but this bears the shade of Radcliffe's *surnaturel expliqué* and vanishes as abruptly as it had been introduced (1801, 60).

17. Note, once again, the near-repetition of names between this chapbook and Drake's *Captive of the Banditti*.

18. The bottom right-hand corner of the illustration adverts to vol. 4, ch. 9, p. 382.

19. Throughout the discussion of the illustrations, I have chosen to use stage directions in keeping with the theatricality I descry. Stage right and left indicate the *actor's* perspective, not the viewer's. Those more comfortable with conventional art terms can mentally substitute foreground, middleground, and background to interpret the figures' positioning.

20. Cited as vol. 1, ch. 1, p. 25.

21. Vol. 3, ch. 1, p. 21.

22. The difference in lighting can be compared to the different key lights used for romantic versus horror scenes.

23. Backscheider (1993), 190–2.

24. Naming Byron as author and thereby assuring its success, a canard perpetuated either by the editors, the publisher (Colburn), or Polidori himself.

25. Robert's father shows a misplaced forward-thinkingness. Asked by his son whether Margaret's nuptials with the false Ruthven have been called off, the old steward replies 'that the young people were not forced to follow such whims,' and that he himself plans to take the place of the Baron in giving away the bride (1820, 126).

26. For a discussion of the Union's repercussions, see Lenham (1984), *passim*.

27. On the link in Polidori between Ruthven and Byron, see Bleiler (1966), xxxvii–xxxviii. We can only speculate whether Polidori's allusive naming was malicious payback for Byron's domineering patronization, or whether his 'mis'-attribution of the novelette to Byron and his subsequent half-hearted disavowal aimed to salve Polidori's conscience for having stolen Byron's fragment in the famous Diodati competition. Regardless, both seem highly successful means of gaining even more money for his publication by doubly encoding his novelette as a *roman-à-clef*. The need for money consumed Polidori throughout his life, and led to his suicide in 1821, his finances made desperate by gambling debts.

28. Adshead reports that, by 1800, English consumption had risen to twenty pounds per capita, 'a single market second only to that of France' (1992, 106).

29. For specific years of increase, see Kennedy (1964), 160. On theories of taxation and social economy in general, see 99ff. See also Brewer (1988), 129, 149, 193, 214. Kames in his *Sketches* (1774) and Burke in his *Letters on a Regicide Peace* contributed to the taxation debate, just as they participated in one way or another in debates over Gothic liberties and values.

30. Contributing to the impression that the chapbook examines notions of citizenship is the setting of the tale at the time of war with Flanders. As

Hobsbawm notes, the Low Countries were some of the very few states not only to embrace Jacobinism, but also to stand a reasonable chance of effecting revolutionary reform on their own (1996, 81). The Baron's service to the King in rooting out such disaffection takes on new coloring in the post-Revolutionary climate.

Chapter 7 From Innkeepers to Puppet Masters: Staging the (Heroic) Author

1. See also Ross (1992), Eagleton (1991), and Lloyd and Thomas (1998); cf. Clery (1995), 7–9, 35, 64–7, 134–43. The copyright debate, to be discussed below, yields a concrete, material causality for some of the more abstract claims made regarding the hegemonic influence of culture, even though temporally precedent.
2. See also La Vopa (1992), 108–9.
3. As did authorial claims to intellectual property. On this, and on the position that the creation of the 'author' was a phenomenon coincident with the late-eighteenth century, see Woodmansee (1984), 426, 430; Rose (1988), 54.
4. Publishers, too, seized on the nexus between Gothic and public authority: William Lane profited handsomely from his *The Soldier's Companion* when war with France resumed in 1803 (Blakey, 1939, 20). Hookham advertised his circulating library, the Literary Assembly, as a heroic endeavor: '[his] most strenuous exertions have been uniformly and unremittingly directed to promote the interest of society by the encouragement and dissemination of Literature' (*Romance of the Forest*, vol. 3 [1796], 4–6).
5. This movement, from the flourishing to the atrophying of the author function, swims against the observations of Foucault: see 'What is An Author?' (1994), 342, 352.
6. Ross (1992), 1, 19.
7. The copyright laws spawned consequences in serial magazine publication. Productions like Harrison's *Novelist's Magazine*, running in various 'new' incarnations throughout the 1780s, had to rely on older works of fiction to fill their pages free of cost. Because the serial chapbooks bludgeoned their sources out of legal recognition, they could afford to be more up to date (Mayo, 1962, 366–9).
8. On the nexus of literature, economics, and circulation as a trope, see Shell (1978).
9. Working in the seventeenth century, Ezell (1999) and Spufford (1981) have sparked recognition of the need to recover 'literary environment.'
10. Gallagher (1994), 228; she draws on Blackstone. See Rose (1988), 63–4.
11. For notions of homogeneity and homogeneous time, see Gellner (1983) and B. Anderson (1991).
12. For an analogous reification of the book in the colonial situation, see Bhabha (1995), esp. 102, 107.
13. Cf. Gallagher (1994), 209–10, 212–13.
14. On Walpole and Shakespeare, see Lewis (1973), 1. xiii; on editors, see Iliffe (1995), 168 and *passim*, and Brewer, 'This' (1995), 14.
15. See Chapter 1, n. 45.

16. Marshall hints that the original priestly author wrote his tale 'to enslave a hundred vulgar minds,' at the same time he avers that fidelity to the *manners* of the times required the inclusion of the miraculous prodigies the story contains.
17. Parks (1974), 12–13.
18. For example, the encounter between Fredric and the 'Spectre' contains verbal echoes of Hamlet's meeting with the shade of his father (I. iv.9, 57, 91). The hermit's adjuration to 'forget Matilda' rewrites Hamlet's renunciation of Ophelia as a class defense. On the continuing use of Shakespeare to solidify nationalist aspirations, especially in the post-Waterloo period, see Foakes (1991), 148–9.
19. See Lewis (1973), 3. 303, 308; Gattrell (1994), 33.
20. See Darnton (1984), chapter 2, esp. 116–24.
21. Setting a pattern that will be traced out again by women's actions during the wars against Revolutionary and Napoleonic France. See Colley (1992), 262.
22. See also *Progress* (1930), I: 75; II: 85, 100
23. Oswald even gossips (1883, 33).
24. See also the Preface to *The Phoenix*, dedicated to Queen Charlotte as 'Patroness of Virtues, Arts, and Science.'
25. Her strategy finesses the way aesthetic theoreticians hierarchized the senses by distinguishing between appeals to distance versus proximity. Because proximity is identified with the feminine (in psychoanalytic terms), Christian Metz holds it no 'accident that the main socially acceptable arts are based on the sense at a distance, and that those which depend on the sense of contact are often regarded as 'minor' arts (culinary arts, art of perfumes, etc.)' (1975, 60).
26. Such instances of self-reflexivity underpin postmodern readings of the Gothic, in that they lend themselves to Derridean notions of the trace and to poststructuralist interpretations about the constructed nature of meaning.
27. On the economics of Lewis's desire, see Wein (1999).
28. See Talfourd (1976), 5–7 and *The New Monthly Magazine* (1826): 533. For a more generalized reason for the pressure to reticence and respectability, see McKillop (1932).
29. The pendulum swings most wildly in the tribunal scene of *The Italian* (1981, 335). The narrator's ejaculations of 'perhaps' and 'probable' in imagining outcomes combine with her use of the conditional to warn us against taking these consequences as fixed and inevitable. But if horrific outcomes are not fated, neither are they precluded. This duplicity is all the more strongly marked in contrast to the tone of authority the narrator acquires from the precise legal terms and distinctions employed (337). See also the same trick, pages 356 and 365, and the insistence that the countess had died from the wound inflicted by Schedoni (363). This deliberateness of duplicity and manipulation contradicts some feminist criticism of 'Female Gothic.' Cf. Gardiner (1982), 185.
30. In her journal entries of tours, as recorded in the Memoir prefixed to *Gaston* (vol.I, 1976), Radcliffe makes frequent mention of Gilpin, at times contradicting his ideas of the picturesque (e.g. 47; 55, where she criticizes Gilpin's preference for a tower to the 'sublime Cathedral' of Salisbury; on 56, she cites him approvingly as a historian of gothic pillars).

31. Journal entry, 19 October 1801, *Gaston*, 1976, 81–2.
32. More sophisticated than most chapbooks, *Vildac* continues in first-person and includes an intradiegetic tale, also told in first-person.
33. On Thompson's possible identity, see Davidson (1985).
34. Vol. Three, chapter 12, of *Melmoth* begins with an epigraph from Shurley's *St. Patrick for Ireland*, asking 'Who brought you first acquainted with the devil?' (245). Since this is the same John Shurley who was a bookseller and promoter of romance, the question and the citation have a nice resonance.
35. Conversely, Maturin cements this sweep by physicalizing the postures of teller and listener.
36. See, for example, 12, 18, 42, 240, 405, 418, 421, 431, 458. The painterly comparisons seem to multiply in the later intradiegetic narratives, beginning with Monçalada's relation of Melmoth's recitals in 'The Tale of Guzman's Family' and 'The Lover's Tale.'
37. Empirical details include the references to historical events contemporary with the narrative, and the inclusion of dates in Robert's diary (e.g. 1986, 124). These dates offer at one and the same time the most concrete and the most oblique evidence for the nationalist undertones of the tale, for through them we can work out that Robert's pleas to be left alone and Gil-Martin's ominous assertion of their eternal amalgamation occur in 1707, the year in which Union took force. See also 71, 64 (and its gloss on), 247; 187, 220, 222. For the motif of 'adoption,' one which we've already seen connected to a political sense in Chapter 5, see 42–3; both meanings seem spurious.
38. *The Spy*, LII (24 August 1811; qtd by Simpson, 1962, 21).
39. This linguistic seesaw continues in the novel, where the 'editor' furnishes English translations of Scottish terms (1986, 231).
40. Even himself (1986, 236).
41. Among the reductions trumpeted, the editor reports the promised 'repeal of the salt duties within a brief period' (1986, 185).
42. Stuart Hall lists Said's definition of 'an imaginative geography and history,' which 'helps intensify its own sense of itself by dramatising the difference between what is close to it and what is far away' as being congruent with Anderson's idea of 'imagined community' (Hall, 1994, 399).
43. Thus, Hogg includes a tale about a Robin Ruthven, a name already rife in our accounts of Scottish Gothicism, who has lived with the fairies, making him a local hero akin to Robert in *The Bride of the Isles* (1986, 195–99).

Chapter 8   The Afterlife of the Gothic Nation

1. Nelson's state funeral crystallized the national esteem in which he was held, just as the proliferation of mementos instanced the tendency to commodify heroes. This esteem and commodification alike wiped away any recollection of the man's personal peccadilloes to refashion Nelson as a hero possessing the most 'pure benevolence' and 'active virtue' (Obituary, *Morning Chronicle*, 7 November 1805, qtd by Hibbert, 1996, 383; see also 382–3, 392–5).
2. For Beckford, see Hibbert (1996), 233–4; for Victoria and Albert, see Edwin Landseer's painting.

3. For accounts of the building projects of George III and others, as well as George IV's coronation, see Girouard (1981), esp. chapter 1. Although not specifically characterizing his findings in terms of a Gothic revival, his book on chivalry remains a valuable survey of the spread of what I have deemed 'Gothic' ideals. Any general sense of the phenomenon cannot afford to over-look Kenneth Clark's 1962 work on Gothic architectural infiltration into middle-class standards, or the European reach of Germann (1972).

4. For the Brass Founder's procession, see Girouard (1981), 68; see also Clark (1990).

5. Kuchta (1996), 71, 77, n. 75.

6. For continental comparisons, see Robson-Scott (1965).

7. Unlike the Silver Fork novels, which detailed aristocratic vice, the later sen-sation novels of the 1860s, spurting up just prior to passage of the second Reform Bill, fastened their gaze on the flagrant sexual transgressions of the middle classes. See Hughes (1980), 8.

8. See Duncan (1992), *passim*. Dorothy Wordsworth's letters record amusing, if outraged, reactions to Scott's fame on the part of some Romantics in 1810 (Moorman, 1969, II: 458–9).

9. The *Literary Review* of September 1826 advertises the fact that the publisher Galignani had pirated sketches from an incomplete run of the Ballantyne edition; the reviewer urges Ballantyne to return the compliment in order to recoup his losses (349).

10. See also Scott's conflation of Scots history with chivalry (*Essays on Chivalry*, 1887, 19).

11. See Temple, 'Of Heroic Virtue' ([1690] 1963). For the medieval history of Odin in the genealogy of English kings, see Kliger (1952), 212.

12. For a description of the two poles around which cultural studies operates, see Morris (1994).

Works Cited

Primary works

Analytical Review or History of Literature, Domestic and Foreign, vol. 19, no. 11 (June 1794). Review of *The Mysteries of Udolpho*: 140–45.

——. vol. 24 (October 1796). Review of *The Monk*: 403–4.

Anonymous, *Adolphus and Louisa, or The Fatal Attachment, A Tale of Truth*. W. Mason, n. d.

——. *All the Talents. A Satirical Poem in Three Dialogues*, by Polypus, 2nd edn. London: John Joseph Stockdale, 1807.

——. *Canterbury Tales*, Lemoine, 1802. Private collection known as *The Entertainer*.

——. *Gothic Legends. A Tale of Mystery*. A. Seale, 1802.

——. *The Abbey of Saint Asaph*. Lane, 1795.

——. *The Bride of the Isles* (1820). Rptd in Haining (1978).

——. *'The Duke of Shoreditch; or, Barlow's Ghost.'* London: J. Asperne, 1803.

——. *The Gothic Story of De Courville Castle* (1810? 1818?). Private collection known as *Tales and Romances*, vol. I.

——. *The Life and Horrid Adventures of The Celebrated Dr. Faustus* (1810). Rptd in Haining (1978).

——. *The Midnight Assassin; or, Confession of the Monk Rinaldi* (1802). London: Printed for William Gilbert, *The Marvellous Magazine*.

——. *The Midnight Groan or the Spectre of the Chapel: Involving an Exposure of the Horrible Secrets of the NOCTURNAL ASSEMBLY. A Gothic Romance*. London: T. and R. Hughes, 1808.

——. *The Mysteries of Udolpho, A Romance, Founded on Facts*. London: W. Mason, n. d. In *Tales and Romances*.

——. *The Spectre Mother: Or, the Haunted Tower*. Rptd in Haining (1978).

——.*The Three Ghosts of the Forest, A Tale of Horror*. London: S. Ker, T. Hughes, N. and J. Muggeridge, and S. Eliot, 1803.

——. *Vildac, or, The Horrid Discovery*. London: W. Mason, 1800.

——. *Young Grigor's Ghost. To which is Added, The Wheel of Life*. Edinburgh, 1770, 1779.

The Anti-Jacobin, or Weekly Examiner, Prospectus, 20 November 1790.

——. 7 May 1798: 203.

——. 21 May 1798: 219–20

Barbauld, Anna. *The British Novelists Series*. London, 1820.

Barrett, C. F. *The Great Devil's Tale; or, The Castle of Morbano* (1802? 1805?). In *Canterbury Tales*.

Barruel, Abbé. *Mémoires pour servir à l'Histoire du Jacobinisme*; i.e., *Memoirs illustrating the History of Jacobinism*, Parts I and II. London: De Boffe, & c. 1797.

Bibliotheca Lindesiana. Aberdeen University Press, 1902.

Blackwood's Edinburgh Magazine, XIV (August 1823). *The Tory*, No. II: 184–7.

——. The Ettrick Shepherd, *A Scots Mummy*: 188–90.

Boaden, James. *Fontainville Forest, A Play, in five Acts (Founded on the Romance of the Forest), as Performed at the Theatre-Royal Covent-Garden*. London: Hookham & Carpenter, 1794.

Bolingbroke, *The Craftsman*, no. 222 (2 October 1730). London: R. Francklin, 1731.

British Critic, IV (1794). Review of *Udolpho*: 110–21.

——. IV (1794). Review of Godwin's *Caleb Williams*: 70–1.

——. X (July–December 1797). Review of *The Italian*: 266–70; Review of Matthias's *The Pursuits of Literature*: 303–6.

——. XII (July–December 1798). Review of Joseph Fox's *Santa-Maria; or, The Mysterious Pregnancy*: 183–4; Review of George Moore's *Grasville Abbey*: 305; Review of *Impartial Strictures on the Poem called 'the Pursuit of Literature,' and particularly a Vindication of the Romance of 'The Monk'*: 318–19.

Burke, Edmund. *Reflections on the Revolution in France*. New York: Doubleday, 1989.

——. *Selected Writings of Edmund Burke*, ed. Walter J. Bate. New York: Random House, 1960.

Burney, Frances. Preface to *Evelina* (1778).

Carlyle, Thomas. *On Heroes, Hero-Worship and the Heroic in History* (1840). London: Chapman & Hall, n.d.

Coleridge, Samuel. *Letters*, ed. E. H. Coleridge, 2 vols. London, 1895.

——. Review of Radcliffe's *The Mysteries of Udolpho*. *Critical Review*, N.S., vol. 11 (August 1794): 361–72.

Critical Review, vol. 19 (January 1765). Review of *The Castle of Otranto*: 50–1.

——. vol. 43 (January 1778). Review of *The Laws Respecting Women*: 44–50.

——. vol. 45 (July–December 1777). Review of *The Champion of Virtue*: 154.

——. vol. 45 (June 1778). Review of Warton's *The History of English Poetry*: 422.

——. vol. 46 (September 1778). Review of Burney's *Evelina*: 203–4.

——. vol. 49 (January 1780). Review of *The History of a French Louse*: 51–5.

——. vol. 50 (November 1780): 340.

——. vol. 51 (January 1781). Review of 'The Ancient Briton': 72.

——. vol. 53 (March–June 1782). 'The British Hero in Captivity': 229; Review of *A Seaman's Remarks on the British Ships of the Line*: 308; Review of 'The Prophecy of Queen Emma': 419–20.

——. vol. 54 (May 1782). Review of John Sinclair, M.P., *Thoughts on the Naval Strength of the British Empire*: 308.

——. vol. 67 (August 1789). Review of Richard Hole's *Arthur; or, The Northern Enchantment*: 85–86.

——. vol. 68 (September 1789). Review of *The Castles of Athlin and Dunbayne*: 251.

——. vol. 69 (April 1790). Review of *Substance of a Speech on the Debate on the Army Estimates, House of Commons, 9th February 1790, Comprehending a Discussion of the Present Situation of Affairs in France*, 4th ed., and *A Letter from Earl Stanhope, to the Right Honorable E. B.: Containing a Short Answer to his late Speech on the French Revolution*, 2nd ed.: 475.

——. N.S., vol. XI (July 1794). Review of Flammenberg's *The Necromancer*: 469.

Crookenden, Isaac. *Fatal Secrets, or Etherlinda di Salmoni* (1806).

——. *Horrible Revenge, or, The Monster of Italy!* London: Harrild (1812).

——. *The Distressed Nun* (1802).

——. *The Mysterious Murder* (1806).

——. *The Nocturnal Assassin* (1806).

——. *The Vindictive Monk; Or, The Fatal Ring*. Clerkenwell: S. Fisher, 1802. Rptd in Haining (1978).

Croly, George. *Salathiel. A story of the past, the present, and the future*. London: H. Colburn, 1829.

Davenport, Selina. *Italian Vengeance and English Forbearance. A Romance*. A. K. Newman, 1828.

DNB, vols XII and XVII, eds Sir Leslie Stephen and Sir Sidney Lee. Oxford and New York: Oxford University Press, 1921.

Drake, Nathan. *Captive of the Banditti* (1801).

——. 'On the Government of the Imagination.' In *Literary Hours, Or Sketches Critical and Narrative*, 2nd edn. London: T Cadell, Jr and W. Davies, 1800.

Dunlop, John. *History of Prose Fiction*, vol. II (1814), ed. Henry Wilson. New York: Burt Franklin, 1970.

Fenn, Eleanor (Mrs Teachwell or Mrs Lovechild). *The Female Guardian*. London, 1784.

Fielding, Henry. *Tom Jones*, ed. Fredson Bowers. Middletown, CT: Wesleyan University Press, 1975.

Gentleman's Magazine, vol. LXXIV (January–June 1804): 22; 46–7; 128.

——. vol. LXXXVI (February 1816): 164.

Graves, Richard. *The Spiritual Quixote*. London, 1771.

Hamilton, Elizabeth. *Letters: Addressed to the Daughters of a Nobleman on the Formation of Religious and Moral Principle*. London, 1806.

Hogg, James. *The Private Memoirs and Confessions of a Justified Sinner*, ed. John Wain. Harmondsworth: Penguin Books, 1986.

Hurd, Bishop Richard. *Letters on Chivalry and Romance*, ed. Hoyt Trowbridge. Augustan Reprint Society, Publication No. 101–02, 1963.

——. *Letters on Chivalry and Romance with the Third Elizabethan Dialogue*, ed. Edith J. Morley. London: Henry Frowde, 1911.

Kames, Henry Home. *Elements of Criticism*. New York: Collins & Hannay, 1830.

Leland, Thomas. *Longsword, Earl of Salisbury. An Historical Romance*, ed. John C. Stephens. New York: New York University Press, 1957.

Lewis, Matthew. *Journal of a West India Proprietor kept during a residence in the Island of Jamaica* (1815–17). New York: Negro Universities Press, 1969.

——. *The Monk*, ed. Louis F. Peck. New York: Grove Press, 1952.

——. *The Castle Spectre*. Rptd in *Seven Gothic Dramas 1789–1825*, ed. Jeffrey N. Cox. Athens: Ohio State University Press, 1992.

MacKenzie, Henry. *The Man of Feeling*. Edinburgh: James Ballantyne & Co., 1823.

Maturin, Charles. *Melmoth the Wanderer*, ed. Douglas Grant. London: Oxford University Press, 1989.

Monboddo, James. *Of the Origin and Progress of Language*. London: T. Cadell, 1786.

Monthly Magazine, vol. XXXIII (1798): 508.

The Monthly Review, vol. XXXII (1765). Review of *The Castle of Otranto*: 97.

——. vol. LXIII (April 1778). Review of *The Champion of Virtue*: 85

——. N.S., vol. 8 (May–August, 1792). Review of *The Romance of the Forest*: 82–5 .

——. N.S., vol. 15 (November 1794). Review of *Udolpho*: 278–83.

——. N.S., vol. 18 (September–December 1795). Review of *The Abbey of Saint Asaph*: 229; Reviews of *A Remonstrance in Favour of British Liberty* and *A Letter to the High Sheriff of the County of Lincoln, respecting the Bills of Lord Grenville and Mr. Pitt, for altering the Criminal Law of England, and respecting Treason and Sedition.*

——. N.S., vol. 22 (March 1797). Review of *The Italian*: 282–4.

——. N.S., vol. 23 (August 1797). Review of *The Monk*: 451. Review of *Mémoires pour servir à l'Histoire du Jacobinisme*: 528–40.

——. N.S., vol. 26 (May–August 1798). Review of *Adeline de Courcy:* 107; Review of Francis Lathom's *The Midnight Bell, a German Story:* 340; Review of *Letter from Citizen Gregoire*: 454–6.

Murray, Hugh. *Morality of Fiction; or, An Inquiry into the Tendency of Fictitious Narratives, with Observations on Some of the Most Eminent.* Edinburgh, 1805.

The New Monthly Magazine and literary journal, vol. 16, no. 65 (May 1826). London: Henry Colburn. 'On the Supernatural in Poetry': 145–52.

——. vol. 16, no. 66 (June 1826). 'Mrs. Radcliffe's Posthumous Romance': 532–6.

Percy, Thomas. *Northern Antiquities* (1770).

——. 'Essay on the ancient Metrical Romances,' prefixed to *Reliques of Ancient English Poetry*. London: Dodsley, 1775.

Piozzi, Hester. *The Correspondence of Hester Lynch Piozzi 1784–1821*, vol. II (1792–98), eds Edward A. and Lillian D. Bloom. Newark: University of Delaware Press, 1989.

Polidori, John. *The Vampyre*. In Bleiler (1966), 257–283.

Pyne, W. H. *Costume of Great Britain* (1808).

Radcliffe, Ann. *A Sicilian Romance*, ed. Alison Milbank. Oxford and New York: Oxford University Press, 1993.

——. *Gaston de Blondeville; or, The Court of Henry III Keeping Festival in Arden. A Romance* (London: Henry Colburn, 1826). New York: Georg Olms Verlag, 1976.

——. *Journey through Holland and the Western Frontiers of Germany*. New York: Georg Olms Verlag Hildesheim, 1975.

——. *L'Italien, ou le confessional des penitens noirs*. Paris: Jeune, Maradan, 1797.

——. *The Castles of Athlin and Dunbayne*, ed. Alison Milbank. Oxford and New York: Oxford University Press, 1995.

——. *The Italian; or, the Confessional of the Black Penitents*, ed. Frederick Garber. Oxford: Oxford University Press, 1981.

——. *The Mysteries of Udolpho*, ed. Bonamy Dobrée. Oxford and New York: Oxford University Press, 1970.

——. *The Romance of the Forest*. London: Hookham & Sons, 1796.

——. *The Romance of the Forest*, ed. Chloe Chard. Oxford and New York: Oxford University Press, 1986.

Radcliffe, William. *The English Chronicle and Universal Evening Post*, 13 July 1789; 18–21 July 1789; 30 July–1 August 1789; 28 November–1 December 1789; 4–6 March 1790; no. 2123, 6–8 December 1792.

Reeve, Clara. *The Old English Baron*, printed with *The Castle of Otranto*. London: J. C. Nimmo and Bain, 1883.

——. *The Phoenix; or the History of Polyarchus and Argenis*. London, 1772.

——. *The Progress of Romance* (1785). New York Facsimile Text Society Edition, 1930.

Scott, Walter. *Ballantyne Novelist's Library*. Edinburgh, 1827.

——. *Essays on Chivalry, Romance, and the Drama*. London: Fred Warne & Co., 1887.

——. *The Miscellaneous Prose Works*, 3 vols. Vol. I. Edinburgh: Robert Cadell, 1867.

——. *Waverley*, ed. Andrew Hook. Harmondsworth: Penguin Books, 1985.

Seward, Anna. *Letters 1784–1807*. Edinburgh and London: n.p., 1811.

Smith, Charles Hamilton. *Selections of the Ancient Costume of Great Britain and Ireland from the Seventh to the Sixteenth Century, Out of the Collection in the Possession of the Author* (1814).

—— and Samuel Rush Meyrick. *The Costume of the Original Inhabitants of the British Islands* (1815).

Talfourd, T. Noone. Memoir, 'The Life and Writings of Mrs. Radcliffe,' in *Gaston de Blondeville*. New York: Georg Olms Verlag, 1976.

Temple, Sir William. *Five Miscellaneous Essays by Sir William Temple*, ed. Samuel Holt Monk. Ann Arbor: University of Michigan Press, 1963.

——. *An Essay upon the Original and Nature of Government*. The Augustan Reprint Society: William Andrews Clark Memorial Library, University of California, Los Angeles, 1964.

Utterson, Sarah Elizabeth Brown. *Tales of the Dead, Principally Translated from the French*. Printed by S. Hamilton, Weybridge. London: White, Cochrane & Co., 1813.

Walpole, Horace. *The Castle of Otranto*. New York: Holt, Rinehart & Winston, 1963.

——. *Historic Doubts on the Life and Reign of Richard the Third*. Gloucester: Alan Sutton, 1987.

——. *Memoirs of the Reign of George III*, ed. Sir Denis le Marchant. London: R. Bentley, 1845.

——. *Correspondence of Horace Walpole*, ed. W. S. Lewis. New Haven, CT: Yale University Press, 1973.

Warton, Thomas. *The History of English Poetry*, vol. 2. London: Dodsley, 1774–81.

Wilkinson, Sarah. 'The Mysterious Novice; Or, Convent of the Grey Penitents.' John Arliss, 1800. Rptd in Haining (1978).

Wordsworth, William. Preface to *Lyrical Ballads* (1802). *Norton Anthology of English Literature*, vol. II. New York: Norton, 1993

Secondary works

Adshead, S. A. M. *Salt and Civilization*. London: Macmillan, now Palgrave, 1992.

Altick, Richard D. 'The Sociology of Authorship: The Social Origins, Education, and Occupations of 1,100 British Writers, 1800–1935.' *Writers, Readers, and Occasions: Selected Essays on Victorian Literature and Life*. Columbus: Ohio State University Press, 1989: 95–109.

Anderson, Benedict. *Imagined Communities: Reflections on the Origin and Spread of Nationalism*. London and New York: Verso, 1991.

Anderson, Howard. 'Gothic Heroes.' In Folkenflik (1982): 205–21.

Anderson, Patricia. *The Printed Image and the Transformation of Popular Culture 1790–1860*. Oxford: Oxford University Press, 1991.

Ariès, Philippe. *Centuries of Childhood: A Social History of Family Life*, trans. Robert Baldick. New York: Vintage Books, 1962.

Backscheider, Paula. *Spectacular Politics: Theatrical Power and Mass Culture in Early Modern England*. Baltimore, MD: Johns Hopkins University Press, 1993.

Bakhtin, Mikhail. *The Dialogic Imagination*, trans. Caryl Emerson and Michael Holquist. Austin: University of Texas Press, 1981.

——. *Speech Genres and Other Late Essays*, trans. Vern McGee. Austin: University of Texas Press, 1986.

Baldick, Robert. *The Duel*. London: Chapman & Hall, 1965.

Balibar, Etienne. 'The Nation Form: History and Ideology.' In *Race, Nation, Class: Ambiguous Identities*, eds Etienne Balibar and Immanuel Wallenstein, trans. Chris Turner. London and New York: Verso, 1991: 86–106.

Bartlett, Thomas. 'Protestant Nationalism in Eighteenth-Century Ireland.' In O'Dea and Whelan (1995): 79–88.

Baudrillard, Jean. *The Mirror of Production*, trans. Mark Poster. St Louis, Mo: Telos Press, 1975.

——. *Simulations*, trans. Paul Foss, Paul Patton, and Philip Beitchman. New York: Semiotext(e), 1993.

Bayer-Berenbaum, Linda. *The Gothic Imagination: Expansion in Gothic Literature and Art*. Teaneck, NJ: Fairleigh Dickinson University Press, 1982.

Beasley, Jerry C. *Novels of the 1740's*. Athens: University of Georgia Press, 1982.

Beattie, J. M. *Crime and the Courts in England 1660–1800*. Princeton, NJ: Princeton University Press, 1986.

Beer, Gillian. *The Romance*. London: Methuen, 1970.

Bender, John. *Imagining the Penitentiary: Fiction and the Architecture of Mind in 18th-Century England*. Chicago: University of Chicago Press, 1987.

Benjamin, Walter. *Illuminations*, trans. Harry Zohn. New York: Harcourt, Brace & World, 1968.

Bermingham, Anne. 'Elegant Females and Gentleman Connoisseurs. The Commerce in Culture and Self-Image in Eighteenth-Century England.' In Bermingham and Brewer (1995): 489–513.

—— and John Brewer (eds). *The Culture of Consumption 1600–1800. Image, Object, Text*. London and New York: Routledge, 1995.

Bhabha, Homi K. *The Location of Culture*. London and New York: Routledge, 1995.

Black, Jeremy (ed.). *Britain in the Age of Walpole*. London: Macmillan, 1984.

Blakey, Dorothy. *The Minerva Press 1790–1820*. London: Printed for the Bibliographical Society at the University Press, Oxford, 1939.

Bleiler, E. F. (ed.). *Three Gothic Novels*. New York: Dover, 1966.

Bossy, John. *The English Catholic Community 1570–1850*. London: Dorton, Longman & Todd, 1975.

Botting, Fred. *Gothic*. New York and London: Routledge, 1996.

Bourdieu, Pierre. *Distinction: A Social Critique of the Judgement of Taste*, trans. Richard Nice. Cambridge, MA: Harvard University Press, 1984.

——. *In Other Words: Essays Towards a Reflexive Sociology*, trans. Matthew Adamson. Stanford, CA: Stanford University Press, 1990: 123–39.

Bray, Alan and Michel Rey. 'The Body of the Friend: Continuity and Change in Masculine Friendship in the Seventeenth Century.' In Hitchcock and Cohen (1999): 65–84.

Brewer, John. 'Commercialization and Politics.' In *The Birth of a Consumer Society. The Commercialization of Eighteenth-Century England*, eds Neil McKendrick, John Brewer, and J. H. Plumb. Bloomington: Indiana University Press, 1982: 197–262.

——. '"The Most Polite Age and the Most Vicious." Attitudes Towards Culture as a Commodity, 1660–1800.' In Bermingham and Brewer (1995): 341–61.

——. *The Sinews of Power: War, Money, and the English State, 1688–1783*. Cambridge, MA: Harvard University Press, 1988.

——. 'This, That and the Other: Public, Social and Private in the Seventeenth and Eighteenth Centuries.' In *Shifting the Boundaries: Transformations of the Languages of Public and Private in the Eighteenth Century*, eds Dario Castiglione and Lesley Sharpe. Exeter: University of Exeter Press, 1995: 1–21.

Bunn-Heidler, Joseph. *The History, from 1700 to 1800, of English Criticism of Prose Fiction.* University of Illinois Studies in Language and Literature No. 2 (May 1928).

Butler, Marilyn. 'Culture's Medium: the Role of the Review.' In *The Cambridge Companion to British Romanticism,* ed. Stuart Curran. Cambridge: Cambridge University Press, 1993: 120–47.

——. *Romantics, Rebels, and Reactionaries: English Literature and its Background, 1760–1830.* Oxford University Press, 1982.

Byars, Jackie. *All that Hollywood Allows: Re-reading Gender in 1950s Melodrama.* London: Routledge, 1991.

Carter, Margaret L. *Specter or Delusion? The Supernatural in Gothic Fiction.* Ann Arbor, MI and London: UMI Research Press, 1987.

Castle, Terry. 'The Female Thermometer.' *Representations,* 17 (Winter 1987): 1–27.

Cawelti, John. *Adventure, Mystery and Romance.* Chicago: University of Chicago Press, 1976.

Chard, Chloe (ed.) *The Romance of the Forest.* Oxford and New York: Oxford University Press, 1986.

Christensen, Jerome. *Lord Byron's Strength: Romantic Writing and Commercial Society.* Baltimore, MD: Johns Hopkins University Press, 1993.

Clark, Anna. 'Queen Caroline and the Sexual Politics of Popular Culture in London, 1820.' *Representations,* 31 (Summer 1990): 47–65.

Clark, Kenneth. *The Gothic Revival: An Essay in the History of Taste.* New York: Charles Scribner's Sons, 1962.

Clery, E. J. 'Introduction.' *The Castle of Otranto.* Oxford: Oxford University Press, 1996.

——. *The Rise of Supernatural Fiction 1762–1800.* Cambridge: Cambridge University Press, 1995.

Cohen, Michèle. 'Manliness, Effeminacy and the French: Gender and the Construction of National Character in Eighteenth-Century England.' In Hitchcock and Cohen (1999): 44–61.

Colley, Linda. 'Britishness and Otherness: An Argument.' In O'Dea and Whelan (1995): 61–77.

——. *Britons. Forging the Nation 1707–1837.* New Haven, CT and London: Yale University Press, 1992.

Connors, Robert J. 'Genre Theory in Literature.' In Simons and Aghazarian (1986): 25–44.

Corfield, Penny. 'The Democratic History of the English Gentleman.' *History Today,* 42 (1992): 40–7.

Cottom, Daniel. *The Civilized Imagination.* Cambridge: Cambridge University Press, 1985.

Couturier, Maurice. *Textual Communication. A Print-Based Theory of the Novel.* London and New York: Routledge, 1991.

Craft-Fairchild, Catherine. *Masquerade and Gender. Disguise and Female Identity in Eighteenth-Century Fictions by Women.* University Park: The Pennsylvania State University Press, 1993.

Cunningham, Hugh. 'The Language of Patriotism.' In Samuel (1989), vol. I, *History and Politics:* 57–89.

——. *Leisure in the Industrial Revolution.* London: Croom Helm, 1980.

Dabhoiwala, Faramerz. 'The Construction of Honour, Reputation and Status in Late Seventeenth- and Early Eighteenth-Century England.' *Transactions of the Royal Society*, 6 (1996): 201–13.

Darnton, Robert. *The Great Cat Massacre and Other Episodes in French Cultural History*. New York: Vintage Books, 1984.

——. Review of Roger Chartier's *Forms and Meanings: Texts, Performances, and Audiences from Codex to Computer*, and of Alvin Kiernan's *Shakespeare, the King's Playwright: Theater and the Stuart Court, 1603–1613*. *NYRB*, xlii, 10 (6 June, 1996): 52–7.

Davidson, Caroline. *The World of Mary Ellen Best*. London: Chatto & Windus, The Hogarth Press, 1985.

Davis, Robert Con and Ronald Schleifer. *Contemporary Literary Criticism: Literary and Cultural Studies*, 3rd edn. New York and London: Longman, 1994.

Deane, Seamus (ed.). *Nationalism, Colonialism, and Literature*. Minneapolis: University of Minnesota Press, 1990.

——. 'Virtue, Travel and the Enlightenment.' In O'Dea and Whelan (1995): 275–95.

Debord, Guy. *The Society of the Spectacle*, a Black and Red translation. Detroit MI: Black & Red, 1983.

DeLamotte, Eugenia C. *Perils of the Night. A Feminist Study of Nineteenth-Century Gothic*. New York and Oxford: Oxford University Press, 1990.

Deleuze, Giles and Felix Guattari. 'Kafka: Toward a Minor Literature.' Reprinted in Richter (1994).

Dobson, Austin. *Horace Walpole, A Memoir*. New York: Dodd, Mead & Co., 1890.

Dole, Carol M. 'Three Tyrants in *The Castle of Otranto*.' *ELN*, 26, 1 (September 1988): 26–35.

Donoghue, Frank. 'Colonizing Readers. Review Criticism and the Formation of a Reading Public.' In Bermingham and Brewer (1995): 54–74.

Doughty, Oswald (ed.). *The Castle of Otranto*. London: Scholartis Press, 1929.

Dowling, William C. 'Burke and the Age of Chivalry.' In *Heroes and the Heroic. The Yearbook of English Studies*, vol. 12 (1981): 109–24.

Downie, J. A. 'Walpole, "the Poet's Foe."' In Black (1984).

Duncan, Ian. *Modern Romance and the Transformations of the Novel. The Gothic, Scott, Dickens*. Cambridge: Cambridge University Press, 1992.

Durant, David S. *Ann Radcliffe's Novels. Experiments in Setting*. New York: Arno Press, 1980.

Eagleton, Terry. *Ideology*. London and New York: Verso, 1991.

——. 'Nationalism: Irony and Commitment.' In Deane (1990).

Ellis, Kate Ferguson. *The Contested Castle: Gothic Novels and the Subversion of Domestic Ideology*. Chicago: University of Illinois Press, 1989.

Ezell, Margaret. *Social Authorship and the Advent of Print*. Baltimore, MD: Johns Hopkins University Press, 1999.

Feather, John. 'The Commerce of Letters: The Study of the Eighteenth-Century Book Trade.' *ECS*, 17, 4 (Summer 1984): 405–24.

Ferguson, Moira. *Subject to Others: British Women Writers and Colonial Slavery, 1670–1834*. New York: Routledge, 1992.

Fitzpatrick, Martin. 'Patriots and Patriotism: Richard Price and the Early Reception of the French Revolution in England.' In O'Dea and Whelan (1995): 211–29.

Fleenor, Juliann (ed.). *The Female Gothic*. Montreal and London: Eden Press, 1983.

Flint, Christopher. *Family Fictions: Narrative and Domestic Relations in Britain, 1688–1798*. Stanford, CA: Stanford University Press, 1998.

Foakes, R. A. 'Coleridge, Napoleon and Nationalism.' In *Literature and Nationalism*, eds Vincent Newey and Ann Thompson. Savage, MD: Barnes & Noble Books, 1991: 140–51.

Folkenflik, Robert (ed.). *The English Hero, 1660–1800*. Newark: University of Delaware Press, 1982.

Foucault, Michel. *Discipline and Punish: The Birth of the Prison*, trans. A. Sheridan. Harmondsworth: Penguin, 1979.

——. *The History of Sexuality*, vol. I. Harmondsworth: Penguin, 1990.

——. 'What is an Author?' trans. Josué V. Harari. Reprinted in Davis and Schleifer (1994): 342–53

Foyster, Elizabeth. 'Boys Will Be Boys? Manhood and Aggression, 1660–1800.' In Hitchcock and Cohen (1999): 151–66.

Gadamer, Hans. *Truth and Method*. New York: Continuum, 1975.

Gallagher, Catherine. *The Industrial Reformation of English Fiction. Social Discourse and Narrative Form 1832–67*. Chicago and London: University of Chicago Press, 1985.

——. 'Marxism and the New Historicism.' In *The New Historicism*, ed. H. Aram Veeser. New York: Routledge, 1989.

——. *Nobody's Story. The Vanishing Acts of Women Writers in the Marketplace, 1670–1820*. Oxford: Clarendon Press, 1994.

Gardiner, Judith Kegan. 'On Female Identity and Writing by Women.' In *Writing and Sexual Difference*, ed. Elizabeth Abel. Chicago: University of Chicago Press, 1982: 177–91.

Gattrell, V. A. C. *The Hanging Tree: Execution and the English People 1770–1868*. Oxford: University Press, 1994.

Gellner, Ernest. *Nations and Nationalism*. Ithaca, NY: Cornell University Press, 1983.

Genette, Gerard. *Narrative Discourse*, trans. Jane Lewin. Ithaca, NY: Cornell University Press, 1980.

Germann, Georg. *Gothic Revival in Europe and Britain: Sources, Influences, and Ideas*, trans. Gerald Onn. Cambridge, MA: MIT Press, 1972.

Gilmore, David. *Manhood in the Making*. London and New York: Yale University Press, 1990.

Girouard, Mark. *The Return to Camelot: Chivalry and the English Gentleman*. New Haven, CT: Yale University Press, 1981.

Gramsci, Antonio. *Selections from the Prison Notebooks*, eds and trans. Quintin Hoare and Geoffrey Nowell-Smith. New York: International Publishers, 1971.

Greenblatt, Stephen J. *Learning to Curse: Essays in Early Modern Culture*. New York: Routledge, Chapman & Hall, 1992.

Greene, Donald. *The Age of Exuberance*. New York: Random House, 1970.

Gregory, Jerome. '*Homo Religiosus*: Masculinity and Religion in the Long Eighteenth Century.' In Hitchcock and Cohen (1999): 85–110.

Habermas, Jürgen. *The Structural Transformation of the Public Sphere*, trans. Thomas Burger with Frederick Lawrence. Cambridge, MA: MIT Press, 1992.

Haining, Peter. *Tales from the Gothic Bluebooks*. Kent: Gothic Head Press, 1978.

Halimi, Suzy. 'La Femme au Foyer, Vue par Clara Reeve.' *Bulletin de la Société d'études anglo-americaines des dix-septième et dix-huitième siècles*, 20 (June 1985): 153–66.

Hall, Stuart. 'Cultural Identity and Diaspora.' In Williams and Chrisman (1994): 392–403.

Harfst, Betsy P. *Horace Walpole and the Unconscious: an Experiment in Freudian Analysis.* New York: Arno Press, 1980.

Harris, Michael. 'Print and Politics in the Age of Walpole.' In Black (1984).

Hazen, Allen T. *A Catalogue of Horace Walpole's Library*, vols 1–3. New Haven, CT: Yale University Press, 1969.

Herzfeld, Michael. *Cultural Intimacy: Social Poetics in the Nation-State.* New York and London: Routledge, 1997.

Hibbert, Christopher. *Nelson. A Personal History.* New York: Addison-Wesley, 1996.

Hill, Christopher. *Puritanism and Revolution.* London: Secker & Warburg, 1958.

Hitchcock, Tim. 'Sociability and Misogyny in the Life of John Cannon, 1684–1743.' In Hitchcock and Cohen (1999): 25–43.

—— and Michèle Cohen (eds). *English Masculinities 1660–1800.* London and New York: Addison Wesley Longman, 1999.

Hoagwood, Terence. *Politics, Philosophy, and the Production of Romantic Texts.* DeKalb: Northern Illinois University Press, 1996.

Hobsbawm, Eric. *The Age of Revolution 1789–1848.* New York: Vintage Books, 1996.

——. 'Introduction: Inventing Tradition.' *In The Invention of Tradition*, eds Eric Hobsbawm and Terence Ranger. Cambridge: Cambridge University Press, 1983.

——. *Nations and Nationalism since 1780: Programme, Myth, Reality.* Cambridge, MA: Harvard University Press, 1992.

Horrocks, Roger. *Male Myths and Icons: Masculinity in Popular Culture.* New York: St. Martin's Press, 1995.

Howard, Jacqueline. *Reading Gothic Fiction: A Bakhtinian Approach.* Oxford: Clarendon Press, 1994.

Hughes, Peter. 'Wars Within Doors: Erotic Heroism in Eighteenth-Century Literature.' In Folkenflik (1982): 168–94.

Hughes, Winifred. *The Maniac in the Cellar: Sensation Novels of the 1860's.* Princeton, NJ: Princeton University Press, 1980.

Hume, Robert D. 'Gothic vs. Romantic: A Revaluation of the Gothic Novel.' *PMLA*, 84 (1969): 282–90.

Hunter, J. Paul. *Before Novels: The Cultural Contexts of Eighteenth-Century English Fiction.* New York: Norton, 1990.

Iliffe, Robert. 'Author-Mongering. The "Editor" between Producer and Consumer.' In Bermingham and Brewer (1995): 166–92.

Jameson, Fredric. *The Political Unconscious.* Ithaca, NY: Cornell University Press, 1981.

——. 'Reification and Utopia in Mass Culture (1979).' From *Signatures of the Visible*. London and New York: Routledge, 1992: 9–34.

Johannesson, Kurt. *The Renaissance of the Goths in Sixteenth-Century Sweden: Johannes and Olaus Magnus as Politicians and Historians*, trans. James Larson. Berkeley: University of California Press, 1991.

Johnston, Arthur. *Enchanted Ground. The Study of Medieval Romance in the Eighteenth Century.* London: Athlone Press, 1964.

Jones, Charles W. *Saint Nicholas of Myra, Bari, and Manhattan. Biography of a Legend.* Chicago: University of Chicago Press, 1978.

Kandiyoti, Deniz. 'Identity and Its Discontents: Women and the Nation.' In Williams and Chrisman (1994): 376–91.

Karl, Frederick. *The Adversary Literature: The English Novel in the Eighteenth Century.* New York: Farrar, Strauss & Giroux, 1974.

Keir, Sir David Lindsay. *The Constitutional History of Modern Britain since 1485.* New York: W. W. Norton, 1966.

Kelly, Gary. *English Fiction of the Romantic Period, 1789–1830.* New York: Longman, 1989.

Kelly, Patrick. 'Nationalism and the Contemporary Historians of the Jacobite War in Ireland.' In O'Dea and Whelan (1995): 89–102.

Kennedy, William. *English Taxation 1640–1799.* London: Frank Cass, 1964.

Kiernan, V. G. *The Duel in European History: Honour and the Reign of Aristocracy.* Oxford: Oxford University Press, 1988.

Kilgour, Maggie. *The Rise of the Gothic Novel.* London and New York: Routledge, 1995.

Killen, A. M. 'L'évolution de la legende de Juif errant.' *Revue de la Litterature Comparée*, v (1925): 5–36.

Klancher, Jon. *The Making of English Reading Audiences, 1790–1832.* Madison: University of Wisconsin Press, 1987.

Klein, Lawrence. 'Gender and the Public/Private Distinction in the Eighteenth Century: Some Questions About Evidence and Analytic Procedure.' *Eighteenth Century Studies*, 29, 1 (Fall 1995): 97–109.

——. 'Politeness for Plebes. Consumption and Social Identity in Early Eighteenth-Century England.' In Bermingham and Brewer (1990): 362–82.

——. *Shaftesbury and the Culture of Politeness: Moral Discourses and Cult Politics in Early Eighteenth-Century England.* Cambridge and New York: Cambridge University Press, 1994.

Kliger, Samuel. *The Goths in England: A Study in 17th and 18th-Century Thought.* Cambridge, MA: Harvard University Press, 1952.

Kuchta, David. 'The Making of the Self-Made Man: Class, Clothing, and English Masculinity, 1688–1832.' In *The Sex of Things*, eds Victoria de Grazia and Ellen Furlough. Berkeley: University of California Press, 1996: 54–78.

La Chance, Charles. '*Don Juan*, "a problem like all things."' *Papers on Language and Literature*, 34, 4 (Summer 1998): 273–300.

Laugero, Greg. 'Infrastructures of Enlightenment: Road-Making, the Public Sphere, and the Emergence of Literature.' *ECS*, 29, 1 (Fall 1995): 45–67.

La Vopa, Anthony. 'Conceiving a Public: Ideas and Society in Eighteenth-Century Europe.' *Journal of Modern History*, 64, 1 (March 1992): 79–116.

Lenham, Bruce. 'A Client Society: Scotland between the '15 and the '45.' In Black (1984): 69–95.

Lewis, W.S. (ed.) *The Castle of Otranto.* New York: Holt, Rinehart & Winston, 1963.

——. *Selected Letters of Horace Walpole.* New Haven: Yale University Press, 1973.

Lloyd, David and Paul Thomas. *Culture and the State.* New York and London: Routledge, 1998.

Lovell, Terry. 'Subjective Powers? Consumption, the Reading Public, and Domestic Woman in Early Eighteenth-Century England.' In Bermingham and Brewer (1999): 23–41.

Lynch, James J. *Henry Fielding and the Heliodoran Novel.* Teaneck, NJ: Fairleigh Dickinson University Press, 1986.

MacAndrew, Elizabeth. *The Gothic Tradition in Fiction.* New York: Columbia University Press, 1979.

McDermott, Hubert. *Novel and Romance: The* Odyssey *to* Tom Jones. Basingstoke: 1989.

McKeon, Michael. *The Origins of the English Novel 1600–1740.* Baltimore, MD: Johns Hopkins University Press, 1987.

McKillop, A. 'Mrs. Radcliffe on the Supernatural in Poetry.' *Journal of English and Germanic Philology,* 31, 3 (July 1932): 352–59.

McNeil, David. *The Grotesque Depiction of War and the Military in Eighteenth-Century English Fiction.* Newark: University of Delaware Press, 1990.

Macherey, Pierre. *A Theory of Literary Production,* trans. Geoffrey Wall. London, Henley, and Boston: Routledge & Kegan Paul, 1978.

Malchow, H. L. *Gothic Images of Race in Nineteenth-Century Britain.* Stanford, CA: Stanford University Press, 1996.

Mangan, J. A. and James Walvin (eds). *Manliness and Morality: Middle-Class Masculinity in Britain and America, 1800–1940.* New York: St. Martin's Press, 1987.

Martin, James. *Gramsci's Political Analysis. A Critical Introduction.* London: Macmillan, now Palgrave, 1998.

Mason, John Hope. 'Thinking about Genius in the Eighteenth Century.' In Mattick (1993): 210–39.

Mattick, Paul (ed.) 'Art and Money.' In Mattick (1993): 152–77.

——. *Eighteenth-Century Aesthetics and the Reconstruction of Art.* Cambridge: Cambridge University Press, 1993.

Mayo, Robert D. *The English Novel in the Magazines 1740–1815.* Evanston: University of Illinois Press, 1962.

Metz, Christian. 'The Imaginary Signifier.' *Screen,* 16, 2 (Summer 1975).

Milbank, Alison (ed.) *The Castles of Athlin and Dunbayne.* Oxford and New York: Oxford University Press, 1995.

——. (ed.) A Sicilian Romance. Oxford and New York: Oxford University Press, 1993.

Miles, Robert. *Gothic Writing 1750–1820. A Genealogy.* London and New York: Routledge, 1993.

Moorman, Mary (ed.). *Letters of William and Dorothy Wordsworth,* 2nd edn, Vol. II: *The Middle Years,* Part I (1806–11). Oxford: Clarendon Press, 1969.

Moretti, Franco. *The Way of the World. The Bildungsroman in European Culture.* London: Verso, 1987.

Morris, Meaghan. 'Banality in Cultural Studies.' In Davis and Schleifer (1994): 642–66.

Mulvey, Laura. 'Visual Pleasure and Narrative Cinema' and 'Afterthoughts on "Visual Pleasure and Narrative Cinema"' inspired by *Duel in the Sun.*' In *Feminism and Film Theory,* ed. C. Penley. New York: Routledge, 1988.

Nairn, Tom. *Faces of Nationalism: Janus Revisited.* London and New York: Verso, 1997.

Napier, Elizabeth. *The Failure of Gothic: Problems of Disjunction in Eighteenth-Century Literary Form.* Oxford: Clarendon Press, 1987.

Nelson, Lowry Jr. 'Night Thoughts on the Gothic Novel.' *Yale Review,* LII, 2 (Winter 1963): 238–52.

Neuberg, Victor. *The Penny Histories: A Study of Chapbooks for Young Readers Over Two Centuries.* New York: Harcourt, Brace, & World, 1969.

Newman, Gerald. *The Rise of English Nationalism. A Cultural History 1740–1830.* New York: St. Martin's Press – now Palgrave, 1997.

Norton, Robert. E. *The Beautiful Soul: Aesthetic Morality in the Eighteenth Century.* Ithaca, NY: Cornell University Press, 1995.

Novak, Maximillian E. 'Gothic Fiction and the Grotesque.' *Novel* 13, 1 (Fall 1979): 50–67.

O'Dea, Michael and Kevin Whelan. *Nations and Nationalisms: France, Britain, Ireland and the Eighteenth-Century Context.* Oxford: Voltaire Foundation, 1995.

Ousby, Ian. 'Carlyle, Thackeray, and Victorian Heroism.' In *Heroes and the Heroic. Yearbook of English Studies*, v, 12 (1981): 152–68.

Park, Roberta J. 'Biological Thought, Athletics, and the Formation of a "Man of Character": 1830–1900.' In Mangan and Walvin (1987): 7–34.

Parks, Stephen (ed.). *Horace Walpole's Political Tracts 1747–48, with Two by William Warburton on Literary Property (1747 and 1762).* New York: Garland Press, 1974.

Parreaux, André. *The Publication of* The Monk. *A Literary Event 1796–98.* Paris: Libraire Mariel Didier, 1960.

Parry, Graham. *The Trophies of Time: English Antiquarians of the Seventeenth Century.* Oxford and New York: Oxford University Press, 1995.

Paulson, Ronald. 'Gothic Fiction and the French Revolution.' *ELH,* 48(1981): 532–54.

Pawlowicz, Peter H. 'Reading Women. Text and Image in Eighteenth-Century England.' In Bermingham and Brewer (1999): 42–53.

Pickett, Terry H. *Inventing Nations. Justifications of Authority in the Modern World.* Westport, CT: Greenwood Press, 1996.

Plumb, J. H. *The Commercialisation of Leisure in Eighteenth-century England.* University of Reading, 1973.

Pocock, J. G. A. *The Ancient Constitution and the Feudal Law.* Cambridge: Cambridge University Press, 1957.

——.*Virtue, Commerce, and History. Essays on Political Thought and History, Chiefly in the Eighteenth Century.* Cambridge: Cambridge University Press, 1985.

Pocock, Tom. *Battle for Empire: The Very First World War 1756–63.* London: Michael O'Mara Books, 1998.

Poovey, Mary. *Uneven Developments: The Ideological Work of Gender in Mid-Victorian England.* Chicago: University of Chicago Press, 1988.

Porte, Joel. 'In the Hands of an Angry God: Religious Terror in Gothic Fiction.' *In The Gothic Imagination: Essays in Dark Romanticism,* ed. G. R. Thompson. Pullman, WA: Washington State University Press, 1974: 42–64.

Preston, John. *The Created Self. The Reader's Role in Eighteenth Century Fiction.* London, Heinemann, 1970.

Punter, David. *The Literature of Terror: A History of Gothic Fictions from 1765 to the Present Day.* London: Longman, 1980.

Railo, Eino. *The Haunted Castle: A Study of the Elements of English Romanticism.* London: Geo. Routledge & Sons, 1927.

Raven, James. *Judging New Wealth: Popular Publishing and Responses to Commerce in England, 1750–1800.* Oxford: Clarendon Press, 1992.

Richards, Jeffrey. '"Passing the love of women": Manly Love and Victorian Society.' In Mangan and Walvin (1987): 92–122.

Richter, David (ed.). *Falling into Theory: Conflicting Views on Reading Literature.* Boston: Bedford Books of St. Martin's Press – now Palgrave, 1994.

————. *The Progress of Romance: Literary Historiography and the Gothic Novel.* Columbus: Ohio State University Press, 1996.

Robertson, Fiona. *Legitimate Histories: Scott, Gothic, and the Authorities of Fiction.* Oxford: Clarendon Press, 1994.

Robson-Scott, W. D. *The Literary Background of the Gothic Revival in Germany.* Oxford: Clarendon Press, 1965.

Rodger, N. A. M. *The Wooden World: An Anatomy of the Georgian Navy.* New York and London: W. W. Norton, 1996.

Rogers, Katherine. *Feminism in Eighteenth Century England.* Brighton: Harvester Press, 1982.

Rose, Mark. 'The Author as Proprietor: *Donaldson* v. *Becket* and the Genealogy of Modern Authorship.' *Representations,* 23 (Summer 1988): 51–85.

Ross, Marlon, 'Romancing the Nation-State: The Poetics of Romantic Nationalism.' In *Macropolitics of Nineteenth-Century Literature: Nationalism, Exoticism, Imperialism,* eds. Jonathan Arac and Harriet Ritvo. Philadelphia: University of Pennsylvania Press, 1991: 56–85.

Ross, Trevor. 'Copyright and the Invention of Tradition.' *ECS,* 26,1 (Fall 1992): 1–27.

Roughead, William. *The Riddle of the Ruthvens and Other Studies.* Edinburgh and London: Moray Press, 1919.

Rubin, Gayle. 'The Traffic in Women.' In *Toward An Anthropology of Women,* ed. Rayna R. Reiter. New York: Monthly Review Press, 1975: 157–210.

Rudé, George. *Wilkes and Liberty: A Social Study of 1763 to 1774.* Oxford: Clarendon Press, 1965.

Rush, Philip. *The Book of Duels.* London: George G. Harrap, 1964.

Samara, Donya. 'Gothic Criticism(s).' *Novel,* 29,2 (Winter 1996): 243–7.

Samson, John. 'Politics Gothicized: The Conway Incident and *The Castle of Otranto.'Eighteenth Century Life,* 10,3 (October 1986): 145–58.

Samuel, Raphael. 'The figures of national myth.' In Samuel (1989), vol. 3: xi–xxxvi.

————. (ed.). *Patriotism: the Making and Unmaking of British National Identity,* 3 vols. London and New York: Routledge, 1989.

Scarry, Elaine. *The Body in Pain.* Oxford: Oxford University Press, 1992.

Schama, Simon. *Citizens. A Chronicle of the French Revolution.* New York: Knopf, 1989.

Schmitt, Cannon. *Alien Nation: Nineteenth-Century Gothic Fictions and English Nationality.* Philadelphia: University of Pennsylvania Press, 1997.

Sedgwick, Romney. 'Horace Walpole's Political Articles 1747–49.' In *Horace Walpole, Writer, Politician, and Connoisseur: Essays on the 250th Anniversary of Walpole's Birth,* ed. W. H. Smith. New Haven, CT: Yale University Press, 1967: 45–55.

Shell, Marc. *Children of the Earth: Literature, Politics, and Nationhood.* New York and Oxford: Oxford University Press, 1993.

————. *The Economy of Literature.* Baltimore, MD and London: Johns Hopkins University Press, 1978.

Shoemaker, Robert B. 'Reforming Male Manners: Public Insult and the decline of violence in London, 1660–1740.' In Hitchcock and Cohen (1999): 133–50.

Shusterman, Richard. 'Of the scandal of taste: social privilege as nature in the aesthetic theories of Hume and Kant.' In Mattick (1993): 96–119.

Sickels, Eleanor. *The Gloomy Egoist*. New York: Columbia University Press, 1932.

Simons, Herbert and Aram Aghazarian (eds). *Form, Genre, and the Study of Political Discourse*. Columbia, SC. University of South Carolina Press, 1986.

Simpson, David. *Romanticism, Nationalism, and the Revolt Against Theory*. Chicago: University of Chicago Press, 1993.

Simpson, Louis. *James Hogg: A Critical Study*. New York: St. Martin's Press – now Palgrave, 1962.

Smith, D. A. *National Identity*. London, 1991.

Smith, Nelson C. *James Hogg*. Boston: Twayne Publishers, 1980.

Spacks, Patricia Meyer. *The Female Imagination*. New York: Avon, 1976.

———. *Imagining a Self: Autobiography and Novel in Eighteenth-Century England*. Cambridge, MA: Harvard University Press, 1976.

Spector, Robert D. *The English Gothic: A Bibliographic Guide to Writers from Horace Walpole to Mary Shelley*. Westport CT and London: Greenwood Press, 1984.

———. *English Literary Periodicals and the Climate of Opinion During the Seven Years' War*. The Hague: Mouton, 1966.

Spufford, Margaret. *Small Books and Pleasant Histories. Popular Fiction and its Readership in Seventeenth-Century England*. London: Methuen, 1981.

Stevenson, John Allen. *The British Novel, Defoe to Austen*. Boston: Twayne, 1990.

Stone, Lawrence. *Family, Sex, and Marriage in England 1500–1800*. New York: Harper & Row, 1977.

Summers, David. 'Why Did Kant Call Taste a "common sense"?' In Mattick (1993): 120–51.

Summers, Montague. *The Gothic Quest: A History of the Gothic Novel*. London: The Fortune Press, 1938.

Tarr, Sister Mary Muriel. *Catholicism in Gothic Fiction. A Study of the Nature and Function of Catholic Materials in Gothic Fiction in England (1762–1820)*. Washington, DC: Catholic University of America Press, 1946.

Thompson, E. P. *The Making of the English Working Class*. Harmondsworth: Penguin, 1978.

Todd, Janet. *Men By Women*. New York: Holmes & Meier, 1981.

———. *The Sign of Angelica: Women, Writing and Fiction 1660–1800*. London: Virago Press, 1989.

Tompkins, J. M. S. *The Popular Novel in England, 1770–1800*. London: Constable, 1932.

Tosh, John. 'The Old Adam and the New Man: Emerging Themes in the History of English Masculinities, 1750–1850.' In Hitchcock and Cohen (1999): 217-38.

Tracy, Ann. B. *The Gothic Novel 1790–1830*. Lexington: University Press of Kentucky, 1981.

Varey, Simon. *Space and the Eighteenth-Century English Novel*. Cambridge: Cambridge University Press, 1990.

Venturi, Franco. *Utopia and Reform in the Enlightenment*. Cambridge: Cambridge University Press, 1971.

Walvin, James. *A Child's World*: London, 1982.

———. *Fruits of Empire: Exotic Produce and British Taste, 1660–1800*. New York: New York University Press, 1997.

———. 'Symbols of Moral Superiority: Slavery, Sport, and the Changing World Order, 1800–1950.' In Mangan and Walvin (1987): 242-60.

Watkins, Daniel P. 'Social Hierarchy in Matthew Lewis's *The Monk*.' *Studies in the Novel* 18, no. 2 (Summer 1986): 115–124.

Wein, Toni. 'Gothic Desire in Charlotte Brontë's *Villette.*' *Studies in English Literature* 39.4 (Autumn 1999): 733–46.

——. 'Legal Fictions, Legitimate Desires: The Gothic Law of Narrative in Ann Radcliffe's *The Romance of the Forest.*' *Genre*, 30, 4 (Winter 1997): 289–309.

——. 'Tangled Webs: Horace Walpole and the Practice of History in *The Castle of Otranto.*' *English Language Notes*, XXV, no. 4 (June 1998): 12–22.

Weinbrot, Howard D. *Britannia's Issue. The Rise of British Literature from Dryden to Ossian.* Cambridge: Cambridge University Press, 1993.

Wiesenfarth, Joseph. *Gothic Manners and the Classic English Novel.* Madison: University of Wisconsin Press, 1988.

Williams, Anne. *Art of Darkness: A Poetics of Gothic.* Chicago: University of Chicago Press, 1995.

Williams, Ioan. *Novel and Romance.* London: Routledge & Kegan Paul, 1970.

Williams, Patrick and Laura Chrisman (eds). *Colonial Discourse and Post-Colonial Theory.* New York: Columbia University Press, 1994.

Williams, Raymond. *Culture and Society 1780–1950.* New York: Columbia University Press, 1958.

Williamson, Margaret. 'The Greek Romance.' In *The Progress of Romance. The Politics of Popular Fiction,* ed. Jean Radford. London and New York: Routledge & Kegan Paul, 1986: 23-45.

Wilson, Kathleen. 'Citizenship, Empire, and Modernity in the English Provinces, c. 1720–1790.' *Eighteenth Century Studies,* 29,1 (Fall 1995): 69–96.

——. 'The Good, the Bad, and the Impotent. Imperialism and the Politics of Identity in Georgian England.' In Bermingham and Brewer (1995): 237–62.

Winter, Kari J. 'Sexual/Textual Politics of Terror: Writing and Rewriting the Gothic Genre in the 1790s.' In *Misogyny in Literature,* ed. Katherine Anne Ackley. New York: Garland, 1992: 89–103.

Woodmansee, Martha. '"Art" as a Weapon in Cultural Politics: Rereading Schiller's *Aesthetic Letters.*' In Mattick (1993): 178–209.

——. *The Author, Art, and the Market: Rereading the History of Aesthetics.* New York: Columbia University Press, 1994.

——. 'The Genius and the Copyright: Economic and Legal Conditions of the Emergence of the "Author."' *Eighteenth-Century Studies,* 17, 4 (Summer 1984): 425–48.

Wright, Eugene P. 'A Divine Analysis of *The Romance of the Forest.*' *Discourse,* 13 (Summer 1970).

Zerilli, Linda M. G. 'Text/Woman as Spectacle: Edmund Burke's "French Revolution."' *The Eighteenth Century,* 33 , 1 (1992): 47–73.

Index

Chapbook Titles

General